LOSING MY VIRGINITY

RICHARD BRANSON

LOSING MY VIRGINITY

How I Survived, Had Fun, and
Made a Fortune Doing Business My Way

CROWN
BUSINESS
NEW YORK

CROWN BUSINESS is a trademark and CROWN and the Rising Sun colophon
are registered trademarks of Random House, Inc.

Originally published in hardcover in slightly different form in Great Britain
by Virgin Books Ltd., London, and in hardcover in the United States by Crown
Business, an imprint of the Crown Publishing Group, a division of Random
House, Inc., in 1998. Subsequent revised editions were published in paperback
in Great Britain by Virgin Books Ltd., London, in 2002, 2005, and 2007.

Crown Business books are available at special discounts for bulk purchase for
sales promotions or corporate use. Special editions, including personalized
covers, excerpts of existing books, or books with corporate logos, can be
created in large quantities for special needs. For more information, contact
Premium Sales at (212) 572-2232 or e-mail specialmarkets@randomhouse.com.

Library of Congress Cataloging-in-Publication Data is available upon request.

ISBN 978-0-307-72074-0

Printed in the United States of America

Cover design: Toby Clarke
Cover photograph: Dustin Rabin, originally published in *Power* magazine

10 9 8 7 6 5 4

First Crown Business Paperback Edition

Dedicated to Alex Ritchie and his family

A special thank-you to Edward Whitley for
helping me pull this project together.
Edward spent two years in my company,
practically lived in my house, waded through
25 years of scribbled notebooks and helped
bring them to life.

Contents

LOSING MY
VIRGINITY

Prologue
'Screw it. Let's do it.'

Tuesday 7 January 1997, Morocco

5.30a.m.

I WOKE BEFORE JOAN and sat up in bed. From across Marrakech I heard the wavering cry of the muezzins calling people to prayer over the loudspeakers. I still hadn't written to Holly and Sam, so I tore a page out of my notebook and wrote them a letter in case I didn't return.

> Dear Holly and Sam,
> Life can seem rather unreal at times. Alive and well and loving one day. No longer there the next.
> As you both know I always had an urge to live life to its full. That meant I was lucky enough to live the life of many people during my 46 years. I loved every minute of it and I especially loved every second of my time with both of you and Mum.
> I know that many people thought us foolish for embarking on this latest adventure. I was convinced they were wrong. I felt that everything we had learnt from our Atlantic and Pacific adventures would mean that we'd have a safe flight. I thought that the risks were acceptable. Obviously I've been proved wrong.
> However, I regret nothing about my life except not being with Joan to finally help you grow up. By the ages of twelve and fifteen your characters have already developed. We're both so proud of you. Joan and I couldn't have had two more delightful kids.

You are both kind, considerate, full of life (even witty!). What more could we both want?

Be strong. I know it won't be easy. But we've had a wonderful life together and you'll never forget all the good times we've had.

Live life to its full yourselves. Enjoy every minute of it. Love and look after Mum as if she's both of us.

I love you,

Dad

I folded the letter into a small square and put it in my pocket. Fully clothed and ready, I lay down beside Joan and hugged her. While I felt wide awake and nervous, she felt warm and sleepy in my arms. Holly and Sam came into our room and cuddled into bed between us. Then Sam slipped off with his cousins to go to the launch site and see the balloon in which I hoped shortly to fly round the world. Joan and Holly stayed with me while I spoke to Martin, the meteorologist. The flight, he said, was definitely on – we had the best weather conditions for five years. I then called Tim Evans, our doctor. He had just been with Rory McCarthy, our third pilot, and had bad news: Rory couldn't fly. He had mild pneumonia, and if he was in a capsule for three weeks it could get much worse. I immediately called up Rory and commiserated with him.

'See you in the dining room,' I said. 'Let's have breakfast.'

6.20a.m.

By the time Rory and I met in the hotel dining room, it was deserted. The journalists who had been following the preparations for the launch over the previous 24 hours had already left for the launch site.

Rory and I met and hugged each other. We both cried. As well as becoming a close friend as our third pilot on the balloon flight, Rory and I had been joining forces recently on a number of business deals. Just before we had come out to Morocco, he had bought a share in our new record label, V2, and had invested in Virgin Clothes and Virgin Vie, our new cosmetics company.

'I can't believe I'm letting you down,' Rory said. 'I'm never ill – never, ever.'

'Don't worry,' I assured him. 'It happens. We've got Alex, who weighs half what you do. We'll fly far further with him on board.'

'Seriously, if you don't come back,' Rory said, 'I'll carry on where you left off.'

'Well, thanks!' I said, laughing nervously.

Alex Ritchie was already out at the launch site supervising the mad dash to get the capsule ready with Per Lindstrand, the veteran hot-air balloonist who had introduced me to the sport. Alex was the brilliant engineer who had designed the capsule. Until then, nobody had succeeded in building a system that sustained balloon flights at jet-stream levels. Although it was he who had built both our Atlantic and Pacific capsules, I didn't know him well, and it was too late to find out much about him now. Despite having no flight training, Alex had bravely made the decision to come with us. If all went well with the flight, we'd have about three weeks to get to know each other. About as intimately as any of us would want.

Unlike my crossings with Per of the Pacific and Atlantic oceans by hot-air balloon, on this trip we would not heat air until we needed to: the balloon had an inner core of helium which would take us up. Per's plan was to heat the air around that core during the night,

3

which in turn would heat the helium, which would otherwise contract, grow heavy and sink.

Joan, Holly and I held hands and the three of us embraced. It was time to go.

8.30a.m.

We all saw it at the same time. As we drove along the dirt road out to the Moroccan air base, it looked as if a new mosque had sprouted overnight. Above the bending, dusty palm trees, a stunning white orb rose up like a mother-of-pearl dome. It was the balloon. Men on horseback galloped along the side of the road, guns slung over their shoulders, heading for the air base. Everyone was drawn to this huge, gleaming white balloon hanging in the air, tall and slender.

9.15a.m.

The balloon was cordoned off, and round the perimeter railing was an amazing collection of people. The entire complement of the air base stood off to one side in serried ranks, dressed in smart navy-blue uniforms. In front of them was the traditional Moroccan collection of dancing women in white shawls, hollering, wailing and whooping. Then a group of horsemen dressed in Berber costume and brandishing antique muskets galloped into view and lined up in front of the balloon. For an awful moment, I thought they would fire a celebratory salvo and puncture the balloon. Per, Alex and I gathered in the capsule and did a final check of all the systems. The sun was rising rapidly and the helium was beginning to expand.

10.15a.m.

We had done all the checks, and were ready to go. I hugged Joan, Holly and Sam one last time. I was amazed at Joan's strength. Holly had been by my side for the last four days, and she too appeared to be totally in control of the situation. I thought that Sam was as well, but then he burst into tears and pulled me towards him, refusing to let go. I almost started crying with him. I will never forget the anguished strength of his hug. Then he kissed me, let go and hugged Joan. I ran across to kiss Mum and Dad goodbye. Mum pressed a letter into my hand. 'Open it after six days,' she said. I silently hoped we would last that long.

10.50a.m.

There was nothing left to do except climb up the steel steps into the capsule. For a second I hesitated and wondered when and where I would put my feet back on solid ground – or water. There was no time to think ahead. I stepped in through the hatch. Per was by the main controls; I sat by the camera equipment and Alex sat in the seat by the trap door.

11.19a.m.

Ten, nine, eight, seven, six, five ... Per counted down and I concentrated on working the cameras. My hand kept darting down to check my parachute buckle. I tried not to think about the huge balloon above us, and the six vast fuel tanks strapped round our capsule. Four, three, two, one ... and Per threw the lever which fired the bolts which severed the anchor cables and we lifted silently and swiftly into the sky. There was no roar of the burners: our ascent was like that of a child's party balloon. We just rose up, up and away and then, as we caught the morning breeze, we headed over Marrakech.

The emergency door was still open as we soared up, and we waved down at the, by now, little people. Every detail of Marrakech, its square pink walls, the large town square, the green courtyards and fountains hidden behind high walls, was laid out below us. By 10,000 feet it became cold and the air grew thin. We shut the trap door. From now on we were on our own. We were pressurised, and the pressure would mount.

Our first fax came through the machine just after midday.

'Oh God!' Per handed it over. 'Look at this.'

'Please be aware that the connectors on the fuel tanks are locked on,' I read.

This was our first mistake. The connectors should have been locked off so that, if we got into trouble and started falling, we could jettison a one-ton fuel tank by way of ballast.

'If that's our only mistake, we're not doing badly,' I said, in an attempt to cheer Per up.

'We need to get down to 5,000 feet and then I'll climb out and unlock them,' Alex said. 'It's not a problem.'

It was impossible to lose height during the day because the sun was heating the helium. The only immediate solution was to release helium, which, once released, would be impossible to regain. We couldn't afford to lose any helium. So we agreed to wait for nightfall to bring the balloon down. It was a nagging worry. We didn't know how this balloon would fly at night, and with our fuel tanks locked on our ability to escape trouble was limited.

Although Alex and I tried to brush off the problem of the locked canisters, it sent Per into a fierce depression. He sat slumped by the controls in a furious silence, speaking only when we asked him a direct question.

We flew serenely for the rest of the day. The views over the Atlas Mountains were exhilarating, their jagged peaks capped with snow gleaming up at us in the glorious sunshine. The capsule was cramped, full of supplies to last us eighteen days. It emerged that failing to lock off the connectors was not the only thing we'd forgotten. We'd also neglected to pack any lavatory paper, so we had to wait to receive faxes before we could go down the tiny spiral staircase to the loo. And my Moroccan stomach was in need of a lot of faxes. Per maintained his glowering silence, but Alex and I were just grateful that we knew about the canisters then rather than finding out the hard way.

As we approached the Algerian border we had a second shock when the Algerians informed us that we were heading straight for Béchar, their top military base. They told us that we could not fly over it: 'You are not, repeat not, authorised to enter this area,' said the fax.

We had no choice.

I spent about two hours on the satellite phone to Mike Kendrick, our flight controller, and tried various British ministers. Eventually André Azoulay, the Moroccan minister who had ironed out all our problems for the launch in Morocco, came to the rescue again. He explained to the Algerians that we could not change our direction and that we did not have powerful cameras on board. They accepted this, and relented.

As the good news came through, I scribbled down notes in my logbook. As I turned over another page, there was a handwritten note from Sam, in thick black ink and Sellotaped to the page: 'To Dad, I hope you have a great time. Safe journey. Lots and lots of love, your son Sam.' I recalled that he'd slipped into the capsule without me the previous night, and now I knew why.

By 5p.m. we were still flying at 30,000 feet. Per started firing the burners to heat the air inside the envelope. Although we burnt for an hour, just after 6p.m. the balloon started losing height steadily.

'Something's wrong with the theory here,' Per said.

'What's the matter?' I asked.

'I don't know.'

Per was firing the burners continuously, but the balloon was still heading down. We lost 1,000 feet, and then another 500 feet. It was getting colder all the time as the sun disappeared. It was clear that the helium was rapidly contracting, becoming a dead weight on top of us.

'We've got to dump ballast,' Per said. He was frightened. We all were.

We pulled levers to dump the lead weights which were on the bottom of the capsule. These were meant to be held in reserve for about two weeks. They fell away from the capsule and I saw them on my video screen dropping like bombs. I had a horrible feeling that this was just the start of a disaster. The capsule was bigger than the Atlantic and Pacific ones, but it was still a metal box hanging off a giant balloon, at the mercy of the winds and weather.

It was now getting dark. Without the lead weights, we steadied for a while, but then the balloon started falling once more. This time the fall was faster. We dropped 2,000 feet in one minute; 2,000 feet the next. My ears went numb and then popped, and I felt my stomach rising up, pressing against my ribcage. We were at only 15,000 feet. I tried to stay calm, focusing intently on the cameras and the altimeter, rapidly going through the options available. We needed to jettison the fuel tanks. But, as soon as we did so, the trip was over. I bit my lip. We were somewhere over the Atlas Mountains in darkness, and we were heading for a horrible crash-landing. None of us spoke. I made some rapid calculations.

'At this rate of fall we've got seven minutes,' I said.

'OK,' Per said. 'Open the hatch. Depressurise.'

We opened the trap door at 12,000 feet, dropping to 11,000 feet, and with a breathtaking rush of freezing air the capsule depressurised. Alex and I started throwing everything overboard: food, water, oil cans, anything that wasn't built into the capsule. Everything. Even a wodge of dollars. For five minutes, this stalled our fall. There was no question of continuing. We just had to save our lives.

'It's not enough,' I said, seeing the altimeter drop to 9,000 feet. 'We're still falling.'

'OK, I'm going out on the roof,' Alex said. 'The fuel tanks have got to go.'

Since Alex practically built the capsule, he knew exactly how to undo the locks. In the panic I realised that, if Rory had been on board instead, we'd have been stuck. We would have had no choice but to parachute. Right now we'd be tumbling out into the night over the Atlas Mountains. The burners roared overhead, casting a fierce orange light over us.

'Have you parachuted before?' I shouted at Alex.

'Never,' he said.

'That's your ripcord,' I said, pushing his hand to it.

'It's 7,000 feet and falling,' Per called out. '6,600 feet now.'

Alex climbed through the hatch, on to the top of the capsule. It was difficult to feel how fast we were dropping. My ears had now blocked. If the locks were frozen and Alex wasn't able to free the fuel cans, we'd have to jump. We had only a few minutes left. I looked up at the hatch and rehearsed what we would have to do: one hand to the rim, step out, and jump into the darkness. My hand instinctively felt for my parachute. I checked to see that Per was wearing his. Per was watching the altimeter. The numbers were falling fast.

9

We had only 6,000 feet to play with and it was dark – no, 5,500 feet. If Alex was up there for another minute, we'd have 3,500 feet. I stood with my head through the hatch, paying out the strap and watching Alex as he worked his way round the top of the capsule. It was pitch-dark below us and freezing cold. We couldn't see the ground. The phone and fax were ringing incessantly. Ground control must have been wondering what the hell we were doing.

'One's off,' Alex shouted through the hatch.

'3,700 feet,' Per said.

'Another one,' Alex said.

'3,400 feet.'

'Another one.'

'2,900 feet, 2,400.'

It was too late to bale out. By the time we'd jumped, we'd be smashing into the mountains rushing up to meet us.

'Get back in,' Per yelled. 'Now.'

Alex fell back through the hatch.

We braced ourselves. Per threw the lever to disconnect a fuel tank. If this bolt failed, we'd be dead in about sixty seconds. The tank dropped away and the balloon jerked to an abrupt halt. It felt like an elevator hitting the ground. We were flattened into our seats, my head crammed down into my shoulders. Then the balloon began to rise. We watched the altimeter: 2,600, 2,700, 2,800 feet. We were safe. In ten minutes we were up past 3,000 feet and the balloon was heading back into the night sky.

I knelt on the floor beside Alex and hugged him.

'Thank God you're with us,' I said. 'We'd be dead without you.'

They say that a dying man reviews his life in the final seconds before his death. In my case this was not true. As we hurtled down towards becoming a fireball on the Atlas Mountains and I thought that we were going to die, all I could think of was that, if I escaped with my life, I would never do this again. As we rose up towards safety, Alex told us a story of a rich man who set out to swim the Channel: he went down to the beach, set up his deck chair and a table laid with cucumber sandwiches and strawberries, and then announced that his man would now swim the Channel for him. At that moment, it didn't sound like such a bad idea.

Throughout that first night, we fought to keep control of the balloon. At one point it started a continuous ascent, rising for no apparent reason. We finally realised that one of the remaining fuel tanks had sprung a leak: we had been unwittingly jettisoning fuel. As dawn approached, we made preparations to land. Below was the Algerian desert, an inhospitable place at the best of times, more so in a country in the middle of a civil war.

The desert was not the yellow sandy sweep of soft dunes which you expect from watching *Lawrence of Arabia*. The bare earth was red and rocky, as barren as the surface of Mars, the rocks standing upright like vast termites' nests. Alex and I sat up on the roof of the capsule, marvelling at the dawn as it broke over the desert. We were aware this was a day that we might not have survived to see. The rising sun and the growing warmth of the day seemed infinitely precious. Watching the balloon's shadow slip across the desert floor, it was hard to believe it was the same contraption that had plummeted towards the Atlas Mountains in the middle of the night.

The still-attached fuel tanks were blocking Per's view, so Alex talked him in to land. As we neared the ground Alex shouted out:

'Power line ahead!'

Per shouted back that we were in the middle of the Sahara and there couldn't possibly be a power line. 'You must be seeing a mirage,' he bawled.

Alex insisted that he come up and see for himself: we had managed to find the only power line in the Sahara.

Despite the vast barren desert all around us, within minutes of our landing there were signs of life. A group of Berber tribesmen materialised from the rocks. At first they kept their distance. We were about to offer them some water and the few remaining supplies, when we heard the clattering roar of gunship helicopters. They must have tracked us on their radar. As quickly as they had appeared, the Berber vanished. Two helicopters landed close by, throwing up clouds of dust, and soon we were surrounded by impassive soldiers holding machine guns, apparently unsure where to point them.

'Allah,' I said, encouragingly.

For a moment they stood still, but their curiosity got the better of them and they came forward. We showed their officer around the capsule, and he marvelled at the remaining fuel tanks.

As we stood outside the capsule, I wondered what these Algerian soldiers thought of it. I looked back, and saw it for a moment through their eyes. The remaining fuel tanks were painted like vast cans of Virgin Cola and Virgin Energy in bright red and yellow. Among the many slogans on the side of the capsule were ones for Virgin Atlantic, Virgin Direct (now Virgin Money), Virgin Territory and Virgin Cola. It was probably lucky for us that the devoutly Muslim soldiers could not understand the writing round the top of the Virgin Energy can: DESPITE WHAT YOU MAY HAVE HEARD THERE IS ABSOLUTELY NO EVIDENCE THAT VIRGIN ENERGY IS AN APHRODISIAC.

* * *

As I looked at the capsule standing in the red sand, and relived the harrowing drop towards the Atlas Mountains, I renewed my vow that I would never attempt this again. In perfect contradiction to this, at the back of my mind I also knew that, as soon as I was home and had talked to the other balloonists who were trying to fly round the world, I would agree to have one last go. It's an irresistible challenge and it's now buried too deeply inside for me to give up.

The two questions I am most often asked are, Why do you risk your neck ballooning? and, Where is the Virgin Group going? In some ways the sight of the ballooning capsule standing in the middle of the Algerian desert, with its cluster of Virgin names plastered over it, summed up these prime questions.

I knew that I would attempt another balloon flight because it's one of the few great challenges left. As soon as I've banished the terrors of each actual flight, I once again feel confident that we can learn from our mistakes and achieve the next one safely.

The wider question of where the Virgin Group will end up is impossible to answer. Rather than be too academic about it all, which is not the way I think, I have written this book to demonstrate how we made Virgin what it is today. If you read carefully between the lines you will, I hope, understand what our vision for the Virgin Group is, and you will see where I am going. Some people say that my vision for Virgin breaks all the rules and is too wildly kaleidoscopic; others say that Virgin has become one of the leading brand names of the century; others analyse it down to the last degree and then write academic papers on it. As for me, I just pick up the phone and get on with it. Both the series of balloon flights and the numerous Virgin companies I have set up form a seamless series of challenges which I can date from my childhood.

When I was searching for titles, David Tait, who runs the American side of Virgin Atlantic, suggested that I call it *Virgin: The Art of Business Strategy and Competitive Analysis.*

'Not bad,' I told him, 'but I'm not sure it's catchy enough.'

'Of course,' he said, 'the subtitle would be *Oh Screw It, Let's Do It.*'

1 'A family that would have killed for each other.'

1950–1963

M Y CHILDHOOD IS SOMETHING of a blur to me now, but there are several episodes that stand out. I do remember that my parents continually set us challenges. My mother was determined to make us independent. When I was four years old, she stopped the car a few miles from our house and made me find my own way home across the fields. I got hopelessly lost. My youngest sister Vanessa's earliest memory is being woken up in the dark one January morning because Mum had decided I should cycle to Bourne-mouth that day. Mum packed some sandwiches and an apple and told me to find some water along the way.

Bournemouth was fifty miles away from our home in Shamley Green, Surrey. I was under twelve, but Mum thought that it would teach me the importance of stamina and a sense of direction. I remember setting off in the dark, and I have a vague recollection of staying the night with a relative. I have no idea how I found their house, or how I got back to Shamley Green the next day, but I do remember finally walking into the kitchen like a conquering hero, feeling tremendously proud of my marathon bike ride and expecting a huge welcome.

'Well done, Ricky,' Mum greeted me in the kitchen, where she was chopping onions. 'Was that fun? Now, could you run along to the vicar's? He's got some logs he wants chopping and I told him that you'd be back any minute.'

Our challenges tended to be physical rather than academic, and soon we were setting them for ourselves. I have an early memory of learning how to swim. I was either four or five, and we had been on holiday in Devon with Dad's sisters, Auntie Joyce and Aunt Wendy, and Wendy's husband, Uncle Joe. I was particularly fond of Auntie Joyce, and at the beginning of the holiday she had bet me ten shillings that I couldn't learn to swim by the end of the fortnight. I spent hours in the sea trying to swim against the freezing-cold waves, but by the last day I still couldn't do it. I just splashed along with one foot hopping on the bottom. I'd lunge forward and crash beneath the waves before spluttering up to the surface trying not to swallow the seawater.

'Never mind, Ricky,' Auntie Joyce said. 'There's always next year.'

But I was determined not to wait that long. Auntie Joyce had made me a bet, and I doubted that she would remember it the next year. On our last day we got up early, packed the cars and set out on the twelve-hour journey home. The roads were narrow; the cars were slow; and it was a hot day. Everyone wanted to get home. As we drove along I saw a river.

'Daddy, can you stop the car, please?' I said.

This river was my last chance: I was sure that I could swim and win Auntie Joyce's ten shillings.

'Please stop!' I shouted.

Dad looked in the rear-view mirror, slowed down and pulled up on the grass verge.

'What's the matter?' Aunt Wendy asked as we all piled out of the car.

'Ricky's seen the river down there,' Mum said. 'He wants to have a final go at swimming.'

'Don't we want to get on and get home?' Aunt Wendy complained. 'It's such a long drive.'

'Come on, Wendy. Let's give the lad a chance,' Auntie Joyce said. 'After all, it's my ten shillings.'

I pulled off my clothes and ran down to the riverbank in my underpants. I didn't dare stop in case anyone changed their mind. By the time I reached the water's edge I was rather frightened. Out in the middle of the river, the water was flowing fast with a stream of bubbles dancing over the boulders. I found a part of the bank that had been trodden down by some cows, and waded out into the current. The mud squeezed up between my toes. I looked back. Uncle Joe and Aunt Wendy and Auntie Joyce, my parents and sister Lindi stood watching me, the ladies in floral dresses, the men in sports jackets and ties. Dad was lighting his pipe and looking utterly unconcerned; Mum was smiling her usual encouragement.

I braced myself and jumped forward against the current, but I immediately felt myself sinking, my legs slicing uselessly through the water. The current pushed me around, tore at my underpants and dragged me downstream. I couldn't breathe and I swallowed water. I tried to reach up to the surface, but had nothing to push against. I kicked and writhed around but it was no help.

Then my foot found a stone and I pushed up hard. I came back above the surface and took a deep breath. The breath steadied me, and I relaxed. I had to win that ten shillings.

I kicked slowly, spread my arms, and found myself swimming across the surface. I was still bobbing up and down, but I suddenly felt released: I could swim. I didn't care that the river was pulling me downstream. I swam triumphantly out into the middle of the current. Above the roar and bubble of the water I heard my family clapping and cheering. As I swam in a lopsided circle

17

and came back to the riverbank some fifty yards below them, I saw Auntie Joyce fish in her huge black handbag for her purse. I crawled up out of the water, brushed through a patch of stinging nettles and ran up the bank. I may have been cold, muddy and stung by the nettles, but I could swim.

'Here you are, Ricky,' Auntie Joyce said. 'Well done.'

I looked at the ten-shilling note in my hand. It was large, brown and crisp. I had never held that amount of money before: it seemed a fortune.

'All right, everyone,' Dad said. 'On we go.'

It was then that I realised he too was dripping wet. He had lost his nerve and dived in after me. He gave me a massive hug.

I cannot remember a moment in my life when I have not felt the love of my family. We were a family that would have killed for each other – and we still are. My parents adored each other, and in my childhood there was barely a cross word between them. Eve, my mother, was always full of life and galvanised us. Ted, my father, was a rather quieter figure who smoked his pipe and enjoyed his newspaper, but both my parents had a love of adventure. Ted had wanted to be an archaeologist, but his father, a High Court judge, wanted him to follow Branson tradition and enter the law. Three generations of Bransons had been lawyers. When Ted was at school, my grandfather engaged a careers officer to talk to him and discuss possible careers. When it emerged that Ted wanted to be an archaeologist, my grandfather refused to pay the careers officer's bill on the grounds that he hadn't done his job properly. So Ted reluctantly went up to Cambridge to read law, and continued as a hobby to build up his collection of ancient artefacts and fossils which he called his 'museum'.

When the Second World War broke out in 1939, Ted volunteered for the Staffordshire Yeomanry, a cavalry regiment organised around the Inns of Court. His regiment fought in Palestine and Ted fought in the Battle of El Alamein in September 1942, and subsequent battles in the Libyan desert. He was then involved in the invasion of Italy and fought at Salerno and Anzio. Before Ted went to war, he devised a code to let my grandparents know where he was: they agreed that, in letters home, the cellar would be the world and certain drawers in the cupboards would represent certain countries. Ted would write and ask his mother to pull out his old riding gloves from the top left-hand shelf of the right-hand cupboard, which had been designated Palestine – unsurprisingly, the censors never picked this up and my grandparents could tell where he was.

When Ted joined up, his uncle, Jim Branson, had already become quite notorious in the army because he advocated eating grass. Great-uncle Jim had owned an estate in Hampshire which he had finally split up among the tenants and then gone to live in Balham, which in 1939 was a distant suburb of London. He was obsessed with eating grass, and *Picture Post* ran a story with a picture of him in his bathroom in Balham, where he grew tubs of grass which he made into hay. Whenever Jim was invited out to eat – which was increasingly often as he became a celebrity – he brought his nosebag with him and ate grass. In the army, everyone mocked my dad: 'You must be Jim Branson's son! Here, have some grass! You're a sprightly looking colt. When are they going to geld you?' and so on.

Ted hotly denied any involvement with Uncle Jim. However, as the war progressed, David Stirling set up the Special Air Service, a crack regiment designed to operate behind enemy lines. The SAS had to travel light, and soon it became known that Jim Branson was advising David Stirling and his elite troops on how to live off grass and nuts.

From then on, whenever Ted was asked, 'Branson? Are you anything to do with Jim Branson?' he puffed out his chest with pride: 'Yes, actually he's my uncle. Fascinating what he's doing with the SAS, isn't it?'

Ted actually enjoyed the five years away from home, and found it quite difficult to knuckle down to the law again when he returned to Cambridge. A few years later, as a young barrister, he arrived rather late at a cocktail party where he was greeted by a beautiful blonde girl called Eve who swooped across the room towards him, picked up a tray of honeyed sausages, and said, 'The way to a man's heart is through his stomach. Here, have some of these!'

Eve Huntley-Flindt had picked up some of her dazzling energy from her mother Dorothy, who holds two British records: aged 89 Granny became the oldest person in Britain to pass the advanced Latin-American ballroom-dancing examination, and aged 90 she became the oldest person to hit a hole in one at golf.

Granny was 99 when she died. Shortly before that, she had written to me to say that the previous ten years had been the best of her life. That same year, on her way round the world on a cruise ship, she had been left behind in Jamaica with only her swimming costume on. She had even read *A Brief History of Time* (something which I've never been able to manage!). She never stopped learning. Her attitude was, you've got one go in life, so make the most of it.

Mum had inherited Granny's love of sports and dancing, and aged twelve she appeared in a West End revue written by Marie Stopes, who later became famous for her work with women's health education.

Some time later Mum was almost obliged to strip for another stage job: dancing for *The Cochran Show* at Her Majesty's Theatre in the West End. Sir Charles Cochran's shows were notorious for having the most gorgeous girls in town, and they took their clothes off. It was wartime and work was scarce. Eve decided to take the job on the grounds that it was all a lot of harmless fun. Predictably, my grandfather violently objected and told her that he'd come storming up to Her Majesty's and pull her out of the show. Eve relayed this to Sir Charles Cochran, who allowed her to dance without stripping. Then, as now, she was able to get away with pretty much anything.

Eve started looking for other, daytime, work, and went out to Heston where a gliding club taught RAF recruits to glide before they became pilots. She asked for a job as a pilot, but was told that these jobs were available only to men. Undeterred, she chatted up one of the instructors, who relented and secretly gave her the job so long as she pretended to be a boy. So, wearing a leather jacket, a leather helmet to hide her hair, and adopting a deep voice, Eve learnt how to glide and then began to teach the new pilots. In the last year of the war she joined the Wrens as a signaller and was posted to the Black Isle in Scotland.

After the war Eve became an air hostess, at the time a most glamorous job. The qualifications were challenging: you had to be very pretty and unmarried, aged between 23 and 27, speak Spanish, and be trained as a nurse. Undaunted that she couldn't speak Spanish and wasn't a nurse, Mum chatted up the night porter at the recruitment centre and found herself on the training course to be a hostess with British South American Airways, BSAA. BSAA operated two kinds of plane between London and South America: Lancasters, which carried 13 passengers; and Yorks, which carried 21. They had wonderful names, *Star Stream* and *Star Dale*, and the air hostesses were known as Star Girls. When the plane taxied down the runway, Mum's first job was to offer round chewing gum, barley sugar, cotton wool and Penguin paperbacks, and explain to the passengers that they had to blow their noses before taking off and landing.

The cabins were not pressurised, and the flights were marathons: five hours to Lisbon, eight hours to Dakar, and then fourteen hours across to Buenos Aires. For the Buenos Aires to Santiago leg the York aircraft was exchanged for the more robust Lancaster, and everyone had to wear oxygen masks over the Andes. After she had been with BSAA for a year, it was taken over by BOAC, British Overseas Airways Corporation, and Eve began working on Tudor aircraft. *Star Tiger*, the first plane to leave for Bermuda, exploded in midair. Her plane was next and arrived safely. But the plane after hers, *Star Ariel*, vanished without trace in the Bermuda Triangle and all Tudor aircraft were grounded. It was later discovered that their fuselages were too weak to withstand the recently installed pressurisation.

By this time Ted probably thought that, if he didn't marry Eve and so disqualify her from being an air hostess, she would be likely to disappear somewhere over the Atlantic. He proposed to her as they roared along on his motorbike, and she shouted, 'Yes!' at the top of her voice so that the wind wouldn't blow the word away. They were married on 14 October 1949, and I was conceived on their honeymoon in Majorca.

My parents always treated my two sisters, Lindi and Vanessa, and me as equals whose opinions were just as valid as theirs. When we were young, before Vanessa's arrival, if my parents went out to dinner they took me and Lindi with them lying on blankets in the back of the car. We slept in the car while they had dinner, but we always woke up when they started the drive back home. Lindi and I kept quiet and looked up at the night sky, listening to my parents talk and joke about their evening. We grew up talking as friends to our parents. As children we discussed Dad's legal cases, and argued about pornography and whether drugs should be legalised long before any of us knew what we were really talking about. My parents always encouraged us to have our own opinions and rarely gave us advice unless we asked for it.

We lived in a village called Shamley Green in Surrey. Before Vanessa was born, Lindi and I grew up in Easteds, a cottage covered with ivy which had tiny white windows and a white wicket gate which led out on to the village green. I was three years older than Lindi, and nine years older than Vanessa. My parents had very little money during our childhood and, perhaps because Mum wasn't greatly interested in cooking, or perhaps because she was saving money, I remember eating a good deal of bread and dripping. Even so, traditions were still upheld and we were not allowed to leave the table until we had finished all our food. We were also given onions which grew in the garden. I always hated them and used to hide them in a drawer in the table. This drawer was never cleaned out, and when we moved house ten years later it was opened and my pile of fossilised onions was discovered.

Food was not as important at meals as company. The house was always full of people. In order to make ends meet, Mum invited German and French students over to learn English in a typical English household, and we had to entertain them. Mum always had us working in

23

the garden, helping her prepare meals and then clearing up afterward. When I wanted to escape, I ran off across the village green to see my best friend Nik Powell.

At first the best thing about Nik was that his mother made amazing custard, so after a meal spent stuffing onions into the table drawer I would slip away to Nik's house, leaving the Germans trying to speak English with my family laughing and helping them out. If I timed it right, which I made sure I did, pudding and custard were already on the table. Nik was a quiet boy with straight black hair and black eyes. Soon we started doing everything together: climbing trees, riding bikes, shooting rabbits and hiding under Lindi's bed to grab her ankle when she turned out the light.

At home Mum had two obsessions: she always generated work for us, and she was always thinking of ways to make money. We never had a television and I don't think my parents ever listened to the radio. Mum worked in a shed in the garden, making wooden tissue boxes and wastepaper bins which she sold to shops. Her shed smelt of paints and glue and was stacked with little piles of painted boxes ready to be sent off. Dad was inventive and very good with his hands, and he designed special pressing vices which held the boxes together while they were being glued. Eventually Mum began supplying Harrods with her tissue boxes, and it became a proper little cottage industry. As with everything she did, Mum worked in a whirlwind of energy which was difficult to resist.

There was a great sense of teamwork within our family. Whenever we were within Mum's orbit we had to be busy. If we tried to escape by saying that we had something else to do, we were firmly told we were selfish. As a result we grew up with a clear priority of putting other people first. Once a boy came for the weekend whom I didn't particularly take to. During the church service on Sunday I slipped out of our pew and went across the aisle to sit with Nik. Mum was furious. When we got home she told Dad to beat me, and we duly went into his study and closed the door. Rather than towering over me in a rage, Dad just smiled.

'Now make sure you cry convincingly,' he said, and clapped his hands together six times to make great smacking noises.

I ran out of the room, bawling loudly. Mum adopted a severe look to imply that this was in my best interests, and resolutely carried on chopping onions in the kitchen – my portion of which was duly stuffed into the table drawer during lunch.

Great-uncle Jim wasn't the only maverick in the family: irreverence for authority ran on both sides. I remember that we acquired an old gypsy caravan which we kept in the garden, and sometimes gypsies came by and rang the doorbell. Mum always gave them something silver and let them rummage around in the barn for anything they needed. One year we were all taken to the Surrey County Show at Guildford. It was thronging with gleaming show-jumpers and men in tweed coats and bowler hats. As we walked past one of the stalls Mum saw a group of gypsy children in tears and we went over to see what was the matter. They were all crowded around a magpie which was tied to a piece of string.

'The RSPCA has ordered us to bring the bird in to be put down. They say it's illegal to own wild birds,' they said.

Even as they told us what was happening, we saw an RSPCA official walking towards us.

'Don't worry,' Mum said. 'I'll save it.'

She picked up the bird and wrapped it in her coat. Then we smuggled it out of the showground past the officials. The gypsy children met us outside and they told us to keep the magpie since they would only be stopped again. Mum was delighted, and we drove it home.

The magpie loved Mum. It sat on her shoulder when she was in the kitchen or working in her shed, and would then swoop out to the paddock and tease the ponies by sitting on their backs. It dive-bombed Dad if he sat down to read *The Times* after lunch, flapping the pages so that they scattered over the floor.

'Damned bird!' Dad would roar, waving his arms at it to shoo it away.

'Ted, get up and do something useful,' Mum said. 'That bird's telling you to do some gardening. And, Ricky and Lindi, run along to the vicar and ask him if there's anything you can do to help.'

Apart from spending summer holidays with Dad's family at Salcombe in Devon, we also went to Norfolk to stay with Mum's sister, Clare Hoare. I decided that when I grew up I wanted to be like Aunt Clare. She was a close friend of Douglas Bader, the Second World War fighter ace who had lost both his legs in a plane crash. Aunt Clare and Douglas owned an old biplane which they flew together. Sometimes Aunt Clare would parachute out of the plane for fun. She smoked about twenty small cigars a day.

When we stayed with her, we swam in the millpond at the bottom of her garden. Douglas Bader would unstrap his legs and haul himself into the water. I used to run off with these tin legs and hide them in the rushes by the water's edge. Douglas would then pull himself out of the water and come lunging after me: his arms and shoulders were immensely powerful and he could walk on his hands. When he had been held a prisoner of war in Colditz, after two failed escapes the Nazis had confiscated his legs.

'You're as bad as the Nazis,' he'd roar, swinging himself after me on his hands like an orang-utan.

Aunt Clare was as much of an entrepreneur as Mum. She was obsessed with Welsh Mountain sheep, which were then an endangered species, and she bought a few of these black sheep in order to save them from extinction. She eventually bred up a large flock and managed to bring them off the endangered list. She then set up a business which she called The Black Sheep Marketing Company and started selling pottery decorated with pictures of black sheep. The mugs with the nursery rhyme 'Baa Baa Black Sheep' written round the side began to sell rather well. Soon Aunt Clare had all the old ladies in the village knitting her black wool into shawls and sweaters. She worked very hard to build up Black Sheep as a trade name, and she succeeded: over forty years later it's still going strong.

Some years later, in the early days of Virgin Music, I received a call from Aunt Clare: 'Ricky, you won't believe this. One of my sheep has started singing.'

Initially my mind reeled, but it was the sort of thing I had come to expect from her.

'What does it sing?' I asked, imagining a sheep singing, 'Come on, baby, light my fire.'

' "Baa Baa Black Sheep" of course,' she snapped at me. 'Now I want to make a recording. The sheep probably won't do it in a studio so can you send some sound engineers out here? And they'd better hurry since it could stop at any time.'

That afternoon a bunch of sound engineers headed up to Norfolk with a 24-track mobile studio and recorded Aunt Clare's singing sheep. They also amassed an entire choir of sheep, ducks and hens for the chorus, and we released the single 'Baa Baa Black Sheep'. It reached number four in the charts.

My friendship with Nik was based on affection but also on a strong element of competition. I was determined to do everything better than he did. One summer Nik was given a brand-new bike for his birthday. We immediately decided to take it down to do the River Run, a game in which you raced straight downhill, braked at the last moment and skidded to a halt as close to the edge of the riverbank as possible. This was a highly competitive game and I hated losing.

Since it was his bike, Nik went first. He did a very creditable skid, curving round so that the back wheel came to within a foot of the water's edge. Nik generally tried to spur me on to do even more outlandish things, but this time he tried to stop me.

'You can't do better than that skid,' he said. 'Mine was perfect.'

I thought otherwise. I was determined to do a better skid than Nik. I took his bike up the hill and launched myself towards the river, pedalling madly. As I approached the bank it became apparent that I was out of control and had no chance of stopping. In a fast-moving blur I caught sight of Nik's open mouth and horrified expression as I hurtled past him. I tried to brake, but it was too late. I somersaulted head over heels into the water, and the bike sank beneath me. I was swept downstream by the current, but finally managed to clamber back ashore. Nik was waiting for me, enraged.

'You've lost my bike! That's my birthday present!'

He was so furious that he was sobbing with rage. He pushed me back in the water.

'You'd damn well better find it,' he shouted.

'I'll find it,' I spluttered. 'It'll be OK. I'll fish it out.'

'You bloody well better had.'

I spent the next two hours diving down to the bottom of the river and groping around the mud and weeds and stones trying to find his new bike. I couldn't find it anywhere. Nik sat on the bank, hugging his knees up to his chin, glaring at me. Nik was epileptic, and I'd been with him on a couple of occasions in the past when he'd experienced fits. Now he was furious, and I hoped his anger would not spur another one. But eventually, when I was so cold that I could barely talk and my hands were white, numb and bleeding from bashing into rocks on the riverbed, Nik relented.

'Let's go home,' he said. 'You'll never find it.'

We walked back home and I tried to cheer him up: 'We'll buy you another one,' I promised him.

My parents must have groaned because the bike cost over £20, nearly a month's supply of tissue boxes.

When we were eight years old, Nik and I were separated when I was sent away to board at Scaitcliffe Preparatory School in Windsor Great Park.

On my first night at Scaitcliffe, I lay awake in my bed, listening to the snorings and snufflings of the other boys in the dormitory, feeling utterly lonely, unhappy and frightened. At some point in the middle of that first night, I knew I was going to be sick. The feeling came on so fast that I didn't have time to get out of bed and run to the bathroom; instead I vomited all over the bedclothes. The matron was called. Instead of being sympathetic, as my mother would have been, she scolded me and made me clear it up myself. I can still remember the humiliation I felt. Obviously, my parents thought they were doing the right thing in sending me there, but at that moment I could feel only confusion and resentment towards them, and a terrible fear of what lay in store for me. Within a couple of days, an older boy in my dormitory had taken a liking to me and got me into his bed to play 'feelies'. On my first weekend home I matter of factly told my parents what had happened under the sheets. My dad calmly said, 'It's best not to do that sort of thing,' and that was the first and last time such an incident happened.

My father had been sent to boarding school at the same age, and his father before him. It was the traditional way for a boy from my background to be educated, to cultivate independence, self-reliance – to teach someone to stand on their own two feet. But I loathed being sent away from home at such an early age, and have always vowed to myself that I would never send my children to boarding school until they were of an age to make up their own minds about it.

In my third week at Scaitcliffe I was summoned to the headmaster's study and told that I had broken some rule; I think I had walked on to a patch of hallowed grass to retrieve a football. I had to bend down and I was caned across my bottom six times.

'Branson,' the headmaster intoned. 'Say, "Thank you, sir."'

I couldn't believe my ears. Thank him for what?

'Branson.' The headmaster lifted up his cane. 'I'm warning you.'

'Thank you ... sir.'

'You're going to be trouble, Branson.'

'Yes, sir. I mean, no, sir.'

I was trouble – and always in trouble. Aged eight I still couldn't read. In fact, I was dyslexic and short-sighted. Despite sitting at the front of the class, I couldn't read the blackboard. Only after a couple of terms did anyone think to have my eyes tested. Even when I could see, the letters and numbers made no sense at all. Dyslexia wasn't deemed a problem in those days, or, put more accurately, it was only a problem if you were dyslexic yourself. Since nobody had ever heard of dyslexia, being unable to read, write or spell just meant to the rest of the class and the teachers that you were either stupid or lazy. And at prep school you were beaten for both. I was soon being beaten once or twice a week for doing poor classwork or confusing the date of the Battle of Hastings.

My dyslexia was a problem throughout my school life. Now, although my spelling is still sometimes poor, I have managed to overcome the worst of my difficulties through training myself to concentrate. Perhaps my early problems with dyslexia made me more intuitive: when someone sends me a written proposal, rather than dwelling on detailed facts and figures I find that my imagination grasps and expands on what I read.

However, my saving grace was outside the classroom: I was good at sports. It is difficult to overestimate how important sport is at English public schools. If you are good at sports, you are a school hero: the older boys won't bully you and the masters won't mind you failing all your exams. I was intensely keen to succeed at sports, possibly because it was my only opportunity to excel. I became captain of the football, rugby and cricket teams. Every sports day I won a series of cups for sprinting and hurdling. Just before my eleventh birthday, in 1961, I won all the races. I even decided to go in for the long jump. I had never done a good long jump before, but this time I decided to just have a go. I sprinted down the track, took off from the wooden plank and soared through the air. After I landed in the sand the master came up to me and shook me by the hand: it was a new Scaitcliffe School record. That summer day I couldn't put a foot wrong, and my parents and Lindi sat and clapped in the white marquee afterward as I went up to collect every cup. I won the Victor Ludorum. Who cared if I couldn't spell? Not me.

The next autumn term I was playing in a football match against another local school. I was running rings round the defender and had already scored one goal. I put my hand up and yelled for the ball, which was booted upfield and bounced over both of us. I turned and sprinted after it, controlled it and was bearing down on the goal when the defender caught up with me and floored me with a sliding tackle. My leg was caught beneath him as he fell across me. I heard a ghastly scream and for a split second I thought that he was hurt until I realised that it was me. He rolled off me and I saw my knee twisted at a horrible angle. My parents had always told us to laugh when we were in pain, so half laughing but mainly screaming I was carried off the field to the school matron, who drove me to hospital. My agony stopped only after they gave me an injection. I had badly torn the cartilage in my right knee and they were going to have to operate.

I was given a general anaesthetic and fell uncon-scious. I awoke to find myself out in the street. I was still in my hospital bed, and a nurse was holding a drip above my head, but my bed, together with several others, was parked outside. I thought I was dreaming, but the nurse explained that there had been a fire in the hospital during my operation and all the patients had been evacuated on to the street outside.

I went home for a few days to recover. Lying in bed, I looked at my silver cups on the mantelpiece. The doctor told me that I would not play sports again for a very long time.

'Don't worry, Ricky,' my mother said as she swept

into the room after the doctor had gone. 'Just think of Douglas Bader. He hasn't got any legs at all. He's playing golf and flying planes and everything. You don't want to be lying there in bed doing nothing all day, do you?'

The worst aspect of this injury was that it immediately showed up how bad I was in the classroom. I was bottom in every subject and would clearly not pass the Common Entrance exam.

I was sent to another school, a crammer on the Sussex coast called Cliff View House. It had no sports to distract boys from the grim and usually hopeless task of preparing for Common Entrance. If you couldn't spell, or couldn't add up, or couldn't remember that the area of a circle is 'Pi' R squared, then the solution was simple: you were beaten until you did. I learnt my facts in the face of unflinching discipline and with a black and blue backside. I may have been dyslexic, but I had no excuse. I just couldn't get it right. When I gave the inevitable wrong answer it was either more lines or a beating. I grew almost to prefer the beatings since at least they were quick.

There were no games apart from an early-morning run, and, as well as for any faults in class, we were also beaten for almost anything else, such as not making our beds properly, running when we should be walking, talking when we should be quiet, or having dirty shoes. There were so many possible things to do wrong that, although we learnt most of them, we accepted that we would be beaten for some obscure misdemeanour almost every single week.

My only consolation was the headmaster's eighteen-year-old daughter, Charlotte. She seemed to take a fancy to me and I was delighted that I, out of all the boys, should have caught her attention. We soon established a routine of nocturnal visits. Every night I would climb out of my dormitory window and creep over to her bedroom in the headmaster's house. One night, as I climbed back through the window, I was horrified to see one of my teachers watching my progress.

The next morning I was summoned to the head-master's study.

'What were you doing, Branson?' he asked.

The only answer I could think of was the worst one I could possibly have given: 'I was on my way back from your daughter's room, sir.'

Not surprisingly, I was promptly expelled and my parents were told to come and collect me the following day.

That evening, unable to think of any other way to escape the wrath of my parents, I wrote a suicide note saying that I was unable to cope with the shame of my expulsion. I wrote on the envelope that it was not to be opened until the following day but then gave it to a boy who I knew was far too nosy not to open it immediately.

Very, very slowly, I left the building and walked through the school grounds towards the cliffs. When I saw a crowd of teachers and boys beginning to run after me, I slowed down enough for them to catch me up. They managed to drag me back from the cliff and the expulsion was overturned.

My parents were surprisingly relaxed about the whole episode. My father even seemed quite impressed that Charlotte was 'a very pretty girl'.

2 'You will either go to prison or become a millionaire.'

1963–1967

AFTER THE CRAMMER HAD served its purpose by beating me into shape, I moved to Stowe, a big public school in Buckinghamshire for over 800 boys. There I faced a daunting prospect. Fagging was still in place: this was an archaic practice in which the younger boys were expected to run errands and do minor chores for the older ones; in effect, to be their servants. Bullying was rife. Your reputation – and ability to avoid being picked on – was helped enormously by being able to score a goal or hit a six. But I couldn't play any games as my knee buckled whenever I tried to run. Since I was also unable to cope with the academic work, I was very quickly sidelined. Being out of the sports teams and bottom of the class was an unenviable position. It seemed as if all the challenges my parents had set me were now irrelevant.

I found refuge in the library, where I went every afternoon and started writing a novel. I sat in the most wonderful splendour, surrounded by leather-bound books and two globes, overlooking the ornamental lake into which the last head boy had dived and never surfaced. I wrote the most lurid sexual fantasies I could conjure up, amazing erotic stories all about a young boy who couldn't play sports due to a knee injury, but who was befriended and then gloriously and expertly seduced by the young Scandinavian school matron. In my mind's eye she used to creep up behind him when he was working in the library ... But, sadly for me, no matter what incredible sexual encounters I dreamt up, there wasn't a girl, let alone a Scandinavian, within miles of Stowe, and matron was sixty years old.

As I sat in the library panting at my own prose and scribbling faster and faster, I became aware of another regular visitor to the library: Jonathan Holland-Gems. In comparison with most of the boys at Stowe, Jonny was extremely worldly and sophisticated, widely read and staggeringly knowledgeable about the arts. He came from London, where his parents knew journalists and writers: when Jonny read *Private Eye* he knew half the people mentioned in it. His mother was a successful playwright. It was through Jonny that my interest in the world of newspapers began to grow, and I began to think that I would like to be a journalist.

Halfway through the term I read a school announcement about an essay competition called the Junior Gavin Maxwell Prize which had been set up by the author, an old boy from Stowe. I momentarily put aside my pulsating pornography and wrote a short story which won the prize. The complete absence of competition must have helped.

Gavin Maxwell, the author of *Ring of Bright Water*, came to present the prize at Stowe. He arrived with Gavin Young, the *Observer*'s war correspondent and later the author of *Slow Boat to China*. After the ceremony they drove back to Surrey and dropped me off at Shamley Green. I stayed in touch with them. They were very supportive of me, partly, I think, because they fancied me. But once they realised I wasn't that way inclined they still remained good and helpful friends. After winning the prize, my English began to improve and I soared up the class to third out of twenty-one. I was still eighteenth in Latin, and bottom in maths, physics and chemistry. 'He tries hard but has very great difficulty in understanding even the simplest mathematical process and in retaining any new topic covered,' read one end-of-term report.

One Easter holiday, I decided to follow my mother's example and make some money. Undeterred by the school's lack of faith in my ability with numbers, I saw an opportunity to grow Christmas trees. We had just moved house from one side of Shamley Green to the other, from Easteds Cottage to Tanyards Farm, which was a rambling building with many barns and sheds and some land. I went round to talk Nik into the plan. He was also on holiday from his school, which was at Ampleforth in Yorkshire. We would plant 400 Christmas trees in the field at Tanyards Farm. By the Christmas after next, they would have grown to at least four feet and we would be able to sell them. Nik and I agreed to do the work together, and share the profits equally.

That Easter we furrowed the ground and planted the 400 seedlings in the field above Tanyards Farm. We worked out that, if they all grew to six feet, we would make £2 a tree, creating a grand total of £800, compared with our initial investment of just £5 for the seedlings. In the following summer holiday, we went to investigate the trees. There were one or two tiny sprigs above ground, but the rest had been eaten by rabbits. We exacted dire revenge and shot and skinned a lot of rabbits. We sold them to the local butcher for a shilling each, but it wasn't quite the £800 we had planned.

The following Christmas Nik's brother was given a budgerigar as a present. This gave me the idea for another great business opportunity: breeding budgies! For a start, I reasoned, I could sell them all year round rather than just during the fortnight before Christmas. I worked out the prices and made some calculations about how fast they could breed and how cheap their food was, and persuaded my father to build a huge aviary. In my last week at school I wrote to Dad and explained the financial implications:

> So few days now until the holidays. Have you ordered any material we might want for our giant budgerigar cage? I thought our best bet to get the budgerigars at reduced rate would be from Julian Carlyon. I feel that if the shops sold them for 30sh., he would get say 17sh. and we could buy them off him for 18 or 19sh. which would give him a profit and save us the odd 10sh. per bird. How about it?

My father reluctantly built the aviary and the birds bred rapidly. However, I had overestimated the local demand for budgies. Even after everyone in Shamley Green had bought at least two, we were still left with an aviary full of them. One day at school I got a letter from my mother breaking the bad news that the aviary had been invaded by rats which had eaten the budgies. It was only many years later that she confessed she had been fed up with cleaning out the aviary so one day had left the cage door open and they all escaped. She didn't try too hard to recapture them.

But, while neither of these schemes had the effect of making money, they did teach me something about maths. I found that it was only when I was using real numbers to solve real problems that maths made any sense to me. If I was calculating how much a Christmas tree would grow, or how many budgies would breed, the numbers then became real and I enjoyed using them. Inside the classroom I was still a complete dunce at maths. I once did an IQ test in which the questions just seemed absurd. I couldn't focus on any of the mathematical problems, and I think that I scored about zero. I worry about all the people who have been classified as stupid by these kinds of tests. Little do they know that often these IQ tests have been dreamt up by academics who are absolutely useless at dealing with the practicalities of the outside world. I loved doing real business plans – even if the rabbits did get the better of me.

I think my parents must have instilled a rebellious streak in me. I have always thought rules were there to be broken, and Stowe had as many rules and regulations as the army – many of them, it seemed to Jonny Gems and me, completely anachronistic and pointless. There was the outmoded practice of fagging, for one thing. Then there was the CCF (Combined Cadet Force), in which boys dressed up as soldiers and paraded around with antiquated rifles; and compulsory church attendance on Sundays. I managed to dodge the latter by skipping the first service of the new term: my name was left off the register, and I was never missed from then on.

During January and February 1966, Jonny and I began to talk about how to change the school rules. We were fifteen years old, but we believed that we could make a difference. My parents had brought me up to think that we could all change the world, so when I looked at how Stowe was run I felt sure that I could do it better. Stowe was actually reasonably liberal in encouraging boys of all ages to contribute to the running of the school.

Jonny and I were particularly incensed by the rule that anyone who wasn't playing games had to go and watch the school team when they were playing another school. Although we were able to go to the library during weekday afternoons, we were still forced to watch the school teams play most Saturdays. I knew that if I hadn't been ruled out by my weak knee I would be in the teams, so I felt doubly frustrated. I wrote to the headmaster:

> I am against the utter waste of time that is spent in compulsory watching of matches. If one is unable to play for the First XI one should be able to spend one's time in better ways than that. I know this sounds a frightful break against tradition etc., but I feel very strongly about this. If 450-odd people watching matches spent that time in Buckingham cleaning windows, for instance, they would gain at least something more than 'watching others achieving something'.

I also tried to reorganise the system of school meals:

> I feel that to improve Stowe one has first got to do it socially, even before religiously. There are many boys who are thirsting for knowledge through interesting conversations. One of the best times to talk is at meals, but at Stowe this is practically impossible. One goes into hall, sits down at one's allotted table next to the same boys every day. A canteen must be constructed in one of the dining rooms. Then boys could choose their own food; they would be free to sit down where they wish; and they could put their forks and plates in a box when they go out. The food waste at the moment is fantastic, and with a canteen system you could cut down on at least half the Italian and Spanish waiters.
>   I would be very interested in your views on this, and any money saved could possibly be put towards my next plan ...

And I went on to explore the idea of a sixth-form bar.

The headmaster suggested that I air my views in the school magazine, but Jonny and I wanted to set up an alternative magazine with a fresh attitude. We wanted to campaign against fagging, corporal punishment, and compulsory chapel, games and Latin. All these ideas were far too 'revolutionary' to be aired in the school magazine, *The Stoic*, a name which seemed only too apt to its long-suffering readers. We then thought about linking up with other schools that had similar rules. Gradually the idea of an interschool magazine was hatched. We would link up with other schools and swap ideas. I jotted down a few titles in a school notebook: *Today*, *1966*, *Focus!*, *Modern Britain*, and *Interview*. Then I wrote out what I wanted to publish and did some more sums in which, once again, I enjoyed thinking about the implications of the maths:

Letters to write.

300 Public school masters: 3×300 = 600d.
+ Envelopes. } 300d
Writing Paper :

12) 900d
75 sh.

Other Debts.

1000 copies Profit £75. at 1/6.
But postage per copy. Profit £58 at 1/2.
Also demands from Shops. Profit £45 at 1½d

Also Publication debts.

1000 copies £45-£60 — ?

I wrote out a list of 250 MPs whom I found in *Who's Who*, and a list of possible advertisers whom I found by going through the telephone book. I also wrote to WH Smith asking whether they would be prepared to stock the magazine. Thus, with contributors, advertisers, distributors and costs all in place – at least on paper – I had written my first business plan.

The numbers looked too small to work, so Jonny and I decided to involve more schools, and technical colleges and universities: it would open up the magazine to more people, and encourage advertisers. We thought that if we aimed the magazine at university students then sixth-formers would buy it; but if we published a magazine for sixth-formers then students wouldn't be interested.

We settled on the name *Student*, which seemed a good one since at the time there was a great deal of talk about 'student power'. This was the period of student sit-ins, occupations and demos at universities and polytechnics. It was an exciting time to be young. My mother lent me £4 as a float against the cost of telephone calls and letters, and Jonny's father arranged for headed notepaper with STUDENT – THE MAGAZINE FOR BRITAIN'S YOUTH printed across the top with the symbol of a rising sun. We set to work writing to all the contributors and possible advertisers.

Student was a perfect vehicle: it gave us a new lease of life. There was so much to organise. I began to set up an office in my study at school and asked the headmaster for a telephone in my room – he unsurprisingly refused. As a result I had to make telephone calls from a call box, but I quickly discovered a useful trick: if I called up the operator and told her that the machine had taken my money but my call had been disconnected, I was able to get a free call. As well as a free call, I was able to avoid the telltale 'pip – pip –

"Today"
"1966"
MODERN
BRITAIN
"Focus!" "INTERVIEW"

<u>Public school</u>.

A new political magazine with the aim of getting every Public School boy more interested in politics and to know about the improvements and "goings on" at every other public school in the country.

To be a 100 pages long 15"x 9" wide and on the same sort of paper as "The Economist" or "Punch".

To be 1/6 in price and strongly advertised before first edition comes out on Saturday June 4th (Stowe's Speech day.)

To be bought out every 4 months with the aim of cutting that down after a year.

4000 copies to be published the first 3 months.

To have data ready for the next magazine as the first comes out.

To have three representatives from each Public School writing + headmasters and other masters.

To have a large collection of M.P.'s writing.

To have famous authors writing.

To have members of the public contributing

pip' as the coins went in. Better still, the operator sounded like a secretary: 'I have Mr Branson for you.'

I drew up lists and lists of people to call, and slowly worked my way down them. Most of them rejected the idea of paying for advertising in an unpublished magazine, but gradually I began to find ways of attracting their attention. I would call up National Westminster Bank and tell them that Lloyds Bank had just taken out a full-page advertisement; would they like to advertise alongside Lloyds Bank? *Student* would be Britain's biggest magazine for young people, I added. I called up Coca-Cola and told them that Pepsi had just booked a big advertisement but that the back page was still free. I called up the *Daily Telegraph* and asked them whether they would prefer to advertise before or after the *Daily Express*. Another tack was to ask an innocuous question that they couldn't easily deny: 'Are you interested in recruiting the highest-calibre school-leavers and university graduates?' No personnel manager would ever admit that they were looking for mediocre recruits. 'Then we're publishing just the magazine for you ...'

In order to avoid the operator coming back on the line to cut me off, I learnt how to pack all this into five minutes. I started speaking faster and pushing harder. My voice had broken early, and nobody guessed that they were talking to a fifteen-year-old schoolboy standing in a public telephone box. I gave my address at Shamley Green, and when I sent out letters I wrote them by the dozen and posted them to my parents, who in turn asked Elizabeth, an old friend in the village, to type them.

My schoolwork was going from bad to worse, but I was giving myself a wonderful lesson in confidence-building. Had I been five or six years older, the sheer absurdity of trying to sell advertising to major companies, in a magazine that did not yet exist, edited by two fifteen-year-old schoolboys, would have prevented me from picking up the phone at all. But I was too young to contemplate failure.

During the holidays I told Nik all about *Student*. He was equally excited and agreed to help distribute it in Ampleforth. He would also try to find contributors for it. Nik recognised that *Student* was really my and Jonny's creation, so he stood back a little bit, but he was as enthusiastic as we were about its potential. We were fifteen years old and felt we could do anything.

By April 1966 and the run-up to O levels, I was able to drop a number of subjects that I had no chance of passing and put even more time into *Student*. To my relief and that of my Latin and science teachers we went our separate ways: 'He is a very weak candidate indeed at Latin and he has now given it up' and 'His interest in science was obviously minimal. Although I am far from convinced that he could not have done better than he did, it was quite evident that he was never going to make much progress.' I was doing better at history, French and English, but not at maths, which was compulsory: 'In spite of much apparent effort he is finding difficulty in retaining methods of attack on problems from one week to the next. He will need a lot of luck with the questions in July.'

However, the main excitement in my life was writing the hundreds of letters which I started sending out from Stowe, and waiting on tenterhooks for the answers. For all my enthusiasm and new-found guile, it took a long time to find any advertisers willing to commit themselves to taking space in *Student*. Jonny and I sent letters out all summer term, continued in the holidays and through the following autumn term. By April 1967, with my single ancient-history A level looming in the summer (I was to take it after only one year in the sixth

45

form), we were still no nearer pulling a magazine together. Jonny and I had been working on *Student* for over a year, and all we had to show for it were dozens of letters of support from various headmasters and teachers, and various vague promises to contribute from politicians, but no advertisements or hard copy. I refused to bow to the inevitable. My letter home dated 27 April 1967 apologised for the small amount of time I had spent with my family over Easter:

It was a wonderful holiday these last four weeks and more was achieved than ever before. I only hope you do not feel too annoyed with me for not being home longer and for not making the time to do more in the garden. I, possibly wrongly, see a divided duty: one to my home, and one to *Student*. It is a difficult decision. Anything I do in life I want to do well and not half-heartedly. I feel I am doing my best in *Student* – as well as the time allows. Yet that leaves little time for my other duty. To me I saw a danger of falling between two stools and still do. Of being a failure in everything I had and having to search for priorities if I am to get anywhere. I am also still only sixteen. Although it sounds a terribly 'I' thing to say, and I only say it in defence, what do most sixteen-year-olds do? No one I know here did anything more last holidays than I used to do two or three years ago, flicks in the evening, mucking about during the day. What did you do when you were a boy of sixteen? Shoot, fish, swim, go out with girls on one side and possibly your museum and helping around the garden on the other side. You had time to help around the garden. You did not see the world as it is today when you were sixteen. Your career was almost lined up. Today it is one long struggle.

You say *Student* is selfish and self-centred of me. 'Possibly,' I say. But is it any more selfish than anything else one does in life? It is, in my opinion, a career like anything else. It could benefit many many more people than going to the films etc. It is a beginning to my life like university or your finals were to yours. It might sound really foul of me bringing this up in my first letter, but I've had little else on my mind over the last two weeks and felt it made sense to get it down on paper.

I was lucky. I always felt that I could speak to my parents as if they were my closest friends. Rather than closing down on me, they reacted very well to this letter and we kept open our lines of communication. At about this time I noticed that a good many of my friends stopped confiding in their parents, but I never felt embarrassed or rebellious towards mine. They always encouraged me to go ahead and do whatever I wanted to do, and if they did not always praise my projects they never expressed less than sympathy and support. The last thing my father wanted to do was to spend his weekends building a cage for my budgerigars, but he never told me. My mother was extremely keen to help me with *Student*, and wrote articles, gave me pocket money that she could scarcely spare and thought of people whom I should approach. Once when I told her that I wanted to get in touch with David Frost, she spent weeks asking all her friends whether they knew anyone who knew anyone who knew David Frost.

Then we had our first breakthroughs: we received our first hard copy, a £250 cheque for an advertisement, and Gerald Scarfe agreed to draw a cartoon for us and be interviewed. *Student* was finally changing from a gleam in my mind's eye to a real magazine.

* * *

The other thing that changed from a bright gleam to a reality was sex. I had a number of girlfriends during the holidays and came tantalisingly closer and closer to losing my virginity at parties, when the lights went out and everyone lay around on cushions.

I finally found a girl who was reputed to go the whole way, and at one party we slipped upstairs into a remote bedroom. I was amazed when she let me push up her skirt and take off her knickers. As we began to make love, she started to moan and groan. She was clearly having a very erotic time. I was pretty pleased by how well I must be performing since she was panting and tossing her head from side to side as she fought to control her breathing. I put up a great show and finally came with equally impressive gusto, roaring and shouting and huffing and puffing. Then I rolled off her. To my astonishment she carried on panting, apparently having what I took to be ecstatic multiple orgasms. Just as I was beginning to feel a little bemused and somewhat redundant, I finally realised that she was panting for a reason.

'Asthma!' she wheezed in breathless panic. 'Inhaler! Ambulance!'

Happily my first steady girlfriend was healthy and Dutch. Rudi was a Dutch 'revolutionary', and in my last term I invited her to Stowe: she slipped into the school grounds and secretly pitched her tent in the middle of the wood. For one glorious week I crept out every night and walked past the lake to the woods where Rudi would be smoking pot and cooking over a tin stove. We lay out under the stars and talked about what we would do to change the world. Rudi was passionately interested in world politics. She became *Student*'s grandly titled 'Dutch overseas correspondent' and went on to write some powerful pieces about the Baader Meinhof terrorist gang.

After dropping all subjects except ancient history, I had even more time for *Student* magazine. Soon Jonny and I were regularly taking the train to London to interview people. However, I had to take my A level, and I was having difficulty remembering facts that struck me as meaningless and abstract. I had bought some fact-file cards on ancient history which contained all the necessary information about Greece and Rome. In preparation for the exam I cut the edges off these and put them in various pockets, even sliding one under my watch strap. When I looked at the questions in the exam, the most difficult thing was remembering which pocket the relevant facts were in. Then I pulled the card out of my pocket and held it curled in the palm of my left hand as I wrote with my right. As it happened, I was too preoccupied with *Student* to care about what grade I achieved. I was just intent on leaving Stowe as quickly as possible and starting life as a journalist in London.

When I left Stowe in 1967 aged almost seventeen, my headmaster's parting words to me were: 'Congratulations, Branson. I predict that you will either go to prison or become a millionaire.'

The next and final time I heard from Stowe was six months later in a letter from the headmaster dated 16 January 1968:

Dear Branson,

I have been pleased to see that the press have given you a good send-off and I was very interested to see a copy of your first issue. May I send you congratulations and all good wishes for the future.

Yours,

R Drayson

The first issue of *Student* was published in January 1968.

49

3 Virgins at business

1967–1970

A T THE END OF the summer term, 1967, Jonny Gems and I moved into the basement of his parents' house in Connaught Square, just off the Edgware Road in London. We managed to persuade Vanessa Redgrave to change her mind from merely sending us her best wishes for the success of *Student* to giving us an interview. The interview was a turning point for us since we could now use her name as a magnet to attract other contributors. As the list of contributors grew to include people like David Hockney and Jean-Paul Sartre, it became correspondingly easier for me to persuade some of the possible advertisers that *Student* would be a worthwhile place for them to appear.

Jonny and I lived in the basement all summer. The room was dark, dank, and sparsely furnished. We slept on mattresses on the floor. The place quickly began to look a complete shambles, scattered with papers, dirty coffee cups and fish-and-chip wrappers. We were always hungry. Sometimes we would slip upstairs to raid Jonny's parents' fridge. Mum would occasionally burst in through the door carrying a picnic hamper.

'Red Cross delivery!' she would shout. 'When did you two last wash?'

We would spread a counterpane on the floor and pile into her picnic.

One day she brought us £100 in cash. Mum had found a necklace on the road near Shamley Green and taken it into the police station. When nobody had claimed it after three months, the police told her she could have it. She knew we had no money, so she came up to London, sold it and gave us the money. Her £100 paid off our telephone and postage bills and kept us going for months. Without it we could have collapsed.

Peter Blake, who was famous for designing The Beatles' *Sergeant Pepper* album cover, drew a picture of a student for our first edition. It was a plain white cover with only two splashes of red: on the title, *Student*, and the red tie the student wore. As well as giving us this illustration, Peter Blake also gave us an interview. He began in arresting style: 'A very pretty girl with no clothes on is a marvellous subject, and one I'm particularly interested in. It is one of those things, along with perspective and anatomy, which teaches you how to draw.'

While I rapidly considered the advantages of becoming an artist, he went on to point out the dangers of 'student power' – which struck a controversial note at the time:

> I don't think the students should have any more power over the teachers than they have already. Just at the moment I don't really like students as a group of people. I think they rather overrate themselves. They seem to talk a lot and protest a lot, and have too many rights. I think one could get overinvolved in the activity of being a student. After all, students are not so important – they are really only there to learn how to be adults. Students shouldn't feel that they *have* to complain.

Perhaps because we were so young and not as aggressive as the usual professional interviewers they faced, some of our contributors made very revealing and graphic remarks. Gerald Scarfe described his work: 'I'll always draw – it's a matter of energy. I could never stop. It's as much a part of me as eating. When I get an idea it has to come out – it is like being sick, a bodily function.' When I asked Dudley Moore what he thought of students he answered: 'The only thing I hate about your generation is your age.' He had been an organ scholar at Magdalen College, Oxford, but when I mentioned classical music he said: 'I'd much rather roll about in the mud with six women all day than sit down at the piano.'

Mick Jagger and John Lennon also agreed to be interviewed. Both were demigods to the student population. *Student* gave a grandiose introduction to the Jagger interview:

> Recently *Melody Maker* wrote: 'Jagger is rather like Dostoyevsky's brother Karamazov who, when told by his venerable brother that pain must exist so that we might learn of goodness, replied that, if it was necessary that one small child should suffer in order that he should be made more aware, he did not deny the existence of God, but merely respectfully returned his ticket of admission to heaven. That is Mick Jagger's kind of rebellion.'

I can't imagine what we were thinking of when we quoted that. I certainly didn't understand it.

I nervously went along to his house on Cheyne Walk, and was shown into the living room by Marianne Faithfull, who then tantalisingly disappeared upstairs. Mick and I smiled at each other genially but were both equally at a loss for words:

RB: Do you like giving interviews?

MJ: No.

RB: Why did you ask *Student* to interview you?

MJ: I don't know. I've got no idea. I don't usually give interviews. I mean, hardly ever.

RB: You're not interested in politics?

MJ: No.

RB: Why not?

MJ: Because I've kind of thought about it for a long time and decided that I haven't got time to do that and understand other things. I mean, if you get involved in politics you get really fucked up.

RB: Do you think people can be influenced by music?

MJ: Yeah, I think they probably can because it's one of those things – it's repetitive, the same thing over and over again. It gets into your brain and influences you.

Our interview with John Lennon was another 'classic'. Jonny and I went along together, and Jonny tried to make a literary allusion:

JG: A critic has written about 'A Day In The Life' as a kind of miniature *Waste Land*.

JL: Miniature what?

JG: TS Eliot's poem, *The Waste Land*.

JL: I don't know about that. Not very hip on me culture, you know.

Ironically, the interview with John was almost the end of *Student*. After Jonny and I had met him, I had the idea of asking whether John and Yoko would provide the magazine with an original recording which we could distribute with *Student* as a flexidisc.

I contacted Derek Taylor, The Beatles' press officer.

At that time, The Beatles had just set up the Apple Foundation for the Arts, with the idea of funding struggling artists and musicians. Most of Derek's day was spent sitting in his office in Savile Row, interviewing a long procession of supplicants, all with a hundred different reasons why they thought The Beatles should give them money. He was like a lord chamberlain at the court of the king. A sweet man, Derek would listen patiently to every request, no matter how far-fetched or nonsensical.

When I told him what we wanted to do, Derek agreed without a moment's hesitation. John and Yoko would be delighted to provide something, he said. He introduced me to Ron Kass, the managing director of Apple, and to a manufacturer of flexidiscs, and we arranged a delivery date.

I rushed back to Connaught Square with the good news. Not only did we have a John Lennon interview: we would soon have an original, unreleased John Lennon song. It was a fantastic promotional coup for *Student*. We contacted Alan Aldridge, the most fashionable illustrator of the day, and commissioned him to design a special front cover, leaving a white space where the flexidisc would be attached. And we made plans to print 100,000 copies of the magazine – our largest ever print run.

The weeks went by, and still no record arrived. In mounting anxiety I called Derek. 'Don't worry, Richard,' he said. 'We've had a few problems. But I promise you'll get something.' In fact, I could hardly have chosen a worse time to tax the Lennons' goodwill. Yoko had just lost the baby she was expecting; John had been busted for possession of cannabis; and the couple were lying low at their mansion in Weybridge.

I was in trouble myself. Our plans for the special issue had put *Student* on the brink of bankruptcy. I was getting desperate. For the first time in my life, I contacted a lawyer, Charles Levison, who wrote to Derek, threatening to sue Apple and the Lennons for breach of promise.

A few days later, I received a telephone call from Derek. 'Come round to Apple, Richard,' he said. 'We've got something for you.'

That afternoon I sat in the basement studio at Apple, with Charles, Derek, John and Yoko, listening to the recording they'd provided. The hiss of the tape recorder was followed by a steady, metronomic beat – like the sound of a human heart.

'What is it?' I asked.

'It's the heartbeat of our baby,' said John.

No sooner had he spoken than the sound stopped. Yoko burst into floods of tears and hugged John. I didn't understand what was going on, but before I could speak John looked over Yoko's shoulder straight into my eyes.

'The baby died,' he told me. 'That's the silence of our dead baby.'

I went back to *Student* with no idea what I should do. I felt unable to release this private moment as a record. Perhaps I was wrong because, as Derek said, it was 'conceptual art' and would have become a collector's piece. We had to scrap the covers and redesign the magazine. It cost a lot of money, but somehow we managed to scrape it together. I considered taking legal action against the Lennons, but they'd had enough problems and, anyway, they'd honoured the agreement in their own particular way, even if I couldn't see the value of it at the time. After our dispute over the recording, Derek wrote a note apologising for all the trouble I'd been caused. His sign-off was a phrase he put on all his correspondence: 'All you need is love ...'

Jonny read extensively. I hardly read at all. I never

seemed to have the time. I would spend the days on the telephone, trying to sell advertising space, persuading people to write for *Student* for nothing, or to be interviewed. Throughout my life, I've always needed somebody as a counterbalance, to compensate for my weaknesses, and work off my strengths. Jonny and I were a good team. He knew who we should interview, and why. I had the ability to persuade them to say yes, and the obstinacy never to accept no for an answer.

In many of the interviews I conducted for *Student* I just turned the tape recorder on and let the interviewee say whatever they wanted. Before meeting the Scottish psychiatrist RD Laing, I had tried to read his bestseller, *The Politics of Experience*. Like most people, I suspect, I had understood hardly a word of it. I aimed the microphone at him and he spoke without stopping for an hour and a half, staring at a corner of the ceiling behind my head. I had no idea what he was rabbiting on about; I was just grateful that there wasn't any room for me to ask him a single question. At the end, when it became apparent that he had finished, I thanked him profusely, went back to the office and transcribed it. It turned out that he had just quoted pages from *The Politics of Experience*, almost verbatim.

After a few issues, the number of people involved with *Student* began to grow. Jonny and I would sometimes go to nightclubs and chat up girls. Sometimes we could even persuade them to come back to the flat, 'for coffee'. If they stayed the night, the next morning we would try to persuade them to help out. For some reason, they often seemed to take pity on us. Word of mouth spread: old friends turned up from school; friends of friends, or people who had read the magazine, wanted to be involved. Increasingly, the basement resembled a squat. We all worked for no money, living off whatever was in the fridge and going out for cheap curries.

All sorts of people helped to distribute the magazine. The basic idea was that they would take away bundles of magazines and sell them for 2/6d a copy, and then come back and give us half the proceeds, 1/3d for each copy sold. They were meant to pay us in advance, but it rarely seemed to work like that. But I never really worried about how much profit *Student* made: I was just determined to have enough cash in the kitty to produce the next issue and pay our bills. I thought that, the more copies we sold, the more word of mouth would spread and ultimately the more advertising we would be able to attract.

Although I hardly realised it at the time, my ambition to be a journalist was beginning to be pushed to one side by the imperatives of keeping the magazine afloat. Jonny ran the editorial side while I ran the business and sold advertising space and argued with the printers. I was becoming an entrepreneur almost by default, although if anybody had mentioned the word to me then I would probably have had to ask Jonny what it meant. I certainly didn't regard myself as a business-man. Businessmen were middle-aged men in the City obsessed with making money. They wore pinstripe suits and had wives and 2.4 children in the suburbs. Of course, we wanted to make money on *Student* too – we needed money to survive. But we saw it much more as a creative enterprise than a money-making one.

Later, it became apparent to me that business could be a creative enterprise in itself. If you publish a magazine, you're trying to create something that is original, that stands out from the crowd, that will last and, hopefully, serve some useful purpose. Above all, you want to create something you are proud of. That has always been my philosophy of business. I can honestly say that I have never gone into any business purely to make money. If that is the sole motive then I believe you are better off not doing it. A business has to be involving; it has to be fun, and it has to exercise your creative instincts.

Running *Student* was certainly fun. Each day unfolded to the deafening strains of Bob Dylan, The Beatles or The Stones blaring out of the hi-fi system, shaking the walls of the basement. When Jonny and I went out to sell copies of the magazine, we would celebrate a single sale of the magazine for 2/6d by going and buying two hamburgers for 1/3d each. Every now and then I would look out of the grimy basement window and see that it was a beautiful day. I would turn off the music and tell everyone we had to go out for a walk. We would wander across Hyde Park and then somehow someone would end up in the Serpentine and we'd all have a swim.

Tony Mellor was one of the main assistant editors, and we all respected him because he had been a trade-union official. Tony was rather older than the rest of us, and was extremely articulate about socialism. As everyone argued over the exact wording of some of the more political pronouncements in the magazine, I was beginning to be aware of a wider picture: the politics of survival. In some ways I became an outsider on the magazine. While the others would be talking about the 'LSD guru' Timothy Leary, Pink Floyd and the latest convolutions of student politics, I would be worrying about paying the printers and telephone bills. As well as spending time on the telephone trying to persuade leading figures of the day to write for *Student*, just for the love of it, I also had to spend hours calling up companies such as British Leyland or Lloyds Bank, trying to convince them to buy advertising space. Without their money, *Student* would collapse.

The responsibility made me grow up fast. You might almost say that I was old before my time. While the others might happily sit around in the evening getting stoned, unconcerned about waking up late the next morning with a hangover, I was always aware of the need to keep a clear head.

My parents and Lindi came up to help us sell copies of the magazine. Mum took a bundle to Speaker's Corner in Hyde Park and pushed them into the unsuspecting hands of tourists. Lindi and I walked up and down Oxford Street selling copies of *Student* to anybody we could stop. I was once with Lindi when a tramp came up and asked for money. We had no money – that's exactly what we were looking for too – but in a histrionic fit of idealism I stripped off most of my clothes and gave them to him. I spent the rest of the day walking around in a blanket.

'Poor old tramp!' Dad chuckled when he heard the story. 'That'll teach him. All he wanted was some loose change, and he got a set of infested clothes from you!'

Student began to attract a high profile, and one day a German television channel asked me whether I would make a speech at University College, London, along with the activist Tariq Ali and the German student leader Danny Cohn-Bendit. The brief was to talk about people's rights. A vast crowd welcomed these two firebrand revolutionaries. I stood and listened as Danny Cohn-Bendit made a brilliant speech full of intellectual depth and passion. Everyone around him was cheering and roaring their approval. Then Tariq Ali stood up, and he too made a passionate speech. The crowd stamped and shouted at the tops of their voices as if they were about to descend upon the Bastille. I began to feel a little queasy.

At Stowe there had been a very cruel tradition. Each boy had to learn a long poem and stand up in front of the entire school and recite it. If you made the slightest mistake or paused for a moment, the master hit a gong, and you had to leave the stage accompanied by great boos and jeers all round: you were 'gonged' off. Since I was mildly dyslexic I found it extremely difficult to learn anything by heart, and for several years was gonged off with relentless regularity. As I watched Danny Cohn-Bendit and Tariq Ali making their inspiring speeches, surfing on the goodwill of the crowd and milking the television camera for all it was worth, I felt the same sickening feeling in my stomach as I had felt when I was waiting to recite my Tennyson piece in the sure knowledge that I would be 'gonged' off stage and loudly booed.

Finally Tariq Ali finished his speech. There was pandemonium. Everyone cheered; somebody hoisted him on their shoulders; pretty girls waved admiringly up at him and the camera swivelled in his direction. Then somebody beckoned to me: it was my turn. I hopped up to the podium and nervously took the microphone. I had barely spoken in public, let alone made a speech before, and I felt chronically nervous. I had absolutely no idea what to say. I had prepared a speech but, under the scrutiny of a thousand expectant faces turned towards me like sunflowers, my mind had gone completely blank. Dry-mouthed, I mumbled a few words, gave a sick smile, and realised with a mounting feeling of panic that I could not do it. There was nowhere to hide. I gave a final inarticulate mumble, somewhere between a cough and a vomit, dropped the microphone, leapt off the podium and disappeared back into the safety of the crowd. It had been the most embarrassing moment of my life.

Even now, whenever I am interviewed or have to give a speech, I feel the same trepidation and I have to overcome the same sense of shyness. If I'm talking on a subject that I know a little about, or that I feel passionately about, then I can be reasonably fluent. But, when I'm asked to talk about something I know very little about, I become extremely uncomfortable – and it shows. I have come to accept that I will never have all the smooth instant answers that a politician would have. I try not to fight my stutters or inability to leap to a perfect answer. Instead, I just try to give the truthful answer, and, if it takes a little time to work out that answer, I hope that people will trust a slow, hesitant response more than a rapid, glib one.

The wars in Vietnam and Biafra were the two leading issues of the late 1960s. If *Student* was to be a credible publication we had to have our own reporters in both countries. We had no money to send any reporters out there, let alone pay for them to stay in hotels and telex back articles, so we had to think laterally. We finally came up with the idea that if we chose very young reporters then they might be a story in themselves. So I called up the *Daily Mirror* and asked whether they would be interested in running an exclusive story about a seventeen-year-old reporter going to Vietnam. They bought the story and paid for Julian Manyon, who was working with us at *Student*, to go to Vietnam. Julian went there, filed some great articles about the Vietnam War, and subsequently went on to become a famous ITN reporter. We managed to make the same arrangement with sending a sixteen-year-old reporter to Biafra. These two ventures were my first experience of leveraging up the *Student* name: we put in the name and the people, and the other side put up the money to fund it.

I felt very passionately about the campaign to end American involvement in Vietnam. In October 1968 all the *Student* staff joined Vanessa Redgrave on the student march to Grosvenor Square, to protest outside the American embassy. I marched alongside Vanessa and Tariq Ali. It was tremendously exciting to be marching for something I believed in, along with tens of thousands of others. The mood of the crowd was exhilarating, but at the same time slightly frightening. You felt at any moment that things could get out of control. And they did. When the police charged the crowd, I ran like hell. A photograph of the demonstration later appeared in *Paris Match*. It shows me, back arched, an inch away from the outstretched hand of a policeman who was trying to catch me as I sprinted across the square.

While I opposed Vietnam, I didn't feel as passionately left-wing on other issues as most of my fellow demonstrators.

'I suppose I am left-wing,' I told a reporter from the *Guardian*. 'Well, only to the extent that I think left-wing views are sane and rational.'

Student was not a radical magazine in the political sense. Nor were we an 'underground' magazine, like *Oz* and *IT*. We weren't advocating putting LSD in the water supply, as they might have done from time to time – although I think there was just as much free love in our offices as there was in theirs.

I tried to maintain a balance between the views of the left and the right, but what I hoped was balance some people saw as prevarication. The writer and poet Robert Graves wrote to me from Deià, Majorca, where he lived:

Your hands seem tied tighter than students deserve.
In the Biafra story, for instance, you don't once
mention what the war is *really* about in the
international context. But that is because you have to
keep pals with the 'overthirties' and the Big Business
Boys, or the journal couldn't survive. Yes, you do
your best.

In fact, the 'Big Business Boys' weren't being as
friendly as I'd hoped. The struggle to secure advertising
had always been much more difficult than finding
contributors. We were pleased to be able to interview
the actor Bryan Forbes or publish Gavin Maxwell's
article, but they didn't bring in money to help us run
the magazine and distribute it. We charged £250 for a
whole-page advertisement, down to £40 for an eighth of
a page. For example, after countless calls I had
managed to get nine companies to take out full-page ads
in the first edition: J Walter Thompson, Metal Box, the
Sunday Times, the *Daily Telegraph*, The Gas Council (the
forerunner to British Gas), *The Economist*, Lloyds Bank,
Rank Organisation, and John Laing Builders. These
nine advertisements had brought in £2,250 and had
been wrung out of a list that started off with over 300
possible companies. But it had been enough to cover the
cost of printing the 30,000 copies of the first issue. With
these funds I had opened an account at Coutts, where
my family had always banked, as our clearing bank. I
must have been their only customer who walked in
barefoot and asked for a £1,000 overdraft. Throughout
the life of *Student*, selling advertising space was always
an uphill struggle.

For all our efforts, it was clear that *Student* wasn't
making money. I began to think of ways to develop the
magazine, and the *Student* name, in other directions: a

Student conference, a *Student* travel company, a *Student* accommodation agency. I didn't just see *Student* as an end in itself, a noun. I saw it as the beginning of a whole range of services, an adjective, a word that people would recognise as having certain key values. In 1970s language, *Student* magazine and everything *Student* promoted should be 'hip'. *Student* was a flexible concept and I wanted to explore this flexibility to see how far I could push it and where it would lead. In this way I was a little removed from the rest of my friends, who concentrated exclusively on the magazine and the student politics they wanted to cover.

It seems Peter Blake was right in saying that student revolution would go out of fashion – and students with it. However, looking at the early editions of *Student* thirty years later, I'm amazed by how little has changed. *Student* then had cartoons of Ted Heath by Nicholas Garland; he was still being caricatured right up until his death by Nicholas Garland. David Hockney, Dudley Moore and John Le Carré still make good copy, and Bryan Forbes and Vanessa Redgrave, or at least their daughters, are still in the news.

Life in the basement was the kind of all-embracing, glorious chaos in which I thrived and have thrived ever since. We never had any money; we were incredibly busy; but we were a close-knit team. We worked together because it was fun, because we felt that what we were doing was important, and because we had great lives together.

Soon a number of journalists from the national papers came to interview me to see what all the buzz was about. We developed a foolproof way of impressing them. I sat at my desk, the telephone at my elbow.

'Great to meet you. Take a seat,' I would say, waving the journalist down into the beanbag opposite me. As they shuffled around trying to retain their dignity, get comfortable, and remove the drips of houmous and piles of cigarette ash from the folds, the telephone would ring.

'Can someone take that, please?' I would ask. 'Now –' I turned my attention to the journalist '– what do you want to know about *Student*?'

'It's Ted Heath for you, Richard,' Tony would call across.

'I'll call him back,' I'd say over my shoulder. 'Now, what did you want to know about *Student*?'

By this time the journalist was craning round to watch Tony tell Ted Heath that he was sorry but Richard was in a meeting and he'd call him back. Then the telephone would ring again, and Tony would pick it up.

'David Bailey for you, Richard.'

'I'll call him back, but will you ask if he can change that lunch date? I've got to be in Paris. OK –' I'd flash an apologetic grin at the journalist '– now, how are we doing?'

'I just wanted to ask you –'

The telephone rang again.

'I'm sorry to interrupt,' Tony would apologise, 'but it's Mick Jagger for you and he says it's urgent.'

'Please excuse me for a minute,' I'd say, reluctantly picking up the phone. 'Mick, hello. Fine thanks, and you? Really? An exclusive? Yes, that sounds great ...'

And on I went until Jonny couldn't stop laughing in the call box opposite or the pips went.

'I'm sorry,' I'd say to the journalist. 'Something's cropped up and we've got to dash. Are we finished?'

The journalist would be ushered out in a daze, passing Jonny on the way, and the telephone would stop ringing.

Journalists swallowed our scam hook, line and sinker: 'Photographers, journalists, writers from papers throughout the world seem to have fallen over themselves in assisting *Student*,' wrote the *Sunday Telegraph*, 'and a massive voluntary distribution organisation has grown throughout schools and universities, allowing, perhaps, over half a million students to read the magazine.'

'An amazing number of top-class contributors. Its scope is limitless,' said the *Observer*. While the *Daily Telegraph* said, 'It seems probable that *Student*, the glossy publication that has attracted a lot of well-known writers, will become one of the largest circulated magazines in the country.'

By autumn 1968 Jonny's parents had understandably had enough of having almost twenty teenagers squatting in their basement and asked us to find somewhere else to live. We moved to 44 Albion Street, just round the corner from Connaught Square. Jonny left to go back to school and take his A levels. He felt guilty about abandoning me, but he was under pressure to continue his education, and his parents sensibly worried that working on a small magazine from their basement was hardly the perfect foundation on which to earn much of a living.

Without Jonny, *Student* almost fell to pieces. There was too much for me to do, and nobody else whom I could really trust to help me out. After a few weeks, I asked Nik to come and help. Nik had finished at Ampleforth, but was due to go to Sussex University at Brighton. He agreed to delay going to university and come to *Student*'s aid.

With Nik's arrival, *Student* was put back on the rails. He started controlling the cash, and, rather than having a large biscuit tin full of money which anyone could dip into to buy food or drink or dope, Nik used our Coutts account properly. He started writing cheques and then checking the stubs off against the bank statements. Nik had lost a front tooth, and with his long black hair he looked rather terrifying. I think he kept away a lot of debt collectors.

The commune, which had been very cramped in Jonny's basement, now spread up and down the new house. People made dens and there were mattresses and joss sticks everywhere. By now most of the people working with *Student* were nineteen or twenty, and there was lots of talk about free love, and lots of practice of it. I installed a large brass bed on the top floor, with a telephone running off a long extension lead which looped down through the banisters. Some days I did all my business from bed.

I'd put the house in my parents' name so that the owners – the Church Commissioners – would not think we were running a business from it. My parents loved the excitement of journalism and, although Dad was a barrister with short hair who wore a blazer and tie to church on Sundays, he and Mum never had any problem talking to people who had hair halfway down their backs and hadn't shaved or washed for a month. Lindi came to stay in Albion Street every half term and during some of her holidays. She helped distribute *Student* and fell in love with a series of men working on the magazine.

I had a short relationship with Debbie, one of the girls living at Albion Street and working on the magazine. One day she told me she was pregnant. We were both very shocked and realised that a baby was the last thing we could cope with. Debbie decided that she wanted to have an abortion. After a few telephone calls it became clear that this would be very difficult to arrange. Debbie could not have an abortion on the National Health Service unless she had proven psychiatric or medical problems. We grew frantic phoning around all the National Health hospitals trying to see if there was any way this could be overcome. When we tried to find a private doctor to help, we found it would cost over £400 – money we didn't have. I was at my wits' end when I finally tracked down a kind doctor in Birmingham who told me that she would arrange the operation for £50.

After the operation, Debbie and I realised that there must be a host of young people who had faced the same problem and had nowhere to turn for help. It would surely be much better if there were one telephone number you could ring to be referred to the right doctor. It wasn't just unwanted pregnancies that were the problem: what if you needed psychological help, or had a venereal disease but were scared of admitting it to your nice family doctor, or had run away from home and had nowhere to live? We drew up a long list of the sorts of problems that students faced, and decided to do something about it. We would give out our telephone number, work out a list of all the best and most helpful doctors, and see who called.

GIVE US YOUR HEADACHES was the slogan for the Student Advisory Centre. We handed out leaflets along Oxford Street and advertised in *Student*. Soon the calls started coming in. A number of doctors, both in the National Health Service and the private sector, agreed to give their services for free or a minimal charge, so we built up a network of professionals to whom we could refer people. Worries about pregnancy and contraception formed many of the calls, but we also became quite a centre for gay men and lesbians to hang around. It soon became clear that they were not as interested in asking our advice as in finding ways of meeting each other, revealing how difficult it was for gay people to lead a normal social life.

The Student Advisory Centre began to take up more time than *Student* magazine. I would be talking to possible suicides for an hour at three in the morning, advising pregnant girls as to who was the nicest doctor they could go and see, writing to someone who was terrified that he had caught venereal disease but didn't dare tell his parents or go and see a doctor – and in what little time was left, trying to run the magazine. One of the biggest problems we found ourselves dealing with was that teenagers were unable to confide in their parents. Hearing others' stories made me realise how lucky I was in my relationship with my own parents. They had never judged me, and always supported me, always praised the good things rather than criticised the bad things: I had no qualms about admitting my problems, worries and failures. Our work was to try to help out those who were in trouble but with nowhere to turn.

With both the Student Advisory Centre and *Student* magazine, life at Albion Street remained frantic and the numbers of people coming in and out of the house at all times of day and night continued to drive our neighbours to distraction. Due to complaints from the neighbours, we were visited on a regular basis by the Church Commissioner inspectors to check that we were not carrying out any kind of business. These visits had all the clockwork tension of a West End farce. The Commissioners had to give us 24 hours' notice before an inspection, and as soon as we received it the whole *Student* staff and my mum immediately wheeled into action.

All the telephones were piled into a cupboard, and the desks and chairs and mattresses were covered by dust sheets. The *Student* staff would pull out paint pots and paintbrushes, put on overalls and start painting the walls of the house. Mum would arrive from the country with Lindi, eight-year-old Vanessa and an armful of toys. By the time the Church Commissioners arrived they would find a friendly crew of painters cheerfully decorating the house, the furniture all swathed in dust sheets, while a mother and her family huddled upstairs. The little girl would be playing with some toys in a rather bemused way, while Lindi and I were engrossed in Monopoly. If Vanessa ever looked as if she might ask us what was going on, Mum would rapidly shoo everyone out of the room, saying it was time for Vanessa's bed.

The Church inspectors would look at this happy domestic scene and wonder what all the fuss was about. They would scratch their heads and say what a lovely girl little Vanessa was, drink their tea and have a nice chat with my mum. As soon as they had disappeared down the street, Mum went back home; we put away the Monopoly, yanked off the dust sheets, plugged in the telephones and got back to work.

The end came on one fatal visit when we forgot to unplug the telephones. By then it was their fifth visit and the inspectors must have suspected something. They stayed for their ritual cup of tea and were just about to leave when two of the telephones started ringing inside the cupboard. A shocked silence fell.

'And just listen to that,' I improvised quickly. 'Can you hear that telephone? The walls are so thin in these houses we can hear everything that goes on next door!'

The inspector strode forward and pulled open the cupboard door. Five telephones, a switchboard and a tangle of wires all tumbled out on top of him. Not even a big family needed a switchboard. That was the end of 44 Albion Street. Vanessa and her collection of dolls and toys were taken down to Shamley Green for the last time, and Lindi and I packed up the Monopoly set. *Student* magazine had to find somewhere else to use as an office.

We scoured the neighbourhood looking for somewhere to rent. The best deal was offered by the Reverend Cuthbert Scott. He liked the work of the Advisory Centre and offered us the use of the crypt at St John's Church, just off the Bayswater Road, for no rent at all. I put an old slab of marble across two tombs to make my desk, and everyone found themselves somewhere to sit. We even charmed the local Post Office engineer into connecting the telephone without our having to wait the normal three months. After a while none of us noticed that we were working in the dim light of the crypt surrounded by marble effigies and tombs.

In November 1969 I received a visit from two plain-clothes policemen from Marylebone Police Station. They had come to draw my attention to the 1889 Indecent Advertisements Act and the 1917 Venereal Disease Act, in case I was unaware of them, which, not surprisingly, I was. They told me that it was illegal to advertise any help or remedy for venereal disease. These Acts had originally been introduced to stop quack doctors from exploiting the large numbers of people who came to them for expensive and ineffective cures for venereal disease. I argued that I was only offering a counselling service and that I passed on anyone who had VD to qualified doctors at St Mary's Hospital. But the policemen were adamant: if the Student Advisory

Centre continued to mention the words 'venereal disease' in public, I would be arrested with the prospect of two years' imprisonment.

The week before, we had successfully prosecuted a policeman from Marylebone Police Station for planting drugs on one of the Student Advisory Centre's clients. The policeman had been sent down, and so I suspected that this visit was connected. I was amazed that the police had trawled through this old legislation to find some obscure law that we were breaking.

We duly changed the mention of venereal disease in the leaflets we distributed around London and started describing it as 'social disease'. Then we got a huge number of inquiries from people who were suffering from acne, and the number of people calling us for help over VD dropped from sixty a week to ten. We decided that the police were bluffing and that helping the remaining fifty people a week was worth risking the Metropolitan Police's threats: we reinserted the mention of VD. We were wrong. The police came back to the crypt again, in December 1969, and arrested me.

John Mortimer, a barrister who had established a reputation for his support of libertarian causes after his defence of *Oz* magazine and his role in the *Lady Chatterley's Lover* trial, offered to defend me. He agreed that the law was ridiculous and that the police were merely being vindictive. John reminded us that every public lavatory carried a government notice on the inside of the door offering advice to those suffering from venereal disease. If I was guilty then so was the government. I was duly prosecuted on two counts: under the Indecent Advertisements Act 1889, which prohibited advertisements of an 'indecent or obscene nature' and deemed references to syphilis and gonorrhoea to be indecent, and the Venereal Disease Act

1917, which banned advertisements offering treatment or advice or mentioning the words 'venereal disease'.

At the first hearing on 8 May 1970 at the Marylebone Magistrates Court, Tom Driberg, the flamboyant Labour MP until 1974, gave a dramatic plea on my behalf. Chad Varah, the founder of the Samaritans, also gave evidence pointing out how many people the Student Advisory Centre had referred to his charity. John Mortimer made his argument that, if I was found guilty, I would have no option but to prosecute the government and all the local authorities, since they had also put up notices in public lavatories. The magistrate dismissed the charge under the Venereal Disease Act on the grounds that the Student Advisory Centre did not offer to cure people but referred them to qualified doctors. He adjourned the other charge until 22 May.

As the court case was proceeding, statistics were released revealing that the number of people with venereal disease had risen dramatically in the previous year to a post-war peak. Lady Birk, the chairman of the Health Education Council, used the statistics together with the example of my prosecution to try to amend the 1889 Indecent Advertisements Act in the House of Lords.

'It's ludicrous that outmoded laws should restrict responsible efforts to stop the spread of these serious diseases,' she said.

By the time of the second court case a number of newspapers had declared how idiotic it was that I was being prosecuted. There was a strong movement to change the law. The magistrate reluctantly found me guilty under the strict letter of the law, but he made it clear that he considered the law was absurd by fining me just £7, some way short of the two years' imprisonment with which the police had been threatening me. John

Mortimer made a statement to the press outside the court in which he called for the law to be changed or we would have no alternative but to prosecute the government for mentioning VD on the doors of public lavatories. The newspapers all joined forces behind us, and Lady Birk's amendment to the law was incorporated into government legislation at the next sitting of parliament. Reginald Maudling, the home secretary, sent me a personal letter apologising for the Crown Prosecution.

That court case taught me that, although I was young, wore jeans and had very little money behind me, I need not be afraid of being bullied by the police or the Establishment. Particularly if I had a good barrister.

One day in 1970 I came back to my desk and found that Nik had been sitting at it. By mistake he had left a draft of a memo which he was writing to the staff. It was a plan to get rid of me as publisher and editor, take editorial and financial control of *Student* and turn it into a cooperative. I would become just part of the team, and everyone would share equally in the editorial direction of the magazine. I was shocked. I felt that Nik – my closest friend – was betraying me. After all, *Student* had been my and Jonny's idea. We had started it at Stowe and against all odds we had managed to publish it. I knew what I wanted to do with *Student*, and it seemed to me that everyone was happy working there. We all drew equal salaries, but ultimately I was the editor and publisher and it was up to me to make the decisions.

I looked around at everyone working. They all had their heads bent down studiously over their desks. I wondered how many were part of this. I put the memo in my pocket. When Nik came back I stood up.

'Nik,' I said. 'Will you come outside for a quick chat?'

I decided to bluff my way through the crisis. If Nik had already whipped up support from the ten other people it would be difficult for me to stop them. But, if they were undecided, I could drive a wedge between Nik and the rest of them and cut Nik out. I had to put our friendship to one side, and get rid of this challenge.

'Nik,' I said, as we walked down the street, 'a number of people have come up to me and said that they're unhappy with what you're planning. They don't like the idea, but they're too scared to tell you to your face.'

Nik looked horrified.

'I don't think that it's a good idea for you to stay here,' I went on. 'You're trying to undermine me and the whole of *Student*. I think that we should remain friends, but I don't think you should stay here any more.'

I still don't know how I managed to say those words without blushing or my voice cracking. Nik looked down at his feet.

'I'm sorry, Ricky,' he said. 'It just seemed a better way to organise ourselves ...' he trailed off.

'I'm sorry too, Nik.' I folded my arms and looked straight at him. 'Let's see each other down in Shamley Green, but *Student* is my life.'

Nik left that day. I told everyone that Nik and I had disagreed over how to run *Student*, and they were free to leave, or to carry on, whatever they wished. They all decided to stay with me, and life at the crypt went on without Nik.

This was the first real disagreement I ever had. Although I felt anguished, I knew I had to confront it. I hate criticising people who work with me, and I try to avoid doing so. Ever since then I have always tried to avoid the issue by asking someone else to wield the axe. I admit that this is a weakness, but I am simply unable to cope with it.

Nik was my best friend and I deeply hoped that he would remain so. When I was next down in Shamley Green I went round to see Nik and found him eating one of his mum's puddings. We sat down together and polished it off.

Apart from the fact that he was my oldest friend, Nik had taken charge of the distribution of the magazine and made sense of it. I missed him terribly. Until Nik had arrived, the distribution had only ever been casually handled, with bundles being sent out to volunteers in schools and universities. For over a year *Student* carried on without Nik and we put out four more editions. When Nik told me that he was standing for a student election at Sussex University, I used *Student*'s purchasing power with the printers to run off some cheap campaign posters. Nik won the election but was later disqualified because he had got outside support for his campaign.

One thing I knew from everyone who came in to chat or work for us was that they spent a good deal of time listening to music, and a good deal of money buying records. We had the record player on constantly, and everyone rushed out to buy the latest Rolling Stones, Bob Dylan, or Jefferson Airplane album the day it was released. There was tremendous excitement about music: it was political; it was anarchic; it summed up the young generation's dream of changing the world. And I also noticed that people who would never dream of spending as much as 40 shillings on a meal wouldn't hesitate to spend 40 shillings buying the latest Bob Dylan album. The more obscure the albums were, the more they cost and the more they were treasured.

Up to this point I had been interested in making money only to ensure *Student*'s continuing success and to fund the Student Advisory Centre, but it struck me as a very interesting business opportunity. When I heard that, despite the government's abolition of the Retail Price Maintenance Agreement, none of the shops were offering discounted records, I began to think about setting up a record distribution business. The number of people working on *Student* had grown to around twenty and we all still lived together in 44 Albion Street and worked in the crypt.

I thought about the high cost of records and the sort of people who bought *Student* magazine, and wondered whether we could advertise and sell cheap mail-order records through the magazine. As it turned out, the first advertisement for mail-order records appeared in the final edition of *Student*. Without Nik to manage *Student*'s distribution, it was floundering, but the offer of cheap records brought in a flood of inquiries and more cash than we had ever seen before.

We decided to come up with another name for the mail-order business: a name that would be eye-catching, that could stand alone and not appeal just to students. We sat around in the church crypt trying to choose a good one.

'Slipped Disc' was one of the favourite suggestions. We toyed with it for a while, until one of the girls leant forward:

'I know,' she said. 'What about "Virgin"? We're complete virgins at business.'

'And there aren't many virgins left around here,' laughed one of the other girls. 'It would be nice to have one here in name if nothing else.'

'Great,' I decided on the spot. 'It's Virgin.'

4 'I am prepared to try anything once.'

1970–1971

AND SO WE BECAME Virgin. Looking back at the various uses to which we've since put the Virgin name, I think we made the right decision. I'm not sure that Slipped Disc Airways, Slipped Disc Brides or Slipped Disc Condoms would have had quite the same appeal.

Our tiny sample of market research proved correct: students spent a good deal of money on records and they didn't like spending 39 shillings at WH Smith when they found out that they could buy them from Virgin for 35 shillings. We started giving out leaflets about Virgin Mail Order records along Oxford Street and outside concerts, and the daily post increased from a bundle of letters to a sack. One of the best things about mail order for us was that the customers sent their money in first: this provided the capital for us to buy the records. Our bank account at Coutts started to build up a large cash balance.

As Virgin Mail Order grew, I tried to sell *Student* to another magazine group. IPC Magazines emerged as the only interested buyer, and we had long negotiations which culminated in a meeting where they asked me to stay on as editor. I agreed to do so, but then made the mistake of telling them all about my future plans. Fantasising about the future is one of my favourite pastimes, and I told the meeting that I had all sorts of other plans for *Student*: I felt that students were given a raw deal by banks, and I wanted to set up a cheap student bank; I wanted to set up a string of great nightclubs and hotels where students could stay; perhaps even offer them good travel, like student trains or even, who knows, a student airline. As I warmed to my theme, I saw that their eyes had glazed over. They thought I was a madman. They decided they did not want to keep such a lunatic on as editor of *Student*, and in the end they decided they did not even want to buy it. *Student* died a quiet death, and my plans for the future had to be shelved for the time being.

We switched all our attention to Virgin Mail Order. One look at the huge numbers of orders coming in and the need to organise where to buy the records from and how to send them out to the customers persuaded me that I needed someone to help me. Although we all had great fun at Albion Street, I was increasingly aware that I was the only one who had to worry about paying all the wages. Even though these were small amounts of money, it was difficult to make sufficient profit even to cover that cost. There was only one person I could turn to: Nik. I wanted my old friend back again.

I buried the episode when Nik had tried to throw me out, and offered him 40 per cent of the newly formed Virgin Mail Order Records company if he came to work with me. He agreed immediately. We never negotiated over the 60–40 split. I think we both felt that it was a fair reflection of what we would each put into the business.

Although Nik was not a trained accountant, he was meticulous at counting the pennies. He also led by example: he never spent any money, so why should any of us? He never washed his clothes, so why should anyone else? He scrimped and saved every penny; he always turned lights off when he left a room; he made only rapid phone calls, and he handled our bills with great skill.

'It's fine to pay bills late,' he said, 'so long as you pay them regularly.'

So we paid our bills on the nail, except that it was always the last nail. Apart from Nik and me, there were no other permanent employees in the crypt. A rotating band of casual workers came in and were paid £20 a week, before drifting on. Throughout 1970 Virgin Mail Order Records thrived.

Then, in January 1971, we were almost ruined by something entirely out of our control: the Post Office workers went on strike. Led by Tom Jackson, the general secretary of the Union of Post Office Workers, the postmen went home and the Post Office taped up the letterboxes. Our mail-order business was set to go bust: people couldn't send us cheques; we couldn't send out records. We had to do something.

Nik and I decided that we should open a shop to carry on selling the records. We had to find a shop within a week before we ran out of money. At the time we had no idea about how a shop works. All we knew was that we had to sell records somehow or the company would collapse. We started looking for a site.

In 1971 music retailing was dominated by WH Smith and John Menzies, both of which were dull and formal. The record departments were generally downstairs and they were staffed by people in drab brown or blue uniforms who appeared to have no interest in music. Customers chose their records from the shelves, bought them and left within ten minutes. The shops were unwelcoming; there was little sympathetic service and prices were high. Although rock music was very exciting, none of that feeling of excitement or even vague interest filtered through to the shops that sold the records. The dowdy staff registered no approval or interest if you bought the new Doors album: they just rang it up on the till as if you had bought Mantovani or Perry Como. It was all the same to them. Nor did they seem particularly enthused about putting in a special order for the Van Der Graaf Generator or Incredible String Band record that had been reviewed in *Melody Maker* that week. None of our friends felt at home in record shops: they were just rather functional places where they had to go to buy their favourite records. Hence the appeal of a cheap mail-order business.

We wanted the Virgin Records shop to be an extension of *Student*; a place where people could meet and listen to records together; somewhere where they weren't simply encouraged to dash in, buy the record and leave. We wanted them to stay longer, chat to the staff, and really get into which records they were going to buy. People take music far more seriously than many other things in life. It is part of the way they define themselves, like the cars they drive, the films they watch, and the clothes they wear. Teenagers spend more time listening to music, talking about their favourite bands and choosing records than almost anything else.

Virgin's first record shop had to incorporate all these aspects of how music fitted into people's lives. In exploring how to do this, I think we created the conceptual framework of what Virgin later became. We wanted the Virgin Records shop to be an enjoyable place to go at a time when record buyers were given short shrift. We wanted to relate to the customers, not patronise them; and we wanted to be cheaper than the other shops. To achieve all this was a tall order, but we hoped the extra money which went on creating the atmosphere, and the profits we forfeited by selling cheaply, would be more than made up for by people buying more records.

Nik and I spent a morning counting people walking up and down Oxford Street compared with people walking along Kensington High Street. Eventually we decided that the cheaper end of Oxford Street would be the best site. We knew that we couldn't rely on people knowing about the Virgin Records shop and making a special trip to buy a record, so we had to be able to attract passers-by into the shop on impulse. At the exact point where we counted the most people walking along the street, we started looking for an empty property. We saw a shoe shop with a stairway leading up to what looked like an empty first floor, so we went upstairs to see what it was like.

'What are you doing?' a voice called up to us.

'We're looking to set up a shop,' we said.

'What kind of shop?'

Nik and I came back down the stairs and found the owner of the shoe shop blocking our way.

'A record shop,' we said.

The owner was a large, square Greek called Mr Alachouzos.

'You'll never pay the rent,' he said.

'No, you're right,' I said. 'We can't afford any rent. But we'll attract lots of people past your window and they'll all buy shoes.'

'What kind of shoes?' Mr Alachouzos's eyes narrowed.

'Jesus sandals are out,' Nik said. 'Do you sell any Doc Martens?'

We agreed that we would fit out the record shop and that we could occupy it for no rent until somebody else came along and wanted it. It was, after all, just an empty space. Within five days we had built shelves, put piles of cushions on the floor, carried a couple of old sofas up the stairs and set up a till. The first Virgin Records shop was ready for business.

The day before opening, we handed out hundreds of leaflets along Oxford Street offering cut-price records. On the first day, a Monday, a queue over a hundred yards long formed outside. I was on the till when the customers started coming through. The first customer bought a record by Tangerine Dream, a German band which we had noticed selling very well through mail order.

'Funny bloke you've got downstairs,' he said. 'He kept trying to sell me a pair of Doc Martens as I waited in the queue.'

At the end of the day I took the money to the bank. I found Mr Alachouzos hovering outside the shop.

'How's business?' I asked, trying to make light of the heavy bag of cash I was carrying.

He looked at me and then back at his shop window, which was still piled high with unsold Doc Martens.

'Fine,' he said firmly. 'Couldn't be better.'

During 1971 Nik was running the Oxford Street record shop; Debbie was running the Student Advisory Centre from Piccadilly, and I was generally looking to do anything I could to expand. We were in the process of changing from *Student* ideas to Virgin, and in due course we renamed the Student Advisory Centre as a new charity called HELP! It continues to operate to this day, but now under the guise of Virgin Unite, which undertakes a very broad range of charitable activities.

I knew very little about the record industry, but from what I saw at the record shop I could see that it was a wonderfully informal business with no strict rules. It had unlimited potential for growth: a new band could suddenly sweep the nation and be a huge hit, as the sudden crazes for The Bay City Rollers, Culture Club,

The Spice Girls or Busted show. The music business is a strange combination of having real and intangible assets: pop bands are brand names in themselves, and at a given stage in their careers their name alone can practically guarantee hit records. But it is also an industry in which the few successful bands are very, very rich, and the bulk of bands remains obscure and impoverished. The rock business is a prime example of the most ruthless kind of capitalism.

As a record retailer, Virgin was immune to the success or failure of an individual band, just so long as there were bands whose records people were keen to buy. But we were restricted to living off our retail margin, which was small, and I saw that the real potential for making money in the record industry lay in the record companies.

For the time being Nik and I concentrated on building up the image of our shop. We continued to work on different ideas to make our customers as welcome as possible. We offered them headphones, sofas and beanbags to sit on, free copies of *New Musical Express* and *Melody Maker* to read, and free coffee to drink. We allowed them to stay as long as they liked and make themselves at home.

Word of mouth began to spread, and soon people began to choose to buy records from us rather than from the big chains. It was as if they thought that the same album by Thin Lizzy or Bob Dylan somehow had a greater value if bought at Virgin rather than at Boots. I felt enormous pride whenever I saw people carrying Virgin paper bags along Oxford Street. Our staff began to report that the same people were coming back every couple of weeks. With a loyal customer base, Virgin's reputation began to grow.

* * *

At the other end of the spectrum from buying records – the recording studios – I heard that conditions were extremely formal. Bands had to check in at an appointed time, bring all their own equipment and set it up, and then leave according to the set timetable, taking all their equipment with them. Since the studios were so overbooked, bands would often have to record straight after breakfast. The idea of The Rolling Stones having to record 'Brown Sugar' straight after finishing their bowls of cornflakes struck me as ridiculous. I imagined that the best environment for making records would be a big, comfortable house in the country where a band could come and stay for weeks at a time and record whenever they felt like it, probably in the evening. So during 1971 I started looking for a country house that I could convert into a recording studio.

In one copy of *Country Life* I saw a fairy-tale castle on sale in Wales for just £2,000. It seemed a bargain. I drove off to see it with Tom Newman, one of the early recruits to the Virgin Mail Order company. He was a singer who had already released a couple of records, but was more interested in setting up a recording studio. When we arrived at the castle we realised that the sales details had inexplicably forgotten to point out that this castle was actually in the middle of a housing estate.

Feeling tired and disappointed, Tom and I turned back and set off on the five-hour drive back to London. Thumbing through *Country Life* on the way home, I saw an advertisement for another property, the old manor house at Shipton-on-Cherwell, some five miles north of Oxford. We turned off the road, followed the signs to Shipton-on-Cherwell, drove through the village, and then turned down a dead end which led to the Manor. The gates to the Manor were locked, but Tom and I climbed over the wall and found ourselves in the grounds of a beautiful seventeenth-century manor house built with yellow Cotswold stone which glowed in the late-afternoon sunshine. We walked round the outside of the house and both realised that this would be perfect.

When we called the estate agent the next morning, we discovered that the Manor had been on the market for a long time. With over fifteen bedrooms it was too big for a family house but too small to be converted into a hotel. The asking price was £35,000, but he agreed £30,000 for a quick sale. I went in to see Coutts, this time wearing a suit and a pair of black shoes, and asked for a loan. I showed them the sales figures which Virgin Mail Order and the Virgin shop on Oxford Street were achieving. I don't know how impressed they were by them, but they offered me a mortgage of £20,000. Some years later Coutts told me that, if I ever came in to see them looking remotely smart, they knew I was in trouble.

The Coutts loan was a breakthrough for me: it was the first time a bank had trusted me with a large amount of debt and I could see that I was almost in a position to buy the Manor. Although I had no money myself, my parents had put £2,500 aside for me, Lindi and Vanessa respectively for when we were thirty. I asked them if I could draw on it early and use it to buy the Manor. They both agreed, even though there was a risk that, if the recording studio went bust, the bank would sell the Manor over my head at a knockdown price and the money would be lost. I was still looking at a shortfall of £7,500.

We were talking about the Manor over Sunday lunch at Shamley Green when my dad suggested that I go and see Auntie Joyce. Auntie Joyce had no children of her own, and had always been devoted to us. Her fiancé had been killed in the war and she had never fallen in love again. She lived in Hampshire and I drove over to see her that afternoon. As always she was both very straightforward and very generous. She had arranged everything.

'Ricky, I've heard about this Manor,' she told me. 'And I gather that Coutts have lent you some money.'

'Yes.'

'But not quite enough.'

'No.'

'Well, I'll step in with the balance. I want the same interest as Coutts,' she said. 'But you can delay paying it to me until you are able to.'

I knew that Auntie Joyce was being extraordinarily kind to me and had probably accepted that she would never see the money again. What I didn't know was that she had remortgaged her house to raise the £7,500 to pass on to me, and was having to pay interest on it herself. When I started thanking her she brushed me aside.

'Look,' she said, 'I wouldn't lend you the money if I didn't want to. What's money for, anyway? It's to make things happen. And I'm sure you'll make things happen with this recording studio just as you won that ten shillings off me when you learnt to swim.'

I promised to myself that, whatever happened, I would repay that money to her, with interest on top.

I had only dealt with the estate agent over the telephone, but after the money was transferred and I had bought the Manor I went to pick up the key. I wandered into his office.

'Can I help you?' he said, no doubt wondering what a scruff like me could possibly want in a smart estate agent's office.

'I've come to pick up the key to the Manor,' I said.
'I'm Richard Branson.'

He looked astonished.

'Yes, Mr Branson.' He pulled out a large iron key.
'Here you are. The key to the Manor. Please sign here.'

And, with a flourish on his paper, I picked up the key
and drove off to take possession of the Manor.

Tom Newman together with his friend Phil Newell
immediately set about converting the Manor outhouse
into a recording studio. He wanted to install a
state-of-the-art sixteen-track Ampex tape machine
together with the best of everything else he could think
of: a twenty-channel desk, quadraphonic monitoring,
phasing and echo facilities, and a grand piano. We both
wanted to ensure that everything was as good as the best
studio in London. The Manor gradually took shape.
Every weekend I drove up with Nik and we would camp
on the floor and knock out the partitions which had
been put across the fireplaces, strip off the lino to get
down to the original flagstone floors, and paint the walls.
Lindi also came up and helped, as did most of the people
involved in Virgin Records. Mum arrived one day with a
grandfather clock she had just bought at Phillips.

'You'll need this,' she said.

We put it in the hallway and kept our money in the
casement. It's now standing in the Virgin Upper Class
lounge at Heathrow, but without the money stuffed
inside.

When the lease on Albion Street expired I moved in
with some friends around Notting Hill for a while, as we
carried on working in the crypt. Soon we were too
crowded to stay in the crypt, and we found an old
warehouse in South Wharf Road, near Paddington
Station, which became the base for Virgin Mail Order.

One day I found myself driving beneath the Westway and into Maida Vale. As I drove over a humpback bridge I saw a line of houseboats moored along the canal. With the water, lines of trees, boats brightly painted in reds and blues with flowerpots on their rooftops, and various ducks and swans nosing around, it felt as if I was suddenly in the countryside.

Since I was brought up running wild in the country, I didn't really like living in London and often felt that I never saw the sunshine or breathed any fresh air. Ever since our summer holidays in Salcombe I had always loved the water and the smells of boats: oil, tar and ropes. I drove round to the local council office. They told me to go to the Water Board, which was responsible for allocating houseboats. They warned me that there was a long waiting list. If I applied now, I might eventually be allocated one in about five years' time. I didn't bother to apply, but drove back to Little Venice, hoping to find somebody on a houseboat who could tell me how to rent one. I felt sure that there must be a way round the system.

As I drove down Blomfield Road along the canal, my car broke down. This was not unusual. I got out and stared hopelessly at the bonnet.

'Do you want a hand with that?' someone called out in an Irish accent.

I turned round and saw an old man on top of a houseboat fiddling with the stovepipe chimney.

'It'll be all right,' I said, wandering towards him. 'What I'd really like a hand with is how to live on one of these boats.'

Brendan Fowley straightened up.

'Well now,' he said. 'There's a thing.'

He took out a pipe and lit it, obviously delighted to have an excuse to stop work.

'You should go along to that boat over there,' he said. 'I've just sold it to someone, and that young lady has moved in. Now I don't know, but there are two bedrooms and she might be looking for a lodger. You'll have to go through a little wooden gate and along the towpath. She's the last boat before the bridge, and she's called *Alberta*.'

I walked along the road, pushed open the leaning wooden door and walked along the narrow towpath. At the last boat, I peered into a round porthole and saw a fair-haired girl bent over in the kitchen.

'Hello,' I said. 'You must be Alberta.'

'Don't be silly,' she said, turning round. 'That's the name of the boat. I'm called Mundy.'

'Can I come in?' I asked. 'My car's just broken down and I'm looking for somewhere to live.'

Mundy was beautiful. Not only was she beautiful but she had just moved a bed on board. We sat down and had some lunch, and before we knew what we were doing we were lying on the bed making love. Her name was Mundy Ellis and I stayed the night with her that night, and moved my suitcase on board the next morning. She had a Labrador called Friday, so with Mundy and Friday I had the week pretty well sewn up. We had the most romantic affair on *Alberta*, having dinner out on the roof in the summer nights, watching the ducks and other boats slip up and down the canal.

Mundy and I lived together for almost a year. She helped out with the Student Advisory Centre, and then with the Manor. At that time nearly everyone was taking drugs, and soon Mundy had taken a couple of LSD trips up at the Manor with Tom Newman. She brought some LSD back to London for me to try, and one evening we and two other friends, Rob and Caroline Gold, settled down on *Alberta* to have a trip.

Rob decided that he wouldn't take any in case anything went wrong. I lived by the dangerous (and sometimes rather foolish) maxim that I was prepared to try anything once, and I took the little paper square. After a while my mind began to race. At first everything was fine. We listened to some music and went outside to watch the evening sky. But when we went back inside everything started to go wrong: my vision began to tilt and Mundy loomed in and out looking like a tiny eight-year-old child. I looked at the others smiling and chatting and laughing. But whenever I caught sight of Mundy all I saw was a wizened creature rather like the red-coated dwarfish murderer in *Don't Look Now*.

I hate being out of control, and I had no idea what to do. Although nearly everyone else at *Student* and then later at Virgin took lots of drugs, I never really joined them. I prefer to have a great time and keep my wits about me. I know that I've got to get up early the next morning and so I've rarely been able to get smashed the night before. Utterly unused to this kind of thing and with the LSD charging through my system, I couldn't think straight. I finally went back outside and lay looking up at the sky. Mundy came out and hauled me into bed. When we started making love, I kept my eyes tightly closed, dreading what I would see if I opened them.

By the time the LSD trip was over, it became clear that my relationship with Mundy was also over. Even though she stopped looking like a murderous dwarf the next morning, I was never able to look at her in the same way again. Soon afterward Mundy left *Alberta* and went up to the Manor to move in with Tom Newman.

5 Learning a lesson
1971

THROUGHOUT THE SPRING OF 1971, Virgin Mail Order attracted many more customers. But, although the company was growing, we were losing money. We offered large discounts on all records and, by the time we had spent money on the telephone calls to order them, paid for the postage, and accounted for the staff and the shops, we weren't keeping up. Sometimes our customers pretended that they hadn't received the records so we would have to send out a second copy, and often a third and a fourth and so on. All in all we were gradually losing money, and before long we were £15,000 overdrawn.

In the spring I received an order from Belgium for a large number of records. I went to the record companies that published those records and bought them without paying the purchase tax which we had to pay on records sold in the UK. I then borrowed a van and drove down to Dover to take the ferry across to France and then drive on to Belgium. Some papers were stamped at Dover to confirm that so many records had been exported, but when I arrived at Calais I was asked for another document, a carnet which proved I wasn't going to sell them en route in France. The British and the French authorities both charged purchase tax on records, while Belgium charged nothing, so the records in my van were effectively bonded stock. I did not have this carnet, and to my disappointment was forced to go back to Dover on the ferry, with the records still in my van.

However, as I drove back to London, it dawned on me that I was now carrying a vanload of records that had apparently been exported. I even had the customs stamp to prove it. The fact that the French customs had not allowed me through France was unknown. I had paid no purchase tax on these records, so I could sell them either by mail order or at the Virgin shop and make about £5,000 more profit than I could have done by the legal route. Two or three more trips like this and we would be out of debt.

As well as the £15,000 debt of Virgin Records, I had taken on the £20,000 mortgage on the Manor, and the cost of converting the outbuildings into a recording studio. It seemed like the perfect way out. It was a criminal plan, and I was breaking the law. But I had always got away with breaking rules before. In those days I felt that I could do no wrong and that, even if I did, I wouldn't be caught. I had not yet reached my 21st birthday, and somehow the normal everyday rules of life didn't seem to apply. On top of all this exuberance, I was about to fall head over heels in love with a beautiful American girl called Kristen Tomassi.

One day at the Manor I was looking for Bootleg, our Irish wolfhound. I couldn't find her anywhere, and went upstairs and along one of the corridors, opening all the bedroom doors and calling out, 'Bootleg! Bootleg!' I flung open the door of one tiny bedroom and found a lovely, tall girl getting changed. Not only was she considerably more attractive than Bootleg, with a rather quizzical, naughty face, but she was by herself and wearing just an old pair of skintight jeans and a black bra.

'You look great just as you are,' I said. 'I wouldn't bother with any more clothes.'

'Whatever are you shouting out about bootlegs for?' she asked.

'Bootleg's my dog. She's an Irish wolfhound.'

Sadly, Kristen did put on a shirt, but I managed to keep her chatting for almost an hour before someone started shouting for me. She had come to England for a summer holiday and met a musician who was doing some backing work at the Manor. She had come along with him for the ride.

We drove back to London in different cars. Kristen was with her musician boyfriend; I was by myself. As I followed her along the road I wondered if we would ever see each other again. I followed them all the way up to London, and finally decided to write a note to her. As I drove along I scrawled a note on a scrap of paper asking her to call me at seven o'clock. I waited until we reached the traffic lights at Acton, then jumped out of my car and ran up to theirs. I tapped on Kristen's window and she rolled it down.

'I just wanted to say goodbye,' I said, leaning in to give her a kiss on the cheek. 'Have a good trip back to the States.'

As I said this I secretly slipped my hand inside the car, reached down, and pushed my note into her left hand. As Kristen's fingers closed round mine, I let go of the note. I smiled across at the boyfriend.

'Hope the recording went well,' I said to him.

I hopped back into my car and drove back to *Alberta*.

I sat by the telephone refusing to make any calls, which was most unlike me, until seven o'clock. Then the phone rang. It was Kristen.

'I'm calling from a payphone,' she said. 'I didn't want John to overhear.'

'Can you step out of the phone box and catch a taxi?' I asked. 'Come on round and see me. I live on a boat called *Alberta*. Ask the taxi driver to take you to Blomfield Road in Little Venice. There's a little wooden door in the fence which leads to the towpath.'

There was a measured pause.

'It sounds like *Alice in Wonderland*,' Kristen said. 'I'll see you in ten minutes.'

And with that Kristen came round and I began my second whirlwind romance on *Alberta*.

The next morning I was due to make what I hoped would be my final trip down to Dover, pretending to export records. By this time I had made three trips and £12,000 profit. This last trip would provide enough money to pay off our overdraft. I could then give up the scam and concentrate on the business. It is impossible to know whether we really would have stopped since making such easy money is addictive, but that was our intention. That morning I loaded up the van with records once again and set off for Dover. This time I was even more casual than normal and after my papers were stamped I didn't even bother going on the ferry but simply drove around the dock and headed back for London. I was anxious to get back to *Alberta* to reassure myself that Kristen was still there. At Little Venice I walked along the towpath to the boat. It was the last week of May 1971, and the apple trees along the towpath were all in blossom.

Kristen had gone. In a panic I called her at her boyfriend's flat and put on an American accent when he answered the telephone.

'I'm looking for a Miss Kristen Tomassi,' I said. 'This is American Airlines.'

'I'll just get her.'

'Kristen,' I hissed, 'it's Richard. Pretend you're talking to a travel agent. And then call me back as soon as you can. Go to a payphone.'

'Thank you very much. I'll do that,' Kristen said, and rang off.

Fifteen minutes later the telephone rang. It was Kristen.

'Just hold the line a minute,' I told her.

'OK, Eddy,' I said, holding my hand over the receiver. 'Time to go.'

Eddy was the Virgin driver who picked up all our record deliveries. He set off for the boyfriend's flat.

'Kristen,' I said. 'What's your number there? This is going to take some time.'

I called her back, and we had a long chat about what we were doing. I spun every yarn I could think of. Twenty minutes later Eddy arrived back from the flat. He had all Kristen's clothes in a suitcase. He had told the boyfriend that Kristen was moving in with me.

'Kristen,' I said. 'You'd better come round here. I've got something to show you. It belongs to you.'

I refused to reveal what it was. Her curiosity kindled, Kristen came round to *Alberta*. She was set upon saying goodbye to me and returning to America.

When she arrived I held up her suitcase. She tried to grab it from me, but I opened it and threw her clothes all around the boat. Then I picked her up and carried her to the bedroom.

While Kristen and I spent the rest of the day in bed, the Customs and Excise officials were planning to raid Virgin. It had never occurred to me that I wasn't the only person who had stumbled across this tax-evasion scam. Many much larger record shops were doing it, and they were being much more sophisticated than I was. I was simply putting the records that should be exported in our Virgin Records shop on Oxford Street, and stocking up the new shop in Liverpool, which was due to open the next week. The big operators were distributing their illegally 'exported' records right across the country.

The telephone rang at around midnight. The caller refused to give his name, but what he had to say was terrifying. He warned me that my bogus trips to the Continent had been noticed and that I was about to be raided by the Customs and Excise office. He said that, if I bought an ultraviolet sun lamp from a chemist's shop and shone it on the records that I had bought from EMI, I would notice a fluorescent 'E' stamped on the vinyl of all the ones that were meant to have been exported to Belgium. He told me that I would be raided first thing tomorrow morning. When I thanked him, he told me he was helping me because I had once stayed up late talking to a suicidal friend of his who had called the Student Advisory Centre. I suspected that he was a customs officer.

I called Nik and Tony and rushed out to buy two sun lamps from a late-night chemist on Westbourne Grove. We met at South Wharf Road and started pulling records out of their sleeves. The ghastly truth was revealed: an 'E' shone up at us from all the records we had bought from EMI for export. We began to run in and out of the warehouse carrying piles of records into the van. We then made a terrible mistake: we assumed that the Customs and Excise officers would just raid the South Wharf warehouse. We therefore drove all the records round to the Oxford Street shop and put them in the racks to be sold. We had no idea that Customs and Excise officers have greater powers of immediate search than the police. I had a similar attitude to when the Church Commissioners used to come to Albion Street: it was all some great game and I found it difficult to take very seriously. By the early hours of the morning we had taken all the 'E'-stamped records to the Oxford

Street shop, and substituted some bona fide records for the warehouse stock.

Kristen and I set off early the next morning and walked from *Alberta* along the Grand Union Canal to South Wharf Road. I wondered when the raid would be. We crossed over the footbridge beside St Mary's Hospital and walked along the path. As we walked by the hospital there was a scream above us. A body fell out of the sky and hit the railings beside us. I caught a glimpse of an old man's grey, unshaven face as he hit the railings. It was horrific. His body seemed to explode and a huge amount of entrails fell on to the ground or hung dripping in red and white shiny rings from the railing. He was naked apart from his white dressing gown, which quickly began to soak up the blood. Kristen and I were too shocked to do anything other than stop and stare. He was clearly dead on impact. His neck hung off from his body and his back seemed to be broken in half. As we stared at the corpse, a hospital nurse came running over from the side door. There was nothing she could do. Someone else came rushing out with a white sheet and covered the body and the bits in the street. Kristen and I stood there, enveloped by silence, until we became aware of the noises of everyday life: traffic, horns blowing, and birdsong.

'Are you all right?' the nurse asked us. 'Do you want a cup of tea?'

We shook our heads and walked on, deeply shaken. It was another surreal twist to the start of our relationship. Two days ago we had met for the first time and I had slipped a clandestine note into her hand. We had enjoyed a fabulous night together on the boat. I had then driven to Dover and back, and arranged for her suitcase to be stolen. I'd spent all last night scrabbling about with the records. Now somebody had killed himself right in front of us. Like me, I think Kristen must have simply suspended her disbelief about what was going on. We were living off adrenaline and bewilderment.

At the South Wharf Road warehouse, we unlocked the doors and walked upstairs. But before we could reach my office there was a knock on the door. I opened it to find seven or eight men in brown macs.

'Are you Richard Branson?' they said. 'We're Customs and Excise and we've got a warrant to inspect your stock.'

These men were rather different from the two dowdy little accountants I had been expecting. They were bulky, tough men, and very threatening. Some of my cocksureness evaporated as I showed them into the warehouse.

'You're meant to have gone to Belgium yesterday,' one of them said. 'You can't get back this quickly.'

I tried to laugh this off as I watched them begin to check all the records with their ultraviolet lamp. They grew increasingly worried when they couldn't find any marked records. I enjoyed their confusion, trying to conceal my hope that we would get away with it. We began helping to check all the records, handing them the records from the sleeves and restocking them on the shelves.

What I didn't realise until it was too late was that they were simultaneously busting our shops in Oxford Street and Liverpool, and finding hundreds of marked records.

'All right.' One of the officers put down the telephone. 'They've found them. You'd better come with me. I'm arresting you. Come down to Dover with us and make a statement.'

I couldn't believe it. I had always thought that only

criminals were arrested: it hadn't occurred to me that I had become one. I had been stealing money from Customs and Excise. It wasn't some great game about my getting one up on the Customs and Excise office and getting off scot-free: I was guilty.

At Dover I was charged under Section 301 of the Customs and Excise Act 1952: 'That on 28 May 1971 at Eastern Docks, Dover, you caused to be delivered to an officer a ship's manifest, being a document produced for the purpose of an assigned matter namely Customs, which was untrue in a material particular in that it purported to show the exportation of 10,000 gramophone records ...'

And so on. I spent that night in a cell lying on a bare, black plastic mattress with one old blanket. The first part of my Stowe headmaster's prediction had come true: I was in prison.

That night was one of the best things that has ever happened to me. As I lay in the cell and stared at the ceiling I felt complete claustrophobia. I have never enjoyed being accountable to anyone else or not being in control of my own destiny. I have always enjoyed breaking the rules, whether they were school rules or accepted conventions, such as that no seventeen-year-old can edit a national magazine. As a twenty-year-old I had lived life entirely on my own terms, following my own instincts. But to be in prison meant that all that freedom was taken away.

I was locked in a cell and utterly dependent on somebody else to open the door. I vowed to myself that I would never again do anything that would cause me to be imprisoned, or indeed do any kind of business deal by which I would ever have cause to be embarrassed.

In the many different business worlds I have inhabited since that night in prison, there have been times when I could have succumbed to some form of bribe, or could have had my way by offering one. But ever since that night in Dover prison I have never been tempted to break my vow. My parents had always drummed into me that all you have in life is your reputation: you may be very rich, but if you lose your good name you'll never be happy. The thought will always lurk at the back of your mind that people don't trust you. I had never really focused on what a good name truly meant before, but that night in prison made me understand.

The next morning Mum arrived to meet me at the court. I applied for legal aid since I had no money to pay for a lawyer. The magistrate told me that if I applied for legal aid I would have to stay in prison as I obviously had no money for bail. If I wanted to be released, I would have to put up bail of £30,000. Virgin itself had no money that we could put up as security. £30,000 was the price of the Manor, but using it as security wasn't an option since it was financed mainly by a mortgage. I had a pile of debt and no real money.

Mum told the magistrate that she would put up Tanyards Farm, her home, as security. I was overwhelmed by the trust she showed in me. We stared at each other across the court and both started crying. The trust that my family had in me had to be repaid.

'You don't have to apologise, Ricky,' Mum said as we took the train back up to London. 'I know that you've learnt a lesson. Don't cry over spilt milk: we've got to get on and deal with this head on.'

Over the summer I confronted the problem with far less shame than I would have done if my parents had added to the burden. I kept a clear head; I was sorry; I wouldn't do it again; and I negotiated an out-of-court settlement with the Customs and Excise office. The tax authorities in the UK are more interested in extracting money than going through expensive court cases.

On 18 August 1971 I agreed to pay £15,000 as an immediate payment, with £45,000 to be paid in three instalments over the next three years. The total was calculated as being three times the illegal profit which Virgin had made from avoiding the purchase tax. If I paid off the sums agreed, I would avoid a criminal record. But, if I failed to pay it, I would be rearrested and tried.

After that night in prison and the subsequent negotiations with the Customs and Excise office, I needed to work twice as hard to make Virgin a success. Nik, Tony Mellor, and my South African cousin Simon Draper and Chris Stylianou, who had both just joined Virgin, resolved to help keep me out of prison. They knew it could have been them and were grateful to me for carrying the can: we were all in it together and it made us even closer. In a desperate attempt to earn money to repay the settlement, Nik started opening Virgin Records shops across the country; Simon began to talk about a record label and Chris started exporting records for real. Incentives come in all shapes and sizes – usually ranging from a pat on the back to share options – but avoiding prison was the most persuasive incentive I've ever had.

Since there was limited growth left in the mail-order business, we concentrated on expanding the record shops. The next two years were a crash course in how to manage cash. From being a completely relaxed company running on petty cash from the biscuit tin and a series of unpaid IOU notes, we became obsessively focused. We used every penny of the cash generated from the shops towards opening up another shop, which in turn was another pound towards paying off my Customs and Excise debt.

Eventually I was able to pay everything and relieve Mum of the bail she had put up. Three years later I was also able to repay Auntie Joyce her £7,500, with £1,000 on top for interest. If I had been unable to pay off Customs and Excise, the rest of my life could have been ruined: it is unlikely, not to say impossible, that someone with a criminal record would have been allowed to set up an airline, or would have been taken seriously as a contender to run the National Lottery.

We knew we had to sell more records, through the shops, overseas and by mail order; attract important artists like Cat Stevens or Paul McCartney to come and record at the Manor, and set up a record label. What we didn't know was that, even as we set out to do this, our first fortune was quietly making its way up the gravelled drive to the Manor in the form of another van. This time it was not carrying illegal records but bringing a young composer and his folk-singing sister from London to act as backing musicians for a band. He was the third reserve guitarist on the musical *Hair*, and she was a folk singer who sang in pubs. At the back of their minds was the hope that they might be able to record some esoteric instrumental music when the rest of the band wasn't using the studio. Their names were Mike and Sally Oldfield.

6 'Simon made Virgin the hippest place to be.'

1971–1972

BEFORE THE POSTAL STRIKE nearly ruined us in January 1971, someone my age with a South African accent walked into my office at South Wharf Road and introduced himself as my cousin. Simon Draper had graduated from Natal University and come over to London with just £100 and the idea of staying for a while. He was thinking of doing a postgraduate degree, perhaps following his brother, who had been a Rhodes Scholar at Oxford, but in the meantime he was looking for a job.

Simon had sat next to my mother at a family dinner party over Christmas and she had told him to get in touch with me. After Simon had exhausted the hospitality of both sides of his family over Christmas and New Year, he moved into a flat in London and tracked down the Virgin Records shop in Oxford Street. Sandy O'Connell, the manager, told him to go over and see me at South Wharf Road. He arrived just before lunch.

We went off to have something to eat at the Greek restaurant round the corner in Praed Street. There, over lukewarm meatballs, chips and peas, Simon explained what he wanted to do. While he had been at Natal University he had also worked on the South African *Sunday Times*. He told me stories of sitting up through Saturday night until the first edition was ready, and then leaving work to go to a jazz club with the first edition tucked under his arm. We swapped stories about journalism and then moved on to music.

Simon was obsessed by music. Because I had left school so young, and had never been to university, I had missed out on those long evenings spent lying around listening to music. Even though music was playing constantly in the *Student* basement, I was too busy calling up advertisers and negotiating with printers to absorb it. If I heard a record, I knew whether I liked it or not, but I couldn't compare it with some other band or recognise that it had been influenced by the Velvet Underground. It seemed to me that Simon had listened to every record released by every band. He didn't just casually enjoy the latest Doors album: he thoroughly understood what they were doing, how they had developed from their previous album and how this album compared with a whole catalogue of music. He had hosted his own half-hour show on Natal Radio, and I soon realised that he knew more about music than anyone I'd ever met.

We also talked about politics. Although I had been involved in various political demonstrations, such as the anti-Vietnam War march to Grosvenor Square, this was nothing compared with the brutality of South African politics. Simon was steeped in both music and politics, and saw music as one way to make a political protest. One of Simon's fellow students at Natal University had been Steve Biko, who was then leading the all-black South African Students Organisation. Simon's tutor, a Marxist, had been shot by government-backed vigilantes in front of his own children. The South African Government then did not tolerate any form of political dissent. Simon was not allowed to play any song with political or sexual connotations, such as those by Jimi Hendrix or Bob Dylan.

By the time we were on our coffee I had persuaded Simon to come and work at Virgin, to be the record buyer for the Virgin Records shop and the Virgin mail-order list. There was no awkward salary negotiation since everyone at Virgin was paid the same, £20 per week.

Tony Mellor had moved from working on *Student* to compiling the mail-order list. We were still trying to sell *Student* to another magazine company, and although it had not been published for over a year Tony kept producing dummies of the next issue with which we tried to impress potential buyers. He was therefore happy to hand the record buying to Simon and revert to the more political question of *Student*'s future. Tony simply gave Simon the one golden, unbreakable rule, 'Virgin doesn't ever, ever stock Andy Williams!', and handed over the first joint of the morning.

'You don't need to worry,' Simon said. 'I'd be the last person to break that one.'

And from then on Simon was on his own. I rather left him to it for the first few months. I was falling in love with Kristen and trying to prevent her going back to finish her architectural course in America. I offered her the job of further renovating the Manor:

'Come on!' I said. 'You don't have to study for six years to qualify as an architect. Just start doing it!'

After not too much persuading she eventually agreed with me and set to work. She was a natural, with perfect taste. With her long blonde hair and fine, almost elfin face, Kristen soon became a familiar figure at all the auction rooms around London as she bid for large remarkable pieces of furniture for the Manor.

While Nik managed the costs of both the mail-order business and the Virgin Records shops, Simon began to define the mail-order list as well as the Virgin Records shops themselves by choosing which records to stock. Simon's taste in music quickly became the single most critical element of the Virgin ethos. A record shop is not just a record shop: it is an arbiter of taste. I had no idea what music to promote, but Simon was full of wonderful plans to bring in unknown foreign albums unavailable elsewhere. There was a thin dividing line between what was 'hip' and what wasn't, and Simon made Virgin the 'hippest' place to be. He started importing records directly from America, flying them in to beat the competition. We only ever dealt in albums because singles were mainly either crass or were loss leaders to promote albums. In the 1970s serious bands such as Pink Floyd, Yes or Genesis rarely released singles. An album was seen as a combination of political statement, art, and a way of life. The serious bands didn't produce dance music: theirs was music to savour while lying down. There was a good deal of discussion about different recordings of the same songs, something which became especially interesting when the American albums arrived with different covers from the British versions, sometimes even different versions of the songs. These days CDs have been standardised to be mass marketed around the world.

As well as imports, notably from Germany, France and America, and a furtive trade in live bootleg recordings, we also made a lot of money by dealing in deletions – recordings which had gone out of stock and were being sold off by the record company. Since we operated a mail-order business, we had hundreds of letters every day asking for special recordings. We thus knew which of these deletions actually had some residual demand, and it was quite simple for us to pick up the popular ones cheaply and sell them on.

Most people assume that a record shop's success lies

in selling records. In fact, Virgin's success both in mail order and the record shops lay in Simon's skill at buying records. He was able to pick out bands that did not sell through the mainstream shops and sell large numbers of them through Virgin. He knew so much about music that he knew which bands would sell even before they were a proven success: he was already using the antennae which enabled us to set up the record label two years later. Without Simon, such a move would have been a step in the dark. Our other genius was John Varnom, who did all the promotion for the records and wrote the advertising slogans for the shops. Virgin began to gain a broader reputation.

With the best music playing in the shops and the warehouse all day, both the staff and the customers lying around smoking dope and talking about how to get hold of the highly prized American recording of *Aerosol Grey Machine* by Van Der Graaf Generator, and everyone enjoying plenty of sex, there was no better place for any self-respecting 21-year-old to be.

But beneath that there was a business to run. At the Manor, building work dragged on. I dreaded every call from Tom Newman, who was fitting all the equipment: he always asked for more money to buy some other piece of recording equipment. At the same time I had the customs fine, the mortgage and the thought of prison hanging over me.

The mail-order business was doing well but mainly seemed to attract the serious music buyers who were looking for quite rare records. It seemed difficult to expand it further. We realised that, if we were going to make money, it would have to come from opening up more Virgin Records shops.

Nik and I began a programme of serious expansion.

Towards the end of 1971 and throughout 1972 we aimed to open a shop every month. By Christmas 1972 we had fourteen record shops: several in London and one in every big city across the country. As well as organising all the records that the shops would stock, advertising the shops, choosing and training the staff to run them, and setting up the accounting systems to keep control of the money, we found that the timing of shop openings was crucial. After negotiating the lease until we were sure that the landlord would go no lower, we would push for a rent-free period for the first three months. This was the single most crucial element. We would not agree to open the shop unless this was in place, and as a result we walked away from a great many opportunities. However, when we opened we knew that the record sales in the first three months would help pay for the rent on the previous shop that we had opened. The sales also demonstrated, without committing to a huge overhead, whether the site we had chosen attracted enough people off the streets to make the shop viable.

As we opened these shops we learnt all sorts of lessons that stood us in good stead for the future. We always looked for the cheaper end of the high street, where we might attract shoppers to come a few extra yards off the beaten track without us having to pay an exorbitant rent. We also chose areas where the teenagers hung out, such as near the Clock Tower in Brighton or Bold Street in Liverpool. We always asked the local teenagers where the best place for a record shop would be. There are many invisible lines in a town which people will not cross: a street can change character in the space of twenty yards.

The other unique thing about record retailing is the speed with which records move. When a big release is out, like the latest David Bowie record, you can measure its sales in hours. You therefore need to keep right on top of the shop to find out what's selling that day. You can then use that information to rearrange the record displays in the other shops. If you run out of the key record that's selling that day, then, of course, the buyer will head off to the next shop to pick it up. Once you've lost that chance to sell a copy of *Hunky Dory*, you never get it back again. There are no repeat sales of the same record. Although you will always stock *Hunky Dory*, up to 70 per cent of your sales of it will happen in the first two weeks of its release.

At first, Virgin promoted its image as a place where people could come and spend time listening to and choosing their records, with a distinct emphasis on elitist, 'hip' taste. As well as the more mainstream records, we wanted to show teenagers more interesting ones. Our shops flatly refused to sell the mass-market teeny-bopper records such as the ones by The Osmonds and The Sweet that were storming the charts. Despite Simon's persuasive arguments about style, our refusal to stock Gary Glitter and all the glam-rock stars always slightly worried me since I could see the short-term income we were turning away. However, Simon assured me that if we stuck to our image we would keep our integrity and build up more customers: 'It's the Andy Williams rule,' he told me. 'We're not in that market.'

The shop at 130 Notting Hill Gate became one of the best Virgin Records shops. Simon started working above it, and we laid our cushions on the floor in the shop so that people could lie around there all day. We knew that we were successful when people started coming up to London just to go to a Virgin Records shop. If we could have sold marijuana, we would have done. In fact, I suspect that some of the staff did. Selling records, chatting up the customers, recommending which music to buy, reaching under the counter for the latest bootleg, heading off to pubs and clubs to hear more bands play: it became a way of life.

When we opened our Virgin Records shop in Bold Street, Liverpool, in March 1972, I proudly saw that we took £10,000 in the first week. A week later the figure was £7,000, and then the following week the takings were down to £3,000. By the middle of the summer they had dropped to £2,000 and I went up there to see what was going wrong. The shop was packed. There were rockers all jammed into one corner, mods in another, and hippies draped all over the floor near the till. All kinds of music were playing. But nobody was buying anything. Everyone was happily stoned and having a great time, but nobody could get to the till and they were keeping other shoppers out of the store. The policy of treating our shops like clubs was out of control. For the next month we had someone at the door who gently warned people as they went in that they were going into a shop, not a nightclub; we put in brighter lights and moved the counter and the till nearer the window. It was a narrow line between maintaining the shop's atmosphere and keeping it profitable. The takings at last recovered.

Throughout this expansion, one of our main difficulties was getting hold of the records to sell. Some record companies, including PolyGram, refused to supply us because we were discounting and therefore offending the main retailers. Other record companies refused to supply us since they doubted our ability to pay. Nik and Chris Stylianou ('Chris the Greek', who had joined as our sales manager) called around all the possible suppliers, and eventually found an extraordinary solution: a record shop in South Woodford called Pop In, run by Raymond Laren. Raymond was prepared to use his account to buy records on our behalf. It was good business for him since he would order all our records on top of his own orders, charge a 5 per cent margin and pass them on to us.

When we first struck this deal with Raymond, we would give him the list of records to add on to his orders; Tony or Simon would drive round and pick them up, and we'd drive them to the three or four Virgin shops. Pop In was a tiny shop with matt black walls and peeling posters of *Sergeant Pepper* and Neil Young. It was difficult to squeeze in and out with the boxes of records, but we managed to cope. Over the next year, as we opened more and more shops, the number of records passing through Raymond's shop grew. Soon Raymond was ordering thousands of records from the record labels and we were sending a lorry to collect them.

We kept trying to deal with the record labels directly, but they continued to ignore us. Soon Virgin became one of the largest record chains in the country and the scenes at Raymond's shop were farcical: a line of vans unloaded hundreds of cases of records at the front door, and people staggered through the shop to the back door, where they were loaded on to another line of vans to take them around the Virgin shops. Something had to give. We were still having to pay an extra 5 per cent to buy our records through Raymond. Finally, Nik and I went back to the record labels and pointed out what was happening. They agreed to sell records to us directly, and Raymond Laren's Ealing-comedy earner was over. His shop reverted to selling a few dozen records each week, and his accountants were left to puzzle over what had gone wrong with his amazing shop.

During 1972 Simon fell in love with a South American

girl and told me that he was going to leave Virgin and go to live in Chile with her. The Manor was at last open for artists to record; there were twenty Virgin Records shops, and the mail-order business was doing well. Simon had been working with me for a year and, although neither of us had ever expected him to stay for more than a few months, I suddenly realised how vital he was to Virgin. His choice in music had established the Virgin Records shops as *the* place to go and buy records. It was 'hip' to go and spend an afternoon mooching around the Virgin Records shop, whereas no self-respecting teenager would go and spend an afternoon hanging around Woolies.

The credibility which Simon had always talked about, and the sales of The Osmonds which we had foregone, had worked. The music press now discussed which artists Virgin was promoting. When we put an eclectic German band called Tangerine Dream in our shop windows, it became a talking point. Record labels started contacting us and asking whether the Virgin Records shops could run special promotions on their bands.

I tried to persuade Simon to stay, but he was set on leaving. His girlfriend went to Chile first, with Simon poised to join her in a month's time. During that month he suddenly received the 'Dear Simon' letter from her which called everything off. He was desperately disappointed, but at the same time it became clear that his future lay in London rather than either South America or even South Africa. Since Virgin now had the record shops and the recording studio, we started talking about the third part of the grandiose dream we had discussed over our first lunch at the Greek restaurant: the Virgin record label.

If Virgin set up a record label, we could offer artists somewhere to record (for which we could charge them);

we could publish and release their records (from which we could make profit), and we had a large and growing chain of shops where we could promote and sell their records (and make the retail profit margin). The three businesses were mutually compatible and would also benefit the bands we signed, since we could reduce prices at the Manor, the manufacturing end, and increase promotion at the shops, the retail end, while still making our own profit.

Simon and I drew up an agreement whereby he would set up and run the new Virgin record label, Virgin Music. He would own 20 per cent of the company, which would henceforth be separate from the Virgin Records shops. And the first person Simon and I wanted to sign up was that third reserve guitarist from *Hair*: Mike Oldfield.

Mike Oldfield had had a difficult childhood with an alcoholic mother. He had often locked himself up in his room in the attic and taught himself how to play all kinds of instruments. At the age of fourteen he had made his first recording with his sister Sally, singing folk music. He and his sister formed a folk duo called Sallyangie and signed to Transatlantic Records. By fifteen he had left home and become a guitarist alongside Dave Bedford with Kevin Ayers' group The Whole World.

For a couple of weeks in October 1971, Mike was signed as a session guitarist to a singer called Arthur Louis who was recording at the Manor. Mike soon started chatting to Tom Newman and one day finally screwed up the courage and gave him a tape of his own music. Mike had recorded this tape himself, laboriously overdubbing many different instruments on to the same tape. It lasted eighteen minutes, was untitled and had no vocals. Tom listened to it and described it as 'hyper-romantic, sad, poignant and brilliant'. Tom then played it to Simon when he was next up at the Manor. Simon was astonished by it. He tried to help Mike approach some record companies, but they all turned him down.

A year later, Simon and I were sitting on the houseboat when we finally decided to start a record company. We called Mike up. To our delight he had still not signed up with anyone. He felt completely rejected by the record industry and was overwhelmed that we seriously wanted to release his music. He came straight over to the houseboat to see us. I suggested that Mike should go back to the Manor and live there, and then whenever the recording studio was free he and Tom Newman could get together and work on his record.

'I'll need to rent some instruments, though,' Mike warned me.

'Like what?' I pulled out my diary and prepared a list.

'A good acoustic guitar, a Spanish guitar, a Farfisa organ, a Fender precision bass, a good Fender amplifier, glockenspiel, a mandolin, a mellotron –'

'What's that?' I drew a circle round it.

'It's not absolutely necessary,' Mike conceded. 'A triangle, a Gibson guitar ... Oh, and some chimes, of course.'

'What are chimes?' I asked.

'Tubular bells.'

I wrote down 'tubular bells' and set about finding all these instruments in a music magazine. The guitar cost £35, the Spanish guitar £25, the Fender amplifier £45, the mandolin £15, and the triangle was a bargain at £1. The tubular bells cost £20.

'£20 for tubular bells?' I said. 'They'd better be worth it.'

7 'It's called *Tubular Bells*. I've never heard anything like it.'

1972–1973

S INCE MIKE OLDFIELD WAS the first artist we signed, we had no idea what sort of a contract to offer him. Luckily, Sandy Denny, who originally sang with Fairport Convention but had now gone solo, had recently recorded at the Manor. She had become a friend of mine and I asked her for a copy of her contract with Island Records. This was apparently a standard Island Records deal, and we retyped it word for word, changing 'Island Records' to 'Virgin Music' and 'Sandy Denny' to 'Mike Oldfield'. It set out that Mike would make ten albums for Virgin Music and receive a 5 per cent royalty on 90 per cent of the wholesale value of the record (10 per cent was kept by the record company to pay for packaging costs and breakages). Since Mike had no money, we put him on the standard Virgin salary which we all received, £20 a week. We would then deduct it from any future royalties, if they ever materialised. Although Simon and I loved Mike's music, we never thought that we'd make any money from it.

It took Mike well into 1973 to record what became known as *Tubular Bells*. It was a fantastically complicated sequence of recordings to make, and he and Tom Newman went over it again and again in the recording studio, mixing, dubbing, and fine-tuning all the different layers of music. Mike played over twenty different instruments and made over 2,300 different recordings until he was happy. In the meantime we were still trying to rent out the Manor to any band we could find, so Mike was often interrupted and had to clear his kit out of the recording studio to make way for The Rolling Stones or Adam Faith.

Frank Zappa had made his reputation as one of the most original, innovative and irreverent performers in rock music. His albums, like *We're Only In It For The Money* and *Weasels Ripped My Flesh*, were filled with biting satire, and when he came up to the Manor to investigate the possibilities of recording there I felt sure he would appreciate a joke.

I drove Frank up from London myself, enthusing about the wonderful manor house in which the studio was situated. But, instead of taking the road to Shipton-on-Cherwell, I made a detour to nearby Woodstock. I turned off the road, under a majestic arch, and drove down a long, gravel driveway to the door of a magnificent house.

'I'll park the car,' I told Frank. 'Just knock on the door and tell them who you are.'

The door was opened by a uniformed footman. Funnily enough, he didn't recognise Frank Zappa and was not amused to be told the long-haired musician had come to stay. Did Zappa know, the footman asked, that he was knocking at the door of Blenheim Palace, the ancestral seat of the Dukes of Marlborough?

Frank got back into the car, swearing that he could see the funny side of it. But he never did record at the Manor.

On 22 July 1972, Kristen and I were married at the tiny church at Shipton-on-Cherwell. I had just turned 22, and Kristen was still 20. We had known each other only since May of the previous year. I still have a copy of the invitation we sent out for the party before the wedding.

It reads: 'Kristen and I have decided to get married, and we thought that this would be a good excuse for a party. There will be a pig on a spit, so please come since the pig will not last. The Scaffold will be playing.' One of the best things about the Manor was that it lent itself to having wonderful parties. We had bands who were happy to play, a river to swim in, huge rooms with ancient fireplaces, and a cloistered courtyard which caught the sun.

Our wedding barbecue was a great feast, with all the villagers from Shipton-on-Cherwell mixing with the Virgin staff and a great many of the rock bands around at the time. The wedding day was extraordinary throughout. As we were waiting at the church for Kristen to arrive, a huge articulated lorry started to squeeze its way down the narrow lane towards us. Nobody could understand what it was doing, until a tiny old lady in a blue suit with a blue hat jammed on to her head climbed out.

'I'm not too late, am I?' Granny called out.

The lorry had crashed into her car coming through Oxford, and she had insisted that the driver take her to our wedding.

My parents gave us a beautiful old Bentley with red leather seats and a walnut dashboard as a wedding present. Although it tended to break down as much as my Morris Minor, it was supremely comfortable to sit in while we were towed along.

One of Kristen's bridesmaids was her sister Meryll, and Nik was my best man. At the reception afterward it became clear that there was a certain chemistry between them, and late that night they headed off towards a room in the Manor. By the time Kristen and I returned from honeymoon, Nik and Meryll had announced that they too were getting married.

Nik and Meryll were married even faster than

Kristen and I: their wedding was in the winter of 1972, just five months after they had met. Kristen and I found this marriage a little claustrophobic: I would spend all day with Nik at South Wharf Road, and then I would also see him and Meryll together in the evenings. Unfortunately, one of the reasons why Kristen had come to England was to escape from her family, and now she found that she and her sister had married two men who practically lived in each other's pocket. Incestuous wasn't the word for it. On top of that, Nik and I, who had run Virgin very much as a singles company, suddenly found ourselves both married: it was something of a culture shock.

Throughout the winter of 1972 and the spring of 1973, Mike Oldfield was living at the Manor and recording *Tubular Bells*. I think this was the happiest time of his life. He was there with Tom Newman, who was obsessed by the technology of recording, and they could endlessly refine the recordings together. Mundy was still living there. When Kristen and I drove up to the Manor on a Friday night, we would find Mike, Tom and Mundy sitting on cushions on the floor, stoking up the vast fire and listening to the latest tapes. They were oblivious to the outside world. *Tubular Bells* was finally ready for release in May 1973.

We knew that we had something extraordinary on our hands when we started selling *Tubular Bells* into the trade. Simon took the recording along to the sales conference at Island Records, who were going to distribute the album. They were all in a large conference room at a hotel near Birmingham. They had already had to listen to hours of music. These men had heard it all before – literally. Simon put on *Tubular Bells* and they listened to the first side in its entirety. When it finished there was an outburst of applause. This was

Simon's first sales conference and so he had no idea that it was unprecedented. He never again heard a roomful of world-weary salesmen applauding a new record.

On 25 May 1973 Virgin Music released its first four albums: Mike Oldfield's *Tubular Bells*; *Flying Teapot* by Gong; *Manor Live*, a jam session from the Manor led by Elkie Brooks; and *The Faust Tapes* by Faust, a German band.

1973 was an extraordinary year for rock and pop music. That summer saw the singles chart dominated by the glam rock of Suzi Quatro, Wizzard, Gary Glitter, and The Sweet. But there was also a large Motown contingent, with Stevie Wonder, Gladys Knight and the Pips, the Jackson Five and Barry White. At the other end of the spectrum from these singers were Lou Reed with 'Take A Walk On The Wild Side' and 10cc with 'Rubber Bullets'.

The album charts were headed by David Bowie at number one with *Aladdin Sane*, the first proof of how he could reinvent himself to stay at the top. Below him were The Beatles with their *1962–1966* and *1967–1970* double albums, Pink Floyd with *Dark Side Of The Moon*, Lou Reed's *Transformer*, and Roxy Music's *For Your Pleasure*.

In the face of this competition, we had to fight hard to attract attention for Virgin's first four releases. But it was *Tubular Bells* that really captured people's imagination: it was completely original and immediately spellbinding. People found it addictive and played it again and again, both to listen to the music and to marvel at how Mike had woven it all together. I remember a review in *NME* that I had to reread several times before I realised that, although I would never understand what the critic was actually saying, he was clearly raving about it. *NME* was the single most influential music paper. With it praising *Tubular Bells*, everyone would look out for it.

Aside from the reviews, I knew that, as soon as we could get people to listen to *Tubular Bells* once, it would take off. As one critic correctly said, 'One hearing should provide sufficient proof.' The problem was getting that hearing. I called up every radio producer I could, trying to persuade them to play *Tubular Bells*. But at that time 3-minute singles dominated radio music: there was no room for a 45-minute piece of music without words. Radio 3 turned it down because it wasn't Mozart and Radio 1 turned it down because it wasn't Gary Glitter.

For the first two weeks, sales of *Tubular Bells* were stillborn. Then I invited John Peel over to *Alberta* for lunch. We had known each other since I had interviewed him for *Student*. He had also started his own record label, Dandelion. He was the only person who played serious rock music on the radio, and his show was our only chance of winning air time for *Tubular Bells*. We all had lunch on *Alberta* and then settled down on the sofas. I put on *Tubular Bells*. He was amazed.

'I've never heard anything like it,' John finally said.

Later that week we listened to John Peel's laconic voice coming out of the radio. I was sitting on the deck of the houseboat with Mike Oldfield and everyone from Virgin.

'Tonight I'm not going to play a whole lot of records. I'm just going to play you one by a young composer called Mike Oldfield. It's his first record and it's called *Tubular Bells*. I've never heard anything like it in my life. It's released by Virgin, a brand-new record label, and it was recorded at Virgin's own studios in Oxfordshire. You'll never forget this.'

With that, *Tubular Bells* started. I was lying on the

sofa. Everyone was lounging around in deep armchairs or on the rug, and we passed round beer and wine, cigarettes and joints. I tried to relax. I could see everyone else lying there totally spellbound by the music. But I kept worrying. I find it impossible to stop my brain from churning through all the ideas and possibilities facing me at any given moment. I wondered how many people were listening to *The John Peel Show*; how many of those would go out and buy *Tubular Bells* the next day; whether they would wait until Saturday or would have forgotten about it by then. Would they come to the Virgin shops or order it from Smith's? How fast would we receive the royalties? How many copies would we have to reprint? How should we break it in America? On one level I was absorbed in the music, but I felt like an outsider. I couldn't lose myself in it like Simon or Nik, or my lovely new assistant Penni, who was a real beauty with long, black wavy hair and a generous smile. I was too aware that Virgin needed to sell a lot of copies to make money for next month's tax repayment. I knew that *Flying Teapot* and *The Faust Tapes* were hardly going to knock The Rolling Stones or Bob Dylan off the charts. But *Tubular Bells* was extraordinary: something must happen from tonight's broadcast. Virgin would never be able to afford to buy such a length of radio time to advertise it.

Mike Oldfield sat in silence. He leant against Penni and stared straight at the radio. I wondered what was going through his head. I had wedged a sleeve of *Tubular Bells* – which showed a giant tubular bell suspended over the sea with a wave breaking in the foreground – above one of the picture frames. Mike stared at it as if he was staring out to sea. A greedy thought swam in the murky depths of my mind: perhaps he was already dreaming up another album?

All the next day the phones rang with orders from record shops for *Tubular Bells*. As well as choosing to break all tradition by playing it in its entirety, John Peel reviewed *Tubular Bells* for the *Listener*:

> On the all too frequent occasions when I'm told that a record by a contemporary rock musician is a work of 'lasting importance' I tend to reach for my hat and head for the wide open spaces. Today these experts would probably tell you that in twenty years' time collectors will still be enthusing over the records of such weighty bands as Yes and Emerson, Lake and Palmer. I'm ready to bet you a few shillings that Yes and ELP will have vanished from the memory of all but the most stubborn and that the Gary Glitters and Sweets of no lasting value will be regarded as representing the true sound of the 1970s.
>
> Having said that, I'm going to tell you about a new recording of such strength, energy and real beauty that to me it represents the first breakthrough into history that any musician regarded primarily as a rock musician has made. Mike Oldfield ...

John Peel had an enormous following, and what he said was picked up by thousands of people across the country.

We arranged for both Gong and Faust to tour the country, but it was the grand *Tubular Bells* concert planned for 25 June which I hoped would bring the national press to witness the music celebrity of the moment. We made the *Tubular Bells* concert into an unmissable event. We managed to have Mick Taylor, then The Rolling Stones' guitarist, Steve Hillage and Hatfield and the North all agree to play various instruments. Viv Stanshall from The Bonzo Dog

Doo-Dah Band agreed to be on stage and announce the instruments as he did on the record.

On the day of the concert Mike came round to see me on the houseboat.

'Richard,' he said quietly. 'I can't go through with this concert tonight.'

'But it's all arranged,' I said.

'I simply can't go ahead,' he repeated in a deathly whisper.

I felt a wave of despair. I knew Mike could be as stubborn as me when he wanted to be. I tried to forget that the whole concert was arranged, the tickets sold and even television coverage agreed. I couldn't use any of that as leverage since it would only strengthen Mike's resolve. I had to be cunning.

'Let's go for a drive,' I said innocuously, and led the way along the towpath and to my old Bentley parked outside. I knew that Mike had always admired this battleship-grey car with its faded red-leather seats. I hoped that a soothing drive past the Queen Elizabeth Hall would put Mike in a different frame of mind. We drove off with Mike sitting bolt upright. After a monosyllabic drive we reached the Queen Elizabeth Hall and I slowed down. There were Mike Oldfield posters everywhere. Already a crowd of people were making their way to the concert.

'I can't go on to the stage,' Mike repeated.

I couldn't tell him that it was in his best interests, that this concert might catapult him into a different league and put him up alongside Pink Floyd. I stopped the car.

'Do you want to drive?'

'All right,' Mike said cautiously.

We drove on, over Westminster Bridge, past Victoria. I watched Hyde Park flash past the passenger window.

Mike turned down Bayswater Road and drove near to the church where I had edited *Student* magazine.

'Mike,' I said. 'Would you like to have this car? As a present?'

'A present?'

'Yes. I'll get out here and walk home. You just keep on driving and the car's yours.'

'Come off it! It was your wedding present.'

'All you have to do is then drive it round to the Queen Elizabeth Hall and go up on stage tonight. It's yours.'

A silence fell between us. I watched Mike as he held the steering wheel and imagined himself driving this car. I knew he was tempted. I hoped he would agree.

'It's a deal,' Mike said.

I would have to tell Kristen and then my parents what I had done with our Bentley, but I knew they wouldn't mind too much. For all its charm and sentimental value, the Bentley was just a car. It was vital to get Mike up on stage and sell copies of *Tubular Bells*. If he was successful, I would be able to pick up any car I wanted. My mother would have approved.

As the last bars of *Tubular Bells* died away at the Queen Elizabeth Hall, there was a momentary silence as people digested what they had just heard. They seemed mesmerised and nobody wanted to break the spell. Then they leapt to their feet in a standing ovation. I was sitting between Kristen and Simon and we stood up and cheered and applauded. Tears ran down my cheeks. Mike stood up in front of the organ, a tiny figure, and just bowed and said thank you. Even the band applauded him. He was a new star.

That night we sold hundreds of copies of *Tubular Bells*. Mike was too shattered to speak to the press.

Looking at all the people cheering and crowding round to buy his record, he said, 'I feel as if I've been raped,' and disappeared off in his new Bentley. Mike refused to go back on stage for many years afterward. Kristen and I walked home. From that night onward, Mike Oldfield's *Tubular Bells* was set to become the most celebrated album of the year. Virgin Music was on the map, and the money started rolling in.

Word of mouth spread and on 14 July *Tubular Bells* entered the album charts at number twenty-three. By August it was number one. For the next fifteen years, whenever Mike Oldfield released an album it reached the top ten. *Tubular Bells* eventually sold over thirteen million copies, making it the eleventh-bestselling album ever released in Britain. The sacrifice of my Bentley was worth it. I never got round to buying another one.

Although overnight Virgin was an established record label, we were a tiny company with a staff of seven and no ability to distribute records to all the record shops across the country. We had two options open to us. The first was to license our records to another, larger, record label. This would work only for fairly successful bands. The other company would give us an upfront payment for the right to promote the record, distribute it and keep the bulk of the profits. If the record recouped its advance, the record company would pay us a royalty, typically around 16 per cent. This was the traditional arrangement for a fledgling record company like Virgin.

The second option was more risky. Virgin would forego the upfront payment and the royalties, and simply pay another record label to manufacture and distribute the records as and when they were ordered by shops around the country. Virgin would be responsible for all the promotion of its records, and carry all the risk if the record failed. Correspondingly, we would have all the upside if the record sold well.

Most small record labels licensed their records since it was easy money: they received 16 per cent royalties from the other company and paid out whatever they had agreed to the artist, say 5 or 10 per cent. But Simon and I decided that we would go for a manufacture and distribution deal (called 'Pressing and Distribution' or 'P&D'). It was a bold move but even then I knew that it is only by being bold that you get anywhere. If you are a risk-taker, then the art is to protect the downside. It seemed to us that *Tubular Bells* was so good that we could promote it ourselves. I felt sure that it would sell enough copies to pay back our investment. With the idea of asking for a P&D deal rather than a straight licensing agreement, we went to see Island Records.

I had first come across Island Records when I was editing *Student* magazine. It had been set up by Chris Blackwell, who was brought up in Jamaica and had almost single-handedly introduced reggae into Britain. Island released Bob Marley, who became the first reggae superstar, and among others they also produced Cat Stevens and Free.

Predictably, at first Island refused to do a P&D deal. They already licensed Chrysalis and Charisma (which had Genesis), and they wanted Virgin too. So they offered us a highly attractive licensing deal with royalties of 18 per cent. We were paying Mike 5 per cent, which meant that if we accepted Island's offer we could collect 13 per cent of the sales of *Tubular Bells* for ourselves. At £2.19 this was 28.5 pence a record, which would mean a total profit to us of around £171,000 if *Tubular Bells* did astoundingly well and sold, say, 600,000 copies – that is to say reached double platinum. A record goes gold at 200,000 copies and platinum at

300,000 copies. If it reached a million copies, then Virgin would make £285,000 without having to pay for any of the costs of promoting and marketing the record. To a seasoned eye Island were far better placed than Virgin to promote this record to all the shops across the country. Most small record companies in our place would have accepted it, and certainly both Island and our lawyers urged us to do so.

But Simon and I felt differently. We had fourteen Virgin shops across the country which could promote *Tubular Bells*. The experience of selling 100,000 copies of *Student* across the country had given me confidence that we could get this record out in quantity. Of course, our job was made much easier because *Tubular Bells* was so good that people wanted to buy it as soon as they heard it.

To an outsider this looked like an enormous gamble. If sales of *Tubular Bells* had faded, Virgin Music would have been dead in the water. But, if we managed to sell 600,000 copies, worth about £1.3 million, Virgin would receive around £920,000 after the shops' retail margin. Of this, we would pay £65,700 to Mike Oldfield as the artist, and £197,100 to Island Records for pressing and distributing the record, leaving us with around £658,000 to divide between promoting the record and keeping as profit to reinvest in other artists. This was the upside.

The intellectual copyright of *Tubular Bells* was our birthright, and we were determined to build on it. So we turned down Island's offer and insisted that we stick to a P&D deal. They would press and distribute the record and we would pay them between 10 and 15 per cent for this. They still held out for a licensing deal until we threatened to go to a rival record company, CBS. So we signed a P&D deal and sacrificed an immediate cash payment which would have been welcomed by Coutts, since the Manor was still in debt. We committed ourselves to selling *Tubular Bells* with our own resources.

Island unwittingly fostered a cuckoo which grew up in their nest: Virgin Music. We became rich beyond our dreams as the sales of *Tubular Bells* shot through silver, gold, platinum, double platinum and then up over a million copies. We grew into a major force in the record industry and eventually became the rival to Island Records. Although the royalty rates we paid Mike Oldfield and Island changed over time, as did the price of the record, *Tubular Bells* went on to sell millions of copies and still sells around the world today. Our gamble that we could promote it ourselves made us our first fortune.

8 'To be second choice means nothing.'

1974–1976

WHEN MIKE OLDFIELD DROVE away in my old Bentley after the concert at the Queen Elizabeth Hall, he was already spinning out of orbit. During all the months in which he had been incarcerated at the Manor with Tom Newman, working in complete privacy and achieving his perfect album, he had been dreaming about everyone buying *Tubular Bells*. But, when he stood up at the Queen Elizabeth Hall and saw the audience giving him a standing ovation, something inside him gave way. He found that, although this adulation was something he had yearned for, now that he had it he couldn't cope with it.

The music industry can make people rich beyond their dreams in a matter of months. Whether he liked it or not, Mike was now caught in that spiral which would make him one of Britain's wealthiest men. The success was devastating to him, and I had to learn to live with that responsibility. I found it impossible to answer the question as to whether I should have pushed him into doing that concert. Mike went to live in a remote part of Wales with a girlfriend, and refused to talk to anyone else except me.

When I first drove down to visit him, I could hardly find the house. It was a tiny stone cottage built on a range of hills called Hergest Ridge. The house had its back to the prevailing winds but it was so remote it was like Wuthering Heights. The whole of the front room was taken up with a grand piano. He took me up on to Hergest Ridge with a six-foot balsawood glider he had made. I watched him as he ran carefully down the hill and then gently launched the huge plane. It hardly seemed to move at first, and appeared suspended above Mike's head, but then the wind caught it and it banked, soaring up and flying away from us down the ridge towards the fields below. Mike watched it, the wind blowing his hair back from his eyes, and for the first time I saw him smile.

I drove back to London and left Mike living on Hergest Ridge. In a sad reversal of my having Kristen's clothes brought round to *Alberta* so that she would have to move in with me, Mike went to the local pub one night and asked a friend to pack up his girlfriend's clothes and take her to the station. For the next ten years, Mike Oldfield lived as a recluse and did no promotion for any of his albums. Fortunately, we had made a film of Mike playing *Tubular Bells*. We made it into a documentary and intercut it with pictures of abstract William Pye sculptures. The BBC showed it three times. Each time this film was broadcast, the sales of *Tubular Bells* and Mike's other records soared. Had Mike spent the next ten years touring, like Pink Floyd, I am sure that he would have become one of the biggest rock stars in the world and John Peel's prediction would have come true. As it was, *Tubular Bells* became more famous than Mike Oldfield, and, although he recorded many other beautiful albums, such as *Ommadawn*, my own favourite, none of them matched the success of *Tubular Bells*.

The other record companies were mystified by Mike's reticence to perform. Ahmet Ertegun, who had eventually, after much negotiation, licensed *Tubular Bells* in America, couldn't understand it:

'You're telling me that you have a film of sculptures for the promo?' he snarled at me. 'I don't get it. I'm not sure anyone over here will get it either. We can all visit the Met if we want to.'

As usual, Ahmet managed to come up with a solution: he sold *Tubular Bells* as the soundtrack for the film *The Exorcist*. As the film became a hit in America, so did the album. It finally reached the top of the American charts a year after it had done so in Britain.

Simon and I developed three key aims when negotiating with bands. We never formally articulated them to each other, but our negotiations over Mike Oldfield taught us these general principles.

First, we set out to own copyright for as long as possible. We tried our hardest never to agree a deal where the copyright reverted to the artist, because the only assets a record company has are its copyrights. We also tried to incorporate as much as possible of an artist's back catalogue into our contract, although often this was tied up with other record labels. Beneath all the glamour of dealing with the rock stars, the only value lay in the intellectual copyright in their songs. We would thus offer high initial sums, but try to tie the artist in for eight albums. Over the life of Virgin Music, we prided ourselves that we had never lost a band. We never lost a band because we always renegotiated their contracts after a few albums, although, ironically, Mike Oldfield was one case where I was too slow to renegotiate and I almost lost him. The vital thing with a new band was, if you built them up, it would often be their third or fourth album that would be the most valuable. One good example of this was The Human League, who had made two albums on Virgin, each of which sold progressively better, but who then broke into the big time with their third album, *Dare*, which sold over 2 million copies. The last thing we wanted was to lose them after a couple of albums only to see them become successful with another record label. After we signed the artist up, we would soon try to extend the contract and, although we might give away 2 or 3 percentage points in royalties, it was a small concession in comparison with the potential of adding another two albums on to the end of the contract.

Right from the start Simon and I tried to position Virgin as an international company, and the second thing we always insisted on was incorporating world-wide copyright to the artist's work in our contracts. We would argue that there was less incentive for us to promote them in Britain if they then used their success here to sell well overseas with someone else.

Our last negotiating point was to ensure that Virgin owned the copyright in the individual members of the band as well as the band itself. It was sometimes difficult to define a band: for example, The Rolling Stones clearly comprised Mick Jagger, Keith Richards, Bill Wyman and Charlie Watts, but a number of other people came and went. The record industry finally defined The Rolling Stones as 'Mick Jagger plus three others'. Some bands split up and became individually successful. Genesis is perhaps the prime example, as Peter Gabriel and Phil Collins both became bigger stars outside Genesis than they had been within the band. We had to ensure that Virgin didn't sign a band only to be left with an empty shell while the lead guitarist went on to succeed as a solo artist on another label.

The only other great truth we found was that, if we wanted a band enough, we had to sign them almost no matter how high the bidding went. An artist on another label remains just that: nothing to do with us. Part of the secret of running a record label was to build up momentum, to keep signing new bands and to keep breaking them into the big time. Even if a high-profile band lost us money, there would be other, intangible, benefits, such as attracting others to sign with us, or opening doors to radio stations for our newer bands.

With these principles in our minds, Virgin began to sign up new bands on the back of Mike Oldfield's success. The bulk of these would inevitably fail. We still paid ourselves tiny wages; we still all lived in each other's pocket, and we reinvested all the money we earned from *Tubular Bells* in new artists and building up the company.

Kristen and I had been married for two years but we were having too many difficulties together and, eventually, we decided to divorce. As well as my marriage breaking up in 1974, Virgin Music was beginning to have some problems. In August 1974 Mike Oldfield's next album, *Hergest Ridge*, went straight to number one. Since *Tubular Bells* was still at number two, money kept coming in. But Virgin was in danger of being seen as just Mike Oldfield's label. In spite of refusing to do any promotion himself, Mike's sales were so large that he eclipsed anyone else.

During that rather awkward patch between 1974 and 1976 when Mike Oldfield was our only superstar, Virgin failed to sign 10cc, The Who and Pink Floyd, despite fighting hard for them. It seemed that we were destined to be forever the second choice, and in music as in so many other things the second choice means nothing. At the end of 1975 I pitched for The Rolling Stones. Word had got about that we had been prepared to pay £350,000 for 10cc: it astonished our rival record labels like Island. When I called up The Stones' manager,

Prince Rupert Loewenstein, he was prepared to listen to me seriously, having heard about our 10cc offer.

'How much are you asking for?' I asked him.

'You'll never be able to afford it,' Prince Rupert told me sympathetically. 'It'll be at least $3 million. And, anyway, Virgin is just too small.'

I knew that the only way to get his attention was to considerably better that offer.

'I'll offer $4 million,' I said. 'As long as there is some back catalogue available.'

Buying the back catalogue would enable Virgin to release a greatest-hits album and would be a good insurance policy if the new record failed.

'I'll send you round the list of the back catalogue that's available,' Prince Rupert said. 'If you can bring a bank guarantee for $4 million to my office by Monday then I'll look at it very seriously. Best of luck.'

It was Friday. Prince Rupert assumed that he had set me an impossible task.

That weekend I travelled around the chain of Virgin distributors we had set up across Europe in France, Germany, Italy, Holland, Sweden and Norway. As I travelled I was constantly on the telephone to those in the rest of the world. I was looking to raise about £250,000 from each distributor. By the end of the weekend I had tracked them all down and asked them to send telegrams to Coutts in London confirming that they would provide the money. By Monday morning I was back in London but still some way short of the $4 million I had promised Prince Rupert. After adding up all the different commitments from the distributors, Coutts promised to make up the difference. I drove round to Prince Rupert's house in Petersham just before eleven o'clock with a bank guarantee for $4 million.

Prince Rupert was dumbfounded. I had caught him

completely off guard. He fingered the $4 million cheque but then gave it back.

'You'll have a chance to match the highest offer,' he promised. 'But you've started an auction.'

In the end EMI won the auction with a bid of $5 million and signed The Rolling Stones. I couldn't raise any more than the $4 million. Although I was disappointed to have failed, I knew that I had done The Stones a good turn by increasing the asking price from the $3 million Prince Rupert would have been happy to accept.

By 1976 the necessity of signing the really big bands was beyond frustration. Virgin had two albums in the top ten: Gong, and Mike Oldfield's *Ommadawn*. These were the days of Genesis's *Trick Of The Tail* and Bob Dylan's *Desire*. Our trouble was that we had spent most of Mike Oldfield's royalties on signing up new bands and, with the exception of Tangerine Dream, had had no major breakthroughs. Tangerine Dream's *Phaedra* had become a top-selling album across Europe, and greatly enhanced Virgin's reputation. Our catalogue was full of wonderful, credible music, but we did not have enough really big sellers. More immediately, we were running out of cash.

On top of that, Mike Oldfield wanted to renegotiate his contract. We were happy to renegotiate but, after we agreed a second version with an increased royalty to him, he instructed another lawyer who began to push for an even higher royalty. Simon and I decided that Virgin couldn't go any higher. We pointed out that Virgin Music as a company was making less money than he was personally. When he asked how this was possible, I made the mistake of being completely honest with him. I told him that we needed successful artists like him to pay for our unsuccessful ones. His sympathy evaporated.

'I'm not giving money away for you to blow on a whole load of rubbish,' he said. 'I'm going back to my lawyer.'

Eventually we agreed another contract and Mike stayed with us. But it was a close-run thing.

In the summer of 1976 we had a crisis meeting with Simon, Nik and Ken Berry. Ken had started in the Notting Hill record shop as a clerk. It was his job to check the shop's takings, but soon he took over a whole range of other jobs. We all found that whenever we needed to know anything – the sales of Pink Floyd that week, the staff wages due, the depreciation on the old Saabs we ran – Ken knew all the answers. Ken became indispensable. He was quiet and unassuming but, as well as dealing with the numbers, his great skill was dealing with people: he was utterly unfazed by negotiating with top rock stars and their lawyers, and soon he became involved in working through the contract negotiations. Simon and I watched him and, as we realised that he would never lose a deal by throwing his ego around and trying to score points off the other side, so we gave him more and more responsibility. The original trio – me, Nik and Simon – made room for Ken, and in many ways he became the link that held us all together.

At that crisis meeting, we went through the figures of the shops, which were trading well but not very profitably. I knew that Nik was pushing them for all he was worth, and we were loath to criticise anything he was doing. Then we started going through the Virgin roster. One by one we debated whether we could afford to keep acts like Hatfield and the North or Dave Bedford that cost us money to promote and looked unlikely ever to break into the big time.

'It's clear to me,' Ken Berry said, adding up a column of figures. 'We have to seriously consider scrapping all our bands apart from Mike Oldfield.'

We looked at him in amazement.

'All our other bands are losing us money,' he went on. 'If we sacked at least half our staff, then we could cope very well, but at the moment Mike Oldfield is bankrolling the entire company.'

I have always believed that the only way to cope with a cash crisis is not to contract but to try to expand out of it.

'What about if we found ten more Mike Oldfields?' I asked, teasing him. 'How would that do?'

Ultimately, we had two options: either tuck away a little money and eke out a living without taking any more risks, or use our last few pounds to try to sign up another band that could break us back into the big time. If we chose the first option, we could get by: we would be running a tiny company, but we could survive and make a living without any risks attached. If we chose the second, Virgin could be bust within a few months, but at least we would have one last chance to break out.

Simon and I wanted to have one last go at breaking a new band. Nik and Ken eventually agreed with us, although I could see that they were reluctant to bet the entire company on a breakthrough. From that night, we were on an emergency footing, desperately searching for The Next Big Thing.

In the meantime we cut back on whatever we could: we sold our cars; we closed down the swimming pool at the Manor; we cut down on the stock in the record shops; we didn't pay ourselves; we dropped a few artists from the record label and made nine staff redundant. This was the most difficult of all, and I shied away from the emotional confrontation and let Nik do it.

One of the artists we reluctantly dropped was Dave Bedford, who was a brilliantly gifted classical composer. Dave reacted very well to the bad news: he wrote a long letter to me saying how much he understood the decision, that he appreciated his records had not sold, that he would have done the same if he had been in my shoes, that he bore Virgin no grudges and wished us all the best for the future. At the same time he wrote a letter to Mike Oldfield in which he described me as a complete shit, an utter bastard, and a vile, tone-deaf, money-grabbing parasite on musical talent. Unfortunately for Dave, he then put the letters in the wrong envelopes.

9 Never mind the bollocks
1976–1977

B Y AUGUST OF 1976 VIRGIN was in real trouble. We were trying to sign some of the aggressive punk bands which were coming on the scene, but we seemed to keep missing out. For instance, we missed getting the Boomtown Rats because I insisted on including the music publishing rights, which they wanted to sell elsewhere. We were unable to find a new band that could lift us out of our rut or dispel our image as a rather hippie label.

Among our other worries we were in the middle of a dispute with Gong over some recording rights. Some of their followers came into the Vernon Yard offices to stage a protest. Our offices were invaded by a host of benign, bearded, long-haired and very peaceful activists wearing kaftans and sandals and smoking joints. They had the appearance of a wandering band of druids and wizards. After an enjoyable afternoon spent slouched on the sofas listening to Gong, Henry Cow and Mike Oldfield, and trying to talk me into signing some petition, they decided to leave. We stood by the front door and thanked them for coming. As they left we gently relieved them of their pickings – mainly records they were trying to conceal in the flowing folds of their kaftans, but one or two of them were making off with posters, tapes, staplers, and even a telephone. They all smiled when they were caught and left in the best of spirits. I followed them out into Portobello Road and watched them wander away through the fruit stalls. One of them stopped to buy some dates. As the stallholder sold him the fruit a man with his hair shaved into a mohican and dyed pink and green walked by.

The kaftaned followers of Gong looked uncomprehendingly at the punk, picked up their dates and walked off, munching slowly.

'I'm going to be out for ten minutes,' I told Penni, my assistant.

I went up Portobello Road and found somewhere to have a haircut.

'How much off?' asked the barber.

'I think it's about time I got some value for money,' I said. 'Take about a foot and half off and let's see what I look like underneath.'

In place of names like Hatfield and the North and Tangerine Dream, a string of new bands had taken over the poster sites. They were called names like The Damned, The Clash, The Stranglers and, most notorious of all, The Sex Pistols.

In the last week of November I was working in my office when I heard this extraordinary song being played in Simon's office directly below me. I had never heard anything like it. I ran downstairs to see him.

'What was that?' I asked.

'It's The Sex Pistols' single. It's called "Anarchy In The UK".'

'How's it doing?'

'Very well,' Simon admitted. 'Very well indeed.'

'Who's signed them up?'

'EMI. I turned them down a couple of months ago. I could have made a mistake.'

There was something so raw and powerful about the song that I was determined to see whether we could win them back. A few days later, I called up Leslie Hill, the managing director of EMI. He was far too busy and important to take my call, so I left a message with his secretary saying that if he ever wanted to get rid of his 'embarrassment', then he should contact me. Half an hour later she called me back to say that EMI were quite happy with The Sex Pistols, thank you.

That very evening, 1 December, at 5.30p.m., The Sex Pistols caused a national furore. They were being interviewed on *Today*, an afternoon television show hosted by Bill Grundy. Bill Grundy had rolled back from a good lunch at *Punch* and realised that the four lads in his studio were fairly drunk as well. He started to mock them, talking about other great composers, Mozart, Bach and Beethoven. It was all a bit silly, until Johnny Rotten spilt his drink in one corner and quietly swore: 'Shit.'

'What did you say?' Grundy asked. 'What was that? Didn't I hear you say a rude word?'

'It was nothing,' Rotten said.

'Come on, what was it?'

Grundy got what he asked for.

'I said, "Shit",' Rotten told him.

'Really?' Grundy said. 'Good heavens, you frighten me to death.'

Then Grundy turned to Siouxsie Sioux, who was the other guest, and asked her whether she would meet him afterward. Steve Jones, one of The Sex Pistols, laughed and called him a dirty old sod. Grundy then turned to him and goaded him into saying more swear words. Jones called him a 'dirty fucker' and a 'fucking rotter', and that was the end of the show.

The next day the national press were once again outraged by The Sex Pistols' behaviour. Nobody criticised Bill Grundy for baiting them into swearing. As I was having my breakfast and reading an article about how someone had kicked in their television in disgust at the show, the telephone rang. It was not yet 7.00a.m. In a wonderful role reversal, the managing director of EMI was now personally calling me.

'Please come and see me immediately,' he said. 'I gather that you're interested in signing The Sex Pistols.'

I went straight round to EMI's offices. Leslie Hill and I agreed that EMI would transfer The Sex Pistols to Virgin, conditional upon Malcolm McLaren, the group's manager, agreeing. We shook hands. Then Malcolm McLaren was ushered in from the next-door room.

'Virgin have offered to take The Sex Pistols on,' Hill said, trying unsuccessfully to keep the relief out of his voice.

'Excellent,' McLaren said, offering me his hand. 'I'll come to your offices later this afternoon.'

I normally make up my mind about whether I can trust somebody within sixty seconds of meeting them. As I watched Malcolm McLaren, with his tight black trousers and pointed boots, I wondered how easy it would be to do business with him. He never showed up at Vernon Yard that afternoon, and never returned my phone calls the next day. I stopped ringing him after four attempts. He knew how to get hold of me, but he didn't call.

On 9 March 1977 McLaren signed The Sex Pistols to A&M records. The ceremony was staged outside Buckingham Palace, where the four punks lined up and screamed abuse at the royal family. The band were just four regular lads, but they were being whipped up by Malcolm McLaren.

I sat at my desk and wondered about Malcolm McLaren. I knew that he had a bestseller on his hands, a band which would transform Virgin's image. If Virgin could sign The Sex Pistols, it would, at a stroke, remove the hippie image which was hanging over us. EMI sneered at Virgin and called us 'The Earl's Court Hippies'. Never mind that we lived nowhere near Earl's Court: the name stuck and I didn't like it. We were stuck with the image of Gong and Mike Oldfield. The royalty cheques were impressive, but I feared that none of the new punk bands would take us seriously if we only had a number of hippie bands. Virgin Music needed to change and to change quickly, and The Sex Pistols could do it for us.

'Every band is a risk,' Derek Green, managing director of A&M, airily told the press. 'But in my opinion The Sex Pistols are less of a risk than most.'

A&M hosted a party to celebrate the signing of The Sex Pistols. Since A&M were 'capitalists' making money out of bands by 'exploiting' them, The Sex Pistols hated them as they hated all record companies – or at least they pretended to. Sid Vicious, then the band's bassist, excelled himself immediately after the signing by wrecking Derek Green's office and being sick all over his desk. As soon as I heard this I reached for my telephone to try one last shot. To my delight, Derek Green told me he was dropping them.

'Can we sign them?' I asked.

'If you can cope with them,' he said. 'We certainly can't.'

The Sex Pistols were given £75,000 by A&M as compensation for the cancelled contract. Together with the £50,000 they had been given from EMI, they had earned £125,000 for doing nothing more than a bit of swearing and vomiting and one single. Once again, The Sex Pistols were looking for a record label.

I began to marvel at how Malcolm McLaren had played his cards so well. The Sex Pistols were now the most shocking band in the country. Among all the punk bands which now rapidly materialised, The Sex Pistols were still the most notorious. They had a single called 'God Save The Queen' which I knew they wanted to release in time for the Queen's Silver Jubilee Day in July 1977.

I watched and waited, knowing that Malcolm McLaren didn't like me. He sneered at me as a hippie who had become a businessman. But, as the weeks passed and Jubilee Day came closer, nobody else came forward to sign The Sex Pistols. I knew that Virgin was perhaps the only record label who could do it. We had no shareholders to protest, no parent company or boss to tell me not to. On 12 May 1977 Malcolm McLaren finally came to see us. The tables had turned. Virgin signed the British rights for The Sex Pistols' first album for £15,000, with a further £50,000 payable for rights for the rest of the world.

'Do you realise what you're getting into?' McLaren asked me.

'I do,' I assured him. 'The question is, do you?'

From the moment we signed The Sex Pistols, McLaren was looking for ways to alienate us so that we'd be sufficiently embarrassed to want to get rid of them. To McLaren's horror and bemusement we refused to be outraged. We released 'God Save The Queen', which was banned by BBC radio and soared to number two in the charts. It would have been number one, but record shops like Virgin and HMV, which would be likely to be selling large quantities of the record, were excluded from the sample taken in order to compile the charts.

On Jubilee Day 1977, Malcolm McLaren rented a Thames pleasure cruiser and steamed upriver towards the House of Commons. The police knew that something was up, and as we set off from Westminster

Pier two police launches shadowed us. The band waited until they were right alongside the House of Commons and then they picked up their guitars and drumsticks and roared out their own version of the national anthem:

God save the Queen,
A fascist regime,
Made you a moron,
A potential H-bomb.
God save the Queen.
She ain't no human being,
There ain't no future in England's dream,
NO FUTURE! NO FUTURE!

The police pulled up alongside and insisted that the band stop playing. This was unwarranted since the boat had a licence for bands to play. It brought back memories of The Beatles' last ever live performance on the rooftop of the Apple studios when the police pulled the plug on them. If it had been Frank Sinatra on board there would have been no problem. The police boarded our boat and steered us back to the pier, where they arrested Malcolm McLaren, mainly because he put up such a spirited fight and started yelling, 'Fascist pigs!'

That week we sold over 100,000 copies of 'God Save The Queen'. It was clearly the number-one record, but *Top of the Pops* and the BBC claimed that Rod Stewart was really the number one. 'God Save The Queen' was banned from the television and radio. From our point of view it was good business: the more it was banned, the better it sold.

The Sex Pistols were a turning point for us, the band we had been looking for. They put Virgin back on the map, as a record company that could generate a huge amount of publicity, and that could cope with punk rock. The Sex Pistols were a national event: every shopper up and down the high street, every farmer, everyone on every bus, every grandmother, had heard of The Sex Pistols. And living close to that kind of public outcry was fascinating. As Oscar Wilde pointed out, 'The only thing worse than being talked about is not being talked about.' The Sex Pistols generated more newspaper cuttings than anything else in 1977 apart from the Silver Jubilee itself. Their notoriety was practically a tangible asset. Most of the press was negative, but so had it been for The Rolling Stones when they had set out fifteen years earlier.

In November 1977 Virgin released *Never Mind The Bollocks, Here's The Sex Pistols*. The lettering on the album sleeve was a brilliant design by Jamie Reid, crudely cut out from newspaper headlines in the same way as kidnappers' notes and hate mail were delivered. Virgin shops put large yellow posters in their windows advertising the record. Not surprisingly, there would always be someone who was offended by this. One day the manager of our shop in Nottingham was arrested under the same Indecent Advertisements Act of 1889 for which I had been arrested nearly ten years previously, when the Student Advisory Centre had advertised help for people suffering from venereal disease. I called John Mortimer, who had defended me then.

'I'm afraid we've fallen foul of the Indecent Advertisements Act again,' I told him. 'The police are saying that we can't use the word "bollocks".'

'Bollocks?' he asked. 'What on earth's wrong with bollocks? It's one of my favourite words.'

'They're making us take down The Sex Pistols' posters saying "Never mind the bollocks, here's The Sex Pistols", and they're threatening to injunct the album.'

He told me that we needed a linguistic adviser, a professor of English who could define the exact meaning of 'bollocks' for us. Since the case had been brought in Nottingham, I called up Nottingham University.

'Please can I speak to your professor of linguistics?' I asked.

'That would be Professor James Kinsley,' said the lady on reception.

I was put through and explained the situation.

'So one of your staff has been arrested for displaying the word "bollocks"?' said Professor Kinsley. 'What a load of bollocks! Actually, the word "bollocks" is an eighteenth-century nickname for priests. And then, because priests generally seemed to speak such a lot of nonsense in their sermons, "bollocks" gradually came to mean "rubbish".'

'So "bollocks" actually means either "priest" or "rubbish"?' I checked, making sure I hadn't missed anything.

'That is correct,' he said.

'Would you be prepared to be a witness in court?' I asked.

'I'd be delighted,' he said.

I enjoyed the court case. The police prosecutor was determined to win what was clearly a case of national importance. Our shop manager was cross-examined and admitted that he had prominently displayed The Sex Pistols' poster in the shop window. The police officer recited how he had arrested him since he was displaying this offensive poster. The policeman had the smug look of someone who was doing the public a great service and expected to be praised for it.

'No questions,' John Mortimer said when he was invited to cross-examine the policeman.

Rather disappointed, the policeman stood down.

'I would like to call my witness,' John Mortimer said when he stood up. 'Professor James Kinsley, professor of linguistics at Nottingham University.'

As Professor James Kinsley explained that 'bollocks' was nothing to do with testicles but actually meant 'priests' and then – due to priests' sermons being full of it – 'rubbish', John Mortimer peered at him myopically and appeared to be struggling to straighten out his thoughts.

'So, Professor Kinsley, are you saying that this expression "Never mind the bollocks, here's The Sex Pistols", which is the basis of this prosecution, should more accurately be translated as "Never mind the priests, here's The Sex Pistols"?' asked John Mortimer.

'I am. Or it could mean "Never mind the rubbish, here's The Sex Pistols".'

John Mortimer allowed a silence to develop in the court. '"Never mind the priests, here's The Sex Pistols",' he mused. 'That is the meaning of this expression. Well, I have nothing further to add. It sounds like a strange title for a record, but I doubt whether the Church would mind.'

'I doubt they would either,' Professor Kinsley agreed.

The prosecutor then pressed Professor Kinsley on this point, asking him how he could be sure that no clergyman would be offended.

Professor Kinsley then played his trump card by folding down his polo neck to reveal a dog collar. Professor Kinsley was also known as Reverend Kinsley.

'That's enough,' snapped the magistrate. He straightened his back, squared his shoulders and, adopting as much magisterial solemnity as he could muster, announced:

'The case is dismissed.'

10 '"I thought I'd move in," Joan said.'

1976–1978

O NE WEEKEND IN EARLY 1976 I met my future wife, Joan Templeman, at the Manor. I make up my mind about someone within thirty seconds of meeting them, and I fell for Joan almost from the moment I saw her. The problem was that she was already married to someone else, a record producer and keyboard player who was producing a Virgin band called Wigwam.

Joan was a down-to-earth Scots lady, and I immediately saw that she did not suffer fools gladly. I knew that I couldn't attract her attention in the same way as I had attracted Kristen. Most of my past relationships with women had been based on great public showmanship, but for the first time I felt that here was a woman who didn't want me to get up to my usual antics.

Joan worked in an antiques shop called Dodo on Westbourne Grove, close to our offices at Vernon Yard. On Monday morning I hovered uncertainly outside the shop, then screwed up my courage and walked in. The shop sold old signs and advertisements. When I asked the lady who owned the shop whether Joan was there, she looked at me suspiciously.

'Are you a customer?' she asked, glowering.

'Yes, I'm fascinated by old signs,' I said, looking uncertainly around the shop.

Joan came through from the back.

'I see you've met Liz,' she said. 'Liz, this is Richard.'

'So what would you like to buy?' Liz pressed me.

There was no way out. Over the next few weeks, my visits to Joan amassed me an impressive collection of old handpainted tin signs which advertised anything from Hovis bread to Woodbine cigarettes. One tin sign read DIVE IN HERE FOR TEA! I also bought a large pig which played the cymbals and had once stood in a butcher's shop. One of my favourite signs was an old picture advertising Danish bacon and eggs which showed a pig leaning casually against a wall listening to a chicken singing. The chicken was celebrating her freshly laid egg and the caption to the scene was NOW, THAT'S WHAT I CALL MUSIC! I gave this to Simon Draper, since he was always terribly grumpy in the mornings until he had eaten a decent breakfast. He hung it over his desk, where it later inspired the title for our annual greatest-hits compilations, *Now That's What I Call Music*. By the time I had bought all my Christmas presents from Dodo, Liz told Joan that she was the best shop assistant she had ever had.

Joan had been married to her husband, Ronnie Leahy, for almost eight years, but they had no children. Ronnie travelled a good deal, and it seemed to me, perhaps conveniently, that he and Joan had begun to drift apart. Whenever Ronnie was away, I called up Joan's friends and asked whether they were seeing Joan.

'Mind if I tag along?' I asked casually.

They soon called me 'Tag-along', which I really didn't mind as long as by tagging along I had the chance to sit somewhere near Joan and talk with her. Our courtship was unlike the other romances I'd had, which I'd been able to control. Joan is an intensely private person, and it was extremely difficult to find out the state of her marriage. While I knew what I felt about her, I had very little idea what Joan made of me. I thought that she might be intrigued by my persistence, but beyond that I was in the dark.

Eventually, Joan agreed to come with me to the Isle of Wight, and we spent the weekend in a tiny hotel in Bembridge. It was the start of our affair. Since Joan was married we both carried on living double lives. She could not see me during the week, when Ronnie was at home, but early one morning she decided to surprise me by dropping round to my house in Denbigh Terrace, where I was still living. As she let herself in, she saw my cleaning lady Martha going up the stairs to my bedroom carrying a tray with two cups of tea on it. Joan knew that I was in bed with another woman – which I was – so she stopped Martha and put a flower on the tray.

'Just say to Richard that Joan says hello,' she said, and then turned on her heel and went back to the shop.

I was mortified. I dashed round to see her at Dodo and persuaded her to have lunch with me.

'So what's all this about undying love?' Joan asked sarcastically.

'Well, I was lonely,' I said lamely. 'I couldn't wait until the weekend.'

'That's a pathetic excuse!' Joan said.

I tried to look ashamed of myself and contrite, but we caught each other's eye and then both burst out laughing.

Our affair continued for almost a year. We were desperate to be with each other, and would call each other up whenever we had five minutes to spare. Joan would slip away from Dodo and I would leave Vernon Yard, and we would meet at Denbigh Terrace, which was right between us. The geography of our affair was very tight-knit: Vernon Yard, Westbourne Grove and Denbigh Terrace all cross Portobello Road within twenty yards of each other, and so Joan and I lived out our affair within a tiny intense triangle.

When we stole twenty precious minutes at lunch, quarter of an hour before a meeting, or a few moments after Dodo shut up shop, we tried to shut the outside world away. But, along with the passion, we were also intensely aware that Joan was married (indeed, on paper, I was in the same situation myself), and that we were in danger of causing pain to Ronnie. In some ways Joan and Ronnie had a similar relationship to Kristen's and mine: Ronnie had wanted to experiment with sleeping with other women and had told Joan that she needed to broaden her horizons, too. Joan had been at a loss because she wasn't able to cope with a series of one-night stands, and so she gradually began to fall in love with me.

Our affair was further complicated when Kristen heard that I was in love with Joan and arrived back in London. By this time I had managed to buy *Duende* back from Kevin Ayers. At more or less the same time, Kristen had left him. She now told me that she wanted to get back together with me. We were, after all, still married. My family has always maintained that you stick with your marriage through thick and thin, and so I felt a great responsibility to agree to Kristen. But I was in love with Joan. It was a nightmarish situation for each of us: Joan felt torn between me and Ronnie; Kristen had been torn between me and Kevin; and I now felt torn between Kristen and Joan. What had started off as a dream affair with Joan in the tiny bedroom in the house at Denbigh Terrace was now beginning to destroy five people's lives.

The tangle of these four relationships finally resolved

itself when I was at a party with both Joan and Kristen. Joan's best friend Linda cornered me:

'So who are you actually in love with?' she demanded. 'This can't go on. You're all killing yourselves and you need to sort it out.'

I saw Joan talking to someone else.

'I'm in love with one woman,' I said, looking across at Joan. 'But she's not in love with me.'

'I'm telling you that she is,' said Linda, following my look.

We left it at that.

The next night I was alone on *Duende*. It was a dark February night and raining hard. I was on the telephone so I didn't hear the sound of knocking. Then the door opened and I swung round. It was Joan.

'I'll call you back later,' I said to the phone, and moved across to hug her.

'Well, I thought I'd move in,' Joan said.

'We've had another Nigerian order,' Chris Stylianou told me. 'They love this guy U-Roy.'

Chris Stylianou was now Virgin's export manager, and throughout the last few months of 1977 had picked up thousands of pounds' worth of business from, of all bizarre places, Nigeria. The Nigerians loved reggae music. At the time, virtually the only British record label that sold reggae was Chris Blackwell's Island Records.

In 1976 I had followed Chris Blackwell's footsteps to Jamaica with a view to signing some reggae acts. After sitting on his veranda for days on end I had finally managed to sign up Peter Tosh, who had sung with Bob Marley, and a performer called U-Roy. *Legalize It*, Peter Tosh's first album with Virgin, had sold well in 1977. But now there was a different sound: Jamaican DJs and radio jocks were cutting their own records and chanting a whole lot of rhyming slang and political slogans to a background beat. It was an early form of rap music. They were called 'toasters' and it was U-Roy, a bejewelled hipster, who was doing so well in Nigeria. I knew that there must be more toasters out in Jamaica and I decided we should go out there and corner the market.

I always like to get away from London in the middle of winter. I've found that sunshine and long-distance travel always gives me a clearer perspective on London life. And this time I had two extra reasons to get away from the city: I wanted to take Johnny Rotten with me because he was having some difficulties with The Sex Pistols and Malcolm McLaren; I also hoped to meet up with Joan, who was going to Los Angeles with Ronnie to give their marriage one last chance. Johnny Rotten was delighted to come since he loved reggae, and Joan and I agreed not to speak until she had resolved her marriage one way or another.

At the last minute, Simon was unable to come with me and I went with Ken. And so, at the start of 1978, a punk rocker, an accountant and a reformed Earl's Court hippie flew together to Kingston, Jamaica, to sign up some reggae bands and look for toasters. Knowing that Jamaicans didn't trust written contracts, we flew in with a briefcase containing $30,000 in cash and set up shop in the Kingston Sheraton. Word soon went around that three gringos were in town looking to audition musicians, and a stream of bands started coming round to the hotel room. Ken sat on the bed with his briefcase; Johnny and I listened to the bands' tapes and chatted to them. Johnny decided which artists we should sign, and then Ken would open up the briefcase and take out the money. American dollars were hard currency in Jamaica, where imports were banned and everything was bought on the black market. Some of the bands were so keen to impress us that they brought their drums and guitars with them. Our room was soon full of tall Rastafarians wearing massive bobble hats in red, yellow and green stripes. One tall singer towered over us and sang lovingly about his spiritual homeland of Ethiopia.

I watched Johnny as he sat on the sofa and nodded his head gently to the music. It was difficult to believe that this was the same man, gaunt and thin as a lightning conductor, who had screeched abuse at everyone, spat at pictures of the Queen, and galvanised a generation of anger. Thinking about the Emperor Haile Selassie, who inspired the Rastafarians, I wondered whether the British royal family hadn't missed a trick.

Over the course of a week we signed almost twenty reggae bands and found a couple more toasters, called Prince Far I and Tappa Zukie, into the bargain. I tried to persuade Johnny Lydon to stay with The Sex Pistols but to no avail. He told me that the group had fallen out among themselves and with Malcolm McLaren; that Sid Vicious was in a tailspin, taking all kinds of drugs and growing violent with Nancy, his girlfriend. Johnny wanted to go solo, and he had a couple of musicians in mind to form a new band called PiL, Public Image Limited. I was sorry since I wanted to build The Sex Pistols as the next classic rock band to follow The Rolling Stones. After all, The Rolling Stones had started off as the most shocking band in the world, with Mick Jagger being arrested for possessing drugs and scandalising public opinion. By 1978 The Stones had been going for more than fifteen years and they had become part of the rock and roll Establishment. And they didn't look like stopping.

Coping with success obviously brings its own difficulties for a rock band, but getting your name into people's minds is almost the hardest thing to achieve. The Sex Pistols had certainly entered the world's vocabulary – if only as a byword for all that most people found revolting – and I felt that they were crazy to throw away that advantage. I tried to persuade Johnny that The Sex Pistols could use their name in slightly different ways, and perhaps move away from the extreme punk image they had made their own. I also wanted to push them overseas: *Never Mind The Bollocks* had sold only 300,000 records overseas, about the same number as it had sold in Britain, and I felt sure that they could do much better with successive albums. After Mike Oldfield's instant success and then his withdrawal from public life, I was determined that The Sex Pistols would not collapse as well. They were Virgin's top band and they had been the catalyst both for Virgin Music's wider success and a whole new wave of rock music. But Johnny was in no mood to listen.

On our final evening we found a Rasta bar up along the coast from Kingston which sold fish in strong jerk sauce. We sat outside watching the sea. A flock of pelicans were dive-bombing in formation, and we watched them methodically work their way through shoals of fish, each one peeling off and diving down, tucking in their wings before plunging into the water. We drank Red Stripe beer and listened to Bob Marley. Although I kept turning the conversation back to what The Sex Pistols could do, Johnny was not really listening.

There was a world of difference between Mike Oldfield and The Sex Pistols. But both of them had found that they could not cope with the pressures of fame. From my point of view, as the head of their record company, there was a further difference: Mike Oldfield had made Virgin Music a tremendous amount of money that we had spent building up the company and signing new acts. We would not be in business without him. Although The Sex Pistols had been number one with 'God Save The Queen', and their album, *Never Mind The Bollocks*, had also been number one, Virgin had not made very much money from the group.

As I sat there with Johnny Rotten on the Jamaican beach, I was forced to accept that Virgin would never make much more money from The Sex Pistols. Malcolm McLaren had arranged for The Sex Pistols to be in a film called *The Great Rock And Roll Swindle*, and I wondered whether there might be a soundtrack which we could release from that, but, otherwise, Simon, Ken and I were going to have to accept that from now on The Sex Pistols were not a going concern.

Although it was highly frustrating to see them falling apart – and in a far worse way than Mike Oldfield, who continued to produce records which sold well – there was some consolation in that, after we had signed The Sex Pistols, Virgin had become the smart record label for punk and new-wave bands to sign with. The music world had seen the promotion which we had put behind The Sex Pistols, and a whole new generation of exciting bands was approaching us. Simon had picked up bands such as The Motors, XTC, The Skids, Magazine, Penetration and The Members which were all selling well, and another band called The Human League were building up a following. Virgin Music Publishing had signed a schoolteacher from Newcastle called Gordon Sumner who used the stage name 'Sting' and sang with a band called Last Exit who were thought to have some promise.

I returned to the Kingston Sheraton, mulling over Virgin's prospects without The Sex Pistols. There was a message from Joan, asking me to call her.

'Shall we meet in New York?' she asked.

I left Jamaica the next morning.

11 Living on the edge

1978–1980

I MET JOAN IN New York. Her attempt to patch up her marriage with Ronnie had failed. We spent a week in Manhattan and felt like refugees. My divorce from Kristen had yet to come through, and Joan had only days previously separated from Ronnie. We were thinking of escaping from New York to spend some time together alone, out of reach from any telephone, when somebody asked me if I had named Virgin Music after the Virgin Islands. The answer was no – but they sounded like just the romantic haven that Joan and I needed.

On impulse, Joan and I decided to fly down to the Virgin Islands. We had nowhere to stay and not very much money, but I heard that if you expressed a serious interest in buying an island the local estate agent would put you up for nothing in a grand villa and fly you all around the Virgin Islands by helicopter. This sounded rather fun. I cheekily made a few calls, and, sure enough, when I introduced myself and mentioned The Sex Pistols and Mike Oldfield and that Virgin Music was really expanding and we wanted to buy an island where our rock stars could come and get away from it all, and perhaps put a recording studio there, the estate agent began to get very excited.

Joan and I flew down to the Virgin Islands, where we were greeted like royalty and ushered into a sumptuous villa. The next day we were flown by helicopter all over the Virgin Islands as the estate agent showed us the islands that were for sale. We pretended we quite liked the first two islands we saw, but we asked him whether there were any more.

'There's one more which is a real little jewel,' he said. 'It's being sold by a British lord who's never been here. It's called Necker Island, but I don't think it's a wise idea because it's miles from anywhere.'

That did it.

'All right,' I said. 'Please can we see it?'

As we flew to Necker Island, I looked down from the helicopter window and marvelled at the clear pale-blue sea. We landed on a white sandy beach.

'There's no water on the island,' said the estate agent. 'The last known inhabitants were two journalists who came here on a survival course. They radioed for help before the week was out. It's the most beautiful island in the whole archipelago, but it needs a lot of money spent on it.'

There was a hill above the beach. Joan and I set off for the top, to get a view over the whole island. There were no paths, so by the time we reached the top our legs were scratched and bleeding from squeezing through the cacti. But the view from the top was worth it: we saw the reef all around the island and noticed that the beach ran most of the way round the shoreline. The estate agent had told me that leather-backed turtles came up to lay their eggs on the beaches of Necker. The water was so clear that we spotted a giant ray flapping its way serenely along the sandy bottom inside the reef. There were thousands of nesting gulls and terns, and a small flock of pelicans fishing in formation. Higher up, a frigate bird came gliding past on an air current, its vast wings spread wide as it carved its way over the thermals. Looking inland, we saw two saltwater lakes and a small tropical forest. A flock of black parrots flew over the forest canopy. Looking across at the other islands, we could see only their green coastlines: there was not a single house in sight. We walked back down the hill to find the estate agent.

'How much does he want for it?' I asked.

'£3 million.'

Our visions of watching the sunset from the top of the hill faded away. 'Nice thought,' Joan said, and we trudged back to the helicopter.

'How much were you thinking of spending?' the estate agent asked, suddenly smelling a rat.

'We could offer £150,000,' I said brightly. '$200,000,' I added, trying to make it sound more.

'I see.'

As we flew back to the villa, it was clear that we were no longer welcome. Talk of $200,000 wasn't enough to secure us a night at the villa. Our bags were left at the door, and Joan and I hauled them across the village to a bed-and-breakfast. It was clear that there were going to be no more helicopter flights over the islands. Yet Joan and I were determined to buy Necker. We felt that it could be our secret hideaway island, somewhere we could always retreat to. So, although we were practically driven off the Virgin Islands as if we were cattle-rustlers, we vowed to return.

Back in London, later, I found out that the owner of Necker Island wanted to sell in a hurry. He wanted to construct a building somewhere in Scotland which would cost him around £200,000. I upped my offer to £175,000 and held on for three months. Finally I got a call.

'If you offer £180,000 it's yours.'

There was never a hint that £180,000 was only a fraction of the £3 million asking price. So I agreed on the spot, and Necker Island was ours. Even at such a low price, there was a snag: the Virgin Islands' government had decreed that whoever bought Necker Island would have to develop it within five years or its ownership would pass to them. It would cost a good deal to build a house and pipe the water across from the neighbouring island, but I wanted to go back there with Joan. I was determined to make enough money to afford it.

Joan and I stayed on Beef Island for the rest of that holiday, and it was there that I set up Virgin Airways. We were trying to catch a flight to Puerto Rico, but the local Puerto Rican scheduled flight was cancelled. The airport terminal was full of stranded passengers. I made a few calls to charter companies, and agreed to charter a plane for $2,000 to Puerto Rico. I divided the price by the number of seats, borrowed a blackboard, and wrote VIRGIN AIRWAYS: $39 SINGLE FLIGHT TO PUERTO RICO. I walked around the airport terminal and soon filled every seat on the charter plane. As we landed at Puerto Rico, a passenger turned to me and said:

'Virgin Airways isn't too bad – smarten up the service a little and you could be in business.'

'I might just do that,' I laughed.

'Richard, I want to get married and I want you to be my best man,' said Mike Oldfield.

'That's wonderful,' I said. 'Who is she?'

'She's the daughter of my therapy teacher.'

Mike Oldfield had been a lifelong introvert. In September 1976 he went on a therapy course in Wales; this seemed to involve being alternately humiliated and praised in front of a group of people. To me, it sounded rather like a crash course in surviving public school or the army. But Mike emerged with his introversion banished. Within days he was posing for some nude photographs in the music press as Rodin's *Le Penseur*. And now he wanted to get married.

'How long have you known her?' I asked.

'Three days.'

'Don't you want to wait?'

'I can't wait,' he said. 'She won't sleep with me until we're married. It's tomorrow at Chelsea Register Office.'

Having failed to persuade him out of it, Joan and I went along to the register office and waited for Mike and his bride. We brought two carved African stools with us as wedding presents. We put them down on the pavement outside and sat on them before Mike's arrival. A stream of men and women passed us and emerged as man and wife. As we sat and waited I could feel the whole idea of marriage becoming less and less appealing. Both Joan and I had suffered failed marriages, and the sight of this production line of wedded couples coming out every six and a half minutes from the register office and, in our jaundiced view, heading for the divorce lawyers put us off saying the vows to each other again. They seemed to ring hollow. I knew that I loved Joan, but I felt we didn't need to say the clichéd words to confirm it.

Mike and Sarah were married and we gave them the two African stools. We had dinner together that night, but the evening ended early since Mike was so clearly intent on getting Sarah into bed. The next morning the phone rang.

'Richard, I want a divorce.' It was Mike.

'What's wrong?'

'We're not compatible,' Mike said, in a voice which brooked no further questions.

Mike and Sarah went more or less straight from the register office to the lawyers, and he ended up paying her over £200,000 in alimony. My mind boggles at what went on that night, but whatever happened it must go down as one of the most expensive one-night stands in history.

In 1977 Virgin as a whole made a pre-tax profit of £400,000; in 1978 the figure increased to £500,000. After the collapse of The Sex Pistols, we were left with a handful of our original artists, the most important being Mike Oldfield, whose albums sold consistently right the way through the advent of punk and new wave. We also had a couple of new signings, both of whom seemed rather esoteric and played synthesiser music: Orchestral Manoeuvres in the Dark and The Human League. While these two bands had yet to sell well, XTC, The Skids and Magazine kept their sales going. We also continued to sell well in France and Germany, particularly with Tangerine Dream.

By 1979, an outsider might have looked at Virgin and come to the conclusion that it was a motley collection of different companies. From our tiny mews house in Vernon Yard, we operated the record shops, which Nik ran; the record company, which was run by Simon and Ken; and the music publishing company, which was run by Carol Wilson. The Manor was going well, and we had expanded our recording business with the purchase of a London recording studio. The original plan to set up everything that a rock star needed, recording, publishing, distribution, and retailing, was beginning to work. On top of this we had also set up Virgin Book Publishing, which was primarily to publish books about music, and biographies and autobiographies of the rock stars.

In lieu of The Sex Pistols' future albums, which would now never be made, we had acquired the rights to the film which Malcolm McLaren was producing, *The Great Rock And Roll Swindle*. This guaranteed one last album, the film soundtrack. In order to pull this film together, we set up Virgin Films, which Nik started to manage.

Another venture that Nik had set up was The Venue, a nightclub where our bands could play and people could eat and socialise while watching them. As the world of rock music grew increasingly sophisticated, it became clear that bands no longer wanted simply to record their songs and then release them. Pop videos were becoming the most effective way of promoting songs, and some cynics observed that pop videos were as important as the music itself. In order to accommodate this, Nik also set up a film-editing studio where our bands could make and edit their own videos.

The other service that Virgin should offer our artists was the ability to sell their records overseas. Although we were a tiny company based in a mews house in Notting Hill, I knew that, if we had no overseas companies, we stood no chance of signing the international bands. One of the beauties of rock music is that at the top end of the market it is a purely international commodity. The best measure of a group's success is how many records they sell overseas. The large multinational companies had a huge advantage over Virgin or Island since, during the negotiation to sign a band, they could point to their sales forces in France and Germany.

One option open to Virgin was not to compete with the multinationals overseas, but purely to concentrate on the domestic UK market and license our bands overseas in the same way in which we had licensed Mike Oldfield when we first set up. Although this was a tempting option in that it saved overheads, I wasn't happy with it. Island and Chrysalis adopted this approach and I felt that it restricted their growth because they were at the mercy of the overseas licensees. Once you have licensed a band away to another record company, you lose all control of their promotion. As well as wanting to control the prospects of our British bands overseas, we also wanted to be able to attract overseas bands to Virgin. We wanted French, German and American bands to feel that they could sign with us for worldwide rights rather than with the large international record labels.

With a skeleton staff at Vernon Yard it was difficult to imagine that we could really take on the multinationals on their own terms. But we decided to give it a go. In 1978, Ken set off to New York to establish the Virgin label in America. Rather as Virgin had grown in London, proliferating itself in a number of small houses around Notting Hill, so I imagined that Virgin America would start off with a house in Greenwich Village, and then move slowly around the country buying houses in Chicago, Los Angeles, San Francisco and other regional centres, so that we didn't build up one monolithic head office.

In 1979 I went to France to meet with Jacques Kerner, the French head of PolyGram. I did not know anybody in the French music industry and, although I was ostensibly seeing him with the idea of asking PolyGram to distribute Virgin records, I was really on the lookout for somebody who could set up Virgin in France. Jacques Kerner introduced me to an intriguing-looking man called Patrick Zelnick who ran PolyGram's record side. Patrick had a vaguely distracted look about him rather like Woody Allen, with thick, wiry, unruly hair and heavy black-framed glasses. Patrick not only looked like Woody Allen, he behaved like him: when we first went out for lunch together, we spent four hours afterward trying to find out where he had parked his car. Patrick told me he had watched Virgin's progress with interest. He had first tried to meet us when we had a stall at the Cannes Music Festival in 1974, but had only been able to find a sign saying GONE SKIING. Patrick had then started coming over to buy records at the Virgin Records shop on Oxford Street, and he loved Mike Oldfield and Tangerine Dream.

Jacques Kerner was offering me £300,000 to license the entire Virgin catalogue in France, with a percentage of royalties on top. Since Virgin had little money at the time, and we had just taken on another loan to pay for Necker Island, the easy option would have been to accept it. But, instead of dutifully taking down the details in my notebook, I wrote down 'Patrick Zelnick: Virgin France'. I surprised Jacques Kerner by asking for some time to think it over.

After the meeting I thanked both men, and asked them to drop by and see me on the houseboat when they were next in London. The next month Patrick came to London and called me up. We had lunch on *Duende*, and I asked him whether he would leave PolyGram and set up Virgin as an independent subsidiary in France. I would give him complete independence to sign whichever French bands he liked. We worked out some rough figures on a piece of paper, and Patrick agreed to do it. He set up Virgin France with a friend of his, Philippe Constantine, who was a wild, ragged individual, on and off heroin but with excellent musical taste. While Patrick did the business, Philippe spent his time with all the bands.

'When you're invited for dinner,' Jacques Kerner said in a reproachful phone call to me when Patrick resigned, 'you're not meant to walk away with the cutlery.'

I apologised for poaching Patrick, but told Jacques that Patrick had made his own decision to set up Virgin. It was only after Patrick had left PolyGram that we looked through the figures again and realised we had miscalculated: we had forgotten to include VAT in our estimations; we had used the wrong retail margin; we had hopelessly overestimated the numbers of records that were sold in Paris. But by then it was too late: Patrick and Philippe were working for Virgin. One of the first bands they signed was called Telephone, who became the bestselling band of the year in France. In later years, Patrick would shake his head in disbelief that he had left the security of PolyGram and joined a virtually bust English record company.

While the negotiations with Patrick were going on, I went back to France to meet the managing director of Arista Records. We were unable to agree a distribution deal, but I pricked up my ears when he started boasting about how Arista was about to sign Julien Clerc, France's biggest pop star. I had no idea who Julien Clerc was, but I excused myself and slipped into the lavatory. I scribbled 'Julien Claire' on my wrist and then carefully pulled down the sleeve of my sweater to hide it. After the meeting was over I rushed to a call box and telephoned Patrick.

'Have you heard of a singer called Julien Claire?' I asked.

'Of course I have,' Patrick said. 'He's the biggest star in France.'

'Well he's free to sign. Let's try to sign him. Can we meet him for lunch tomorrow?'

At the lunch the next day, Patrick and I managed to persuade Julien Clerc to sign with Virgin from under Arista's nose. Within a fortnight I had succeeded in having my name struck off two record companies' lunch lists, but both Patrick and Julien Clerc went on to make fortunes for Virgin France and themselves.

With Ken in New York, Patrick in Paris, Udo in Germany and our own operation in London, we could properly market Virgin as an international record label. Our trouble was that we had no cash reserves, and so any setback could prove fatal. When I visited Coutts Bank in the Strand I now wore shoes and my hair was in no danger of getting caught in the revolving door, but they still treated me like a schoolboy prodigy rather than a businessman. Even looking at Virgin's sales of £10 million, they would shake their heads and smile.

'It's all good pop music, isn't it?' the Coutts manager would say genially. 'My son loves Mike Oldfield. I just wish my other one didn't play all this loud punk stuff. I keep having to yell up at him to turn it down.'

I tried to point out that Virgin was growing into a large company. We had very good sales, and were making as good and steady money as any regular business. But the bankers never saw it like that: 'You're doing jolly well,' the bank manager said. 'But of course the quality of your earnings is so poor. We can't see what they're going to be more than a month in advance.'

In spite of this cheerless analysis, at the end of 1978 we felt quite confident: in the UK we had enjoyed a good year, with a string of top-ten hits and good sales through the record shops. But in 1979 Margaret Thatcher was elected prime minister; interest rates soared, and we were hit by a severe recession. Record sales in Britain dropped for the first time in twenty years, and our chain of shops lost a lot of money. Ken had had no luck in New York: Virgin's first single there cost $50,000 to promote and completely bombed. Reluctantly, we decided to close the office and called Ken back home..

Everything seemed to be going wrong, even at home. In November 1979 Joan called me to say that the houseboat was in danger of sinking. I had left the water pump on and, rather than pumping water out, it had backfired and started siphoning water in. We met at *Duende* and waded around in the water trying to salvage furniture and boxes of files. After we had retrieved all we could, we stood on the towpath chatting to our neighbours about the best way to pull the boat up. One of the neighbours shifted a box, and to our embarrassment a large vibrator fell out. When it hit the ground, it turned itself on and started to vibrate. As we all watched it, it buzzed around and finally fell into the canal, where it zipped through the water like a torpedo before finally vanishing from view.

'Anything to do with you, Richard?' Joan asked caustically.

'No. You?'

'Of course not.'

That box had (of course!) been on *Duende* for years. The circle of ripples where the vibrator had sunk seemed a fitting end to the 1970s.

In 1980 I travelled to Los Angeles to try to interest American record companies in English artists. The trip was a disaster. I took a collection of demo tapes but nobody was interested in anything new. Mike Oldfield was as popular as ever – someone even misspelt his name 'Oilfield', which was certainly closer to the truth for Virgin – but the other bands I was trying to license, such as The Skids, The Motors, XTC, Japan, Orchestral Manoeuvres in the Dark ('Hang on, Richard,' said the buyer at CBS. 'We haven't got all day. Can't we just call them OMD?'), and The Flying Lizards, were listened to with polite interest but few bids.

As I saw that Virgin's income was drying up, I made continual lists of savings we could make. I sold Denbigh Terrace, and put the money into Virgin; we sold two flats we owned in Vernon Yard; we cut back on everything we could think of. I recently came across a list of immediate priorities of the time in my notebook. It brings back the sense of desperation:

1. Remortgage the Manor
2. Turn off the swimming-pool heater
3. Sign Japan [the band]
4. Sell the houses in Vernon Yard
5. Ask Mike Oldfield if we can hold back his cash
6. Sell the houseboat
7. Sell my car
8. Lease all the recording equipment
9. Nik could sell his shares to a merchant bank or Warner Bros
10. Sell The Venue

I wrote to the Virgin staff and told them that we had to tighten our belts urgently:

The good news is that Ian Gillan's new record has gone straight in at number three in the charts. But the bad news is that it's only sold 70,000 copies, which is just a half of what a number-three record would have been last year. Our profits have been reduced by more than half since we have the same overheads.

By Nik's calculations Virgin was heading for a £1 million loss in 1980.

'I can't sell my shares to a merchant bank,' he told me. 'Virgin is losing £1 million this year. The shares are worthless.'

'But what about the brand name?' I asked.

' "Virgin"? It's worth minus £1 million,' he said. 'They won't recognise any value in the brand name. What's the worth of British Leyland as a brand name?'

Virgin was suddenly in desperate trouble. The 1980 recession caught us with all the unexpected ferocity of a squall at sea. For the second time we had to make some staff redundant: nine people, who represented a sixth of the worldwide staff of Virgin Music. This was proportionately less than the cuts being made by other record companies at the time, but it was a gut-wrenching blow for us. Nik, Simon, Ken and I spent hours arguing over what we should do. With no major rock star on the roster to release a hit record, Virgin had no predictable future income. We found ourselves desperately fighting to try to prove Coutts Bank wrong. Once again we went through our catalogue of bands and made several cuts. We had to abandon most of the reggae bands we had signed in Jamaica since a military coup in Nigeria had banned all imports and destroyed our sales.

Tension rose between Nik and Simon as they argued over which bands Virgin should keep. Nik argued that Virgin should drop The Human League, a young band from Sheffield who played synthesisers.

'Over my dead body,' Simon told him.

'But they're so marginal,' Nik argued. 'We can't afford to keep supporting them.'

'The Human League is exactly why I'm in this business,' Simon said, fighting to keep his temper.

'You just spend all the money I save in the shops,' Nik said, wagging his finger in Simon's face.

'Look here,' Simon snapped, rising to his feet. 'Never, ever, wag that fucking finger in my face again. And The Human League are staying.'

I watched Simon and Nik fight it out, knowing that something would have to be done. Nik had been my main partner, my closest childhood friend, and we had worked together since *Student*, when we were sixteen. But he was obsessed with cutting back and saving money, though, admittedly, at a time when we were in deep trouble. But once again I felt that unless we did something dramatic, which meant spending money, we would never get out of trouble.

Nik and Simon reached an angry stalemate and turned to me to arbitrate between them. To Nik's fury, I backed Simon. This was a turning point in the triangular relationship which had worked so well up to this point. I felt that Simon's taste in music was the only thing that could pull Virgin out of the hole we were in. Without Simon's new generation of bands, we would be stuck treading water. Nik thought that we were throwing good money after bad, and he went back to the record shops determined to squeeze even more savings out of them.

At another meeting we argued over a new signing, the drummer from Genesis. In September 1980, Simon wanted to spend £65,000 to sign up Phil Collins as a solo artist. Once again Simon was supremely confident that this was the right move, and he stood up to all the doubts and criticisms Nik threw at him. The reason we even had the chance to sign Phil Collins was our expansion into the recording-studio business. As well as the Manor, we had acquired a studio in West London which we called the Town House. At the back of the Town House we had built a second studio, which was hired out at a lower rate. Rather than having the normal padded walls to kill all acoustic reverberations, we had built it with stone walls. When Phil Collins wanted to record some solo material he decided that he couldn't afford the top-of-the-range studio, so he booked the Stone Wall studio instead. There he found he managed to get the most extraordinary recordings of his drumming for 'In The Air Tonight'. It sounded fantastic. And Phil got on so well with the sound engineers that soon he found himself talking to Simon, and before we knew what had happened he was ready to sign up with us.

Nik made Simon do all kinds of sales analysis to try to work out how many copies of a solo album by Phil we could sell. Nik was worried that Genesis fans would not buy him, but Simon proved that, even if just 10 per cent of known Genesis fans bought Phil's debut solo album, we would make money. As we stared with dismay at our overdraft and the wretchedly low sales figures of our other bands, we knew the gamble we were making. To his credit, Nik agreed that we should sign Phil Collins, even taking money from the shop tills to make up enough for the advance. Phil proved to be an extraordinarily gifted musician and singer. His voice was haunting and his lyrics poignant: he was destined to become more successful than Genesis itself.

In the meantime, *New Musical Express* mentioned that Virgin Music was in financial trouble. If Coutts read *NME*, which I doubted, they might think twice about extending the loan I wanted. I immediately tried to squash the idea with a letter to the editor: 'Since in your last issue you speculate that I am in deep financial trouble you will appreciate my need to sue you in order to acquire some interest-free money rather than approach the merchant banks ...' Although *New Musical Express* was hardly the *Financial Times*, I recognised that if rumours like that are not hit hard on the head they have a horrible habit of becoming self-perpetuating. Worse still, they were true.

A couple of months after the arguments over The Human League and Phil Collins, I came across two deals that I thought were irresistible. They both involved nightclubs. The first one was The Roof Garden in Kensington, which was being offered for sale at £400,000. Virgin of course had no money, but the brewer who supplied beer to The Roof Garden was prepared to offer us an interest-free loan if we continued to stock their wines, beers and spirits. The other nightclub was Heaven, a large gay nightclub under Charing Cross Station. The owner was a friend of my sister Vanessa and he wanted to sell it to someone who would respect it and keep it as a gay club. Through my work at the Advisory Centre, he knew that he could trust me to do this. His asking price was £500,000 and once again the brewer was prepared to give us an interest-free loan to cover the entire purchase price, in return for stocking their beers. I had no idea why the brewers did not want to acquire these clubs outright, and I jumped at the chance to buy them.

I knew that Nik would oppose these purchases, so I signed the contracts without telling him. He was furious. He thought that I was squandering money. He looked at the £1 million extra liability which the purchase of these clubs represented and thought that I was ruining Virgin.

'It'll sink us,' he argued.

'But we don't have to pay any interest,' I said. 'It's free money. When someone offers you a Rolls-Royce for the price of a Mini you have to take it.'

'There's no such thing as a free lunch and there's no such thing as free money,' Nik told me. 'It's still debt. We can't possibly pay it off. We're practically bust as it is.'

'This money is free,' I said. 'And I think there is such a thing as a free lunch. We'll trade out of trouble.'

Nik disagreed with me so vehemently that it became clear we had to go our separate ways. He thought that I was leading Virgin headlong into bankruptcy. He wanted to protect the remaining value of his 40 per cent share of the business before it was too late. For my part, in spite of our history, I had been unhappy with our professional relationship for two or three years. Nik and I had always been best friends but, as Virgin had grown bigger and moved from being a record retailer to a music label, I felt that he had become out of his depth. Nik thought that we were all out of our depths, which we may well have been. There was no room for him in the record label, and in any event he wasn't comfortable doing all the socialising with the musicians which Simon, Ken and I did. I rather suspected that Nik's puritanical outlook made him resent every pound that was thrown away on ordering another bottle of champagne, even if by charming and so winning the band on to Virgin Music we would reap vast benefits. I felt that Nik was always trying to stop me doing the things I wanted to do, most of which, admittedly, involved risking money on new bands. It is probably an interesting litmus test of our relationship that I don't think Nik came on staff skiing holidays after about 1977. I have always wanted the Virgin staff to have a great time, and I'll be the first one to make a fool of myself in any way if I think that it'll help the party go with a swing. Nik found all that side of life difficult to enjoy. We knew each other so well we could write pages about each other's good and bad points. In the end we both realised that it was best to separate while we were still friends. That way we could remain friends, rather than waiting until we had grown into implacable enemies.

I raised another loan from another bank, and bought out Nik's shareholding in Virgin. As well as this cash,

Nik also took with him some of his favourite parts of the Virgin Group: the Scala cinema and the film- and video-editing studios. Nik's real interest lay in the film world, and when he left he set up Palace Pictures with a view to making movies. With his talent he soon started making wonderful films such as *The Company of Wolves*, *Mona Lisa* and the Oscar-winning *The Crying Game*.

With our separation settled, Nik and I hugged each other and made up. We had both got what we wanted, and to celebrate our 'divorce' we threw a leaving party at The Roof Garden. In many ways we managed to get the best of both worlds: we remained great friends, saw a lot of each other, and both managed to thrive without the other. Although I had acquired Nik's 40 per cent of Virgin, I was well aware that there was no difference between owning 100 per cent and 60 per cent of a busted company. Nik was right about Virgin's trading losses for 1980: we lost £900,000.

12 'Success can take off without warning.'

1980–1982

AS WELL AS PARTING from Nik, I came dangerously close to splitting up with Joan in 1980. I was working frantically to keep Virgin afloat and I knew that Joan was growing increasingly frustrated. No matter how late I got home, the telephone rang. Every time we woke up on a Saturday morning it rang again. One night I returned home to the houseboat to find it empty. Joan had gone and left me a note: 'I am pregnant. I am afraid to tell you. I have run away from home. If you miss me, call me at Rose's.'

As I looked at the note, I realised that my life had changed. I sat down and thought about what to do. After Kristen had left me, I had had a number of affairs. I loved the variety and the freedom. Ever since she had moved in with me, I feared I had taken Joan too much for granted. My marriage to Kristen had made me sceptical about long-term relationships, and at that time I had not made the same commitment as Joan. I was also under pressure from my parents to get back together with Kristen or, if not, then to marry some kind of university-educated, tennis-playing girl from Surrey – which Joan emphatically was not.

I remember telling my parents that Joan had moved in with me. Dad was fishing on the shore of a lake, and Mum was pointing out a rising trout.

In the ensuing silence Dad flunked his cast, which landed in a tangle.

'That's torn it,' he said.

But when I sat in the houseboat holding Joan's scribbled note and thinking about our unborn baby, I realised that I really loved her. Until that moment I had been guilty of wanting to have my cake and eat it: having a great relationship without making a commitment to it. I had enjoyed a number of different relationships, and had never thought about the consequences. I think lots of men would happily drift through life without having children unless their partners forced the issue. I called Rose, Joan's sister, and dashed round to be with Joan.

About six months into Joan's pregnancy I was in France while Joan was on holiday in Scotland. She had an attack of appendicitis in Fort William. I flew to Scotland to be with her while she was having the operation. In fact, she did not have appendicitis but an ovarian cyst which had burst, but the doctors decided to go ahead and remove her appendix as well – a dangerous operation at the best of times but more so on a six-months-pregnant woman. The operation triggered Joan into labour. She was put on a drip to try to reduce the contractions, and we immediately set off in an ambulance to try to reach a more modern hospital at Inverness. The drive across Scotland in the snow was a nightmare. Every jolt of the road set Joan into further contractions. By the time we arrived she was in agony with the pain of the operation, the pain of the contractions, and desperately trying to keep the baby in.

At Inverness Hospital it became clear that Joan would have to give birth to the baby. There was going to be little chance of the baby surviving as it was three months premature. A baby girl was born who weighed just four pounds, and we called her Clare after my aunt.

Clare could scarcely feed and the hospital did not have the necessary equipment to keep her alive.

Although Clare did open her lovely, deep milky-blue eyes, she died after four days. All I can remember of her now is her tiny size. Neither of us was allowed to hold or touch her. Her brief home was in an incubator. She was so small she would have fitted into the palm of my hand. We pored over her face, and marvelled at her tiny hands and the determined set to her face as she slept. But now that memory has faded. When I try to remember Clare, my mind is cluttered by the antiseptic smell of the hospital, the metal chairs in our room scraping over the lino, and the look on the nurse's face as she came to tell us that Clare had died.

Clare inhabited a world of her own, and came in and out of our lives leaving only despair and emptiness and love behind her. She was so small and lived for so little time that she was almost never here at all, but in that heartbreaking time she brought Joan and me intensely close together. Until I had seen Clare's tiny fragile body, dwarfed by the tiniest nappy, and seen how beautiful she was, and known that she was our baby, I had never thought I would want to have a child.

After Clare's death, Joan and I were determined to have another baby, and to our delight Joan became pregnant again within a year.

Once again Joan went into labour early, this time by six weeks. Both of us were taken by surprise. I was at a party at The Venue and arrived home at three in the morning, roaring drunk. I fell into a deep sleep, and only reluctantly woke when I felt Joan slapping me about the face and shouting that she was having contractions. I fell out of bed and managed to drive her to hospital. The doctors examined Joan and led her to the maternity ward. 'You look fine,' they reassured her.

Then they looked at me.

'You look terrible. You'd better take these aspirins and go to bed.'

Some time later that morning, I was woken up to find four doctors peering at me through their masks. I assumed that I had had a terrible accident and was in a casualty ward somewhere.

'Joan is well into labour,' they said. 'You'd better come with us.'

Holly was born, under six pounds in weight. It was the most incredible experience I had ever been through. By the end of it (I believe!) I was even more exhausted than Joan. I pledged to myself that I'd never miss the birth of one of our children. However, after what had happened to Clare, our immediate concern was keeping Holly alive.

We drove back to the houseboat on a freezing-cold November morning in 1981, and Joan wrapped Holly up with her in bed. For the rest of the winter they stayed more or less in the bedroom the whole time while I worked in the room next door. Penni used to walk through the bedroom to her desk, which was tucked between the bilge pump and the stairs.

In 1981 Virgin Music finally began to earn some money. Japan had had hit albums with *Gentlemen Take Polaroids* and *Tin Drum*. Some of our recent hit singles were XTC's 'Generals And Majors' and 'Sgt Rock', and Ian Gillan's 'Trouble' and 'New Orleans'. The Professionals and The Skids were also successes. We still didn't know what Phil Collins would come up with, and – twenty-fourth in my list of things to do that month – I arranged to go up to Scotland to a concert by one of our new bands, Simple Minds. Simple Minds' album, *New Gold Dream*, was a bestseller.

The best news of 1981 was that Simon's prediction about The Human League was proved right. Their first two albums were quite experimental and built up a loyal cult following. When we noticed that their sales kept steadily rising we knew that we had every chance of breaking through. Their third album, *Dare*, powered into the top ten and then went to number one. *Dare* sold over 1 million copies in Britain and 3 million around the world. The hit single 'Don't You Want Me, Baby?' was played over and over again and became ingrained on everyone's mind.

Almost as quickly as they had run out, Virgin's cash balances were now restored. Whenever Virgin has money I always renew my search for new opportunities. I am continually trying to broaden the Group so we are not dependent on a narrow source of income, but I suspect this is more down to inquisitiveness and restlessness than sound financial sense. This time I thought I saw a perfect opportunity. Since Virgin was an entertainment company, I thought we could publish our own listings magazine called *Event*. Unfortunately, it was launched at the same time as the highly successful *Time Out*, and *Event* lost the battle.

It is always difficult to admit to a failure, but the one positive thing about the *Event* episode was that I realised how important it was to separate the various Virgin companies so that, if one failed, it would not threaten the rest of the Virgin Group. *Event* was a disaster, but it was a contained disaster. Every successful businessman has failed at some ventures, and most entrepreneurs who run their own companies have been declared bankrupt at least once. Rather than defaulting on our debts, we paid them up and shut down the magazine.

The money that *Event* magazine lost Virgin was

rapidly repaid to us by The Human League, Simple Minds, Phil Collins' enormously successful debut solo album, *Face Value*, and then, most spectacularly, by a young singer who called himself Boy George.

I first heard of Boy George and Culture Club after Simon went to see them perform at a recording studio in Stoke Newington in 1981. The music publishing rights had already been signed by Virgin, and Simon was intrigued by the startling appearance of their lead singer, a beautiful young drag queen, and the soft, easy-going white reggae they played. Simon invited the band back to Vernon Yard, where they agreed a recording contract.

When Simon introduced me to George O'Dowd, I found myself shaking hands with somebody who looked utterly unlike anyone I had ever met before. His long hair was braided like a Rastafarian; he had a pale white face, huge arched eyebrows, and wore the ornate robes of a geisha girl.

Although we knew that Culture Club was an extraordinary creation, their first single, 'White Boy', was stillborn. Virgin released it on 30 April 1982 but nothing much happened: it sold around 8,000 copies and reached 114 in the charts. We didn't mind. We really felt that, as soon as Boy George was properly photographed or if we could get him on to *Top of the Pops*, his records would take off. People just had to see Boy George and they would want to buy his music. Teenagers would go mad for him. As well as looking astonishing, George had a fabulous voice and was very witty and charming: he was a rebel in a totally different way from The Sex Pistols or James Dean, but a rebel nonetheless. Virgin brought out Culture Club's second single, 'I'm Afraid Of Me', in June, and although it sold better than 'White Boy' it still only reached 100 in the charts. Culture Club carried on recording their album, *Kissing To Be Clever*, which they had largely written before they signed with us.

When we released Culture Club's third single, 'Do You Really Want To Hurt Me?', on 3 September 1982 it was our final attempt to launch the band. Funnily enough, Radio 2 played the song before Radio 1, and general reviews of the single were poor: 'Watered-down fourth-division reggae,' wrote *Smash Hits*. 'Awful.' But with the Radio 2 exposure it crept up the charts, up to number 85 in its first week, and number 38 in its second week. We plugged him as hard as we could, but the BBC refused to interview Boy George, calling him a 'transvestite'. Then we heard about a cancellation on *Top of the Pops*. We did everything we could to get Boy George into that slot, and when *Top of the Pops* finally agreed, we suspected we had a sensation in the making.

With his white face, his swaying robes, his felt hat and impossible arched eyebrows, Boy George beat every other sophisticated romantic band, such as Spandau Ballet, at their own game. He appealed to all teenagers, both male and female, as well as to children as young as eight or nine and their grandmothers to boot. It was impossible to define why he was so popular: parents wanted to mother him; girls wanted to be as beautiful; boys wanted their girlfriends to be as beautiful; it's impossible to quantify. The next day the telephones rang off the desks and the orders for the single came pouring in. 'Do You Really Want To Hurt Me?' rose to number three. George then appeared on *Noel Edmonds' Late Late Breakfast Show* and Noel asked him whether he was a great fan of Liberace. 'Not any more,' George said, implying that the roles had now been reversed. The single reached number one. When George announced that he preferred a cup of tea to sex, he became an international icon.

For Christmas 1982, we released Culture Club's first album, *Kissing To Be Clever*, which sold 4 million copies around the world. And then came another amazing breakthrough: their sixth single, 'Karma Chameleon', was the top-selling single of 1983, selling over 1.4 million copies in the UK and reaching number one in every country around the world that had a chart, over thirty countries to our knowledge. Culture Club was a worldwide pop phenomenon, and their second album, *Colour By Numbers*, sold almost 10 million copies.

Virgin's finances were thrown upside down: from the £900,000 loss in 1980, we made a profit of £2 million in 1982 on sales of £50 million. In 1983 our sales shot up to £94 million and our profits soared to £11 million. Once we had started the Boy George fan club, it was impossible to control it, and in 1983 40 per cent of our profits came from Boy George. For the first two years the Culture Club story was the perfect model. The extraordinary thing about the record industry is how success can take off without warning. One minute nobody had heard of Boy George; the next minute every person around the world from Ireland to Korea and Japan to Ghana was humming 'Karma Chameleon'. Boy George's success was measured literally by the speed of sound. Many people find such a vertical run frightening, and they would be right in thinking it creates havoc in a company. Happily, I have always thrived on havoc and adrenaline, and so I felt perfectly at home as we fanned the flames of Culture Club's success.

13 'You go ahead with this over my dead body.'

1983–1984

IT IS ALWAYS EASIER to live with the benefit of hindsight. People often point out that Nik sold his 40 per cent stake in Virgin at the wrong time. But when Nik and I split up he was as aware of the sales figures and profit forecast as I was and things were in bad shape. At the time Nik and I were both happy: Nik was happy to leave a company that looked as if it was heading into trouble, and I was happy to have virtually full control of my destiny, even if I knew that Virgin was on a knife edge. Soon after Nik left, two things happened that could not have been foreseen. Firstly, compact discs became widespread and so we were able to resell our back catalogue on CD. Many people replicated their entire record collection on compact disc, and certainly an artist like Mike Oldfield sold tremendously well on CD; The Sex Pistols less so.

The second change was that Virgin itself became the undisputed leading independent record label. Simon's taste in music finally triumphed: Virgin Music started to dominate the top-ten singles and albums charts. From being seen as a one-band record label that had made an incongruous leap from Mike Oldfield to The Sex Pistols, Virgin Music was now the envy of the record industry. All Simon's signings of the last couple of years took off at once: we had The Human League as well as their spin-off, Heaven 17; Simple Minds; Boy George; Phil Collins; China Crisis and Japan. The wonderful thing about these artists was that we had broken them all ourselves. I was still determined to sign a classic act of the calibre of Bryan Ferry or The Rolling Stones, but the beauty of our roster was that it was all home-grown, and was finally beginning to sell well overseas.

As I watched the money pouring into the bank, I began to think of other ways to use it. Although I was closely involved in signing bands, I felt that I knew as much as I wanted to about negotiating record contracts. I needed another challenge. I had the opportunity to use our cash to set up more Virgin companies and widen the basis of the Group so that all our eggs would not be in one basket if we were hit by another recession. I also wanted to expand the Virgin name to stand for more than a record label, and become more involved in all kinds of media. It was only three years since Virgin had almost gone bust, and two years since Nik had left. From having had very little money with which to play over the last three years, I now had cash mounting up in the bank and I wanted to reinvest it as fast as possible.

When I began looking for other businesses to start up, I thought about expanding our tiny book-publishing business. I knew that the music-publishing side of Virgin Music made a very good living from publishing the music and collecting royalties, and I wondered whether a properly managed book-publishing division would be as successful. At the back of my mind was the thought that, if a rock star is famous, there should be all sorts of other activities that they could explore, including books and videos, appearances in films, and soundtracks.

Vanessa, my younger sister, had been going out with Robert Devereux since he was at Cambridge University. Robert had become part of the family. Although Virgin is not a family company in the traditional sense, in that it has not been passed down vertically from generation to generation, it is a family company in a horizontal sense, in that I always involve my wider family in whatever I do, and I listen to their opinions as closely as anyone else's. I know that a number of businessmen shut their families off from their work: they hardly ever invite their children into their office, and when they are at home they never discuss what they do at work. It is a British characteristic not to discuss money over a meal, but when this boils over into never discussing business then I think it represents a lost opportunity. Business is a way of life. It is small wonder that there are so few business entrepreneurs when business is excluded from the family circle.

When I was wondering what to do about Virgin Books, Vanessa suggested that I talk to Robert, who had been working at Macmillan Publishers for three years. Robert came around to *Duende* with his boss Rob Shreeve, and I asked them whether they would come and work at Virgin Books. I had no clear idea what Virgin Books should do, apart from somehow exploit the growing success of the Virgin rock stars. Robert suggested that books and videos could be sold through the same outlets, and he had the idea that Virgin Books could form part of a wider Virgin interest in the media, which could involve television, radio, films and videos as well as books. Undaunted by the reality that he was actually joining a tiny little publisher, Robert left his job and came to join us at Virgin. Rob Shreeve decided to stay at Macmillan for the time being.

When Robert arrived at Virgin Books he immediately put a stop to the line of novels we were selling. He recast Virgin Books as a nonfiction specialist in books about rock music and sport. A few years later he decided to buy another publishing house, WH Allen, which he put together with Virgin Books. With hindsight, this was a mistake: we tried to do too much, and in 1989 the publishing business ran into difficulties and had to be radically cut back. It was one of our early acquisitions, and it gave us first-hand experience of all the pain that comes with laying off staff in order to turn a company round. It also demonstrated the benefits of growing a company from scratch, when you employ exactly those people you want, and really establish the kind of atmosphere you want.

A year later, Rob Shreeve joined Virgin Books as managing director, with Robert as chairman. Together they relaunched the business as Virgin Publishing, concentrating on our core strengths of music and entertainment. Within a few years the company had become a highly successful publisher of books on entertainment, and probably the world's leading publisher of books on popular music.

In February 1984 a young American lawyer called Randolph Fields asked me whether I was interested in operating an airline. Randolph was looking for investors to finance a new airline that would use the Gatwick to New York route, which had become vacant following the collapse of Sir Freddie Laker's airline in 1982. He sent me a proposal which I took up to read at Mill End. It was obvious that he had contacted lots of other investors before me – a record-label owner is hardly going to be his first call – so as I skimmed through the proposal I kept saying to myself, 'Don't get tempted; don't even think about it.'

In the same way that I tend to make up my mind about people within thirty seconds of meeting them, I also make up my mind about whether a business proposal excites me within about thirty seconds of looking at it. I rely far more on gut instinct than researching huge amounts of statistics. This might be because, due to my dyslexia, I distrust numbers, which I feel can be twisted to prove anything. The idea of operating a Virgin airline grabbed my imagination, but I had to work out in my own mind what the potential risks were.

Throughout that weekend I mulled over the proposal. Randolph's idea was to offer an all-business-class airline, but this didn't appeal. I worried about what would happen on the days when businessmen don't fly: Christmas, Easter, Bank holidays, the entire Thanksgiving week. I thought that we would have to have holiday-makers to fill the plane in those weeks. If we were going to be different from other airlines, with their first, business and economy classes, perhaps we could offer just two classes: business and economy? I wondered what the implications of that would be. We'd get both businessmen and tourists – who would we miss? I wrote out a list of things I wanted to understand about how the aircraft leasing would work. If I could lease the plane for one year and then have the chance to return the plane, we would have a clear escape route if it all failed. It would be embarrassing, but we would limit the amount of money we lost. By the end of the weekend I had made up my mind: if we could limit everything to one year – the employment contracts, the leasing of the aircraft, the exchange exposure, and anything else that starting up a New York route involved – then I wanted to have a shot at it.

The only airline that was offering cheap fares across the Atlantic in 1984 was People Express. I picked up the phone and tried to call them. Their number was engaged. It was impossible to get through on their reservations line all morning. I reasoned that either People Express was very poorly managed, in which case they would be an easy target for new competition, or that they were so much in demand that there was room for new competition. It was that continual engaged tone on my telephone throughout Saturday more than anything else which triggered my belief that we could set up and run an airline.

I called up Simon on Sunday evening.

'What do you think about starting an airline?' I jauntily asked him. 'I've got a proposal here –'

'For God's sake!' he cut across me. 'You're crazy. Come off it.'

'I'm serious.'

'You're not,' he said. 'You're mad.'

'OK,' I said. 'I won't go into it now. But I think we should have lunch.'

On Monday morning I called up international directory inquiries and asked for the number for Boeing. Boeing is based in Seattle, and due to the time difference I couldn't speak to them until late that afternoon. They were rather bemused to hear an Englishman asking what kinds of deals were available on a jumbo. I spent all afternoon and all evening on the phone to Boeing, and eventually I spoke to someone who could help me. They told me that Boeing did lease aircraft, and that they had a second-hand jumbo that they would seriously consider taking back after a year if things didn't work out. With this extremely basic, not to say sketchy, information I prepared to face Simon and Ken.

The lunch the next day was not a success. After I told them about how impossible it had been to get through to People Express and that Boeing had planes to lease, they looked shocked. I think they realised I had done all the market research I felt I needed to do and had made up my mind. They were right: I had worked myself up into a state about it.

'You're a megalomaniac, Richard,' Simon said. 'We've been friends since we were teenagers, but if you do this I'm not sure that we can carry on working together. What I'm telling you is that you go ahead with this over my dead body.'

Ken was less outspoken, but he too thought that the idea of combining a record company with an airline was anathema.

'I can't see the connection,' he said. 'And, if you're looking for losses to offset against our profits, we could always invest in new bands.'

'All right, then,' I said. 'We won't combine it. We'll keep the two companies separate. We can arrange the financing so that Virgin Music is scarcely at risk. I've spoken to Boeing, and they can offer a lease whereby they take the plane back after a year if it doesn't work. The most Virgin would lose would be £2 million.'

Simon and Ken remained resolutely opposed.

'Come on,' I ploughed on. 'Virgin can afford to make this step. The risk is less than a third of this year's profits. Money from Culture Club is pouring in. And it'll be fun.'

Simon and Ken both winced when I said 'fun', which is a particularly loaded word for me – it's one of my prime business criteria. Since I had made up my mind, I knew I had to convince them. I carried on arguing that we would only have one plane, that we could just dip our toe into the water, and that if the water was too hot we could cut our losses. I explained that the beauty of starting up from scratch rather than buying an existing airline was that we could easily retreat if it didn't work. In my mind it was that simple. Simon was most worried that I was risking the value of his shareholding in the Virgin Group, and I think Ken thought I had gone way over the top.

In the same way that the argument over The Human League had been a turning point in Simon's and my relationship with Nik, the argument that lunchtime was a turning point in my relationship with Simon. Over the years I had unnerved him several times, but this time he felt that I was prepared to bet the company and all our accumulated wealth on a scheme that he thought was totally harebrained. Simon's interest and love for life comes from the arts, from music, books, his collection of paintings and beautiful cars. My interest in life comes from setting myself huge, apparently unachievable, challenges and trying to rise above them. From a purely commercial perspective, Simon was absolutely right; but from the viewpoint of wanting to live life to the full, I felt I had to attempt it. From that lunchtime onward a tension sprang up in our relationship which has never fully dissolved.

Randolph was proposing to call the airline British Atlantic, but if I was going to be involved I wanted to bring 'Virgin' into the title. We agreed to differ on that until the airline was a little closer to reality. There was a lot to learn, so I asked Sir Freddie Laker, a man I've always admired, whether he could help me. Sir Freddie came to have lunch on *Duende* and explained the mechanics of an airline. He quickly confirmed my suspicions about the limitations of starting an airline that was exclusively business class.

'And you don't want to be all no-frills economy service either,' he pointed out. 'That was my mistake. You'll be vulnerable to the simple cost-cutting attack which put me out of business.'

We began a discussion on the philosophy of the

business-class service at that lunch. We talked about offering a first-class service at business-class fares, and building in all kinds of extra services for the cost. Two of the best ideas that came out of our lunch were to offer a limousine pick-up as part of the service and offer a free economy ticket to anyone who flew business.

Freddie also warned me to expect some fierce competition from British Airways.

'Do all you can to stop BA,' he said. 'Complain as loudly as possible, use the Civil Aviation Authority to stop them, and don't hesitate to take them to court. They're utterly ruthless. My mistake was that I never complained loudly enough. They destroyed my financing and it's too late for me now. I sued them and won millions of dollars, but I lost my airline. If you ever get into trouble, sue them before it's too late. Another thing, Richard, is the stress. I'm not kidding, but you should have regular medical checkups. It is very stressful.'

Freddie told me that he was just recovering from cancer of the pancreas.

'You need to go to a doctor and ask him to stick his finger up your bum. He'll be able to tell you what's what,' Freddie said.

I was inspired to see that, despite all his problems, Freddie was still so ebullient. He was unbowed by the experience, and he saw me as his successor, picking up the flag where he had left off. I asked Freddie whether he would object if I called Virgin Atlantic's first aircraft *Spirit of Sir Freddie*, but he laughed it off:

'Not the first one,' he said. 'My name's a liability now and you'd send out the wrong signals. But I'd be honoured when you've got a larger fleet.'

As Freddie left *Duende* he turned round and shouted back at me, 'One last word of advice, Richard. When you're bent over and the doctor's got his finger up your bum, make sure that he hasn't got both his hands on your shoulders!'

Roaring with laughter, he made his way along the towpath.

The first arrangement I made with Randolph was that we would have an equal partnership. I would invest the funds; he would run the airline. Randolph had already recruited two key people from Laker Airways: Roy Gardner, who had run the engineering side of Laker, and David Tait, who had run the American side of the operation.

'What do you think of the name?' I asked David Tait.

'British Atlantic?' He snorted. 'Just what the world needs: another BA!'

Using David's reaction, I managed to get Randolph to agree to change the name to Virgin Atlantic Airways, and then we formed our joint partnership.

'What do you think of the new name?' I asked David Tait.

'Virgin Atlantic?' He snorted. 'Nobody will ever set foot inside a plane called "Virgin". It's ridiculous. Who'd fly an airline that's not prepared to go the full distance?'

Within a couple of weeks it became clear that the arrangement between Randolph and me would not work. At our first meeting in front of the Civil Aviation Authority, who monitor the safety of airlines, Randolph went in to talk about his plans for the new airline. Colin Howes, my lawyer from Harbottle and Lewis, was there. After watching Randolph blustering for a few minutes, Colin slipped out of the hearing to call me and advise me to get across to Kingsway in Holborn:

'It's not going very well,' Colin said. 'I think that Randolph is digging a hole for himself.'

I came into the hearing and saw that Randolph was

being fiercely cross-examined by British Caledonian, who were objecting to our licence application. Our airline was purely an idea, a paper airline, so it was easy for them to run rings round us, asking what we intended to do about safety drills, how we were going to maintain our plane, how we could guarantee our passengers' safety. Randolph was an impatient man, and I could see that he was growing angry and confused in the face of this sustained questioning. Equally, the CAA were looking rather sceptical about Randolph's ability to get an airline off the ground. When the CAA came on to the question of finances, the British Caledonian lawyer looked across the room at me and said:

'You'll have to have a lot of hits on *Top of the Pops* to keep the airline going.'

'Actually,' I pointed out tartly, 'Virgin made profits of £11 million last year – more than twice those of your client, British Caledonian.' I decided not to mention that we were having to pay out large sums of money to continue making *1984*.

The CAA specified that the new airline would have to have working capital of £3 million and gave their permission for us to fly in theory. This was the official blessing. Of course, the CAA could withdraw their permission at any time if we failed to meet safety requirements. We would have to have another CAA test once we had leased the aircraft, but for now we had the go-ahead to establish the airline. We rented a warehouse near Gatwick Airport, where we based Roy Gardner and his engineering team, and started recruiting pilots and cabin staff. We rented office space in the Air Florida office on Woodstock Street, just off Oxford Street, where we piggybacked on their computer-reservations system and created a dummy file for the Virgin Atlantic flights.

David Tait moved his family up from Miami back to their home in Toronto and started living at Virgin Music's office in New York. A team of lawyers representing Boeing came over to London to start negotiating over the lease of the aircraft, and soon they were spending most of their days with me on the upper deck of *Duende*, while Joan and Holly lived on the lower floor.

The houseboat was becoming increasingly crowded with the addition of Holly, and the comings-and-goings to do with the airline. Joan and I decided to look for a home on land for the family, and settled on a large, comfortable house off Ladbroke Grove.

The first casualty of Virgin Atlantic Airways was my relationship with Randolph Fields. Two things became clear. The first was that, since Virgin Group was being asked to guarantee the entire finances of Virgin Atlantic, Coutts Bank would only countenance extending credit to us if we had control of Virgin Atlantic. They would not lend us money if we controlled only half the new airline. Since Randolph was not putting up any money, he saw the sense of this and reluctantly agreed that Virgin should have a controlling share of the airline.

A far more difficult problem with Randolph came about in his relations with the new Virgin Atlantic staff. Perhaps if we had had a longer time than the four months we gave ourselves it would have been different. But we felt that, if we were to survive the first year, we had to launch in June in order to take advantage of the heavy summer traffic and build up reserves and cash flow to keep us going through the lean winter months. It was a virtually impossible timetable, and demanded that we work flat out. One moment we might be choosing the design of the air hostesses' uniform or working out the menu; the next we were arguing over some legal clause in the 96-page document about the lease of the aircraft we were negotiating with Boeing.

I first got wind of serious trouble from David Tait, whom Randolph had employed in America and who was going to be crucial to our chances of succeeding.

'I've resigned,' he told me. 'I'm sorry, but Randolph is impossible to work with.'

'What's the matter?' I asked. I knew that, without David selling tickets in America, Virgin Atlantic would be stillborn.

'I can't tell you everything,' David said. 'It's just impossible. I'm sorry, but I wish you all the best and hope that it's a great success.'

I could tell that David was about to ring off, so I begged him to come over to London to see me. He had no money to buy a ticket, so I sent him one and he came two days later. When he arrived at *Duende* he found me holding Holly, who was feverish and screaming. Joan had gone off to buy more Calpol. We smiled at each other above the noise as I cuddled Holly.

'You may think that's loud,' David said. 'But I can tell you that Randolph can scream louder. I can't work for him.'

David's experience confirmed the growing realisation that we had to move Randolph to one side if we were going to get the airline started. David had taken a great gamble in joining Virgin Atlantic. He had moved his young family away from Miami back to Toronto, and was living by himself on the top floor of the Greenwich Village house that Ken Berry had bought. All he had was a desk, a telephone and a tiny bedroom, and he had to try to sell tickets to Americans for a start-up airline. Since he was unable to advertise Virgin Atlantic without an American licence (which was to come only the day before we took off), David had tried to alert New Yorkers by advertising in the sky above Manhattan. On a cloudless spring afternoon, a formation of five small planes had planned to squirt out white and red smoke printing WAIT FOR THE ENGLISH VIRGIN across the sky. Unfortunately, just as they were finishing, a single cloud blew over and obliterated the final letter, so New Yorkers craned their necks and wondered what the cryptic message WAIT FOR THE ENGLISH VIRGI meant.

David's falling-out with Randolph had been over the ticketing system. Randolph wanted to avoid all travel agents, who charged 10 per cent of the fare for their services, and instead sell every ticket through a theatre booking agency called Ticketron. David had looked at Ticketron, who charged only $5 for issuing a ticket, but had refused to deal with them.

The staff from the Woodstock Street ticketing office had also complained about Randolph's behaviour. They told me that he kept bursting into the room and asking everyone to leave it so that he could make telephone calls in private. I realised that Randolph was not the right person to run the new airline. I promised David Tait that, if he stayed, he would soon have no more trouble from Randolph.

'He won't be here much longer,' I said. 'You can deal with me directly.'

As we worked through April and May, more and more of the airline staff dealt with me directly. Randolph was cut out of the operation. He became increasingly difficult to cope with. Eventually my lawyers advised me to change the locks on the ticketing office to keep him out. As the inaugural flight fixed for June drew nearer, Randolph and I were on a war footing.

I still wonder how we packed everything into those last few days. The newly trained cabin crew came up to the Woodstock Street office to man the telephones, which were ringing off the hook. The lease with Boeing was finally wrapped up, including a complete maze of legal conditions, but basically allowing us to return the aircraft to them after a year and be reimbursed for at least the original cost. If the aircraft had risen in value then we would receive the increased price. After two months of negotiation I think Boeing were rather surprised at our tenacity: 'It's easier to sell a fleet of jumbos to an American airline than just one to Virgin,' admitted their negotiator after we had finished. The continual negotiation of music recording contracts had stood me in good stead. As a side agreement to the lease contract, we had a currency agreement to protect us if the pound fell in value against the dollar (our exposure was in dollars).

At one point I took Boy George in to meet all the staff in the Woodstock Street office. He was dressed in his usual bizarre collection of robes, with his hair plaited and braided and tied with ribbons and his gloves festooned with huge diamond rings. For a minute he stood watching the complete chaos as everyone answered the phones, made out tickets, told passengers about our timetable, invited celebrities and journalists for the inaugural flight, and worked on dummy copies of the in-flight magazine. Then he said:

'I'm pleased that I've got my feet squarely on the ground.'

14 Laker's children

1984

ON 19 JUNE 1984, three days before we were due to launch, I went down to Gatwick for our final CAA approval, a test flight. *Maiden Voyager* stood by a departure gate and I marvelled again at her size. I also wondered at the size of the Virgin logo on her tail fin. It was huge – the largest version that I had seen. I remembered back to the early 1970s when Simon and I asked Trevor Key to come up with some ideas for a new logo. Having drawn a blank, Trevor briefed graphic designer Ray Kyte, of design consultants Kyte & Company, who created the concept and supplied the visual styling for a signature-style logo which can be interpreted as my personal endorsement, the 'V' forming an expressive tick. Some marketing experts once analysed the logo and wrote about the upbeat way it rises from left to right. This, of course, might have been going through Ray's head when he developed the original idea. Seeing it up on the tail fin made me begin to realise what we had started. This thing was going to happen: we had a jumbo.

The entire cabin crew came on board for the ride, as did over a hundred Virgin staff, and I sat at the back with the CAA official. The plane had arrived only the previous day, flown over from Seattle, and until we had received our formal CAA licence to fly, the engines were uninsured. We took off and the crew all burst out clapping and cheering. I could hardly stop myself from shedding a tear: I felt so proud of everyone.

Then there was a loud bang from outside. The plane lurched to the left and a massive flash of flame then a long trail of black smoke poured out from one of the engines.

In that horrible stunned silence, the CAA official put his arm round my shoulders.

'Don't worry, Richard,' he said. 'These things happen.'

We had flown into a flock of birds, and one of the engines had sucked in some of them and exploded. We needed a new engine overnight in order to do the CAA test flight again. Our inaugural flight to New York was due to take off the day after tomorrow with 250 journalists and cameramen on board.

Roy Gardner was with me and he radioed through to the team at British Caledonian who carried out our maintenance. When *Maiden Voyager* had arrived the previous day, Roy had rejected two of the engines on financial grounds and asked for two others to be fitted. Now he recalled one of the engines, which had been taken to Heathrow and was about to be flown back to Seattle.

When we landed I was standing beside the plane trying to think of how to overcome this problem, when a press photographer came up to me smiling broadly.

'I'm sorry,' I apologised. 'I'm not up to it now.'

'I'm sorry too,' he said. 'I saw the flames and smoke pouring out of your engine. I actually got a great shot of it.'

He looked at my dumbstruck face and then said, 'Don't worry though. I'm from the *Financial Times*; we're not that kind of paper.' He opened up his camera, pulled out the film and gave it to me. I couldn't find words to thank him. If that photograph had appeared in the press, it would have been the end of Virgin Atlantic before we'd even begun.

Unfortunately, because Virgin Atlantic did not have a CAA licence, we were uninsured for the engine. We had to pay £600,000 for a new one. After several desperate calls, I realised that there was no alternative. With a sinking feeling, I called up Coutts to let them know that a payment of £600,000 would have to go through.

'You're very close to your limit,' Chris Rashbrook, the manager of our account, said.

Our overdraft limit with Coutts for the entire Virgin Group was set at £3 million.

'It's a terrible freak accident,' I said. 'One of the engines blew up and we can't get our insurance until we get our licence. Without a new engine, we won't be able to get our licence. It's a catch-22 situation.'

'Well, I'm just warning you,' Rashbrook told me. 'You spent a fortune on filming *Electric Dreams* and we're still waiting for the MGM cheque.'

The MGM cheque was the £6 million which MGM had agreed to pay for the American distribution rights to *Electric Dreams*.

'Please can you wait until I get this inaugural flight out of the way?' I asked. 'Let's sort it out when I get home. I'm back on Friday. We'll only be £300,000 over our limit. When the MGM cheque comes through we'll have no overdraft and around £3 million on deposit.'

He said that he'd think about it.

The day before the inaugural flight, *Maiden Voyager* was fitted with another engine and ready to fly again. The CAA official came on board and we took off. This time there was no explosion and we were given our licence. I dashed back up to London to sort out another Randolph Fields crisis. We had offered Randolph £1 million, but he thought that wasn't enough. He had gone to a judge in America and applied for an injunction to stop *Maiden Voyager* from taking off. All through the night we had a damage-limitation meeting with David Tait, Roy Gardner and my lawyers, to try to work out an arrangement whereby we could prevent Randolph from ruining the airline. The judge eventually threw the request out, but not before we had battled all night to keep on top of what he was up to. By dawn we felt that we would win, and at 6a.m. I ran a bath and lay in it. I felt exhausted. I tried to wash my face, but my eyes felt sore and itchy as if a blast of sand had blown into them. David Tait came in and sat on the lavatory and we ran through the final list of things we had to do. David then left to catch Concorde so that he would arrive in New York before us in order to organise the welcoming reception for the flight.

On board for the inaugural flight, I was surrounded by family and friends, the people who had been most important to me, and to Virgin, over the last ten years. I sat next to Joan, with Holly on her lap. Behind us was pretty much everyone from the entire Virgin Group. The aircraft was full of journalists and photographers, along with a collection of conjurors, entertainers and Uri Geller. As *Maiden Voyager* taxied down the runway, the screen at the front of the cabin flickered into life and showed the backs of the pilots and the flight engineer as they sat in the flight deck and manned the controls. Over their shoulders we could see the view through the windscreen. An announcement came over the loudspeakers:

'Since this is our first flight, we thought you might like to share our view from the flight deck, and see what really happens when we take off.'

We could see the view of the runway stretching out in front. Then we started speeding along: the tarmac rushing beneath the windscreen gathered pace until the white lines were just a blur. But the pilots seemed rather relaxed: rather than staring intently ahead and flying the plane, they started looking sideways at each other and smiling. One of them had very long hair beneath his cap; the other was a West Indian. We were now hurtling down the runway, and these two pilots were doing nothing about it. They were simply paying no attention. Everyone watching the screen held their breath: this was all some mad suicide flight by that lunatic Branson. There was a deathly hush. Then, just as the plane's nose rose up and the runway began to disappear from view, the West Indian reached behind his ear, pulled out a joint, and offered it to his copilot. Before anyone was entirely sure that this was a joke, the plane took off and the two pilots took off their caps and turned round to face the camera: they were Ian Botham and Viv Richards. The bearded flight engineer

"They must be good — getting suitable stewardesses can't be easy!"

was me. The whole plane rocked with laughter. We had filmed it the previous day on a flight simulator.

We had loaded seventy cases of champagne on board. This number proved to be just about right for what turned into an eight-hour party. People danced in the aisles as we played Madonna's new hit 'Like A Virgin' and Culture Club and Phil Collins. For a quiet interval we showed the movie *Airplane*, and the cabin crew started a Virgin tradition by giving out choc ices in the middle of the film.

At New York's Newark Airport I realised that, in the excitement of going, I had forgotten my passport. I was almost refused entrance to the reception party in the terminal. By some mistake, the cabin crew had thrown away all the cutlery, so they had to scrabble around up to their elbows in all the rubbish bins retrieving the cutlery to wash it up and then get it back on board the plane. I embarrassed everyone except the Mayor of Newark when I was talking to him as I thought, for some bizarre reason, that he had organised the catering. I took the return flight back to Gatwick and fell into my first long sleep for many weeks. I dreamt about exploding engines, cabin crew offering meals on plates straight from the rubbish bins, and pilots smoking marijuana. When I woke up, I felt sure that nothing else could go wrong. A bad mistake.

A taxi carried me back to London. As we pulled up at my house I saw a rather uncomfortable-looking man sitting on the steps. At first I thought he was a journalist, but then I realised that it was Christopher Rashbrook, my account manager at Coutts. I invited him in, and he sat down in the sitting room. I was exhausted and he was fidgety. I was rather slow to understand what he was saying. But then I suddenly heard him say that Coutts were unable to extend

Virgin's overdraft as requested and would therefore regrettably bounce any cheques that took our overdraft over £3 million. I rarely lose my temper – in fact I can count the times I have lost my temper on the fingers of one hand – but as I looked across at this man in his blue pinstripe suit with his neat little black leather briefcase I felt my blood boil. He was standing there in his highly polished black Oxford brogues and calmly telling me that he was going to put the whole of Virgin out of business. I thought of the numerous times since March when I and the Virgin Atlantic staff had worked through the night to solve a problem; I thought about how proud the new cabin crew were to be flying with a start-up airline; and I thought about the protracted negotiation we had fought with Boeing. If this bank manager bounced our cheques, then Virgin would be out of business within days: nobody would supply an airline with anything such as fuel or food or maintenance if word went about that the cheques were bouncing. And no passengers would fly with us.

'Excuse me,' I said as he was still making excuses. 'You are not welcome in my house. Please get out.' I took him by the arm, led him to the front door and pushed him outside. I shut the door in his bewildered face, walked back into the sitting room and collapsed on a sofa in tears of exhaustion, frustration and worry. Then I had a shower upstairs and called Ken:

'We've got to get as much money in from overseas as possible today. And then we've got to find new bankers.'

Our overseas record subsidiaries saved us that week. We managed to pull in enough money on Friday to keep us just below the £3 million overdraft limit. We gave Coutts no reason to bounce our cheques, and so we stopped them from pushing the various Virgin companies, together with the new airline, into instant insolvency. It was a surreal situation: Virgin Music was set to make £12 million profit that year, and was forecast to make £20 million the following one. We were already one of Britain's largest private companies, but Coutts were prepared to push us into insolvency – and make 3,000 people lose their jobs – for the sake of going £300,000 over our limit, with a cheque for £6 million due to arrive any day from the States.

The Coutts crisis made me realise that we needed a tough financier to replace Nik. We needed someone who could cope with the finances of both Virgin Atlantic and Virgin Music and act as a bridge between the two. By surviving on cash flow and debt, the entire Virgin Group was living too dangerously. The mid-1980s were boom years in the City, and every company seemed able to sell its shares to the public and raise millions of pounds to invest. Perhaps, I began to think, that was the way forward for Virgin.

Apart from the four main operations, Virgin Music, Virgin Records shops, Virgin Vision and the new airline, Virgin Atlantic, there were now a host of new little companies operating under the Virgin umbrella. There was Top Nosh food, which delivered food around industrial estates; Virgin Rags, a line of clothes; Virgin Pubs and Vanson Property, a property-development company which looked after our growing collection of properties and as a sideline was making a lot of money by buying, developing and then selling property. This disparate selection of businesses needed someone to put them in order.

Don Cruickshank was recommended to us by David Puttnam, the English film-maker. He was a chartered accountant who had worked at the management consultants McKinsey for five years before moving to be general manager of the *Sunday Times* and then on to

Pearson, where he had been managing director of the *Financial Times*. Robert Devereux, who by now was married to my sister Vanessa, had come across him when dealing with Goldcrest Films, part of Pearson, but Simon knew nothing about him. Don started work in the cramped offices at Ladbroke Grove and was the first person at Virgin who had ever worn a suit and tie. Everyone marvelled at him. With Don as managing director, Virgin began to be organised into a company that could attract outside investors.

Soon Don brought in Trevor Abbott as finance director. Trevor had been with MAM, Management Agency & Music, an entertainment company which had managed the careers of Tom Jones and Engelbert Humperdinck, and had set up its own record label to launch Gilbert O'Sullivan. MAM had then diversified into music publishing, had a chain of hotels, operated a fleet of corporate jets, had nightclubs, and leased out fruit machines and jukeboxes. MAM had a great deal in common with Virgin, but as Trevor left he was already working on the merger between MAM and Chrysalis.

Don and Trevor were soon holding meetings with banks and rearranging both our finances and the internal structure of the Group. As a whole, Virgin's turnover in 1984 was going to exceed £100 million, and each time Don and Trevor saw me they expressed amazement at how things were run. They were aghast at the lack of computers in the Group, the lack of stock control, and the apparently rather casual way Simon, Ken, Robert and I decided on how to invest our money. They came to see us on *Duende* and set out how they proposed to reorganise Virgin with a view to inviting in some outside investors.

The first thing they did was sort out our overdraft facilities. Coutts and their parent company, National

Westminster Bank, had been willing to close us down for exceeding a £3 million overdraft. Taking the same balance sheet to a different consortium of banks, Don and Trevor arranged an overdraft facility of £30 million. They then looked at the structure of the Virgin Group and decided to close down a number of our smaller companies, such as Top Nosh food and the pubs. They divided the Virgin Group into Music, Retail and Vision, and then hived off Virgin Atlantic, together with Virgin Holidays, Heaven, The Roof Garden and Necker Island, into a separate private company. Simon and I were both 33 years old, as were Trevor and Ken. Don was a little older; Robert a little younger. We felt that we could take on anybody, and we now set our minds to take the Virgin Group public. We were going from the rock market to the stock market.

15 'It was like being strapped to the blade of a vast pneumatic drill.'

1984–1986

I AM OFTEN ASKED why I go in for record-breaking challenges with either powerboats or hot-air balloons. People point out that, with success, money, and a happy family, I should stop putting myself and them at risk and enjoy what I am so lucky to have. This is an obvious truth, and part of me wholeheartedly agrees with it. I love life; I love my family; and I am horrified by the idea of being killed and leaving Joan without a husband, and Holly and Sam without a father. But another part of me is driven to try new adventures, and I still find that I want to push myself to my limits.

If I were to think about it more carefully, I would say that I love to experience as much as I can of life. The physical adventures I have been involved in have added a special dimension to my life that has reinforced the pleasure I take in my business. If I had refused to contemplate skydiving, hot-air ballooning or crossing the Atlantic in a boat, I think that my life would have been the duller for it. I never think that I am going to die by accident, but if I were to die then all I can say is that I was wrong, and the hardened realists who kept their feet on the ground were right. But at least I tried.

Apart from the thrill of the actual event, I love the preparation for it. A tremendous sense of camaraderie builds up within the team when we are preparing for a challenge, and if we are going after a record there is not only the technological challenge but also a great feeling of patriotism as the public cheers us on. There used to be a great many British explorers, all in the best tradition of Scott of the Antarctic, and I feel proud to follow in their footsteps.

The first challenge I was involved in was to try to recapture the Blue Riband for Britain. In the Victorian age of steamships, the Blue Riband was awarded to the fastest ship across the Atlantic. In 1893 the Blue Riband was held by the British Cunard Line. Then it went to three German ships, before Cunard won it back again in 1906 with RMS *Lusitania*, later sunk in 1915 by a German U-boat. After the First World War the Germans won it back, and then the Italian ship *Rex* won it in 1933 with an average crossing speed of 29 knots. In order to celebrate this achievement, and to celebrate the whole Blue Riband competition, an English shipowner and member of parliament called Harold Hales commissioned a monumental trophy. From then on, the Hales Trophy was awarded along with the Blue Riband.

In the small print of the conditions of the award, Hales offered it to the fastest boat that crossed the Atlantic, and he defined the Atlantic as the stretch of sea between Ambrose Lightship on the American coast and the Bishop Rock Lighthouse, off the Scilly Isles. Hales made no mention of the size of boat as long as it carried passengers; indeed nobody in those days ever considered that a small boat would have any chance of competing safely with the big ships.

The next ship to win the Hales Trophy was SS *Normandie*, a French liner which crossed the Atlantic on her maiden voyage at an average speed of 30 knots. In 1952, before the age of the big passenger ships came to an end, the SS *United States* won the Hales Trophy with a crossing that took 3 days, 10 hours and 40 minutes. The Hales Trophy was then put away in the American Merchant Marine Museum. Unfortunately, Harold Hales did not live to witness the SS *United States*: with horrible irony he had drowned in a boating accident on the River Thames. The glorious days of passenger liners faded as people began to use the new form of transport, aeroplanes, and everyone forgot about the Hales Trophy.

In 1980 a powerboat builder called Ted Toleman decided to resurrect the Blue Riband competition and attempt to win the Hales Trophy back for Britain. In order to do so, he would have to build a boat that could cross the Atlantic in less than 3 days, 10 hours and 40 minutes. The SS *United States* was a truly impressive ship: she weighed 52,000 tons and needed 240,000 horsepower to shift her. The speed record she set was impressive: an average of 35.6 knots (equivalent to 40 miles an hour). In contrast to this huge 52,000-ton liner with its swimming pool and grand piano, Ted planned a lightweight catamaran.

Sailing a small, fast boat across an ocean is extremely dangerous. For one, you are very vulnerable to waves. In this respect, a larger steamer finds heavy seas much easier: it just slices through them. The passengers may use the excuse of a slight roll to lurch into one another's arms on the dance floor, but the boat's speed is unimpaired. With a small boat, an ill-judged steering move at 30 knots can plunge the prow into the side of the wave and cause the whole boat to go under or break apart.

Ted Toleman designed a 65-foot catamaran, and launched it in 1984. Rather than the SS *United States'* 240,000-horsepower engines, which were the size of small cathedrals, Ted used two 2,000-horsepower engines, which could propel his catamaran at almost 50 knots on calm water. Of course, it is one thing to be able to race across a calm lake at 50 knots; quite another to reach those speeds on the choppy surface of the Atlantic Ocean, where the waves swell to 20 feet or higher. Ted knew that he would be lucky to reach speeds of 35 knots. It would still be a three- to four-day crossing. The challenge was whether it would be three days and nine hours or three days and eleven hours.

During 1984, Ted's budget for the boat overran and he approached me to sponsor the cost of the trip, in return for my being able to name the boat and join him in the challenge. He had already asked Chay Blyth, the round-the-world yachtsman, to help him. Virgin Atlantic had just started flying, and although I was immediately attracted by the idea of winning a trophy back for Britain – Britain doesn't have that many trophies – I also relished the chance to promote our new airline. A successful Atlantic crossing would attract publicity in both New York and London, our sole destinations.

'How fit are you?' Chay asked me.

'Not bad,' I ventured.

'That's not good enough,' Chay said. 'There's no room for passengers. You need to get into shape.'

And so I started the most gruelling fitness programme of my life.

'You're going to be pounded for three solid days,' Ted said as we killed ourselves in the gym. 'You've got to be able to take it.'

We asked Esso to sponsor the trip by providing the fuel, and when they kindly agreed to do so we all went along to a celebratory lunch with their whole board of directors.

'I want to thank you all very much,' I said sincerely.

'It's going to be a great trip, and we're really going to advertise BP as much as we can.' I thought that I heard a collective intake of breath, but I ploughed on regardless. 'We're going to plaster BP all over the refuelling ships, have your logo on the boat, really put BP on the map. Nobody will ever confuse you with that old rival of yours ...'

At this point I looked up at the wall opposite me and noticed the huge Esso logo. I realised my mistake. The Esso executives looked at me with horror, as if I were a ghost. I fell down on the floor and crawled under the table.

'I am sorry,' I said, and started to spit and polish their shoes.

Remarkably, Esso were as good as their word and went ahead with sponsoring the trip.

The boat and the crew were put through their paces for two months until we were finally ready.

Joan was nearly eight months pregnant with our second child, and I was desperately hoping to do the crossing in time to be back for the birth. But we were stuck in New York for three weeks waiting for the stormy weather to clear. In those three weeks I kept flying back to London to be with Joan, and then flying back to New York when they told me we were about to set sail. By the time I had crossed the Atlantic eight times, I felt as though I knew it as well as I wanted to at 30,000 feet.

The storms cleared and we got the green light. Joan told me that she was feeling fine and that I should go. She still had two weeks before the baby was due. We roared out of Manhattan and headed north.

The other crucial difference between *Virgin Atlantic Challenger* and the great liners was comfort: while the passengers in the 1930s danced to jazz bands and played deck quoits, we were strapped in airline seats and pounded relentlessly up and down. With the deafening noise of the engines and the constant reverberation, it was like being strapped to the blade of a vast pneumatic drill. We could hardly talk, let alone move; we just had to stomach an unending sequence of banging, shaking and clattering.

Towards the end of the first day I got a radio message.

'Richard.' It was Penni, who was at the control centre. 'Joan's in hospital and she's just had a baby boy. Rose was with her and it all went fine.'

I'd broken my pledge, but most importantly we'd had a healthy child. We all whooped with joy and Steve Ridgway, another member of the crew, rustled up a bottle of champagne to toast Joan and my new son. Without any extra shaking from me, the bottle exploded and fizzed everywhere. It was impossible to drink. The champagne foamed between our teeth and foamed up and down our throats. Holding on to a lifeline, I staggered to the side and threw the bottle overboard, where it bobbed in the wake. Now I had to power on to see Joan, Holly and our baby boy.

The crossing would have won the record comfortably. We endured three hellish days of mental pile-driving over 3,000 miles. We had three refuelling stops lined up at 800-mile intervals. These fuel boats were enormous ships which loomed over us like skyscrapers. Even with a small swell, the approach to them was terrifying: we drew up about 30 yards away, and they fired a harpoon towards us with a buoy on the end of the line. We hauled this on board and then pulled out from the ship the great hose with the fuel. When this was clamped on, we gave the go-ahead and the fuel was pumped on board. The smell of petrol and the rolling swell made us all sick. And as we staggered to the edge and retched we seemed in danger of smashing into the vast black and rusted cliff face of the fuel boat's side.

As we approached Ireland with only a few hundred miles to go, we hit a ferocious storm. We had been battered solidly for three days, but this was the worst yet. The boat smashed up and down. We held on to our seats and could see nothing. As we approached the Scilly Isles, with only 60 miles left and the Hales Trophy nearly in our hands, we hit a massive wave. A second later there was a shout from Pete Downie, our engineer.

'We're going down. The hull's split right open. Get out fast.'

'Mayday! Mayday! Mayday!' Chay was on the radio in a flash. '*Virgin Challenger* is sinking. We are abandoning ship. Repeat: we are abandoning ship. Hey, Ted!' Chay swung round. 'You're the skipper: you're meant to be the last off!'

Within seconds the boat started to go down. The first life raft we inflated snagged on something and ripped open. We had a backup raft which we threw overboard and pulled the ripcord to inflate.

'Nobody panic!' Chay shouted. 'There's no hurry! Everyone take their time!'

As we edged along the rail to get into the life raft, Chay shouted out, 'Panic! Panic! We're going down. Move it!'

The life raft was like a tiny inflatable coracle with a hooded tent. We huddled together, rocking up and down in the sea like we were on a crazy funfair ride. I was sitting next to the radio, and I picked up the mike. An RAF Nimrod picked up our Mayday. I gave the pilot our position, and he rapidly radioed any ships in the area.

'OK, there are three vessels in the area that are heading towards you,' the pilot came back to me. 'In no particular order, there is the QE2, which is heading for New York; an RAF helicopter from the Scilly Isles has been mobilised, and a Geest boat heading to Jamaica is also on its way. Please take the first one that arrives.'

'Tell him I'm not going in a fucking banana boat to Jamaica,' Chay said. 'Neither am I going back to New York. I want the bloody helicopter.'

'That'll be fine,' I said over the radio, deciding not to pass on Chay's comment, since for once I thought we were in no position to negotiate.

Ted was gutted. He sat there in silence, his dream shattered.

From the tiny hatch door we could see the stern of *Virgin Challenger* sticking out above the water. The rest of the boat was underwater. All you could see was the word 'Virgin'.

'Well, Richard,' Chay said, pointing at the logo, 'as usual you got the last word in.'

As we waited, I started a chorus of 'We're all going on a summer holiday ...' Everyone sang along, even Ted.

Eventually we were picked up by the Geest banana boat on its way to the Caribbean. We were winched up in turn and left the life raft spinning by itself.

'Handy in case anyone else capsizes,' said Chay.

It was dinnertime and the guests were gathering in the captain's quarters. Rather like in the great days of ocean steamers, they were all wearing dinner jackets and evening gowns. We were a bedraggled lot in our damp nylon survival suits.

'My poor boy,' one elderly lady said to me. 'And you haven't even seen your newborn son yet, have you?'

'No,' I said. 'I'm afraid we're heading off to Jamaica so I won't see him for a while.'

'Well, I've got this photograph of him for you.'

To my astonishment, she pulled out that day's edition of the London *Evening Standard*. And there on the front page was a picture of our tiny son wrapped up in a shawl. I have to admit to a tear in my eye as I looked at it.

A salvage team radioed us to ask permission to salvage the boat.

'Of course,' I said, looking out of the porthole to where we could still see the stern sticking up like a tombstone.

'You bloody idiot!' Chay snapped at me. 'You never want to see that boat again. Just a lot of waterlogged electronics which will never work again. You'll never get a penny from the insurers.'

'On second thoughts,' I said, 'perhaps I can call you back?'

'Right you are,' they said.

I put down the phone and Chay and I looked across the sea at *Virgin Challenger*. As we did so, it silently plunged below the surface.

It took a month for the ringing in my ears to stop. I was beginning to think I had permanent brain damage. However, winning the Blue Riband and the Hales Trophy became unfinished business. We were determined to succeed. Chay and I felt that, after what had happened to *Challenger*, we should build a single-hulled boat rather than a catamaran, because it would be stronger. Since Ted Toleman specialised in catamarans, he refused to change the design and dropped out. We formed a new team with three key members of Ted Toleman's original crew, Chris Witty, Steve Ridgway, and Chris Moss, who asked me whether they could come to work for Virgin. Chay Blyth stayed with the project as the presiding sailing expert, and together we designed a new boat.

On 15 May 1986, *Virgin Atlantic Challenger II* was launched by Princess Michael of Kent. The boat was 75-feet long, with a single hull. We were confident that she could cope with the heavy seas much better than her predecessor. But as we sailed her around the south coast on her maiden voyage towards Salcombe, we cannoned off a vast wave which almost spun the boat over. Everyone was hurled across the deck and one of our crew, Pete Downie, broke his leg. The agony on his face was more to do with the realisation that he wouldn't be with us than the pain from his leg. Chay fractured a toe and Steve was almost swept overboard. We arrived at Salcombe like a hospital boat.

We shipped the boat over to New York, and once again waited for good weather. When we left New York Harbour on a bright June morning in 1986 and headed up towards Nova Scotia, we braced ourselves once more for the pounding. It was not as bad as the first time, and the trip up the east seaboard of America was much faster than we hoped. We sped along and after eighteen hours met the first refuelling ship off the coast of Newfoundland.

We refuelled and headed off into the gathering darkness. The summer night was short, and we were travelling northeast, which made it shorter still, so we had just five hours of darkness to cope with. We relied on the radar and trying to squint ahead through the night-vision goggles, but still had no idea what was ahead. Motoring at that speed through the night was like driving blindfold, and we narrowly missed a surfacing whale.

By the second day the adrenaline rush which had kept us going had worn off. It was now just horrible, relentless banging. Each wave smashed us up and down, up and down, until we could no longer grin and bear it: we had to just clench our teeth and bear it.

As we approached *RV2*, the refuelling boat, off the coast of Canada, we also had to keep an intense lookout for icebergs. Large icebergs show up on the radar and can be avoided; it is the 'small' ones, tiny blips above the surface which actually weigh 100 tons and could smash the hull, that are dangerous. Indeed, even an iceberg the size of a beanbag could seriously damage the hull. The difficulty was that, as hour after hour passed and we were deafened by the roar of the engines, it was impossible to keep our concentration going. We still had over 2,000 miles to travel. Each minute of every hour was a battering. This was where the strength of the team came through: we all rallied round to help each other get through it.

As we waved goodbye and revved up the engines to speed away from the second refuelling boat, our engines coughed, choked, and conked out. Eckie Rastig, our new engineer, went below decks to investigate. He came back up horrified: the fuel filters were full of water. This was a disaster. He took a dipstick sample and reckoned that for every 12 tonnes of fuel taken on board we had also taken on about 4 tonnes of water. It was a complete mystery as to how the water had got in with the fuel, but we had no time to worry about that. Maybe it was the Esso directors' revenge for my blunder over BP! The diesel and the water had emulsified together, which meant it was impossible to split the water off from the diesel: we had to drain the entire four fuel tanks and start again. The Esso boat came back alongside and we filled up again, taking another precious three hours.

We restarted the engines but they conked out again.

It was now 11p.m. and we had spent seven hours bobbing up and down next to the refuelling boat in the middle of the freezing ocean. The race was slipping away. The swell grew progressively worse.

'The storm's catching up with us,' Chay said. 'This isn't funny.'

The storm, which was following the wonderful weather we had enjoyed on the first day, was not an abrupt, fierce storm, but just a big spell of filthy weather, our worst nightmare. Soon the boat was riding waves which had grown to 50 feet. We hardly dared stand on deck because one moment we were well beneath the vast Esso ship so that it looked as if it must topple over on top of us; the next moment we were thrown up way above it and we couldn't believe that we wouldn't skate down the edge of the wave and crash into it. By now the suffocating petrol fumes made us all sick. Everyone was retching and puking and doubled up in pain. Our survival suits were soaked with seawater and flecked with vomit; our faces were white and green; our hair was frozen.

'It's not worth going on,' Chay shouted in my ear. 'We've all spoken and we're all gutted. It's over. I'm sorry, Richard.'

I knew that if we failed on this attempt there would be no third time. We had to go for it. I had to persuade them.

'Let's just try to get the engines going and see how far we can get,' I said. 'Come on. We've got to make a stab at this.'

There was an engine specialist called Steve Lawes on board the Esso boat whom I knew. I asked him to come aboard and help us. They set up their winch and swung him out over the side. With the two boats swinging up and down on the giant waves, it was astonishingly brave

223

of him to try. With perfect timing they dropped him on our deck and he snapped off the belt before he could be swept back into the air as another wave drove us down and the Esso boat up. Steve went down to join Eckie in the engine room. There was a tiny space beside the engines, and together they drained the fuel tanks and took on more fuel. I went down to see them, but there was no room for anyone else.

I didn't have to beg Steve to stay with us.

'I'll stay just for the pleasure of the ride,' he said, oil stains already covering his face.

I suddenly felt that we had a chance.

'There's still water in the fuel,' Eckie said. 'But we can filter it out as we go. We're going to have to do it every few hours.'

I hauled myself back upstairs and found Chay of all people throwing up over the side. I pulled him by the shoulder.

'Steve's going to stay,' I shouted in his ear. 'We can go on.'

'It's over, Richard,' Chay shouted at me. 'It's fucking well over. This boat's knackered.'

'We've got to go on,' I yelled.

For a moment we stood there, eyeball to eyeball, clutching on to each other like two old drunks. We had flecks of vomit in our beards; our eyes were red and bloodshot from the salt and the fumes; our faces were drained of colour; and our hands were raw and bleeding. With another lurch of the sea, we staggered against each other, utterly exhausted. We hated this boat; we hated this trip; we hated the sea; we hated the weather; and – right now – we certainly hated each other.

'We've got to go on and do it,' I repeated like a madman. 'We've just got to do it. It's the only way. What are you suggesting? That we get towed home?'

'God, you're worse than me,' Chay said. 'All right. We'll give it one last shot.'

I hugged him and we both fell against the railings.

'Right!' Chay yelled to the crew. 'We're casting off.'

We all summoned up our strength again and went into action. We cast off from the refuelling boat and, with fine-tuning from Eckie and Steve, the engines roared back into life. They were coughing and spluttering and liable to cut out, but at least they worked and we didn't have to get out the oars. We waved up at the Esso boat, and headed off into a grey light. We felt better now that we were away from the oil fumes, but we were all exhausted. I felt as if my stomach had been punched over and over again by a prize fighter. Everyone was now in his own world, fighting to get through each hour. I just kept repeating to myself that we had to get on. As well as fighting the weather and the fuel, we were all immersed in fighting our own will not to collapse.

Every four hours the fuel filters were so clogged up that they needed replacing. We stopped the engines; Steve and Eckie replaced the filters, and on we went. As hour by hour passed, it became clear that we were not going to have enough filters to make the last refuelling stop. The filters would run out and the engines would break down. We would be marooned at sea. I was in touch with a passing Nimrod (as one is!) who had taken us under its wing. These planes spend hour after hour flying over the Atlantic searching for submarines, and we were a welcome diversion. The pilot suggested that another Nimrod could come out and drop a load of filters, but they would need to get clearance from the top. I radioed Tim Powell, who was running the control centre from the Oxford Street Megastore.

'Tim, we need help. We need some fuel filters

dropped. The Nimrod has offered to do it, but they need to get clearance – right from the top.'

Within an hour, Tim had spoken to the right people at Downing Street, and an RAF Nimrod had picked up the filters from Southampton and was flying to meet us.

We didn't hear the plane coming. It just swooped low overhead, coming straight out of the grey cloud behind us. It was huge, and although there was no sun the plane seemed to drain all the light and cast us in shadow. The Nimrod roared over us, with a rumble which shook the boat, and dropped a small drum attached to a buoy in our path. We all danced and whooped with joy. Chay cut back the engines and aimed for the little red marker. Steve picked it up with a long hook, and we hauled it on board: it was a steel drum packed with filters. On top of the filters were some chocolate bars and a little handwritten note which said: 'Good luck!'

We radioed up to the pilot and thanked him.

'I've got a TV crew on board,' he said. 'The whole country's on the edge of their seat. God speed.'

We reached the third Esso ship and, with another set of full tanks and some Irish stew for us, our first hot meal in two days, we approached the last leg of the crossing with rising determination. We calculated that we had to travel at an average speed of 39 or 40 knots for the final twelve hours if we were to break the record. With our engines in the state they were, it was going to be extremely close. We battled through more heavy weather, unable to go faster than 30 knots for three hours, then the sun came out and the sea calmed. Steve and Eckie replaced the filters for the last time, and we opened the throttles and went flat out across the sea, hurtling over the waves towards the Scilly Isles.

When we passed the point where we had sunk on the

previous attempt we all cheered and suddenly knew that we could do it. Five miles out from the Scillies, we were met by a posse of helicopters and then hundreds of boats of all kinds who welcomed us home. We zoomed past Bishop Rock Lighthouse at 7.30p.m. Eckie and Steve staggered up from the engine room. They were the heroes who had endured three days of pounding in a hot cramped engine room, standing ankle deep in oil while they fought to keep the engines going. Dag Pike switched off his navigational system and we all threw our arms round each other. We had done it. Our total journey had lasted 3 days, 8 hours and 31 minutes: in a voyage of over 3,000 miles, we had beaten the Blue Riband record by a mere 2 hours and 9 minutes.

16 The world's biggest balloon
1986–1987

'A FTER THE BIG BANG, how about a little pop?'
By 1986 everyone was heading for the City.
Everyone who had bought shares in British
Telecom had doubled their money.

I will never forget going into the City to see the lines
of people queuing up to buy Virgin shares. We had
already had over 70,000 postal applicants to buy Virgin
shares, but these people had left it until the last day, 13
November 1986. I walked up and down the queue
thanking people for their confidence, and a number of
their replies stuck in my mind:

'We're not going on holiday this year; we're putting
our savings into Virgin.'

'Go on, Richard, prove us right.'

'We're banking on you, Richard.'

At one point I noticed that the press photographers
were taking pictures of my feet. I couldn't understand
it. Then I looked down and noticed with a shock that,
in the rush to get dressed, I had put on shoes that didn't
match.

The flotation of Virgin attracted more applications
from the public than any other stock-market debut
issue, apart from the massive government privatisations. Over 100,000 private individuals applied for our
shares, and the Post Office drafted in twenty extra staff
to cope with the mail sacks. That day we heard that The
Human League had gone to number one in America.

Beneath our euphoria, we were worried to hear that only a small number of City institutions had applied for shares. It was the first sign of the difficulty we were going to have in our dealings with the City.

By 1986 Virgin had become one of Britain's largest private companies, with some 4,000 employees. For the year ended July 1986, Virgin had sales of £189 million, compared with £119 million for the previous year, an increase of around 60 per cent. Our pre-tax profits were £19 million, up from £15 million. Although we were a large company, we had very little flexibility to expand: all we could do was either use up the cash we had earned, or ask our bankers for a bigger overdraft. I watched a number of other private companies sell their shares on the stock market: Body Shop, TSB, Sock Shop, Our Price, Reuters, Atlantic Computers ... There was practically a new company every week, and the stock exchange had to set up a queuing system so that, in between the massive privatisations of British Telecom, British Airways and BP, there was an orderly procession.

When we arrived back from the Atlantic crossing, the entire country seemed to have enjoyed the challenge. Mrs Thatcher expressed an interest in seeing the boat, and I offered her a ride up the River Thames. We managed to win approval to break the five-mile-an-hour speed limit on the Thames, and Tower Bridge opened her gates as *Atlantic Challenger* came whizzing through. We picked up Mrs Thatcher and, together with Bob Geldof and Sting, we did a lap of honour up to the Houses of Parliament and back, as other boats on the river blared their horns and the fire brigade pumped great plumes of water into the air in salute. Mrs Thatcher, the 'Iron Lady', stood on the deck beside me and faced into the keen wind.

'I must admit,' she said, as we accelerated up the river, 'I do enjoy going fast. I love powerful boats.'

I looked across at her. She was indeed enjoying herself. Her profile cut through the wind like a bowsprit, and not a single strand of hair had blown out of place.

Although we had raised £30 million from the stock-market flotation, I soon began to feel that we had made the wrong decision. A few weeks after our flotation in November, our investment banker at Morgan Grenfell, Roger Seelig, was investigated by the Department of Trade and Industry over his role in Guinness's takeover of Distillers, which he had orchestrated in January. Roger resigned from Morgan Grenfell and, although the case against him was eventually abandoned, his career was ruined. Without being able to use Roger as a touchstone, I began to lose faith in the City and the onerous demands they made of us.

Firstly, the City had insisted that Virgin appoint some nonexecutive directors. Sir Phil Harris was recommended. He was a self-made man who had made a fortune from selling carpets. We also appointed Cob Stenham, who had been finance director of Unilever and was a well-respected banker. I found it difficult to comply with all the formality the City insisted we adopt. I was used to chatting with Simon and Ken about which bands to sign, and then letting them get on with it. Virgin board meetings had always been highly informal affairs. We met on *Duende*, or at my house in Oxford Gardens, or while we were on a weekend together. I found our business was not one that could be boxed into a rigid timetable of meetings. We had to make decisions quickly, off the cuff: if we had to wait four weeks for the next board meeting before authorising Simon to sign UB40, then we would probably lose them altogether.

I also had a number of disagreements with Don, notably about dividends. I was extremely reluctant to follow British tradition and pay out a large dividend. I preferred the American or Japanese tradition whereby a company concentrates on reinvesting its profits to build itself and increase share value. To me, a large dividend meant a loss of cash which would be better employed within Virgin than by paying it away. It seemed to me that our outside shareholders had entrusted their money to Virgin in order for us to make it grow, not for us to hand 5 per cent of it back on a plate – which would be taxed as income and so immediately lose 40 per cent of its value.

This may sound like a petty argument, but it illustrates the general loss of control I experienced. Most people think that 50 per cent of a public company is the key to controlling it. While this is true in theory, to a large extent you lose control just by having to appoint nonexecutive directors and generally giving up your time to satisfy the City. Previously, I had always felt confident about any decision we made, but now Virgin was a publicly quoted company, I began to lose faith in myself. I felt uneasy about making the rapid decisions I have always made, and wondered whether every decision should be formally ratified and minuted at a board meeting. In many ways 1987, our year of being a public company, was Virgin's least creative. We spent at least 50 per cent of our time heading off to the City to explain what we were doing to fund managers, financial advisers and City PR firms, rather than just getting on and doing it.

I also felt very responsible to the people who had invested in Virgin shares. Phil Collins, Mike Oldfield and Bryan Ferry had bought shares; Peter and Ceris, my neighbours and close friends at Mill End, had invested some of their life-savings in Virgin; and my family, my cousins, and many people who had come across me in various walks of life, had all bought shares. Trevor Abbott had borrowed £250,000 from me to buy Virgin shares, and, although he knew the figures even better than I, I still felt responsible in case the shares fell in value.

I would not have minded if the City analysts had been correct in their assessment that Virgin was doing badly, or that the management was incompetent. What began to infuriate me was that – no matter how often Simon, Ken or I tried to explain that over 30 per cent of our income came from royalties from the back catalogue, and even if we failed to release another record we would still enjoy a stream of earnings; or that 40 per cent of our earnings in France came from French singers rather than Boy George or Phil Collins, giving us a steady local income – the City continually oversimplified how Virgin worked. The analysts still assumed that Virgin was wholly dependent upon me and Boy George. Simon and Ken started taking recordings to the City analysts' meetings and playing them UB40, The Human League and Simple Minds, but they remained unimpressed. Virgin shares, which had started trading at 140 pence, soon slipped down to 120 pence. The faith which the people in the queue had placed in me, and the faith which the Virgin artists and staff placed in me by spending their own money on buying Virgin shares, began to overwhelm me.

As 1987 progressed, the Virgin share price recovered to around 140 pence but never took off. We began to use the money we had raised from the flotation to make two investments: the first was to establish a proper Virgin subsidiary in America; the second was to start stalking Thorn EMI with a view to launching a takeover bid for the company. Virgin Records America Inc. was not a cheap investment. We had learnt the hard way before and this time we invested heavily. During 1987 we managed to release four top-twenty singles and one gold album in America. Although Virgin America lost us money in 1987, it was a long-term investment and we felt sure that eventually we would make far more money from having our own record company there than from licensing our best artists to American companies.

The second challenge, stalking Thorn EMI, had to be done with care. We felt that the EMI record label was managed in a rather sleepy way and that their incredible back catalogue, which included The Beatles, could be run far more profitably. The Thorn EMI Group as a whole was valued at around £750 million, three times the size of Virgin. Eventually I thought that the best thing to do was go round and have a chat with Sir Colin Southgate, the managing director of Thorn EMI, and ask him in a friendly way whether he would like to sell us EMI Music.

'Shall we come along?' Simon and Ken asked.

'It might be a bit overbearing,' I said. 'I'll slip in and see him face to face, and then if he's keen we can all meet him.'

I called Sir Colin and arranged a meeting at his office in Manchester Square. I was shown up to the top floor of the office building, and ushered into a room. It fell silent. I was confronted by at least twenty unsmiling faces. They lined one side of the table, their pinstriped suits shoulder to shoulder, forming an unbreachable wall. Sir Colin shook my hand and peered over my shoulder to see whether there was anyone else.

'It's just me,' I said. 'Where shall I sit?'

One side of the long, gleaming mahogany table was empty. There were ten or fifteen memo pads and sharpened pencils laid out on it. I sat down and looked across at the sea of faces.

'Well, let me introduce you,' Sir Colin began. He rattled off the names of bankers, lawyers, accountants and management consultants.

'I'm Richard Branson,' I introduced myself with a nervous laugh. 'And the reason I'm here is that I just wondered whether you would like to ... might like to ...' I paused. The necks opposite all craned towards me. 'Might like to sell your EMI subsidiary,' I said. 'It seems to me that Thorn EMI is such a big group and that EMI Music might not be your top priority. You have so much else going on. That's all.'

There was a hushed silence.

'We're quite happy with EMI,' Sir Colin said. 'We are taking all steps to run it as a leading member of the Thorn EMI Group.'

'Oh well,' I said. 'I thought it was worth a try.'

And with that I stood up and left the room.

I went straight round to see Simon and Ken at Vernon Yard.

'They're serious,' I said. 'They're on an emergency footing. They thought I was going to bid for them. They practically had their bayonets fixed. If Sir Colin's so worried that he brought all his heavies along, then they clearly are vulnerable and I think we should have a crack at them.'

Simon and Ken agreed with me. Trevor arranged for us to go and see Samuel Montagu, another investment bank. Samuel Montagu introduced us to Mountleigh, a property group, and suggested that we could make a joint bid. Since Sir Colin would not sell EMI separately to us, we could bid for the whole Group with

Mountleigh and then split it up: in a nutshell, Mountleigh would take the national chain of television-rental shops and we would take EMI Music.

We knew that our first year's profits as a public company were on course to more than double, at over £30 million (despite the cost of setting up in the States), and so we planned to release these results in October at the same time as announcing our bid for Thorn EMI.

During the course of the summer, Trevor arranged a £100 million loan with the Bank of Nova Scotia and we slowly began buying shares in Thorn EMI, paying about £7 a share as we built up a stake which we could use as a launch pad for the bid. As the stock market soared higher through the summer months and some rumours began to circulate that Thorn EMI was vulnerable to a bid, I began to worry that if we left it until October we might be too late. There was not much I could do about it, because I was determined to set off on a challenge which many people thought would be the end of me. A challenge as daunting and as daring as anything in the world of business. Per Lindstrand and I were planning to fly across the Atlantic Ocean in a hot-air balloon. Until I returned safe and sound, nobody was going to take the idea of Virgin bidding for Thorn EMI too seriously.

It all dated from a telephone call I had received on my first day back at the office after the *Atlantic Challenger* crossing.

'It's someone called Per Lindstrand,' Penni said. 'He says that he's got an incredible proposal.'

I picked up the phone.

'If you thought that crossing the Atlantic by boat was impressive,' said a stilted, Swedish voice, 'think again. I am planning to build the world's largest hot-air balloon, and I'm planning to fly it in the jet stream at 30,000 feet. I believe that it can cross the Atlantic.'

I had vaguely heard of Per Lindstrand. I knew that he was a world expert at ballooning and held several records, including one for reaching the highest altitude. Per explained to me that nobody had flown a hot-air balloon further than 600 miles, and nobody had been able to keep a hot-air balloon up in the air for longer than 27 hours. In order to cross the Atlantic, a balloon would have to fly more than 3,000 miles, five times further than anyone had ever managed before, and spend three times longer up in the air.

A balloon filled with helium, like the old zeppelins, can stay in the air for several days. A hot-air balloon relies on the hot air within the envelope rising above the surrounding cold air and taking the balloon with it. But the loss of heat through the balloon's envelope is rapid, and, in order to heat the air, balloonists burn propane. Until Per's proposed flight, hot-air balloons had been hampered by the impossible weight of fuel needed to keep them afloat.

Per thought that we could break the flight record by putting three theories into practice. The first one was to take the balloon up to an altitude of around 30,000 feet and fly along in the fast winds, the jet streams, which move along at speeds of up to 200 miles an hour. This had previously been considered impossible as their power and turbulence could shred any balloon. The second was to use solar power to heat the balloon's air during the day and thus save fuel. This had never been attempted. The third was that, since the balloon would be flying at 30,000 feet, the pilots would be in a pressurised capsule rather than the traditional wicker basket.

As I studied Per's proposal, I realised with amazement that this vast balloon, a huge ungainly thing which could swallow the Royal Albert Hall without showing a bulge, was actually intended to cross the Atlantic Ocean in far less time than our *Atlantic Challenger* boat with its 4,000-horsepower engine. Per reckoned on a flying time of under two days, with an average speed of 90 knots compared with the boat's speed of just under 40 knots. It would be rather like driving along in the fast lane of the motorway only to be overtaken by the Royal Albert Hall travelling twice as fast.

After wrestling with some of the science and the academic calculations about inertia and wind speeds, I asked Per to come and see me. When we met, I put my hand on the pile of theoretical calculations.

'I'll never understand all the science and theory,' I said, 'but I'll come with you if you answer me this one question.'

'Of course,' Per said, stiffening his back in readiness for some incredibly challenging question.

'Do you have any children?'

'Yes, I've got two.'

'Right, then.' I stood up and shook his hand. 'I'll come. But I'd better learn how to fly one of these things first.'

It was only later that I learnt that seven people had already tried to be the first to cross the Atlantic and that five of them had perished.

Per took me for a week's crash course on ballooning in Spain. I discovered that ballooning is one of the most exhilarating things I had ever done. The combination of soaring up over the world, the silence when the burners are off, the sensation of floating, and the breathtaking panoramic views all immediately seduced me. After a week of being shouted at by Robin Batchelor, my instructor, who looked like my double, I had my balloon licence. I was ready.

As the prevailing jet stream flows from west to east, we found a launch site in Maine, close to Boston, about a hundred miles inland to avoid the effect of sea breezes. Per reckoned that by the time we crossed the coast we should be up in the jet stream and above the local weather. Our two key mentors were Tom Barrow, who headed the engineering team, and Bob Rice, an expert meteorologist. Both men were clearly such authorities that I unreservedly put my trust in them. The jet stream parts over the Atlantic, with one branch heading up to the Arctic and another branch swerving down to the Azores and back out to the middle of the ocean. Bob Rice told us that getting our route right was like 'rolling a ball bearing between two magnets'. In the event of running out of fuel or icing up, we would have to ditch the balloon at sea.

'There are flotation collars round the capsule which will keep it buoyant,' Tom Barrow said.

'What if they don't work?' I asked.

'You'll get your money back,' he said. 'Or rather, we'll get the money back on your behalf.'

At our final briefing with Tom at Sugarloaf Mountain, Maine, the day before the balloon went up, he went through the last emergency drills: 'Landing this thing is going to be like freewheeling a Sherman tank without any brakes. It's going to be a crash.'

His last warning was the most telling: 'Now, even though we're here, I can still abort this project if I think it's too dangerous or if you develop health problems.'

'Does that include mental-health problems?' I joked.

'No,' Tom said. 'That's a prerequisite for doing this flight. If you're not completely nuts and scared to death, then you shouldn't be on board in the first place.'

I was certainly scared to death.

17 'I was almost certainly going to die.'

1987–1988

PER AND I TOOK sleeping pills the evening before the launch. When we were woken up at 2a.m. it was pitch-dark, but as we were driven to the launch site we saw the vast balloon lit up by floodlights and towering over the trees. It looked astonishing: the sides were silver and the dome was black. It was monumental. The balloon was fully inflated and straining at the anchors. We were worried that a wind might strike up and tip it over, so we climbed into the capsule and the ground crew set about the final checks.

Inside the capsule, we were unaware of the accident which actually catapulted us upward. A cable became caught round two of the propane tanks and as the balloon strained up and down it pulled them off. Without their weight, the balloon shot up, still trailing a couple of cables carrying sandbags. As we gained height and headed over the Maine forest towards the sea, Per climbed out of the capsule and cut the last two cables. We made rapid progress towards the glowing dawn, soaring along in the jet stream at 85 knots – just under 100 miles an hour. After ten hours we had flown over 900 miles and had easily broken the long-distance record for a hot-air balloon. Over the radio Bob Rice told us to keep at 27,000 feet whatever happened, since that was where the fast winds were.

That first night we hit a storm and came down to calmer weather, but it was snowing and we immediately lost the speed of the jet stream.

'We need to get back up there,' Per said. He fired the burners and we rose again to meet the bad weather. The balloon was buffeted hard by the storm and the capsule was tossed to and fro, but just when we wondered whether we should head back down we shot out into clear weather and reached a speed of 140 knots – over 160 miles an hour. The next morning the Virgin 747, *Maiden Voyager*, arrived and flew in a figure of eight round us. My mother's voice came crackling over the radio:

'Faster, Richard, faster! We'll race you.'

'I'm doing my best, Mum. Please thank the crew and passengers for going out of their way to greet us,' I said.

In fact, we sped along and crossed the coast of Ireland at 2.30 that afternoon, Friday 3 July. It was a dream crossing compared with the boat. We had been in the air for just 29 hours.

The incredible speed of our flight gave us an unexpected problem: we still had three full tanks of fuel attached to the capsule, and they could well explode on landing. We decided to swoop down very low and drop off the fuel tanks in an empty field, and then come down a second time for a controlled landing. Per stopped burning propane and brought the balloon down low so that we could see where we could safely jettison the extra fuel tanks. As we came down, the wind suddenly swirled around us, much harder than we expected. The ground rushed up to meet us. Travelling at a speed of almost 30 knots, 35 miles an hour, our groundspeed was not so much the problem as our sudden plunge downward. We hit the ground and bounced along a field. All our fuel tanks were torn off by the impact, along with our radio aerials. Without the weight of the tanks, we hurtled back upward. I didn't see it, but we narrowly missed a house and an electricity pylon. We had hit the ground in Limavady, a tiny Irish village.

With no fuel tanks we were utterly out of control. Unless we could heat the air, once this rise topped out we would fall rapidly, gathering speed like someone in an unopened parachute. We had one small reserve fuel tank inside the capsule with us, and Per quickly connected it to the burners.

'It's tangled,' Per said. 'The cables are tangled.'

The balloon was rising like a rocket. The top of the dome was forced down by the pressure, and the cable that hung down the middle of the balloon snagged on something and started spinning us round in a knot. The whole balloon was twisting itself into a corkscrew, closing the mouth so that there was no chance of heating the hot air inside. As we began to drift downward, I opened the capsule hatch and climbed out on top. I took my knife and hacked away at the twisted cable.

'Quick!' Per shouted up at me. 'We're falling fast.'

I finally managed to cut the cable, and the balloon whipped round. The dome straightened out, and the hole in the bottom of the envelope was open.

'Get in!' Per yelled.

As I dropped down through the hatch, he fired the burners full blast. We were within 300 feet of the ground, but the burst of heat steadied our descent and we rose again. I tried some switches, but there was no power in the capsule.

'Damn,' I said. 'No lights, no radio, no fuel gauge. Only the altimeter's working.'

'Let's try coming down on the beach,' Per said. 'We can't risk anywhere inland.'

I put on my life jacket and parachute, and attached the life raft to my belt. We saw the coastline approaching and Per vented hot air from the top of the balloon to reduce our height. But once again the ground wind was considerably stronger then we expected and it swept us out to sea. We were heading northeast, and without the radio or electricity in the capsule we were more than ever at the mercy of the wind.

'Hold tight,' Per said.

He let out more air, alternating this with burning propane to try to reduce the speed of our descent through the thick grey cloud. As we finally came out of the fog, I saw the foaming sea rising up to meet us. We'd missed the beach. We were going far too fast. I realised the truth of Tom Barrow's words: it was like trying to stop a Sherman tank without brakes. With horror, I watched the ocean rushing towards us.

We hit the sea, crashing me into Per. We were tilted at a crazy angle, unable to stand upright. The balloon started to drag us across the surface of the ocean. We were being bounced from wave to wave.

'The bolts!' Per shouted.

He grabbed hold of the chair and hauled himself upward. I tried to help push him to his feet, but the capsule was smashing up and down and each time I reached up I was knocked back. I watched Per's hand stretch out, grasp the red lever and pull it down. This was supposed to fire the explosive bolts, which would sever the cables connecting the capsule to the balloon. In theory the balloon would then sail away and crumple into the sea, leaving the capsule to float on the water.

But nothing happened. Per yanked the lever up and down but the bolts did not fire.

'Jesus Christ!' Per yelled. 'The bolts are dead.'

The balloon was now bouncing us across the Irish Sea like a monstrous beachball. I was knocked sideways again and hit the upturned edge of the flight deck.

'Get out!' Per shouted at me. 'Richard, we've got to get out.'

Per braced himself against the hatch, wrenched down the levers and pushed it open. The balloon slowed for a moment as the capsule dug into the water, and Per heaved himself up and climbed through the hatch. As I saw Per's backside squeeze through the hatch and disappear from view, I lunged after him and followed him up the rungs. I noticed that Per was still wearing his parachute. We clutched at the steel hawsers and tried to balance on the tilting capsule.

'Where's your life jacket?' I shouted.

Per didn't seem to hear me. The wind and the roar of the sea blew my words straight back into my face. The balloon was lurching at an angle, one side of it ploughing through the grey sea. It showed no signs of slowing down. Behind us we left a foaming white wake. Then a gust of wind caught us and the balloon lifted off the surface.

Per threw himself off the top of the capsule into the cold black water. The drop seemed at least 100 feet. I was sure that he'd killed himself.

I hesitated. Then I realised with horror that I was too late. Without Per's weight, the huge balloon soared up. I almost fell backward over the edge of the capsule as it swung underneath the balloon like a pendulum. I ducked down, grabbed hold of the railing and watched the grey sea fall away beneath me. I was rising rapidly, and I couldn't see Per. Now that the balloon was sailing with the wind and no longer dragging the capsule through the water, it was much quieter. I watched with mounting dread as I soared upward into thick cloud and lost sight of everything.

I was now by myself, flying in the biggest balloon ever built, and heading towards Scotland. The wind was freezing cold; the sea below me was icy; and I was in thick fog. I had only the tiny emergency fuel tank left.

I climbed back into the capsule. It was now the right way up and I felt reassured to see the screens and controls the way they had been as we crossed the Atlantic. I ran through the options: I could parachute into the sea, where nobody would be likely to find me and I could drown; or I could sail up into the darkening sky and try a night landing, should I be lucky enough to reach land. I picked up the microphone, but the radio was still dead. I had no contact with the outside world.

The altimeter ticked down so I instinctively fired the propane. To my delight, the flame surged up inside the balloon and steadied it. I had assumed that the seawater had killed the burners. I gave a good long blast and the balloon started rising again. I was having difficulty breathing so I put on an oxygen mask. I checked the altimeter: 12,000 feet. Thick white cloud pressed all around me. I had no sense of where I was. All I knew was that the grey foaming sea was waiting for me below. Before Per had ditched the balloon, he had told me that it was unlikely we had enough fuel to reach Scotland before dark. The remaining spare fuel tank gave me only about an hour's worth of flying. Sooner or later I would have to face the Irish Sea again.

I wondered about the explosive bolts. Perhaps they had cut through one, two, three or even four of the five key cables that held the capsule to the balloon. Perhaps even now that last cable was straining and fraying under the weight and might give way. If so, the capsule would plunge straight down into the sea and I would be killed on impact. It was this fear which had prompted Per to jump. The capsule hatch was still open and I gave the propane one good long burn before climbing out once more on to the top of the capsule to look at the cables. It was now completely quiet. I could not see all the cables without leaning out over the capsule railings. Standing amid the swirling white cloud, I felt an overwhelming sense of loneliness. The cables looked intact so I squeezed back inside the hatch.

Whatever I did in the next ten minutes would lead to my death or survival. I was on my own. We had broken the record but I was almost certainly going to die. Per, with no survival suit, was either dead or trying to swim on. I had to get somebody to find him. I had to survive. I cleared my mind and concentrated on the options in front of me. I hadn't slept for over 24 hours and my mind felt fuzzy. I decided to take the balloon up high enough so I could parachute off the capsule. I blasted the burners and then found my notebook and scrawled across the open page, 'Joan, Holly, Sam, I love you.' I waited until the altimeter showed 8,000 feet and then climbed outside.

I was alone in the cloud. I crouched by the railings and looked down. I was still wheeling through the possibilities. If I jumped, I would be likely to have only two minutes to live. If I managed to open my parachute, I would still end up in the sea, where I would probably drown. I felt for the parachute release tag, and wondered whether it was the right one. Perhaps due to my dyslexia, I have a mental block about which is right and which is left, especially with parachutes. The last time I had free-fallen I pulled the wrong release tag and jettisoned my parachute. At the time I had several skydivers around me, so they activated my reserve parachute. But now I was by myself at 8,000 feet. I slapped myself hard across the face to concentrate. There had to be a better way.

'Give yourself more time,' I said out loud. 'Come on.'

As I crouched on top of the capsule, I looked up at

the vast balloon above me. The realisation dawned that I was standing beneath the world's largest parachute. If I could bring the balloon down, then perhaps I could jump off into the sea at the last moment before we crashed. I now knew I had enough fuel for another thirty minutes. It must be better to live for thirty minutes than jump off with my parachute and perhaps live for only two minutes.

'While I'm alive I can still do something,' I said. 'Something must turn up.'

I climbed back inside and took off my parachute. I made up my mind. I would do anything for those extra minutes. I grabbed some chocolate, zipped it into my jacket pocket, and checked that my torch was still there.

Peering out of the capsule into the fog below me, I tried to work out when I should stop burning, when I should open the vent, and when I should leave the controls and climb out on top of the capsule for my final jump. I knew that I had to judge the last burn exactly so that the balloon would hit the sea as slowly as possible. Despite losing all our fuel tanks, the balloon was still carrying a weight of around three tonnes.

As I came out through the bottom of the clouds, I saw the grey sea below me. I also saw an RAF helicopter. I gave a last burn on the propane to slow my descent, and then left the balloon to come down of its own accord. I grabbed a red rag and climbed out through the hatch. I squatted on the top of the capsule and waved the rag at the helicopter pilot. He waved back rather casually, seemingly oblivious to my panic.

I peered over the edge and saw the sea coming up. I shuffled around the capsule trying to work out where the wind was coming from. It was difficult to be sure since it seemed to be gusting from all directions. I finally chose the upwind side and looked down. I was fifty feet away, the height of a house, and the sea was racing up to hit me. I checked my life jacket and held on to the railing. Without my weight, I hoped the balloon would rise up again rather than crashing on top of me. I waited until I was just above the sea before pulling my life-jacket ripcord and hurling myself away from the capsule.

The sea was icy. I spun deep into it and felt my scalp freeze with the water. Then the life jacket bobbed me straight back up to the surface. It was heaven: I was alive. I turned and watched the balloon. Without my weight, it quietly soared back up through the cloud like a magnificent alien spaceship, vanishing from sight.

The helicopter flew over me and lowered a sling. I sat inside it like a swing, but each time it tried to lift me it dunked me back in the water. I couldn't understand what was wrong, and I was too weak to hold on much longer. Eventually it winched me up and someone reached out and pulled me inside.

'You should have put the sling under your arms,' said a Scottish voice.

'Where's Per?' I asked. 'Have you picked up Per yet?'

'Isn't he in the balloon?' the RAF man asked.

'Haven't you got him? He's in the water. He's been there ever since I took off again. About forty minutes ago.'

The pilot pulled a face. He spoke to someone on the radio, but it was difficult to make out what was said. The helicopter spun on its axis and headed off.

'We're taking you to our boat,' the pilot said.

'I want to look for Per,' I said. 'I'm fine.'

If he had survived the fall, Per would still be swimming – or, more likely, drowning – in the Irish Sea. The light was fading and, from the air, only his head would be visible. It was like looking for a football – a grey football in a grey stormy sea. The pilot took no notice of my arguments. Within two minutes we had landed on a ship and I was pulled on board. Without pausing for breath, the pilot took off immediately and headed back over the sea. I was marched across the deck and put into a hot bath. Then I went up to the bridge to see how the search was going. For ten minutes, fifteen minutes, twenty minutes, there was nothing. Then the radio crackled.

'We've spotted him,' the pilot said. 'And he's still swimming. He's alive.'

Per's struggles weren't over. The winch that had pulled me up was now jammed, and so they had to attract a dinghy to rescue him. By the time the dinghy arrived, Per was almost dead. He had been in the water for two hours, swimming as vigorously as possible to keep his circulation going, but making no headway against the tide. He had no life vest on, and by the time of his rescue he was completely frozen and exhausted. It was extraordinary that he'd survived, and he later put it down to his experiences as a child, being forced by his father to swim every day in the icy lakes of Sweden.

We met on board the ship, and fell into each other's arms. Per had been stripped naked and wore a survival blanket. His face looked like white marble. He was blue with cold and he couldn't stop his teeth chattering.

For what it was worth, we were the first to cross the Atlantic in a hot-air balloon. More importantly, we were alive. We could not believe that we had both survived.

During the summer of 1987 British Caledonian had been struggling to stay in business. It took out a series of advertisements which showed businessmen singing 'I wish they all could be Caledonian girls' to the tune of The Beach Boys' 'California Girls', and they made a great play about their cabin crew's tartan. But it was no good: British Caledonian were losing money and in August they announced that they had agreed terms for British Airways to take them over.

It seemed to me that this takeover clearly breached the strictures of the Monopolies and Mergers Commission in that it was the largest and the second largest UK carriers forming one company with a market share across the Atlantic of well over 50 per cent. We complained to the Commission that this deal increased BA's share from around 45 per cent to 80 per cent on several transatlantic routes, but the deal was still given the go-ahead in September. BA and B-Cal made great play that B-Cal would be run independently and the B-Cal cabin crew would continue to wear their tartan uniforms and retain their independence. Without B-Cal offering competition, BA could now turn its full attention to mopping up the last tiny British competitor – us – and then concentrate on dominating the Atlantic routes.

As the BA/B-Cal deal went ahead we realised that, as well as the threat that a larger BA would pose to us, this takeover could contain a hidden opportunity for us. We had already used the increased value of our first jumbo, which had risen in worth by $10 million, to leverage up and lease a second plane, which we were flying to Miami. We wanted to expand further. Under the terms of the Bermuda Agreement, which governs international air traffic between America and Britain, there is provision for two British carriers between America and Britain. Our lawyers also discovered that the Japanese intergovernmental agreement contained the provision for two British and two Japanese carriers to Japan. With B-Cal removed from the scene, Virgin Atlantic was now free to push itself forward and apply to fly these routes as the second carrier.

Just as surely as Mike Oldfield and The Sex Pistols had been turning points for Virgin Music, BA's takeover of B-Cal was a turning point for Virgin Atlantic. Prior to their merger, we flew only to Miami and Newark Airport near New York. Now, as the second British long-haul carrier, Virgin Atlantic was entitled to apply for the routes that B-Cal had served and were duplicated by the BA/B-Cal alliance. Top of our list was to fly to JFK, the main airport at New York; Los Angeles; and Tokyo. Further down, we listed three other destinations that B-Cal had operated: San Francisco, Boston and Hong Kong. In 1987 we had just two aircraft. In order to fly to Los Angeles and Tokyo we would have to lease two more aircraft and double the number of our cabin crew.

In the meantime, as well as stalking B-Cal's routes, we were also continuing to stalk Thorn EMI. In the last week of September, Trevor had finalised our £100 million loan with the Bank of Nova Scotia. Despite the stock market rising all summer, we felt that Thorn EMI was still undervalued. With £100 million at our disposal, we started buying on 25 September 1987. Undaunted by the size of EMI, we started putting in buying orders for 100,000 shares at a time. We decided to buy up to 5 per cent of the company before announcing our takeover bid. Even if our bid failed, we knew that in the long run the 5 per cent stake would increase in value.

Immediately rumours started going around the market that Thorn EMI was going to be bid for. Some days we bought 250,000 shares, costing us £1.75 million; other days we spent £5 million. Sometimes we sold shares to keep people guessing. We were stirring up the pot and ensuring that a high number of Thorn EMI shares were traded, which kept the bid rumours going. By the second week of October, our shareholdings had cost £30 million.

During the night of Thursday 15 October 1987 there was a hurricane in Britain. I remember walking from Oxford Gardens to *Duende* and looking across the green streets – they were carpeted with leaves. With so few people able to get to work as a result, the stock market was closed on Friday. But, in America, the selling of shares which had started on Wednesday became a stampede. I watched with amazement through Friday evening as the Dow Jones fell 95 points, then its largest one-day fall. The full significance of Wall Street's crash did not really hit London and the rest of the world until Monday. The Sunday newspapers were full of optimistic noises, and even encouraged their readers to buy as many BP shares as they could. On Monday the Australian market was the first to open and fell by a fifth; Tokyo fell 1,500 points. I thought that this was a great opportunity to buy more Thorn EMI shares, and I called up our broker and asked him to buy £5 million worth of Thorn EMI shares first thing. I wanted to get in there before anyone else and I was worried that someone else might have seized the opportunity. In the event I needn't have bothered. I don't think that anyone could believe their luck that there was a buyer in the market. The broker filled his order within twenty seconds, and asked me if I wanted to buy any more.

'There're tons more of it where that came from,' he said.

Finally sensing a crisis, I paused. Even as I thought about it, the London stock market fell by 100 points, then another 100 points, then another 50 points – a full day's fall of 250 points. That afternoon the Dow Jones crashed by another 500 points. Within a three-day period, the world stock markets lost around a quarter of their value.

Trevor and I got together. For me the immediate

damage was that the price of Virgin had nearly halved in value from 160 pence to 90 pence. Someone worked out that I had lost £41 million in value on my shares in Virgin Group plc. The actual picture was much worse than this. The share price of Thorn EMI had dropped from £7.30 to £5.80, a drop of over 20 per cent, and the value of our shareholding had crashed to £18 million.

The Bank of Nova Scotia was unamused. With the crash in share prices, they asked for an immediate cash payment of £5 million. Oddly enough, I was still rather confident about buying Thorn EMI. I felt unaffected by the slump in Virgin's own share price since I was never going to sell my shares anyway, and I was absolutely certain that the share price was grossly undervalued. And, since I was focusing more on the profits and cash flow from EMI, I began to see the stock-market crash as a golden opportunity to buy the company. But Mountleigh were blown apart by the crash – their share price collapsed by 60 per cent and they were unable to borrow any more money to buy shares in Thorn EMI, or anyone else for that matter.

That week I had a furious argument with the two nonexecutive directors whom we had brought in to represent the outside shareholders' interests when Virgin went public. Sir Phil Harris and Cob Stenham were utterly opposed to continuing the siege of Thorn EMI and announcing a bid when we released our results later in October.

'But it's a unique buying opportunity,' I said. 'It simply cannot be true that Thorn is now worth only two-thirds of its value on Friday. We know the cash we can earn from its back catalogue, so in terms of straight cash to us it's a bargain.'

'There could be tough times ahead,' they warned me. 'This crash has changed the whole picture.'

'But the people who buy records won't stop,' I said. 'Most people don't hold any shares anyway. They'll carry on buying Beatles and Phil Collins albums.'

But everyone disagreed with me. They all wanted to see where the stock market went next. The Thorn EMI share price continued to fall until it reached £5.30. I was sure that, if we could present a united front, then we would be able to raise the money and buy Thorn EMI at a bargain price. I argued that there was no good reason for the crash, and that share prices would recover soon. I told them that there would never again be such a wonderful opportunity. But they all disagreed, and since I could not persuade them I had to let the matter drop. I expected the Virgin share price to jump up when we released our results. And so, when we announced that Virgin's profits for the year ended July 1987 had more than doubled from £14 million to £32 million, we made no reference to Thorn EMI. As it happened, our share price did not move upward. Anything but. It was difficult to understand how Virgin could have floated with a share price of 140 pence the previous year, and then our share price be halved on the back of doubled profits.

The stock-market crash was the final nail in Virgin's coffin as a public company. I knew that Don would be opposed to changing direction, but Trevor and I had a quiet chat about the logistics of going private again, and Trevor set about working out the finances that such a large buy-back would entail.

In July 1988 we announced that the management of Virgin would conduct a management buyout of Virgin Group plc. We could probably have got away with paying less than the original 140 pence per share, but we decided we would offer the same price we had sold the Group for on the stock market, a large premium over the 70 pence at which shares were changing hands just before our announcement. This meant that nobody who had invested in Virgin when it was floated – all those people in the queue outside the bank who had wished me well – would lose money. Our reputation would stay intact.

Trevor renegotiated the entire financial structure of the Virgin Group, and set in place the mechanics for going private at the end of November 1988. It was a colossal task made no easier when our advisers, Samuel Montagu, approached their parent bank, Midland Bank, to come and join the syndicate of lending banks, but were turned down out of hand.

Trevor decided to dispense with Samuel Montagu's services in all but name. Rather than set up a syndicate of banks which would have had one leading bank as the point of contact and prime negotiator, he began to pull together a consortium of banks, each of whom he approached directly. This meant that he would have to do much more legwork, since he was speaking to them all individually, but it also meant that he could play each of them off against the others. In the end he arranged lines of credit with twenty different banks, and we drew up an overdraft of £300 million. We bought in the outside shareholders' shares, refinanced the debt which had been secured upon our Virgin Group plc shares, and similarly for Virgin Atlantic.

With over £300 million of debt, we were so heavily borrowed that we knew we had to move rapidly if we were going to survive. We had to give up the idea of buying Thorn EMI, so we sold our shares, and concentrated on dealing with our own problems. I had always felt that the City had undervalued Virgin Music, and now we would have to see what its real value was. Don Cruickshank, Sir Phil Harris and Cob Stenham left

Virgin. Don had carried out a superb job in recasting the company as one that could demonstrate clear lines of management. Trevor took his place as managing director.

Trevor and I set about finding other companies who might wish to invest in any of the Virgin subsidiaries as joint ventures. We wanted to replace the shareholders in the City with one or two key partners in various Virgin subsidiaries. The structure of the Virgin Group was about to become extremely complicated.

18 'Everything was up for sale.'

1988–1989

WHEN I HAD BOUGHT back Nik's 40 per cent stake, I had been able to repay my £1 million overdraft because Virgin had suddenly released a string of hits starting off with Phil Collins. At the time I knew I was on a knife edge. Now the sums of money were far more daunting: we had a debt mountain of over £300 million, and we had to reduce it by £200 million within the first year. This pressure meant that everything was now up for sale. There were no sacred cows. If we received a good offer for a part of any Virgin business, then we would take it. Trevor, Ken and I began to put out feelers to see what level of interest there was. One of the first areas we looked at was Virgin Retail.

Trevor and I divided Virgin Retail into three separate divisions: the first comprised the rump of the record shops that we had kept back from selling to WH Smith, the typical high-street shops together with the Oxford Street Megastore; the second comprised Patrick Zelnick's proposed Paris Megastore on the Champs Elysées, where Patrick Zelnick would set up a separate French subsidiary to invest in the shop; the third comprised the plans we had for Ian Duffell, the man who had designed and set up the HMV record shop on Oxford Street, and whom we had managed to persuade to join Virgin.

We offered him the chance to set up Virgin

Megastores anywhere in the world, and we promised to back his judgement and let him have a direct share in the Megastores. Ian was one of the best record retailers in the business: he had excellent plans for the record shops and, for the first time since we opened our earliest batch of Virgin shops, I felt that we could be back on the map. His interest lay in opening a sequence of overseas Virgin Megastores.

We thought about setting up in America, but the retail rents at the time were astronomical and the competition was high. Instead we chose to open the first one in Sydney, which was a quiet market without much competition. There we could open a Megastore and experiment a little with different formulas without losing a lot of money.

In the meantime, the Paris Megastore was the first overseas shop to materialise. Patrick had found a grand old bank dating from the late nineteenth century. It had marble floors, soaring high ceilings and the most spectacular staircase. This grabbed my imagination. We knew that small record shops did not make enough money; they just attracted passers-by who were disappointed by the lack of depth of stock. Now that the 1970s were over and the cushions on the floor had been cleared away, the traditional Virgin shops seemed to have lost their identity and customer loyalty. We had to go for something bigger, where we could offer the best range of products in the world.

Patrick's Paris Megastore was an incredible success. From its opening day it smashed all his sales forecasts and became the most celebrated shop in Paris. Indeed, it became far more than a shop: it became a landmark and a tourist destination. After a few months the Paris Megastore attracted as many visitors as the Louvre. Today it still generates sales per square foot over twice those of any other record store in the world. It seems that every teenaged Japanese and German tourist makes a pilgrimage there and buys huge numbers of CDs, and even the café at the top has become a smart place for French executives to meet. I was delighted for Patrick, but I still had no idea what to do about the British record shops.

We decided that it was time to bring some other people in to turn Virgin Retail around. Giving people their notice is always heart-wrenching, and I hate doing it. I hate confrontation and I hate disappointing people. I always try to give people another chance. But it was clear that this team was out of its depth and losing money without any hope of turning the company round. The final straw came when, after the end of the financial year, they admitted to us that the losses of Virgin Retail would be £2 million more than they had anticipated. By leaving it so late we were stuck.

We asked some head-hunters to draw up a short list of suitable candidates, but I was most intrigued when Simon Burke applied for the job of chief executive. Simon had joined Virgin a couple of years previously as the development manager. His job was to sift through all the business proposals we receive and see whether we want to follow any of them up.

One of the things that I am always trying to do with Virgin is make people reinvent themselves. I firmly believe that anything is possible and, despite Simon's having no obvious qualifications to turn a large chain of unsuccessful record shops into a chain of successful ones, I was certain that, if anyone could do it, he could. And, sure enough, as soon as Simon started work at Virgin Retail in August 1988, things began to change as he started to weed out everything we didn't need or that was losing money.

His strategy began to pay off, and by June 1989 Virgin Retail had produced its first ever profit. In his first presentation to the Virgin board he showed us some slides and asked for £10 million to invest in new shops. He pointed out that Retail was falling apart, and he showed us some pictures of the shops in which tiles were hanging off the roof and the wiring was coming apart. He suggested that, if any airline customers saw this, they would worry about the state of the aircraft. Unfortunately for Simon, Patrick Zelnick was also asking for £10 million, to develop Virgin Megastores in Bordeaux and Marseilles. Flushed with the recent success of the Paris Megastore, I felt more inclined to divert the funding to France than the UK. It must have been galling for Simon. In the meantime, the Sydney Megastore was ready to open, and Ian and Mike were looking at Japan.

In order to create the investment in the UK shops and help pay off the general debt, we set up another joint venture. Ideally we would have liked a financial investor to take a 30 per cent stake but, with the high interest rates and the feeling that high-street retailing was heading for recession, we had no takers. We began talks with Kingfisher, the owner of Woolworth's. As these talks dragged on, WH Smith got wind of them and called me to see whether they could make an offer. And so, just as Simon Burke was getting on with the job of sorting out Virgin Retail for Virgin, he suddenly found himself with a new boss: a two-headed creature comprising both Virgin and WH Smith. WH Smith bought a 50 per cent stake in our ten UK Megastores, which, unlike the earlier shops we had sold to WH Smith, continued to trade under the Virgin name. Their sale raised £12 million, which we immediately used to pay off borrowings in Virgin Atlantic. It was another case of some frantic juggling to keep one step ahead of the bankers.

While the UK retail arm spun off into a joint venture with WH Smith, and the European retail side started to expand from Paris into Bordeaux, Marseilles and then Germany, several different Virgin companies turned their attention towards Japan.

While many British companies complain about how difficult it is to do business in Japan, Virgin has always enjoyed an excellent rapport with the Japanese. I put it down to the success of my first ever trip to Tokyo. I had gone there as a twenty-year-old, before I was married to Kristen, and rather ambitiously arranged a number of meetings with people in the entertainment and media world to see whether we could set up some kind of joint venture distributing records. I think it was before we started Virgin Music, so I didn't even have Mike Oldfield to sell them. I was young, impoverished and had very little to offer. I went along to a number of meetings where immaculate geisha girls served tea, and I sat in my jeans and sweater and enthused about business to kind and patient groups of Japanese businessmen. No business deals were forthcoming, but the great success was at my hotel.

When I arrived at the airport and took a coach into Tokyo, I realised that I could not afford to stay at any of the hotels on the list suggested by the tourist board. So I took a taxi and asked for a cheap local hotel. The hotel looked utterly anonymous from the outside, just a plain little concrete building, and my room was very small. But that night, bored and alone, I saw that room service offered a massage. Two beautiful Japanese girls came up to my room, where they asked me to lie in the bath and gave me the most erotic massage of my life.

We all ended up in my bath tub. When I breathlessly called up for a massage the next night to repeat the experience, I was confronted by two huge women in severe aprons who explained that the other two girls were having a night off. They proceeded to karate chop and pummel me to within an inch of my life. Nowadays I am booked into huge hotels which are very nice, but nothing compares with that first business trip.

By 1988 Virgin had become quite a well-known brand name in Japan. Several of our artists sold well there, particularly Boy George, The Human League, Simple Minds and Phil Collins. After the British Airways takeover of British Caledonian, we successfully applied for the right to fly to Tokyo. When we looked at ways of reducing our overdraft, we realised that we would have to sell shares in both Virgin Atlantic and Virgin Music in order to reduce our mountain of debt.

Our first deal was to sell 10 per cent of the airline to Seibu-Saison, a large Japanese travel group. Virgin Atlantic had just announced doubled pre-tax profits of £10 million, and Seibu-Saison bought the 10 per cent stake for £36 million. At the same time as this deal was going through, Robert Devereux was signing up a longer-term contract with Sega for Virgin Communications to distribute Sega games. It was becoming clear that Japanese companies shared much of the same philosophy as Virgin.

Like us, they tend to operate on long-term objectives. As well as the constrictions of having to report to nonexecutive directors and shareholders, one of my main frustrations with being a public company quoted on the stock market was the short-term view which investors took. We were under pressure to produce instant results, and unless we paid out a large dividend our share price would suffer. Japanese investors do not invest with the dividend payment in mind; they look almost exclusively for capital growth. And, given that it can take a long time for investments to pay off, Japanese share prices are very high in comparison with the company's earnings. Hence, Japanese price-earnings ratios are often three times as high as British ones. I once heard of a Japanese company that was working to a 200-year business plan! It reminds me of Deng Xiaoping's remark in the 1980s, when he was asked what he thought the implications of the 1789 French Revolution were. 'Too early to tell' was his reply.

The next part of the Virgin Group to embrace a Japanese partner was Virgin Music. This was the key sale. If we were going to make any sense of having bought back Virgin Group plc, then we had to raise a good price for Virgin Music. Simon, Trevor and I spoke to a number of American companies about taking a stake in Virgin Music. One of them offered the most money but was not prepared to take the role of a passive, long-term investor. We all gravitated towards a Japanese media company, Fujisankei. I think my mind was made up at a meeting with Mr Agichi of Fujisankei in the garden of our house at 11 Holland Park.

'Mr Branson,' came the quiet question. 'Would you prefer an American wife or a Japanese wife? American wives very difficult – lots of litigation and alimony. Japanese wives very good and quiet.'

19 Preparing to jump

1989–1990

BY SELLING 25 PER CENT of Virgin Music for $150 million – £100 million – we had vindicated our argument that the City had undervalued Virgin. The sale was a clear sign that that company alone was worth at least £400 million, and that was without any value at all placed on the various other companies, such as Retail, which had made up the public Group. This was way above the £180 million at which the City had valued us before we offered to buy the company back, and still way above the £240 million price we had eventually paid to go private.

With Japanese partners in our two main businesses, the airline and music, we then turned to our third business and decided to expand the retail side in Japan as well. Ian Duffell and Mike Inman, along with our Japanese adviser, Shu Ueyama, had already started to do their research. Mike had started learning Japanese in Sydney because his brother had married a Japanese girl. Ian sent him to Tokyo, and he himself headed to Los Angeles, where he started looking for a Megastore site along Sunset Boulevard.

Mike reported that it would be impossible to set up a Megastore in Tokyo by ourselves: Tokyo is a vast city with few distinguishable regions, and it is extremely difficult for outsiders to identify the key parts. Retail, residential and commercial properties are all jumbled up together, unlike in London, which has easily

definable shopping areas – like Oxford Street, Knights-
bridge and Kensington High Street – and where it is
relatively easy to get your bearings. Tokyo all looks the
same. Property is extremely expensive, and in order to
rent a shop you have to put down a huge deposit called
'key money'. Trevor, Ian and Shu had met up with a
great many potential Japanese partners, and eventually
chose to team up with a fashion retailer called Marui.
Trevor formed a fifty–fifty partnership which would be
the start of Virgin Megastores in Japan.

The difficulty with a record shop is that you are trying
to sell an identical product to that of every other record
shop. Virgin had nothing that we could call our own or
that was available only at Virgin shops. We knew that
our competitors were losing a lot of money in Tokyo,
partly because they had had to pay such high

"I was going to pinch Kate Bush's new album but I think I'll forget it."

key-money deposits on their shops, but also because
they had not established any customer loyalty and so
did not get the vital return visits.

In order to avoid these pitfalls, we set up the joint
venture with Marui. They were the first retailer really
to understand the importance of railway stations. They
positioned their stores as close as possible to the large
railway stations, and so ensured a vast crowd of passing
pedestrians. Marui's clothes were aimed at the young,
increasingly affluent generation and they had also
pioneered a popular in-house credit card. Marui
managed to secure us a fabulous site in Shinjuku, a
prime shopping area in central Tokyo, and we took
10,000 square feet. The property belonged to Marui and
we agreed a system whereby we paid them a certain
percentage of our sales instead of a fixed monthly rent.
In this way we avoided paying the ruinous key-money
deposit and, although 10,000 square feet was small by
European standards, it was still larger than any other
record shop in Tokyo. It was the flagship store I wanted.

In order to be different from our competitors, and to
attract customers, we installed listening facilities and
hired a DJ. The DJ was not only an entertainer: by
playing great songs he soon covered his costs by
triggering sales. The Tokyo Virgin Megastore soon
acquired the same kind of cult status as the early shops
in Oxford Street and Notting Hill. Teenagers from
across the city flocked there and it became *the* place to
go. Tokyo is an expensive city and so teenagers enjoyed
being able to spend a cheap afternoon listening to
music, chatting and buying records. The average time
spent in our Tokyo Megastores was forty minutes –
considerably longer than people spend having a meal in
McDonald's. It was almost an extension of our original
1970s retail philosophy. With 10,000 customers a day,

the store was even more successful than we had expected.

With Ian in Los Angeles, Mike was by himself. In due course, he followed in his brother's footsteps by falling in love with a Japanese girl. They got married on Necker Island.

Within the space of two years, between 1988 and 1990, each Virgin subsidiary had set up a deal with a Japanese company. With Sega, Marui, Seibu-Saison and Fujisankei, we were uniquely placed to begin expanding in Japan. I was also about to become involved in an altogether different venture in Japan: Per and I were planning to take off from Japan and fly across the Pacific to America in our second hot-air-balloon adventure.

Per told me his worst fear when it was too late. We were on the plane on our way to Japan when he confessed that he had been unable to test the capsule in a pressure chamber: he was not 100 per cent sure that it would survive at 40,000 feet. If a window blew out at that height, we would have between seven and eight seconds to put on our oxygen masks.

'We'll need to keep them handy,' Per said in his usual understated way. 'And, of course, if the other person is asleep then it'll be necessary to put the mask on and get it going in three seconds and then put on the other person's in three seconds, allowing two seconds for a fumble.'

I didn't fancy a fumble with Per, even for two seconds, and I vowed that I wouldn't go to sleep during the flight.

'Will we have any advance warning about it?' I asked.

'If the capsule decompresses, you'll notice that it suddenly becomes misty. The capsule will appear to fill with fog. You will hear a screaming in your ears and you will experience the sensation of your lungs being sucked out of your chest and through your mouth.'

When a journalist asked me about the dangers of the flight, I recounted Per's words.

'You see, it's essential that one of us stays awake during the flight,' I told the journalist. 'So, rather than using the comfortable Virgin seats which we used to cross the Atlantic, we've asked British Airways for two of theirs.'

We were attempting the flight in November, when the jet stream across the Pacific is at its strongest. However, it is also the time of year when the ocean is extremely stormy. We would take off from Japan and almost immediately be above the sea. We would then have to more than double our Atlantic distance record of 3,000 miles in order to reach America.

Per's team had taken the balloon and capsule to the launch site in Miyakonojo, a small town in the south of Japan which they had calculated lay directly below the jet stream. On my first night there I was called by Tom Barrow, who had fallen out with Per since the Atlantic crossing. We had replaced Tom with Mike Kendrick, but Tom had been following Per's progress and was extremely worried.

'You're going to end up in the water,' he told me. 'Your first priority is to be prepared for a safe, survivable ditch in the sea. If, against all odds, you reach the mainland, you'll have a 60 per cent chance that it'll be dark. In November it's dark for fifteen hours of the day in North America, particularly the further north you go. You can't land in the dark, so you may well have to fly for another fifteen hours. Even at 30 miles an hour this'll take you 1,000 miles inland and you could well be in trouble then. You should assume that there'll be storm conditions – it's hardly likely to be a still, calm day. Up in the north you get people trapped in cabins waiting for the weather to clear, so for God's sake have your search and rescue team in place. Don't be dependent on calm weather for your landing.

'Check all the systems before you take off. Don't get pressured into taking off. Even if everything's well built and works, the flight is still terribly dangerous.'

I thanked Tom for his advice.

'My last word on the matter,' he told me. 'The Atlantic crossing was a successful flight that was out of control. We all know that. It was fully out of control at the end, but both of you survived. You both taught yourselves to fly that balloon as you went along. In the Atlantic you can ditch near a boat. In the Pacific you're dead. So you'll either ditch in the sea and die, or you'll hit land in the dark and that'll be a close call.'

I put down the telephone. I was sweating. I had hardly finished scribbling down what he'd told me when it rang again. It was Joan. It was Holly's eighth birthday. She came on the line:

'I'm keeping a diary, Dad,' she told me. 'We can swap diaries when you come home.'

'Yes, darling,' I said, swallowing hard.

When I mentioned to Per the improbability of surviving if we ditched in the sea, he agreed.

'We don't need to bother with health insurance,' he said casually. 'It's only worthwhile taking out life insurance.'

As Per's team assembled the electrical systems in the capsule, Per and I sat down together and went through the flight operations. It was hard to believe that we were going to be once again incarcerated in this tiny capsule, surrounded by all these gadgets – which were our only means of communication with the outside world.

'Look,' I found myself saying to a reporter who was running through a list of everything that could go wrong, 'it'll either be a piece of cake or it won't.'

The jet stream above the Pacific is a different shape from the one above the Atlantic. The Atlantic one is a V-shaped polar jet stream, like an upside-down Toblerone. As you rise, the jet stream becomes wider and the wind becomes faster, so you gradually increase your groundspeed. At 10,000 feet the air current might be 50 knots, then at 27,000 feet it will be 100 knots, and so on. A balloon can ease into it without being buffeted. The Pacific jet stream is a different beast altogether. It is a subtropical jet shaped like a single-bore cable. At 20,000 feet the air current could be completely still. At 25,000 feet it could be the same. Then suddenly at 27,000 feet you hit the jet stream, which is moving at between 100 and 200 knots. Nobody had ever flown a balloon in the Pacific jet stream before, and we knew there was a danger that when the top of our balloon hit the current it could be sheared off from the capsule suspended below. If that didn't happen we knew it would be a pretty rough buffeting. With the capsule travelling at 5 knots and the balloon at 200 knots, we knew it would initially be like being pulled along by a thousand horses.

If we managed to get into the jet stream, we knew that it would have an inner core which is generally about 4,000 feet in diameter. To keep within this tube would mean constantly monitoring the altimeter, and watching out for any buffeting which would imply that the balloon and capsule were in different streams.

The atmosphere at Miyakonojo was almost like a carnival. A Shinto priest even came to bless the site. My parents had arrived, but Joan had chosen to stay at

home until the balloon went up and then take a plane
to Los Angeles so that she and the children could meet
me at the end of the flight. By Sunday night our
weatherman, Bob Rice, was forecasting perfect conditions for Tuesday, but by Monday these had been
delayed to Wednesday. Per and I spent another day in
the capsule going over and over everything that could
go wrong.

'Keep the fire burning – that's all that matters,' I
wrote across a page in my notebook after one
three-hour session on all the possible outcomes of our
flight.

The delay gave me the chance to revisit the banks of
dials, gauges and switches built into the capsule walls.
It also gave me time to make sure that I remembered
the difference between the switches that released the
empty fuel tanks and the ones that separated the
balloon from the capsule!

'It's code yellow,' Bob Rice announced. 'Expect a
green light by 2100 hours, November 23rd.'

'Is the Pacific Ocean the largest ocean in the world?'
asked Holly down the telephone. 'How many miles is it?
And how long would it take you to fly all round the
world?'

It was time for a sleep. I lay on my hotel bed but
couldn't keep my eyes shut, and so I started to write in
my diary:

> Trying to have a couple of hours' rest. Failing
> miserably. Just looked out of the window to see the
> end of a beautiful day. The smoke from the volcano
> looks like thin cloud in the sky. Cars with
> loudspeakers going through the streets announcing
> the time of our departure. Civic fireworks planned
> for 2.30a.m. for anybody from the town not already

awake. Imagine an English city council doing that!
Still not feeling nervous: elated, excited, but not
really nervous. Everything seems to have gone so
well. Bob feels the crossing and landing conditions
are nearly as good as we can expect. Still have some
nervousness about the inflation. In two hours must
go back to site for a live interview for *News at One*.

When I went back to the site I sensed trouble. The
balloon's envelope was still laid out on the ground:
inflation had not started. The operation room was full
of Per's team being debriefed: 'Too windy, too risky, too
much downwind.' They decided to leave the envelope
laid out on the ground and hope that the wind fell away
by the next night. With the 70-tonne balloon stationary,
a gust of wind could rip the fabric. I went back outside
and asked for our translator. Somebody gave me a
microphone and I apologised to the huge crowd huddled
on the hillside above the launch site. We promised to try
tomorrow.

The next day was long and listless. The jet stream
seemed to be behaving peculiarly and Bob Rice was
struggling to work out whether we would land in
California or Yukon.

'Oh, fuck the weather,' Bob, America's most re-
nowned and sophisticated meteorologist, finally said.
'Just go!'

I went back to the hotel for a final sleep, and once
again I ended up staring out of the window at the
volcano. I heard the drummers starting in town. Then
a fax was pushed under my door. In spidery, slanting
letters, Holly had written:

I hope you don't land in the water and have a bad
landing. I hope you have a good landing and land on

dry land, and Miss Salavesen said to have a good landing too. I hope you have a nice trip.

Love from Holly.

PS. Good luck and I love you too.

I took a sleeping pill and fell on to my bed.

A few hours later Per woke me up and we drove to the site. A crowd of around 5,000 people had come out to watch in the freezing cold. There were families, old ladies, young babies. I heard cheers as the balloon rose from the ground and swung up above the capsule. The burners were roaring now to heat up the air. The wind was still, but we needed to take off as soon as possible in case any gusts caught us on the ground. Hundreds of coal braziers had been brought out on to the slope. Their smoke rose straight up into the starry night air – clear proof of how absolutely still it was.

I was standing with my parents admiring the magnificence of the balloon when a strip of the fabric suddenly peeled off the envelope and hung down.

'What's that?' Dad asked me.

I ran to find Per.

'What's happening?'

'Nothing to worry about,' Per said. 'Just a little heat loss. The balloon's big enough to cope.'

I took Per back into the operation room and Dad grabbed his arm. 'What's that flapping off halfway up the envelope?' he said.

'It's air coming up the side of the balloon,' Per said.

Dad didn't look convinced.

Per and I walked out and stood underneath the balloon. It effectively had a hole where the lamination had peeled off. We went back to the control room and I found Dad.

'Dad, don't tell Mum,' I said, 'but we've got a hole. Per still feels we'll make it to America.'

'You can't fly in that thing,' Dad said.

A minute later, more strips of lamination started falling off.

'Richard, I'm afraid we're going to have to abort the flight,' Per said. 'If we take off, we'll end up in the Pacific.'

I looked out at the crowded hillside. I was going to have to let them all down. With my hands trembling with cold and bitter disappointment, I once again picked up the microphone.

'I'm so sorry,' I said, trying to stop my voice from choking. 'The lamination of the balloon has torn apart. We think that it was because we left the balloon out all last night and the frost got into it ...'

As the translator repeated my words, a groan rose from the crowd. Then there was a gasp and I looked up to see three or four huge chunks of fabric crash off the envelope and fall down on to the burners. Someone pulled them off, but the whole balloon was disintegrating in front of our eyes.

'Shut off the burners!' I yelled. 'Stand back from there.'

Without the burners, the balloon sagged. It fell to one side, hot air seeping out of its holes.

'We'll come back next year,' I promised. 'Please have faith in us.'

'Well, Richard,' said Dad as we all drove back to the hotel, 'holidays with you are never dull.'

Joan was two hours into her flight to Los Angeles when she heard the news.

'Excellent!' she exclaimed. 'Champagne all round, please!'

The pilot pulled back the throttle and the helicopter rose still higher. The pale-blue sea shimmered and glittered beneath us. I watched as we approached

Necker: the white coral reef and then the pale strip of beach, the leaning palm trees and the pointed roof of the Bali house, the deep green of the forest inland. We circled overhead and I saw our family and friends standing on the beach. Most of them were wearing white with wide-brimmed hats. There was a splash of colour from some tropical shirts. I spotted Vanessa and Robert; Lindi and her husband Robin; all the children; Peter and Ceris, my friends and neighbours from Mill End; Ken and his wife Nancy; Simon and his wife Françoise. I waved down at their upturned faces. In the middle of the crowd I saw Joan in her stunning white dress, with Holly and Sam, her sister Rose, her brother John and her mother beside her. Granny was standing with Mum and Dad, waving up at me merrily.

I tapped the pilot on the shoulder and he brought the helicopter round once more.

I picked up the box of Milk Tray and gripped it in my teeth. Everything was in place. I crouched low and paused at the open door. The wind was hot and fast in my face, the beach and silvery-blue sea spinning crazily beneath me, as I stared down. We were hovering over the swimming pool. I gripped the side of the door and looked back at the pilot.

'All because the lady loves Milk Tray!' he shouted.

I took the box out of my mouth for a moment.

'The kids do too!' I shouted back.

I flashed him a thumbs up, took one last look at the swimming pool directly beneath me, and then climbed out on to the struts and swung off them. Joan and I were finally getting married and I didn't want the Milk Tray to melt. I prepared to jump.

20 'Who the hell does Richard Branson think he is?'

August–October 1990

I WAS WOKEN UP by a heavy kick in my back. I had been thumped and prodded all night. Since it was now 5.30a.m., I slipped out of bed and put on my dressing gown. I watched Sam snuggle into my warm hollowed-out pillow, which he had been fighting to occupy all night. He and Holly still often slept in our bed with us. I turned on CNN and put my head close to the screen to hear the news. I didn't need much sound to understand that it was just as bad. Iraq had invaded Kuwait the previous week and the world was in a tailspin. The price of crude oil had soared from $19 a barrel before the invasion to $36. The price of aviation fuel had rocketed from 75 cents a gallon to $1.50, an even sharper increase than the rise in crude oil because the Allied Forces had begun stockpiling aviation fuel in preparation for an airborne attack on Iraq.

Two of the main ingredients of an airline's profitability are the number of passengers and the cost of aviation fuel. All independent airlines were now facing disaster: we were having to operate when the price of fuel – which represents 20 per cent of our total overheads – had more than doubled, and the number of passengers flying had dried up. In the first week following the invasion, Virgin Atlantic received 3,000 cancellations. We had a £25 million overdraft facility with Lloyds Bank which we had just broken. I wondered how far we could go before Lloyds asked us to do something about it. I pushed the worry to the back of my mind.

I wondered how many more passengers would cancel today. The big state-owned airlines were even worse hit since nobody wanted to risk flying on a flag-carrier due to the chance of a terrorist attack. Since Mrs Thatcher had allowed the American jets to refuel in Britain on their Libyan raid, companies that were closely aligned with the government were seen as vulnerable to terrorist retaliation. The bomb on the PanAm jumbo over Lockerbie had shown how devastating such retaliation could be. Despite being a normal public company, British Airways still proclaimed itself as the British flag-carrier, and for the first time this reputation was to our advantage. After the first week of empty flights, I was beginning to feel a glimmer of hope that passengers were cautiously returning: we had noticed a slight preference towards Virgin Atlantic in place of either any American airline or British Airways.

In the summer of 1990 Virgin Atlantic was still a tiny airline. We flew to just four destinations in two countries. Each day we scanned the bookings for these four routes to see whether there was any sign that we were winning passengers back. The Tokyo route was our worst hit. We were allowed to fly only four times a week – and never on Sunday, which is the most popular day for businessmen to travel – and so the route was losing money even before Iraq invaded Kuwait. Throughout the summer we had been lobbying to be awarded the two extra flights to Tokyo which were about to be released, but as always we were up against British Airways. Our flights to Newark and Los Angeles had lost passengers from the first week after the invasion, but now we detected a swing towards Virgin in preference to the American carriers. The best news was that our holiday flights to Miami and Orlando seemed to be largely unaffected.

We had celebrated my fortieth birthday the previous month and, although Joan had arranged a wonderful party on Necker, I had found myself feeling uncharacteristically depressed. I felt that Simon had lost interest in Virgin Music, and I sympathised with him. It was extremely tough negotiating every contract and sometimes it felt rather repetitive going over the same points time and again. Although we had built Virgin Music into one of the major independent record labels, all Simon's wealth was tied up in that single company and I knew that he was worried I might jeopardise it by some new risky venture. Simon wasn't interested in the other projects I talked about and had only ever seen Virgin Atlantic as a huge liability to the rest of the Virgin Group: a business that could be driven to the wall by British Airways or by something out of the blue – something like a war in the Gulf.

Turning forty had also made me wonder what I was doing with my life. After the great leap into setting up Virgin Atlantic, I now found that it was difficult to develop the airline as quickly as I wanted. Although we had had a wonderful year and had been voted Best Business Class Airline, Virgin Atlantic was confined to operating from Gatwick Airport. Due to a single short runway and the lack of connecting flights, Gatwick was less profitable, both for cargo and passengers, than Heathrow. We were struggling to make money. On top of this we had fallen into a maintenance dispute with British Airways which continued to be a large bone of contention.

Given Simon's gradual loss of interest, and our endless struggles to make ends meet at Virgin Atlantic, I began to question whether I should start doing something completely different. I even thought of going to university and studying history: it would be nice to have time to read. When I mentioned this to Joan she squashed the idea by bluntly pointing out that this was really just an excuse to meet a whole lot of pretty girls away from home. I mulled over the idea of setting up as a full-time political campaigner. I thought of studying some of the major issues, such as healthcare and homelessness, understanding what the best solutions were, and then fighting hard for the political change to implement them.

But all these thoughts were pushed out of my mind by Saddam Hussein's invasion of Kuwait. We had the full-blown crisis at the airline, and I found myself caught up in the Gulf War in an extraordinarily personal way.

'Daddy, please can you help me find my shoes?'

It was Holly.

'Which ones?'

'You know, my new trainers.'

As the world on the television continued to disintegrate towards war, and as our half-empty 747 *Maiden Voyager* headed across the Atlantic towards a dawn over Gatwick, my family gathered in bed for breakfast. Joan brought up a huge tray with fried eggs, fried bread, bacon and baked beans. As we ate, some of the Virgin staff let themselves in through the front door. I heard Penni start up the photocopier downstairs. Our new press officer, Will Whitehorn, trooped upstairs to his office. A dynamo of perpetually cheerful energy, Will had already proved himself to be a terrific asset.

Getting Holly and Sam ready for school was always a kind of mad initiative test. Shoes, socks, vests, shirts, blazers and berets had to be found wherever they had inexplicably hidden themselves overnight. They could be conjured up only by the most inspired lateral thinking.

'Here they are!' Joan had somehow thought to look for Holly's shoes inside the large doll's house, which hadn't been used by anyone for as long as I could remember.

'What were they doing there?' I asked.

'No idea,' Holly said, and put them in her school rucksack without further explanation.

'Sam, we're going in *two* minutes,' Joan threatened.

Sam had started to reassemble the Scalextric.

As they finally managed to pick up all their bits and pieces and head for the door, the phone rang. It was Queen Noor of Jordan.

My friendship with Queen Noor was one of the unlikely consequences of my balloon trip with Per across the Atlantic. Queen Noor was the Grace Kelly of Jordan. She was American and had once worked as an air stewardess. Tall, blonde and wholly glamorous, she now lived in a walled and heavily guarded palace in Amman. Queen Noor had heard about our balloon flight and telephoned me to ask whether I would teach her and her family how to fly a balloon. I had gone out to Jordan with Tom Barrow and spent a week at King Hussein's palace teaching the royal family how to fly a hot-air balloon.

We flew over Amman, hovering over the rooftops and looking down on the ancient city with its minarets, whitewashed walls and faded orange-tiled rooftops. Nobody in Amman had ever seen a hot-air balloon before, and they stared up in amazement as we loomed overhead. When they realised that their King and Queen were standing in the wicker basket, they cheered and ran beneath the balloon waving up at us. When we fired the gas burner, all the dogs in the city started barking. With the barking, the cheering and the calls of the muezzins, the city gave in to total pandemonium. King Hussein, Queen Noor and the royal princes waved down as the balloon flew within three feet of the rooftops. I think that the only people who didn't enjoy the trip were King Hussein's bodyguards, who had successfully shielded him from nine assassination attempts but who could do nothing to protect him as he floated around in a wicker basket.

When Saddam Hussein invaded Kuwait, King Hussein of Jordan was one of the few world leaders who refused to condemn him out of hand. King Hussein pointed out that Kuwait had promised Iraq a number of oil wells as part of its contribution towards the long war against Iran. Yet Kuwait had continually reneged on that promise and it had also cheated on its OPEC quotas.

Among all the chaos which followed the invasion, a huge number of foreign workers fled from Iraq into Jordan. There were around 150,000 refugees congregating in a makeshift camp with no water and no blankets. It was extremely hot during the day, when they had no shade; and freezing cold at night, when they had no warmth. A blanket can be rigged up as shade, and wrapped up in for warmth. As soon as I heard about this problem, I had contacted King Hussein and Queen Noor offering to do whatever I could to help. Queen Noor now telephoned me to say that, although the Red Cross was in the process of setting up a water-distribution system, there was still the task of trying to find up to 100,000 blankets.

'A few very young children have already died,' Queen Noor said, 'but it hasn't turned into a full-scale catastrophe yet. I think that we've only got about two or three days' grace before we start to lose hundreds of refugees.'

That day I drove down to Crawley and talked to some of the Virgin Atlantic staff about how we would set about finding and then flying 100,000 blankets to Amman. Everyone at Virgin rallied round. During the course of the day we called up the Red Cross, William Waldegrave at the Foreign Office and Lynda Chalker at the Overseas Development Office, and managed to secure 30,000 blankets, with the promise of more to come from UNICEF in Copenhagen. Now that we had offered to provide the plane, the Red Cross put out an appeal on national radio and from that evening a warehouse at Gatwick started filling up with blankets. On top of that, David Sainsbury promised me that he would supply several tons of rice.

Two days later, all the seats were removed from one of our 747s and replaced by over 40,000 blankets, several tons of rice and medical supplies. The 747 then flew to Amman. The blankets were loaded up into a line of trucks waiting at the airport, and we came back with a number of British nationals who had been stranded in Jordan and wanted to come home.

When I returned to Britain, William Waldegrave told me that he had had a call from Lord King, chairman of British Airways, who had been surprised to see the Virgin Atlantic flight to Jordan featuring on *News at Ten*.

'We should be doing that,' Lord King had told Waldegrave.

William Waldegrave had pointed out to Lord King that I had just offered to help and Virgin Atlantic happened to have an aircraft available to make it possible. The next week British Airways flew some supplies out to Jordan and brought back some more nationals. Christian Aid told us that they were amazed: over many years they had unsuccessfully appealed to British

Airways to help them, but, ever since the Virgin
Atlantic flight to Amman, BA had been practically
suffocating them with offers of help. Healthy competition even benefits charities sometimes.

Since I heard that some of our original shipment had
not reached the refugee camps, I decided to go and stay
in Amman for a few days to watch the procession of the
next delivery of supplies until it finally reached the
camps. Once again I stayed with King Hussein and
Queen Noor at the palace. I had fierce arguments with
the minister for the interior about the need for strict
accountability over these supplies so that the people
who had provided them could be confident that they
reached the camps. I also had several long talks with
King Hussein about the Gulf crisis. King Hussein was
sure that war could be averted, but was worried that the
West wanted diplomacy to fail so that they could defend
Kuwait and protect their oil supply. By the time I
returned home it was clear that there would not be a
full-blown refugee crisis in Jordan. Queen Noor told me
that there were no more deaths from dysentery or
dehydration. Over time the 150,000 refugees slowly
dispersed.

A few days later I was watching the news when I saw
the extraordinary footage of Saddam Hussein surrounded by the British nationals who had been detained
in Baghdad. In one of the most chilling scenes I have
seen on television, he sat down and motioned a young
boy to come and stand by him. He put his hand on this
young boy's head, and then continued to address the
camera while gently patting his shoulder. The boy was
about the same age as Sam. I knew that I had to do
something to help these people. If that boy had been my
son, I would have moved heaven and earth to bring him
back home. The reporters were expecting that the

hostages would be used as 'human shields' and would be incarcerated inside the prime Allied targets.

I had no idea how I would set about helping bring these hostages home, but I knew that Virgin Atlantic had an aircraft and that, if we could somehow obtain permission to fly into Baghdad, we would be able to pick up any hostages whom Saddam Hussein agreed to release. It struck me that, in the same way in which I had been able to help the crisis in Jordan, I might be able to provide the vehicle for releasing these hostages.

The next day I was called by Frank Hessey. His sister Maureen and his brother-in-law Tony were hostages in Baghdad. Tony had severe lung cancer and needed urgent medical attention. He had telephoned every department in the Foreign Office, the Iraqi ambassadors in Europe and even the Iraqi Government in Baghdad, but nobody seemed able to do anything. Frank asked me to help.

As well as being in touch with the Foreign Office over the blankets-to-Jordan flight, I also had my friendship with King Hussein and Queen Noor. King Hussein was one of the few points of contact any government in the West had with Iraq. I had heard that Iraq was short of medical supplies and I wondered whether there were grounds for a deal whereby, if we flew in medical supplies, Iraq could release some foreign detainees. I called Queen Noor and asked her whether she could help me. When I described my proposal, she suggested that I come out to Amman once again and discuss it with King Hussein.

The next three days, which I spent in Amman with King Hussein and Queen Noor, gave me an insight into how a businessman can help in moments of crisis. On the face of it, all I had to recommend me to Saddam Hussein was that I had once taken King Hussein and

Queen Noor up in a hot-air balloon and I owned a tiny airline that operated four Boeing 747s. Although nobody else had taken King Hussein hot-air ballooning, many businessmen own large aircraft. But these two qualifications had propelled me into a unique situation: I was one of the only Westerners whom King Hussein was prepared to confide in, and therefore I had virtually direct access to Saddam Hussein.

I started to draft a letter to Saddam Hussein. I told him that I was staying in Amman, helping out with the repatriation of immigrants and organising some medical and food supplies. I asked him whether he would consider releasing any foreigners who were caught in Baghdad, particularly women and children and those who were sick. As a gesture of goodwill I offered to fly in some medical supplies that Iraq was short of. I mentioned Frank Hessey's brother and his lung cancer. I signed it 'Yours respectfully, Richard Branson'.

Then I went down to the drawing room and King Hussein spoke for an hour about the problems in the Middle East. As I sat there and listened, I looked around and saw a signed photograph of Margaret Thatcher standing beside one of Saddam Hussein. King Hussein pointed out to me why he did not automatically support the Kuwaiti position against Iraq:

'The people of Kuwait are divided into three categories,' he said. 'There are 400,000 Kuwaitis who are either very rich, or very, very rich; and there are 2 million impoverished immigrant workers looking after them.'

He pointed out that there was no free press and no free elections in Kuwait: it was hardly the 'democracy' the West claimed to be defending.

'The Kuwaitis do nothing for the Arab world,' he went on. 'All their money is in Swiss bank accounts, not in

Arabia. I've asked a number of world leaders whether the West would have come to Jordan's rescue if Iraq had invaded Jordan, a country with no oil. Each time there was a silence. I doubt it.' Then he laughed. 'I know that you would, though! Yes, you'd come sailing over the horizon in your balloon with your Virgin planes beside you!

'No, seriously,' he said, 'this is the chance to resolve the entire Middle Eastern question. Kuwait promised Saddam Hussein that it would pay its share of the costs of the war against Iran, which Iraq fought on its behalf. It has reneged on that promise. Originally, Saddam only planned to take the disputed oilfields he thought were rightfully his. He only occupied the whole country because he heard that the Kuwaitis were preparing the landing strips to let the Americans come in and defend them. He is certainly not interested in invading Saudi Arabia.'

King Hussein's peace plan involved Iraq pulling back to the border but keeping the disputed strip of land which he felt that Kuwait owed Iraq. Then in three years' time there should be elections in Kuwait to see whether these border people wanted to be part of Kuwait or Iraq. He told me that the West had little idea of the months of negotiation which had gone on between Iraq and Kuwait, and how the Kuwaitis had continually failed to honour their promises. On top of that, the Kuwaitis had not waived the debts which Iraq had incurred over the Iran war, and the Kuwaitis continued to cheat all the Arab states by overproducing oil and selling it too cheaply.

At the end of dinner, King Hussein took my letter off to his study and translated it into Arabic. He wrote a covering letter to Saddam Hussein, and despatched it by special courier to Baghdad. Before we went to bed, he quoted something his brother had said: 'Why did the sheep bells of the Falkland Islands ring louder than the church bells of Jerusalem?'

Back in London, I began talking to the Foreign Office. I tried to get the medical details of all those people stuck in Baghdad so that we could 'prove' they were ill. I then called around other foreign embassies to alert them that there might be a rescue flight going into Baghdad and that they should try to get some of their people on it by showing 'proof' that they were ill.

Two nights after I returned to England, we got a response from Saddam Hussein. He promised us that he would release the women and children and the sick hostages, but he wanted someone of stature to be flown in to ask him publicly to do so. I telephoned Edward Heath, the previous Conservative British prime minister, and asked him whether he would do so. He agreed. King Hussein contacted Saddam Hussein and put forward Ted Heath's name. Saddam Hussein agreed to him. The next day we flew Edward Heath out to Amman, where King Hussein arranged for him to go to Baghdad.

A day later, King Hussein phoned me:

'I have good news for you, sir,' he said. He was impeccably polite and always addressed people as 'sir' or 'madam', as did his children. 'You can set off for Baghdad. I have Saddam's word that you will be safe.'

We had spent the last few days planning for this call and had already found a brave volunteer crew, whom I'd like to name: Les Millgate, Geoff New, Paul Green, Ray Maidment, Peter Johnson, Jane-Ann Riley, Sam Rasheed, Anita Sinclair, Caroline Spencer, Ralph Mutton, Peter Marnick, Paul Keithly, Helen Burn, Nicola Collins, Janine Swift and Stephen Leitch. We had forewarned passengers that there might be delays on Virgin Atlantic and that we might have to move them on to another airline.

When I told my fellow airline directors that we had permission to fly, they were understandably concerned. They knew that if the plane was delayed in Baghdad for more than a handful of days we could go bust.

'The government has confirmed that they will stand behind our insurance company if the plane is destroyed,' Nigel Primrose, the Virgin Atlantic finance director, confirmed. 'But nobody will give us loss-of-business insurance if the plane is hijacked and kept in Baghdad. Remember, BA have already had one 747 wrecked in Kuwait.'

There was silence round the table as they digested this.

'There is one upside,' David Tait said with a serious face. 'They'll hold Richard there too and spare us any more of his harebrained schemes!'

Everyone laughed.

Although I knew I was risking everything on this flight, I also knew by now that there was no backing out.

We took off from Gatwick at 11a.m. on 23 October 1990 and headed east over Europe. We sat huddled together at the front of the plane, a strange collection of hostage relatives, doctors, nurses, Virgin cabin crew, and one journalist to represent the press. The remaining 400 seats behind us were empty. It was rather eerie. After a couple of hours we all walked up and down the aisles to get some exercise.

The daylight outside rapidly faded and by the time we entered Iraqi airspace it was dark. I looked out into the night and wondered where the Iraqi army was. I imagined the radar monitoring us as we headed towards Baghdad. We would be a single luminous green blob moving slowly across their dark screens. I half expected to see a couple of fighter planes come up and give us an escort, but it remained unnervingly quiet. The plane hummed and shuddered its way towards Baghdad, the first plane in twelve months to do so. Everyone stopped talking. We were entering the most dangerous airspace in the world, the concentrated target of the Allied Forces' planned attack. I wondered when the assault would begin.

I let myself into the flight deck and sat behind the captain, Les Millgate, and the two first officers, Geoff New and Paul Green. They were talking to air-traffic control over the radio but that was the only sign that Baghdad was out there. Ahead of us through the windscreen there was nothing. Iraq had a complete blackout. I wondered who lived down there, whether they could hear us flying overhead and whether they thought that we were the first Allied bomber. We seemed to be the only plane in the sky.

'We're getting close to the city,' Les Millgate said.

I scanned the screens in front of us and watched the altimeters drop as we descended. Flying long haul is deceptive. For most of the time up in the air you are above the cloud level in that magical world of the jet stream, hardly aware that you are moving. Then, as the plane starts coming down, you suddenly realise that you are flying a massive piece of metal at over 400 miles an hour and it has to be brought to a standstill. We came down lower and the plane hurtled through the darkness. Normally an airport is a blaze of orange and silver lights and it is difficult to distinguish the runway lights among them. The runways, ramps, planes and control tower are all brilliant with fluorescent and halogen lighting. But, for the first time, we were flying over a land that was so blacked out we could have been flying over the sea.

Geoff New was being guided in by air-traffic control at Baghdad. He opened the wing flaps and let down the undercarriage. I watched as we came lower and lower. Now we were only 600 feet up, now 500 feet. The disembodied voice of the air-traffic controller started counting out our height. Suddenly, two lines of landing lights lit up in the darkness below us. We aimed straight down the middle; the plane touched down and raced along the tarmac. A few more lights appeared to guide us, and we taxied to the loading gates. I could dimly make out men with machine guns standing alongside a flight of steps. Jane-Ann Riley, our in-flight supervisor, signalled the door was safe to be opened, and I looked out. It was freezing cold.

The steps were being manoeuvred towards us. I led the way down to Iraqi tarmac. Two lines of soldiers fanned out around us. A couple of senior government officials wearing brown camel-hair overcoats greeted us and indicated that the relatives should stay aboard. Baghdad airport is bigger than Heathrow but it was completely deserted: ours was the only aircraft there. I looked back at the incongruous sight of the Virgin cabin crew, with their red miniskirts and red stilettos, walking past the group of Iraqi soldiers in the vast empty airport. Their heels clacked loudly in the silence. We all smiled. The soldiers were a little timid at first, but then grinned back. Without any other planes on the runway, ours looked unnaturally large.

We were taken into a bare departure lounge where all the technology – computer terminals, telephones and even light fittings – had been stripped out. This would have taken some time, and it indicated that the Iraqis were fully expecting to be bombed and had already salvaged everything they wanted from the airport. We handed out some presents we'd brought: boxes of chocolates for the officers and lots of Virgin kids' flightpacks for the soldiers to send home to their families. Then I heard movement outside and Ted Heath came through the glass doors at the head of a large crowd of men, women and children. They looked pale under the fluorescent lights. As soon as they saw us they broke into a cheer and ran forward to embrace us. Ted was smiling and laughing and clasping everybody by the hand.

I soon realised that we weren't going to take all these people back with us. Everyone was laughing and hugging each other, tears streaming down their faces. Outside, the soldiers were unloading the medical supplies we had brought. We opened bottles of champagne and toasted each other and those that were to be left behind. I found Frank Hessey's brother and we hugged. A pregnant Filipino woman who was having to leave her husband behind came up to me. She was in tears. Another man had to hand his three-year-old daughter to his nanny and say goodbye to her. I just hugged him. There was nothing else I could do. We both had tears in our eyes. I was a father too.

After an hour the Iraqis told us to get back on the plane. As we walked across the freezing tarmac I shook hands with the soldiers and gave them more children's packs for their kids. We wished each other well. It was disturbing to think that when we flew away these frail-looking, scared soldiers in their uncomfortable boots and olive-green trousers would still be clutching their guns and keeping guard at what would probably be the first target to be bombed to smithereens.

Most of the hostages walked arm in arm across the

runway to keep warm and support each other. They looked like ghosts. The lone 747 dwarfed them. All the lights had once again been turned off, apart from a single spotlight illuminating the steps. I went up the stairs and turned to wave goodbye.

'You're always late!' said a gruff voice. It was Frank Hessey. He had stayed on board to surprise his sister and brother-in-law. When they saw each other they burst into tears and hugged.

My last sight of the Iraqi soldiers was of them gathering together and starting to pull open the red Virgin packs we had given them. We may well have been the first Westerners they had ever met. They knew that the second lot would soon arrive, roaring overhead and firing missiles. Will Whitehorn had been checking through all the bags the hostages had brought with them. At the last minute he found a bag with a transistor radio which nobody claimed. Just as the plane door was about to be closed he ran towards it and threw the bag down on to the concrete. The soldiers were too startled to do anything. The bag lay there as the doors shut and the plane rolled back off the blocks.

Inside the plane there was a great cheer as the relatives swarmed down the aisles to hug each other. We put on seat belts for takeoff, but as soon as the plane levelled out the party started. We had got away. We were standing around with glasses of champagne and swapping stories when the pilot announced that we had left Iraqi airspace. There was applause.

I grabbed the microphone and pulled Ted Heath's leg by announcing, 'And I've just had word that Mrs Thatcher is *absolutely* delighted that Ted has managed to return safely!' Her *bête noire* was on the way home.

Frank Hessey, his sister Maureen and brother-in-law Tony held hands in a state of disbelief: they couldn't

"THIRTY OF THEM HAVE ASKED TO BE TAKEN BACK TO BAGHDAD!"

believe that they were together and had left Baghdad. Others on the plane were crying – they were delighted to be free but in turmoil over those they had left behind. Two months later Tony was to die of lung cancer, and Baghdad airport was reduced to rubble by the heaviest concentration of firepower ever used by a military force. I hope that the Iraqi soldiers with their badly cut uniforms had somehow managed to escape.

'Who the hell does Richard Branson think he is?' Lord King demanded of William Waldegrave in his second call to him. 'Part of the bloody Foreign Office?'

Lord King's indignation was echoed by some newspapers, who suggested I was doing it only for personal glory. Stung by this criticism, while staying with King Hussein I tried to analyse my motives in my diary:

Feel absolutely shattered. Been burning the candle at both ends. During an interview with ITN about the various people I saw, I choked up. Telling the story of the British father who had to hand his three-year-old child to a nanny at Baghdad airport to take her out of the country, and the woman from the Philippines who had that day left the country to have her second baby. I could only get halfway through telling it.

What are the motives for doing things? Is there any truth in the jibes? One month ago I was doing an interview with *Vanity Fair* and was at an all-time low. I'd seemed to have run out of a purpose in my life. I'd proved myself to myself in many areas. I'd just turned forty. I was seeking a new challenge. I was even considering selling up everything except for the airline. Getting smaller. Being able to focus on one business venture that I loved. But also to have the time to try to use my business skills to tackle issues that I felt I could help, such as in attacking the cigarette companies, cervical cancer, etc.

I felt I'd get better self-satisfaction in this way and would not be wasting the next forty years of my life just running companies, getting bigger – a repeat of the first forty years.

Do I need recognition for this? No, I don't think so. The dilemma is that to campaign on many issues you need to use yourself publicly to get people moving. Television is a very powerful medium. By my speaking on TV, the tons of medicine, the foodstuffs and blankets and tents reached the refugees. The £2 million from Mrs Thatcher's government has come through. An emergency meeting has taken place between the five main charities. Free advertising is to start on the BBC and ITV. I believe that by moving quickly a major disaster in this case has been averted. But, by not speaking out, it would not have been.

The dilemma is how often one can use the press in this way in one small country like England without losing one's appeal to the public. If there should be a hint that I'm doing it for personal glory, then I won't be able to do it at all.

By flying into Baghdad and rescuing the hostages Virgin had again usurped British Airways' traditional role. At the time I had no idea that the Virgin flight into Baghdad would annoy Lord King so much. I was trying to help out – I had an aeroplane at my disposal and I could act quickly. Although this plane was one of just four planes Virgin Atlantic operated, suddenly we looked like a much larger airline. We had successfully negotiated with Saddam Hussein; we had carried in medical supplies; and we had brought back the hostages. I only found out later that Lord King's indignant reaction was the start of an entire campaign by British Airways to try to put Virgin Atlantic out of business.

Above: My fetish for sweaters started at an early age.
Left: I have never liked desks. *Both Private Collection.*

Above: First edition of *Student*, with cover designed by Peter Blake. *Private Collection.*
Left: Speakers' Corner, Hyde Park, 1968. Debating the decade away on a soap box with Jane Butters. *Peter Pearson Lund.*

Above: Kristen and me at the Manor Studios with Bootleg, who was named after those albums in white sleeves we sold under the counter.

Above right: Just what exactly was it that the incredibly handsome Nik saw in Kristen's sister Meryll? *Both Private Collection.*

Above: Roger Dean's original design for our record label—Virgin Records. © *Roger Dean 1972.*

Left: Listening to an early tape of The Rolling Stones with a very young Mick Jagger. *Private Collection.*

Right: *Tubular Bells*—the first release on Virgin Records. It made Mike Oldfield (left) the biggest-selling artist of the 1970s and us our first fortune—to lose. *Private Collection.*

Below: *Tubular Bells* and *Never Mind the Bollocks* record sleeves.

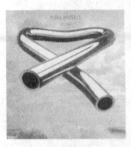

Right: With Boy George before heroin nearly destroyed his life and his musical career. *Rex Features.*

Above: After years of trying, we finally manage to sign The Stones. *Rex Features.*

Above: Making the best of a sad day, Friday March 4, 1992. Signing the deal with Colin Southgate and Jim Fifield of Thorn EMI. *Rex Features.*

Right: I take Janet Jackson on a balloon trip and threaten to use her as ballast. She signs with Virgin instead. *Mark Lockwood/Virgin Airship and Balloon Company.*

Right: I am lucky to share many of my experiences with my long-suffering parents.
Below Right: With father, Ted.
Both by Thierry Boccon-Gibod.

Above: Family album. *Roberta Booth.*
Below: Two loyal sisters, Lindi and Vanessa. *Private Collection.*

Above and left: Family album.
Above by Thierry Boccon-Gibod/left by Frank Spooner Pictures/Thierry Boccon-Gibod.

Below: Our lovely houseboat—home and headquarters.
Rex Features.

Right: Our own Virgin Island. Necker is one of the most beautiful jewels in the Caribbean and, with its great room **(above)** in the house on the hill, it remains my favorite getaway. *Both by Thierry Boccon-Gibod.*

Below: Impressing only the children and a couple of passing sea gulls, I arrive for our wedding with a box of chocolates in my teeth. *Private Collection.*

Left: Our wedding on Necker. A week later Sam said of a friend's wedding, "But they can't be getting married. They haven't had any children yet." *Private Collection.*

Right: Meeting the man I most admire in the world.

Below: With Princess Diana. *Both by Thierry Boccon-Gibod.*

Left: The Royal Navy comes to our rescue. *HMS Gannet, Royal Navy, Crown Copyright.*

Below: Being bounced across the Irish Sea seconds before Per jumped for his life. *Alan Lewis.*

Above: Richard and Per after rescue. *HMS Gannet, Royal Navy, Crown Copyright*

Right: Painful good-bye to Sam. *Thierry Boccon-Gibod*

Above: Balloons, balloons, balloons . . . Inflating the world's biggest balloon is a 48-hour project and a lot can go wrong. *Thierry Boccon-Gibod.*

Left: With Per on yet another photo shoot while we were waiting for the weather to come good for our round-the-world flight. *Rex Features/ Cam II/Virgin.*

Below: A day of contrasts—the beauty of the Atlas Mountains followed by a night of terror. *Thierry Boccon-Gibod.*

Above: Learning the tricks of the trade that Alex Ritchie had used to save our lives. *Frank SpoonerPictures/Thierry Boccon-Gibod.*

Right: Seconds before liftoff on our Atlantic crossing in 1987. *Private Collection.*

Above: Passing Bishop Rock Lighthouse off the Scilly Isles and bringing the Blue Riband back to Britain. *Private Collection.*

Right: Triumphant trip up the Thames with Margaret Thatcher and the crew. *Zoom Photographic.*

Above: Randolph Fields and me at a press conference before the inaugural flight to New York.

Left: Playing a prank during our inaugural flight with cricketers Ian Botham and Viv Richards.

Below: Liftoff! *All by Alan Davidson*

Right: Talking to and learning from passengers. *Thierry Boccon-Gibod.*

Below: Sir Freddie wishes us better luck than he had. *Arthur L. Field.*

Below right: Informal press conference on the plane about BA's dirty-tricks campaign. *Thierry Boccon-Gibod.*

Below: Outside the court. A moment to savor. *Rex Features/Today.*

Left: Lord King of BA and I bump into each other a few days after Virgin's victory. *Rex Features/Richard Young.*

Below: Dave Gaskill's view of our assault on the Iraq's president's stronghold. *Dave Gaskill.*

Above: Former British prime minister Edward Heath and King Hussein helped us to get the hostages out of Iraq. They celebrated in style on the flight home. *Mirror Syndication International.*

Above: Sometimes in the line of duty you have to make a fool of yourself. *Frank Spooner Pictures/Thierry Boccon-Gibod.*

Above right: Launching Virgin Brides—what a drag! *Rex Features/Julian Makey.*

Left: The "pirate" attacks Concorde at Heathrow. *Virgin Atlantic Press Office.*

Below left: Launching Virgin Vie. *Virgin Vie.*

Below: On the South Africa inaugural this friendly cat nearly removed my beard permantly. *Thierry Boccon-Gibod.*

Above: Two acres of Times Square, New York, 1992. How things have moved on since the Notting Hill pillows of 1972. *Thierry Boccon-Gibod.*

Left: On top of the world! *Mark Greenberg/ Visions.*

21 'We would have about two seconds to say our last prayers.'

November 1990–January 1991

E VER SINCE WE HAD abandoned our attempt the previous December, Per had been building the new envelope for the balloon that would attempt to take us across the Pacific Ocean. By the beginning of December it had been shipped out to Miyakonojo to join the capsule and await a good jet stream overhead.

A Japanese balloonist, Fumio Niwa, was challenging us to be the first to cross the Pacific, and was planning to fly a helium balloon. Per and I and our families and the balloon team arrived in Miyakonojo, and Fumio and I talked and joked over the radio as the preparation went on. He too was grounded by the unseasonably slow jet stream, which our weather-forecasting charts implied would leave us stranded somewhere over the Pacific. We waited and practised safety drills. We also watched the mounting tension in the Gulf on CNN. We felt sure that the Allied attack would take place just after Christmas. Per and I agreed that, if the Allied Forces declared war on Iraq, we would cancel the trip for a second time and return home.

As we approached Christmas there was still no war in the Gulf but there was also no sign of a sufficiently strong jet stream to take us across the Pacific. Bob Rice told us it was likely to be at least a week before an improvement. Per flew back to England for Christmas. Joan and I took our family down to Ishigaki, an island off the south Japanese coast.

The island was very quiet and had the classic Japanese landscape of mountains and sea. I spent time with my mother and father, and we watched the cormorant fishermen in their canoes. These fishermen were carrying out a tradition dating back several thousand years. They lined up six or seven birds along the edge of the boat and one by one the cormorants went diving for fish. The birds then brought them back to the boat and opened their beaks for the fishermen to remove the fish. The birds had rings round their necks to stop them swallowing.

I would have loved to have spoken to these fishermen. Probably they were as stressed about their money and families as anyone else, but their life seemed so tranquil and rooted in such an ancient tradition that I felt they must have come to terms with time in a way I never had. I wondered how they would have viewed my constant rushing about, my wish to set up new companies, to challenge myself, and to fly over the Pacific at 30,000 feet in a hot-air balloon.

At the end of our holiday, Joan took the children back to London to start school. Joan does not – understandably – like the idea of my ballooning and likes even less the idea of seeing me take off. I hugged them all farewell at Tokyo's Narita Airport and then braced myself for the trip. As my parents and I walked through the airport to catch an internal flight to Miyakonojo I saw a television screen. In wildly flickering footage the news showed a helicopter hovering over the sea and winching a body on board. From the respectful tone of the reporter, I immediately knew that it was Fumio, and that he was dead.

We had all been on such a high, but this put our lives and the risks I was taking with them into perspective: it could have been us. We found somebody who could speak a little English. They explained that Fumio had taken off the previous morning but had crashed into the sea just off the coast. He had radioed for help from his capsule but he was dead by the time the rescue helicopter arrived. He had died of exposure.

The sight of Fumio's body being winched out of the freezing ocean killed off much of my enthusiasm for the flight. I felt a deep sense of foreboding, but was equally helpless to withdraw. If the weather conditions were right, we would climb into the capsule and take off. I resigned myself to fate, and forced myself to make the best of it.

Later we found out exactly what had happened to Fumio. He had taken off the day before we were due back, hoping to steal a march on us. The strong winds had torn the envelope of his balloon, forcing him to ditch in the Pacific in his capsule. But the ocean was so rough that when the seaplane arrived it was unable to pick him up and had radioed for a helicopter. There was a delay while the rescue services sorted out which helicopter should come. By the time it arrived Fumio was dead. He'd been only about 10 miles into the 8,000-mile journey. It was a salutary warning.

Per and I planned to launch the balloon on Sunday 13 January. The Allied Forces had given Saddam Hussein a deadline of 15 January by which to leave Kuwait, and we felt sure that the attack would take place very soon after that deadline. Unfortunately it was too windy for us to inflate the balloon on Sunday and we postponed it until Monday. The jet stream now picked up speed, and by Monday 14 January it looked as if the flight might be possible. In the evening the weather cleared and we started inflating the balloon.

After taking a sleeping pill that afternoon, Per and I were woken at 2.30a.m. to go down to the launch site.

We made our way through the thousands of people who had come to watch despite the cold. We walked behind a police car which slowly inched along. The Japanese children held up candles and waved Union Jacks at us. They sang 'God Save The Queen' in perfect English accents. Once again people had set up braziers and were barbecuing fish and sweetcorn.

'Don't eat anything,' I warned Per as he was about to accept some fish. 'The last thing I need is you having a bout of food poisoning up there.'

In front of us, absorbing all the attention, the balloon was straining at its steel hawsers. It towered over everyone. This time it was large enough to swallow the dome of St Paul's cathedral. It had been heated to a great temperature, and was ready to soar upward as soon as the cables were cut.

We thanked the people of Miyakonojo for their hospitality and released some white doves as a rather futile peace gesture. Just before I climbed up the steps into the capsule, I sent someone to fetch my parents. Everyone was now very edgy, looking up at the straining balloon as it tried to rise. My parents made their way through the barriers and police and we just hugged each other. My mother gave me a letter which I zipped into a trouser pocket.

'Time to go!' Per yelled.

As we turned we saw Alex, our designer and engineer, emerge from the capsule with the biggest adjustable spanner we'd ever seen. 'I think it'll be OK now,' he said.

We climbed up the steps and ducked down into the capsule.

As the ground crew backed away, we started firing the burners. The pressure to lift grew stronger and stronger, and then Per fired the bolts which released the steel hawsers and we rocketed upward. For the first few breathless minutes we just marvelled at our silent speed. Then the balloon rose above the dark covering of cloud and we saw the silver dawn on the horizon. I got on to the radio and made contact with the ground crew.

'You're up and away!' Will Whitehorn shouted. 'The crowd down here are cheering like crazy. It looks amazing. You're heading up fast.'

Within five minutes we were out of sight of Miyakonojo and heading up into the jet stream. Within half an hour we were well over the Pacific Ocean. Then at 23,000 feet we hit the bottom of the jet stream. It was as if we had struck a glass ceiling. However much we burnt, the balloon refused to go in. The winds were too strong, and they were pushing down the flat dome of the balloon. We kept pushing up against it, and we kept being buffeted back down. We put on our parachutes and clipped ourselves to the life rafts in case the balloon suffered a catastrophic rip. Then, at last, the balloon edged into the jet stream.

The top of the balloon took off ahead of us, and I saw it streaming in front of and even below the capsule. We were knocked to one side. From travelling at 20 knots we were suddenly flying at 100 knots. For a moment I thought we were going to be torn apart, and I remembered my image of the thousand horses dragging us to pieces, but then the capsule came into the jet alongside the balloon and we were righted. The balloon rose above us again and we were safely tucked into the jet. Per's relief didn't give me the greatest of confidence:

'Nobody's done that before,' he said. 'We're in uncharted territory.'

After seven hours it was time to dump an empty fuel tank. We had six tanks of propane bolted to the capsule. The idea was that we would change the fuel tank when one was empty, jettison the dead weight, and fly correspondingly faster. We decided to go down out of the jet stream as we dropped the tank in case anything went wrong.

We had a video camera beneath the capsule which pointed vertically downward – in effect an extra window for us. The sea below us looked dangerous: it was running to great waves, and although we were 25,000 feet above it we could clearly see the white tops and the deep shadows of the troughs.

I looked at the video monitor as Per pressed the button to release the empty fuel tank. Before I could see what happened, the capsule lurched sideways. I was thrown across the capsule and landed on top of Per.

'What's happened?' I cried.

'No bloody idea.'

I crawled back up the sloping floor of the capsule to my seat. We were suspended at an angle of about 25 degrees above the horizontal. Per checked all the controls to see if he could see what had gone wrong. We had no idea if we were hanging by just one steel rope and the capsule was about to part company with the balloon and plummet down into the sea. I reran the video and watched what happened when the fuel tanks fell away. To my horror I saw three tanks falling down to the sea rather than one.

'Per, look at this.'

We watched again in silence.

'Bloody hell!' Per said. 'All the tanks on one side of the capsule have gone.'

Rather than jettisoning one empty tank, we had actually jettisoned one empty tank and two full ones. The implications of this were horrific. We had flown only around 1,000 miles and now we had just half the fuel we had started out with. We had three tanks of propane rather than five to fly us across the most dangerous and remote part of the Pacific Ocean.

'Watch out!' Per said. 'We're rising.'

I looked at the altimeter. Without the weight of the two full tanks of fuel, the balloon was soaring upward. We were once again buffeted as we entered the jet stream, but we hit it with such speed that we carried on rising. The altimeter ticked steadily upward from 31,000 feet to 34,000 feet.

'I'm letting air out,' Per said. 'We've got to come down.'

I stared at the altimeter, willing it to slow down: 35,000, 36,000, 37,000, 38,000 feet. We had no idea how strong the capsule was. We knew that the glass dome was able to withstand pressure of only around 42,000 feet, and even that was something of a guess. If we reached 43,000 feet the glass dome would explode. We would have about two seconds in which to say our last prayers, long enough to see our lungs being sucked out of our chests. After that our eyeballs would pop out of their sockets. We would become a scattering of debris somewhere in the Pacific.

Per had opened the vent at the top of the balloon, but it was still rising. The weight of the three fuel tanks we had dropped and the amount of hot air we'd needed to support them was the problem. It was a race between time and the altimeter. Thank goodness we had gone down out of the jet stream before we had dropped the fuel tanks.

'It's slowing,' I said with helpless optimism. 'I'm sure it's slowing.'

The altimeter ticked up: 39,000, 39,500, 40,000, 40,500, 41,000 feet.

We were now in the realm of the unknown. None of our equipment had been tested at this kind of height and anything could go wrong.

At 42,500 feet the altimeter finally stopped rising. I wondered bleakly whether this was because it had broken and simply could not register any greater height. We were way above the heights flown by all passenger jets except Concorde. But then it clicked down 500 feet. And then some more.

'We don't want to come down too fast,' Per said. 'We'll only have to burn fuel to bring us back up again.'

He shut the vent and the balloon continued to fall, down to 35,000 feet. Then we had to start firing the burners again to stay in the jet stream.

At last we could confront the problem of the lost fuel tanks. Our radio contact with the San José flight centre remained good, and they were clearly as devastated by the loss of the tanks as we were. There were some rapid calculations. If we were to reach land in the time available to us before the fuel ran out, we had to fly at an average speed of 170 miles an hour, twice as fast as any hot-air balloon had ever flown before. The odds against us were over-elming.

'What about Hawaii?' I asked. 'Can we aim to land nearby?'

'It's a needle in a haystack,' Per said. 'We'll never get anywhere near it.'

'I wonder if America is doable,' I whispered.

'Of course it's doable,' he said. 'The question is whether we can do it.'

Per's a precise logician when he wants to be.

I asked over the radio about the conditions below us. Mike Kendrick, the project manager, came on loud and agitated:

'I've just spoken to a cargo ship which is in the area. They said there's a strong wind and high seas. "Atrocious" is the word he used.'

Per leant over and urbanely asked Mike, 'What do you mean by "atrocious"? Over.'

'I mean *fucking atrocious*. You're not going to ditch in there. No boat will turn round to pick you up. There are waves over 50 feet high. The nearest boat says that the seas are running so high their boat would be bust in half if it tried to turn. Do you understand? Over.'

'Keep going on your current altitude,' Bob Rice came on. 'The jet is reasonably strong.'

Then, all of a sudden, the radio cut out.

For the next six hours we had no contact with the outside world. Due to the terrible weather around us we were in a high-frequency blackout spot. We were somewhere over the Pacific, hanging by a few steel hawsers to a vast balloon, the remaining fuel tanks dangling off the side of the capsule like a necklace, and we could not make any contact with anybody. We could barely control where we were going or how fast we were getting there, and we hardly dared move around the capsule. Our three main points of reference were the Global Positioning System, our watches and the altimeter. Every ten or fifteen minutes we took a reading off the GPS and calculated our groundspeed.

As we flew on Per began to show signs of utter exhaustion.

'I'm just going to have a rest,' he mumbled, and lay down on the floor.

I was alone. Unlike during the Atlantic crossing, when I had been more of a passenger than a pilot, I now really understood what was happening. If we were going to make land, our only chance was to keep the balloon absolutely in the centre of the jet stream. The vein of wind there is only a hundred metres wide, just four times the width of the balloon itself. But staying in it was our only hope.

The sky was pitch-black all around us. I scarcely looked out of the capsule and tried to concentrate on the instruments. As I sat there, with Per lying comatose on the floor, it seemed clear that we were both going to die. With just three fuel tanks we would run out of fuel some thousand miles off the American coast and have to ditch in the sea. It could well be night-time; Mike had told us the ground weather was atrocious – fucking atrocious – and nobody would be able to find us. We would have to fly this balloon for another thirty hours if we were going to live. I knew that the only chance of our living was for me to fly the balloon right in the core of the jet stream. I put all thoughts of death out of my head, and for the next ten hours concentrated intently on the dials.

I do not believe in God but, as I sat there in the damaged capsule, hopelessly vulnerable to the slightest shift in weather or mechanical fault, I could not believe my eyes. It was as if a spirit had entered the capsule and was helping us along. As I watched the instruments and calculated our groundspeed, it became clear that we were beginning to fly very fast, close to the necessary 170 miles an hour. Before we had dropped the fuel tanks we had been flying at about 80 miles an hour, which had been very good progress. This was a miracle.

I slapped myself across the face to make sure I wasn't hallucinating, but each fifteen minutes the speeds grew faster: 160 miles an hour, 180, 200, and even 240. This was astounding. I tried not to imagine the size of the balloon above me: I just looked at the dials and pretended that I was driving some kind of weightless car which I had to keep within a ribbon of road. Whenever we dropped speed, I assumed that we had dropped out of the inner core of the jet stream and so I burnt a little gas – as little as possible – and generally we picked up speed again.

Even at this amazing speed, it still takes an hour to fly 200 miles and we had 6,000 of them to fly. I tried not to be daunted by the length of the journey ahead, but concentrated on each fifteen-minute section. I was desperately trying not to fall asleep. My head kept dropping forward and I pinched myself to keep awake. I suddenly saw an eerie light on the glass dome above us. I looked up and marvelled at it: it was white and orange and flickering. Then I yelled: it was fire. I squinted at it and realised that burning white lumps of propane were tumbling all around the glass dome, just missing it.

'Per!' I yelled. 'We're on fire.'

Per lurched awake and looked up. He has incredibly quick reactions, and in spite of his exhaustion it took him a split second to decide what to do:

'Take her up,' he said. 'We've got to get up to 40,000 feet where there's no oxygen. Then the fire'll go out.'

I fired the burners and the balloon began to rise. It seemed to rise too slowly, and the lumps of propane continued to drop all around the glass dome. With the outside temperature at minus 70 degrees and the heat of the fireballs, it would take only one hitting the glass to explode it.

We rose through 36,000 feet, 38,000 feet, and put on our oxygen masks. They were scant comfort. If the glass dome cracked or melted, we would die within seconds from loss of air pressure. We were caught in a catch-22: the lack of oxygen at 40,000 feet would snuff out the flames on the glass dome but it could also snuff out the burners. If the burners went out before the propane fireballs, we'd drift back down to 36,000 feet before we could restart the burners and the propane fire would continue to threaten the glass.

We rose to 43,000 feet. At last the burners spluttered and the fire was snuffed out. Per opened the vent at the top of the balloon and we headed back down. As well as risking the capsule exploding at 43,000 feet, we had wasted precious fuel.

We flew on without radio communication for another hour. I kept myself going by talking into the video camera. I imagined that I was talking to Joan, Holly and Sam, and kept chatting away, telling them how much I loved them and that we were coming back to land in America. The balloon stayed at 29,000 feet, and continued to sweep northeastward towards the West Coast of America. We were in a tiny metal capsule swinging around in the stratosphere above a dark ocean. I was too frightened to eat anything other than apples and some chocolate. I wrote in my logbook:

Flown seventeen hours and four minutes. Feels like a lifetime. Coming near the dateline. When we cross the dateline we beat our world hot-air-ballooning record. However, right now we are about as far away from help as anyone could ever be, sitting in a tilting capsule with half our fuel gone, terrified that if we move the rest will fall off. Not sure whether war has broken out because we have lost all communication with the outside world. Unlikely to reach the coast. But spirits up and the speed we're going is amazing.

As our hours out of contact with San José continued, I wrote, 'Things look pretty desperate. I'm not certain at this moment that we'll get home.'

Then, just as abruptly as we had lost contact, we made it. I heard voices on the radio. By this time radio contact had been down for six hours and ten minutes.

Mike had thought he'd lost us as two of the ships he had steaming towards us had reported sighting wreckage.

'Mike, is that you?'

'Richard! Where are you?'

'Sitting in a tin can over the Pacific.'

We nearly wept with relief.

'We thought that you must have ditched. God, we practically mobilised the airforce and the navy.'

'We're OK,' I lied. 'We've had a fire up on the capsule from propane but it's gone out.'

I gave them our position.

'Any other problems, apart from not having enough fuel to go home?' Mike wanted to know.

'No. We're still tilting. We're certainly not going to fire off any more fuel tanks.'

'War's broken out in the Gulf,' a girl's voice said. It was Penni, who was in the control room with them. 'The Americans are bombing Baghdad.'

I thought of the soldiers I had met at Baghdad airport. The outbreak of the Gulf War meant that, if we did have to ditch, quite rightly we would be the last priority for anyone.

'Thank God we've got hold of you,' Bob Rice said. 'I've worked out your route. You need to come down immediately. Your current jet stream will soon start bending back towards Japan. You'll be marooned over the Pacific. If you come down from 30,000 feet to 18,000 feet you might get the jet that's heading north. It's sweeping up towards the Arctic but at least it's land.'

'Christ!' Mike swore. 'Another half an hour and you'd have been swinging back away from us.'

We cut off the burners and began to descend. After five hours Bob told us to rise again. We went back up to 30,000 feet and sure enough found ourselves heading northwest. We now flew steadily hour after hour. We stayed in the jet stream and kept the fuel we burnt to a minimum. We were still over the Pacific, flying at 200 miles an hour in a lopsided capsule, and we were exhausted, but now we had radio contact I felt that anything was possible. And the miracle continued. Our speeds were extraordinary: 210 miles an hour, 220, 200. We were just beating the average 180 miles an hour we needed. Someone was being very kind to us.

The good news was that we were now heading steadily towards the Canadian coastline. The fuel was lasting well; our speeds kept up; and Per and I began to believe that we might even make land. I was still too frightened to doze off since the only few seconds I had fallen asleep I had terrifying nightmares of skulls and death. We were both exhausted, dehydrated and fighting to keep our concentration.

'You're heading way north,' Mike Kendrick told us. 'The rescue team is chasing you to try to get to where you're going to land. They're in a Learjet. Will's there, and so are your parents.'

After 36 hours of flying, we finally crossed the coast of northern Canada. It was too dark to see, but we felt safer. Even though we were now heading for the Rockies, one of the most inhospitable mountain ranges you could find, at least it was land. We hugged each other and shared a chocolate bar. It was an incredible feeling. As we started flying over the Rockies, we made radio contact with the local ground control, Watson Lake Flight Service.

'Put your rescue beacon on,' they advised. 'You're heading into a blizzard. There's zero visibility and a wind of 35 knots. The Learjet has turned back to shelter at Yellowknife.'

Our exhilaration turned to despair. We put on the rescue beacon, and from then on every five seconds there was an ear-splitting beep. We had been expecting to land in California with an escort of helicopters but we had missed Los Angeles by 3,000 miles and were heading into an Arctic blizzard. We knew we could land safely and then die, just as easily as Fumio had done. Hot-air balloons are fragile things: they are not designed to be flown in blizzards. A bad blizzard could tear up the balloon and we could drop out of the sky. It was just before dawn.

We knew we had to land soon after dawn. If we left it for another two or three hours the sun would heat up the balloon's envelope and we would continue to fly past Greenland, deeper into the Arctic and out of reach of any rescue team.

One of my allotted jobs was to prepare the balloon for landing. When we were at 750 feet, I opened the hatch. Cold air and snow rushed in. I climbed out on to the top of the capsule. We were in the middle of a snowstorm, and whirling along at around 80 miles an hour. It was difficult to keep my balance as we were still hanging at an angle and the top of the metal capsule was frozen. I held on to the steel hawsers and leant across to remove the safety pins which are there to prevent the bolts from firing if we hit a lightning storm. I pulled them out and threw them into the snowstorm. I crouched there for a minute and watched the snow whirl around me.

The only light was the huge orange flame above me. Snowflakes were spinning around me and falling into the flame, where they vanished. One of the most magical things about ballooning is that you do not hear the wind because you are travelling at the same speed as it is. You can be flying at 150 miles an hour and put tissue paper on the capsule which – in theory – shouldn't blow off. And so, although we were in the middle of a snowstorm, it was very quiet. I was mesmerised by the sight of the snowflakes vanishing into the flames. Then I peered around and began to see the ground below us. I realised that one of the reasons why it was so dark was that we were flying over a thick pine forest. I shouted down to Per:

'Don't get too low. It's all forest. We'll never get out of there.'

I stayed on the top of the capsule and shouted down what I could see.

'There's a space ahead. Can you see it?'

'Prepare for landing,' Per shouted, and shut off the burner.

I climbed back into the capsule and we headed down. Our groundspeed was around 40 miles an hour when we crashed to earth with a hell of a bang. We went skidding across the ground before Per managed to fire the explosive bolts. Mercifully, this time they worked and the capsule ground to a halt as the envelope flew off without us. We were strapped in, but in a trice we were struggling to get out. Both of us thought the capsule might blow up with the last of the propane fuel.

We wrenched open the hatch and clambered outside. We hugged each other and danced a little jig in the snow. The silver balloon envelope had draped itself across the pine trees and was being shredded by the wind. Then we realised two things: the capsule wasn't going to blow up, and it was minus 60 degrees outside. Unless we got back inside, we'd get frostbite. We crawled inside the capsule and I made radio contact with Watson Lake Flight Service.

'We've done it. We've arrived. We're all in one piece.'

'Where are you?'

'We've landed on a lake surrounded by trees.'

'It's a frozen lake,' came the laconic Canadian voice. 'It's quite safe. The only trouble is that there are about

800,000 lakes in your vicinity and they've all got plenty of trees.'

We had to wait in our capsule for another eight hours. Per had frostbite in one of his feet, and I had frostbite in a finger. We huddled together, half-asleep, eating our supplies, desperate for warmth as the snow and wind howled around our metal capsule. We had landed over 300 miles from the nearest habitation, 150 miles from the nearest road, in an area of wilderness about 200 times the size of Britain.

'We've flown for 6,761 miles,' Per said with weary triumph. 'We flew for 46 hours and 6 minutes. That makes our average speed 127 knots, 147 miles per hour. These are all significant records. We've flown further than any other balloon has ever flown.'

'I'm dying for a hot drink,' was all I could say, 'and a log fire. And a sunny beach. Why aren't we in California!'

'Next time it's the ultimate flight,' Per started fantasising. 'It's round the world.'

When I peered out of the capsule I thought I saw something move. For a moment I thought that it was a dog and I had a surreal vision of somebody taking their dog for a walk along the frozen lake. As I watched the creature, it came up to the capsule and sniffed at it. It was an otter. It sniffed around us, then turned up its nose as if to say, 'Big deal – a capsule,' and slunk off. It was the only creature to have witnessed that we were the first to cross the Pacific – and it didn't even have a camera.

Every five seconds of those eight hours the emergency bleeper went off, piercing our eardrums. As we huddled together, I relived the flight and wondered why I had trusted Per with my life. We had landed over 2,000 miles away from our destination; we had lost two fuel tanks; we had caught fire; we had flown across the

Pacific in the dark with no radio contact. I remembered the previous flights – the first attempt from Japan had seen the balloon disintegrate and catch fire, and the Atlantic crossing had nearly killed us.

As Per talked about our flying round the world, I wondered whether I was mad to consider ever going with him again. I knew that he had pushed the technological boundaries of balloon flying further forward than anyone, but it was sad that we hadn't developed a stronger bond with each other. I get close to most of the people I spend a long time with. But Per is not a team player. He's a loner. He's often difficult to read. He's someone who is quick to criticise. I'd been brought up to look for the best in people. Per always seemed to find the worst. Despite this, we somehow managed to get on together as two opposites who can respect each other's strengths and weaknesses. And when it comes to ballooning I have plenty of weaknesses for him to respect! He also has had to put up with every project we do being branded a 'Branson' or 'Virgin' challenge, and he copes with that very well. Certainly, we have been through more together than most people experience in a lifetime.

As I tried to imagine us setting off round the world in a high-altitude balloon, I realised that, for all our horrendous moments together, our balloon flights had been some of the greatest adventures of my life. During the rest of my life, I am – to a greater or lesser extent – in control of my destiny. Up in a balloon we are at the mercy of the elements, the technology, the teams of engineers who have built it, and we are 30,000 feet up. The odds are not the best but I have always been unable to resist taking on odds that look formidable and then proving them wrong. And once again fortune had been kind to us.

At last we heard the thudding sound of a helicopter's blades. It got louder and louder, and then the helicopter circled overhead and landed beside us. We had the bags of videos and our logbooks ready, and we staggered over to the helicopter, Per limping with frostbite.

It was another four hours' flight to Yellowknife. When we landed at a tiny airfield, the yellow fluorescent lights made blurred circles in the driving snow. We crunched across the snow to the hangar. Gusts of flakes blew across us as we opened the door and stepped inside.

There was Will, Mum, Dad, Per's wife Helen, and some people from Yellowknife. I almost didn't recognise anyone since they were all wearing strange bulky clothing: bright-red padded jackets and thermal trousers. They roared with delight when we came in.

'Have a cold beer!' Will shouted. 'It's all there is!'

Per and I ripped off the ringpulls and sprayed everyone there.

'You've made it!' said Mum.

'Never again!' said Dad.

'What do you mean?' Per joked. 'We're going round the world next time. If those fuel tanks had stayed on we'd be over England now!'

'Have you got that letter I gave you?' Mum asked me.

It was still in my trouser pocket.

'It was written by some Japanese schoolchildren. You have to give it to the local child closest to where you land.'

One of the ground crew at Yellowknife had brought his six-year-old son along to see these two balloonists who had arrived from Japan, so I knelt down and gave him the letter.

'It's from some children who live in Miyakonojo in Japan,' I told him. 'You'd better go there one day. But perhaps not by balloon!'

Yellowknife town is so cold in January that diesel freezes solid. In order to stop your car from freezing, you either keep the engines running or plug them into special electric supplies which look like parking meters and heat the engines. We had a meal in the town's largest steak house, to which half the people living in Yellowknife turned up. When we came out of the restaurant, we could hardly breathe for exhaust fumes. Most of the shops are in underground shopping malls, which are easier to heat without the wind-chill to worry about. During the meal a fax arrived from the new prime minister, John Major, congratulating us on the flight. Surely Yellowknife was one of the most remote places the 10 Downing Street letterhead has ever found itself.

The next day we said goodbye to the gold miners and fur trappers who had looked after us so well at such short notice. It's not often they have guests ballooning down on them from Japan, and they invited us to come again. We flew to Seattle and then on to the warmth of Los Angeles. From there we caught the plane back to London, and I had a chance to read the newspapers and understand what was going on. The stock market had soared on the back of the invasion, and looking at the amount of firepower the Allied Forces were using it was hard to imagine that Iraq would survive for long. I spent some time talking to the crew and the pilots and heard how empty the flights were. One of the pilots warned me that the Gulf War was actually hiding a recession that was going to last a very long time.

'After all the bombing is over and Saddam Hussein is dead,' he said, 'the world will suddenly realise that it wasn't the "Mother of all Wars" which was the issue, but the "Mother of all Recessions".'

22 Flying into turbulence

January–February 1991

FRIDAY 25 JANUARY WAS the end of a bad week for Sidney Shaw, our account director from Lloyds Bank. He sat on the edge of my sofa fidgeting with his pen and papers, refused to have a cup of coffee and then changed his mind. Trevor and I began to worry. Sidney expressed no interest in last week's Pacific crossing and was reluctant to meet my eye. He was behaving ominously like my old Coutts bank manager.

'I saw Air Europe on Monday and Dan Air on Wednesday,' Sidney began, 'and I suspect that you're in much the same trouble. I'm afraid that we're pulling our loans out of both those airlines, and I don't see why we should support you any more. We can't see how you can possibly keep Virgin Atlantic going.'

It was clear where he was heading. He had come to see us in perhaps the worst week in what would become the worst year of aviation history. Virgin's group overdraft facility with Lloyds Bank was formally set at £20 million but we had now hit £50 million. After a visit by Lloyds Bank on Monday and the subsequent withdrawal of their loans, Air Europe – the largest independent short-haul airline in Europe – run by Harry Goodman, had been declared bust on Wednesday, with 4,000 redundancies. As with Laker, B-Cal, Dan Air and of course Virgin Atlantic, British Airways had managed to keep Air Europe confined to Gatwick.

As the Gulf War continued, the price of aviation fuel

was still over $1.20 a gallon, and passengers were still not flying – and certainly not flying the flag-carriers. To an outsider, the airline industry looked like a disaster. Yet, for the rest of the Virgin Group, the picture was pretty good. Virgin Communications would reach sales of over £150 million that year on Sega equipment alone. Simon and Ken were having no problems in selling records. Indeed Virgin singers Paula Abdul and Steve Winwood were top of the charts in America, and Bryan Ferry was there in Britain. The Gulf War and the gathering recession were not affecting record sales. The Virgin Megastores weren't making much money, but weren't losing anything either.

Virgin Atlantic was our biggest liability in that we had high overheads that we couldn't cut down. But even here the underlying picture was encouraging. Virgin holidaymakers were still all taking their holidays, and Ron Simms, then managing director of Virgin Holidays (since retired), forecast that we would increase this number from 83,000 the previous year to around 100,000 in 1991, a jump of 20 per cent. Ron had built up Virgin Holidays into one of the most profitable parts of Virgin Travel, and since I've never known him make a forecast that he can't comfortably beat by several thousand I took this as a concrete figure. Given that the average value of a Virgin holiday was £730, this meant that we would receive sales of over £73 million from these customers alone, and they would be taking seats that would otherwise be empty. There was equally good news on the cargo side: the rates for cargo to Japan had actually increased. Alan Chambers, who had success-fully built up our cargo division, pointed out that so many airlines had suspended services to the Far East that he was now able to charge a premium to transport cargo to Japan.

'What are we shipping out there?' I asked him.

'You'd never guess,' he said. 'Scottish smoked salmon and whisky are the bulk of it. Then we're bringing back computer games. It's a roaring business.'

It sometimes seems to me that I have spent all my life trying to persuade bankers to extend their loans. Given that Virgin's policy has always been to reinvest our surplus cash back into the business, our profit and loss accounts understate the underlying value of the businesses. This policy has worked over the long term, but whenever there is a crisis it disguises the real picture and means that the banks worry about our short-term profits and ability to pay our immediate interest. Trevor explained to Sidney Shaw that our balance sheet had included no value either for the Virgin brand name itself or for the contracts with the Virgin artists.

'Look,' I told Sidney Shaw. 'In a nutshell, we have very sound businesses. The record company alone will make £30 million profit this year, and that's in spite of the cost of making a massive investment in America. It's forecast to make £75 million next year. Virgin Communications and Virgin Retail are profitable. The airline, the holiday company and the freight company will also make profits by the end of the year. They're just having a bad patch. With the Gulf War and the winter, we've got a cash-flow shortage of £10–20 million. This is a tiny percentage of the total value of the Virgin Group and it'll be ironed out by the end of the year.

'Anyway,' I pointed out, 'we could easily sell some or all of Virgin Music. The latest Citibank valuation shows it to be worth $900 million. Now, are you going to withdraw your loan because of a temporary blip due to a war?'

'No, no, no,' Sidney backed down. 'But you must see it from our point of view.'

I could see it all too clearly from his point of view: Virgin Atlantic had a small cash-flow deficit, which, despite the great value in the rest of the Group, put us at the mercy of Lloyds Bank. Under the British banking system, banks make their money from charging high interest rates rather than taking any kind of equity stake, as they often do in Japan and Germany. British banks therefore have a greater incentive to cut and run from a company than see it through the bad times. It is in desperate times like the middle of a war that perfectly good profitable businesses go bust. The frightening thing about an airline is that it can go bust faster than almost any other business: all it takes is for the telephones to go quiet and for passengers to stop booking flights. Even a large airline can unravel in a matter of days.

By the time Sidney Shaw walked away from Holland Park, he seemed to have had most of his worries put to rest. He wrote me a letter admitting that his worst fears had been unfounded; he even apologised for 'overreacting'. For the time being, Lloyds Bank was back on our side. The only trouble was that the idea of our selling part or all of Virgin Music was now firmly on their agenda.

Trevor had made a number of forecasts for 1991, even the worst of which showed that over the year Virgin Atlantic would make a profit of £7 million. So we ourselves felt quite confident. However, as soon as I arrived back in London I realised that, beyond the immediate concerns of Lloyds Bank, there were some wider rumours going around the City that Virgin was going the way of Air Europe and Dan Air and that I was destined to become another Freddie Laker.

Rather than spending time searching for the right partner to invest in Virgin Music, I had to switch my attention to stamping out a bizarre variety of rumours about Virgin Atlantic. I was closely in touch with journalists, and so, when I started receiving a series of calls from them asking me in one breath whether there was a drugs problem at Heaven nightclub and in another breath about the finances of Virgin Atlantic, I was rather baffled. Up until then journalists had typically asked me about our new services on board the planes, the latest record signing, or what Janet Jackon was really like. And so, when 'serious' newspapers began firing questions about the drug scene at Heaven, and in the same conversation asking about the impact of currency movements on our profit and loss account, I felt that something rather strange was happening. I was bewildered. By the time almost every newspaper had inquired about Heaven, I felt that there must be some kind of campaign against us. It was most odd.

The news coming from the airline was also disturbing: the number of passengers who booked seats and then didn't turn up, the 'no-shows', had increased way beyond the levels any of us remembered since we had set up.

One day Will came into my office looking worried.

'I've just had a call from a friend at Rothschilds,' he said. 'Apparently Lord King was there for lunch yesterday, and he was bad-mouthing Virgin Atlantic.'

An accusation of financial weakness can rapidly become a self-fulfilling prophecy, particularly when it comes from as lofty and authoritative a source as Lord King of Wartnaby, whom nobody would think could ever feel threatened by a tiny airline like Virgin Atlantic. Lord King's accusation of Virgin Atlantic's financial weakness had a number of key audiences. For a start there was the press, which would not be slow to run a story about another successful entrepreneur who, like Alan Bond, Ralph Halpern, George Davis, Gerald Ronson, the Reichmanns and many others, was now overstretched and running into trouble. But, more significantly for us, Lord King would also be listened to by the bankers in the City whom we were considering approaching to place some shares in Virgin Atlantic. We had had some preliminary talks with the American bankers, Salomon Brothers, who were preparing a selling document to raise around £20 million. Rumours of our impending insolvency would pull the carpet from under our feet when trying to negotiate. The third audience whose antennae would pick up this rumour was the aircraft manufacturers and leasing companies: despite the recession we were looking to expand our fleet, but nobody would do business with a crippled airline. The last key audience was in many ways the most important to us in those first months of 1991: the Civil Aviation Authority, which has a duty to ensure that all airline companies are trading viably.

I am no stranger to healthy competition – working hard and playing hard – but there was no love lost between Virgin and BA. Over the last two years we had become embroiled in an increasingly acrimonious dispute over some maintenance BA had carried out on one of our planes. Thanks to their bad servicing, our 747 was grounded for sixteen days in August, the busiest time of the year.

In desperation I had called Sir Colin Marshall, chief executive of BA.

'Your engineering was so bad that it could have brought an aircraft down,' I told him.

'That's one of the perils of being in the aviation business,' he told me coldly. 'If you'd stuck to popular music you wouldn't have had this problem. No, we won't lend you a plane.'

All of which meant that, instead of making good money in the summer and living off it through the winter's lean months, Virgin Atlantic had a terrible summer and alienated passengers. Since we had paid out to lease the replacement aircraft, our cash flow was severely hit. When we tried to agree compensation, BA dragged its heels. They owed us several million pounds of compensation and by delaying payment precipitated a cash crisis at the airline which Virgin Music had to bail out. Just before I set off to Japan for the balloon flight, we had sued BA.

Alongside the maintenance dispute, our major battle with British Airways was our application for two extra flights a week to Japan, which was being negotiated with the Japanese Government. Flight timetables and slots may have no appeal outside the world of aviation, but they form our lifeblood. Without permission to fly somewhere, we literally can't take off. The battle over the slots and routes to Tokyo was a vital one for Virgin to win if we were to expand.

After the B-Cal takeover, their four flights to Tokyo had been transferred to Virgin, but it still wasn't enough. For the route to be viable we needed to be able to fly daily, and from Heathrow. Surely that had to be a priority before BA was allowed to fly twice a day during the week. Two frequencies – four slots – were then offered by the Japanese Government. BA naturally presumed they would be theirs. After consultations with our lawyers, and even though we knew that BA had already lined up for the slots, we made an application. Our future depended on it. If we were successful, Virgin would win not just the routes but – crucially – the slots that BA had arranged for them at Narita Airport, Tokyo.

When news of our application leaked out, British Airways went berserk. This kind of thing had never happened before: small airlines were meant to just let BA walk all over them and be grateful for any slots at all. But to ask for slots that were 'rightfully' theirs! They went into action. Lord King and his team lobbied good and hard that these slots were British Airways' rightful inheritance and that it was illegal to transfer them to Virgin Atlantic. This argument backfired:

'They're not "your" slots,' Malcolm Rifkind, the then secretary for transport, said curtly to British Airways. 'They actually belong to the government and we issue them to you. BA does not own them.'

When British Airways realised that they had lost that argument, they turned to more damaging allegations, pointing out that Virgin Atlantic was not a financially strong enough airline to take on these slots. In fact, they muttered, word was in the trade that Virgin Atlantic was about to go bust. Hence Lord King's comments at the Rothschilds lunch. They also wrote 'confidential' letters to the Department of Transport casting doubts on our finances. This hit the CAA on their Achilles heel. They could not award the frequencies to Virgin Atlantic only to see us suddenly go bust.

We had to battle to persuade the CAA that Virgin Atlantic was a viable airline. Throughout January, as the CAA deliberated whether to award these two Tokyo frequencies to us, I heard an increasing number of rumours about both Virgin and me, all of which implied that we were in trouble.

Finally, in the last week of January, the CAA made two historic decisions in our favour: it awarded the two extra frequencies to Virgin Atlantic, ordering British Airways to hand over to us the slots it had organised at Narita Airport; and it announced that it would recommend to the Department of Transport that Virgin Atlantic should be allowed to operate from Heathrow.

Lord King was furious. As a major donor to the Tory Party's finances, he announced that he had been betrayed and appealed against the Narita decision.

On 29 January, the first television documentary about the rivalry between Virgin Atlantic and British Airways was broadcast by Thames Television. This programme described the battle we were having over the Tokyo frequencies and open access to Heathrow, and also highlighted some of the other complaints Virgin Atlantic had about BA, including our long-standing maintenance dispute. The day after the Thames Television programme, British Airways issued a press release which claimed that Virgin Atlantic was abusing them. It referred to our attack on them as an 'onslaught'.

After hearing of another tirade of abuse from Lord King about me, and recognising that it could indirectly drive Virgin Atlantic bust, I wanted to have the rumours stopped. I didn't mind competition from British Airways or anyone else as long as it was fair competition, but I continued to hear a growing collection of damaging rumours.

On 31 January, I wrote my first letter to Lord King. I hoped that by bringing matters out into the open I would be able to stop the rumours. I have always believed that personal relationships are vital in business and that people should be directly accountable for their actions. If I alerted Lord King to what he had set in motion, I hoped that he would then call me and we would have a quick chat about it and bury the hatchet. I wrote:

> I am writing to put on record to you that I resent the level of personal abuse your people at British Airways have recently resorted to. As chairman of a

323

small independent airline I have behaved no differently than you would have done in my place. I have argued our case with the CAA over Tokyo slots. They have decided in our favour. That decision is now under review. We have argued our case for access to Heathrow. The CAA have decided in our favour and we are waiting on the secretary of state's final decision.

In none of these issues have we behaved improperly. We have sought remedies through the CAA, the Department of Transport, the EEC and the High Court when appropriate. We have not at any stage made offensive personal remarks about you or Sir Colin Marshall. I would expect the same courtesy from your company.

My letter was wishful thinking.

The next week Will was called by a man who introduced himself as Frank Dobson, private detective. He said that he wanted to have an urgent meeting with Will. He suggested a pub underneath Waterloo Station. Will went along with Gerrard Tyrrell, our lawyer from Harbottle and Lewis. Frank Dobson told them that a detective agency called Kroll Associates was investigating me and the whole Virgin Group. Frank Dobson asked Will whether he could work for Virgin to counteract whatever Kroll were up to. Will thanked him for his information but turned down the offer of his help since we never use private detectives.

I received Lord King's reply on 5 February. He merely quoted what he had said to the *Sunday Telegraph*: 'I run my airline; Richard Branson runs his. Best of luck to him.' He added that he intended to say nothing more on the subject.

The letter's brevity was matched only by its

arrogance. It was clear that Lord King treated me with a contempt that would rub off on how everyone at British Airways felt they could treat Virgin Atlantic.

Lord King's letter contained two short sentences. Lord King did not mean me to have the 'best of luck'. Indeed, if he could have anything to do with it, luck would not enter into it. And Lord King would go on to say a great deal about 'the subject' to a number of people.

The other peculiar thing about Lord King's letter was that it did not address me personally but only quoted a response he had made to a newspaper. It was as if he could not bring himself to address me as a person or even acknowledge me. I knew that he had coined the contemptuous expression 'the grinning pullover' to describe me. In the same way that British Airways was trying to steamroller Virgin Atlantic out of sight, it struck me that Lord King was pretending I didn't even exist.

23 Dirty tricks

February–April 1991

I N THE AFTERMATH OF the Thames Television programme, more alarming proof emerged of some
kind of campaign against me and Virgin.

'I've had a call from an ex-British Airways man,' Chris
Moss, our marketing manager at Virgin Atlantic, told
me. 'Peter Fleming saw the Thames Television
programme and says that he can confirm all sorts of
things BA have been up to.'

'Will he write it down?' I asked. 'Is it hard evidence?'

'He says that Virgin is BA's number-one enemy and
that after the Baghdad flight they set up a special team
to undermine you.'

'Can you get it in writing?'

'I'll try.'

Throughout February and March we discussed with
Malcolm Rifkind, the transport secretary, the question
of the disputed Tokyo frequencies and our access to
Heathrow. He was a down-to-earth Scot who gave us a
very fair hearing. I really felt that he was on our
wavelength when he pointed out how vastly improved
the Heathrow–Glasgow shuttle was:

'I now get a decent meal with proper cutlery,' he said.
'It used to be a damp little white sandwich.'

'That's British Midland bringing in some competition,' I
pointed out. 'They've got the slots to do it from Heathrow.'

I thought our lunch meeting had gone well, but right
at the end he floored me:

'Richard,' he said. 'You must admit that BA does do an excellent job.'

'Yes, they're much improved,' I agreed. 'But they have been given everything on a plate: for instance they were given Concorde for nothing with all the debts written off, and they were given the exclusive use of Heathrow.'

'They were,' Rifkind admitted. 'But it's all in the national interest.'

Silence fell between us. To my mind he had just undermined the entire lunch.

'There's no national interest at stake here,' I argued. 'British Airways is just a large airline which is owned by its shareholders. It happens to have a monopoly because that's what it was given while it was nationalised. But it's no longer like Aeroflot. Think of your old white sandwiches on the Glasgow shuttle. And, unlike other privatised monopolies, which have their market dominance reduced by regulators, BA has no regulator and has actually been allowed to increase its dominance since it was privatised.'

I thought that I might have gone too far because Malcolm Rifkind nodded rather awkwardly and made his way to the black Rover outside. I knew that he'd never flown Virgin because all members of parliament, all civil servants, all soldiers, were still encouraged to fly British Airways as if it was somehow still the 'national carrier'. As I watched his car head off back to Westminster, I wondered whether he really believed that British Airways operated in the national interest or whether he had just been playing devil's advocate.

'Good news, Richard,' said Malcolm Rifkind on 15 March 1991. 'I am pleased to say that the government is going to allow Virgin Atlantic to operate from Heathrow. And, on top of this, we are also going to nominate you as the British carrier to operate the two extra flights to Tokyo.'

It was the crucial turning point we had been waiting for.

'Fantastic news!' I shouted. 'Penni, let's have some champagne! Call down Will. Call down everyone!'

As everyone gathered in my office to celebrate, I dialled Hugh Welburn's number. Hugh had written a paper that pointed out the critical importance for an airline of operating from Heathrow. The paper's conclusion was that, due to the single short runway at Gatwick and the lack of connecting flights, an identical route from Heathrow would be 15 per cent more profitable than one from Gatwick. Hugh's paper, and the revelation that Virgin would be able to fly more cargo from the longer Heathrow runways and thus earn more taxable revenue, had made a powerful impression on Malcolm Rifkind.

'We've won,' I told Hugh. 'Well done. We've finally managed to get into Heathrow.'

Hugh was delighted and amazed. He had been a consultant in the aviation industry for a long time, and he had seen the demise of British Caledonian and several other smaller airlines that had failed to make ends meet from Gatwick.

'This is your breakthrough,' he said. 'But watch out. British Airways won't like it at all – they'll go berserk.'

As we drank champagne, the telephone started ringing with calls from journalists who had picked up the story. They were also ringing up Lord King, and the following day and over the weekend I read his reaction with interest:

'Government transport policy?' Lord King snorted in the *Observer*, of which his son-in-law Melvin Marckus was the business editor. 'What transport policy?'

I didn't know whether to laugh at the interview or be annoyed. I read on with growing amazement:

'It seems that every time we build up a profitable route,' Lord King went on to say, 'someone comes along and says, "I'll have some of that," and the government obliges.'

Lord King estimated that Malcolm Rifkind's decision to allow Virgin Atlantic to fly the extra two flights to Tokyo would cost BA around £250 million a year in lost revenue: 'That is £250 million of revenue lost to our public shareholders which has gone straight into Richard Branson's back pocket,' he fulminated.

If only revenue did go straight into my back pocket. Perhaps in his rage Lord King had forgotten that there are costs that unfortunately crop up between revenue and profit.

On the same day the *Sunday Telegraph* commented:

> This week Lord King was breathing fire over the decision finally to allow Virgin into Heathrow. Its long confinement at Gatwick has been a boon to BA and now I can see why. British Airways' approach to its services is hidebound by the managerial thinking of a national airline while Virgin has all the cheek, determination and original thinking of the whippersnapper entrepreneur snapping at the heels of the giant conglomerate. In terms of food and service, upper-class Virgin is like first class.

In the *Observer* Lord King argued, no doubt with a straight face, that each time the government tried to foster a strong second airline it ended in disaster. He gave the examples of Laker Airlines, British Caledonian and Air Europe. This was stunning hypocrisy. British Airways had helped push Freddie Laker out of business

– a grand jury was empanelled to look into the issue but, ultimately, no charges were brought after the intervention of the UK and US Governments. All three airlines had been confined to Gatwick. British Airways championed the benefits of competition, as long as the competition stayed out of sight at Gatwick.

My parents had always drilled into me that the best motto to follow is 'Nothing ventured; nothing gained'. By fighting tooth and claw for access to Heathrow, we had finally won. Virgin Atlantic was still tiny in comparison with British Airways, but we were now a serious threat to their long-term future in a way that British Caledonian had never been.

The demise of PanAm and TWA was also to play a role in the question of our access to Heathrow. American Airlines and United Airlines, the two giant American carriers, moved in to buy the rights to the routes into Heathrow that PanAm and TWA had operated. In order for these routes to be activated, the two airlines asked for the Heathrow slots to be transferred over to them. Under the strict letter of the Traffic Distribution Rules these slots could not be transferred but should revert to the Heathrow Slot Committee. We immediately argued that, if this should happen, then Virgin Atlantic should be allowed to apply for them alongside all other carriers who were interested in flying from Heathrow. Although Malcolm Rifkind had opened up Heathrow in principle, we still had a battle on our hands over how we would actually get the slots to fly from there.

The letter I had asked Chris Moss to try to extract from the British Airways employee, Peter Fleming, came through on the following Monday morning. It added to my sense of unease. Dated 18 March, Peter Fleming's letter said:

There is no doubt that BA's UK sales management had Virgin as public enemy number one. The real crisis was precipitated by the high profile Richard Branson achieved during his campaign to return hostages from the Gulf. During this period I was debriefed from a UK sales management meeting and told that a management team had been set up to undermine the 'Branson image'.

The development of actions in the European Courts [Virgin had put in a formal complaint] has however precipitated a thorough 'cover-up' of activities. In the last few months at BA I was told on three separate occasions to destroy 'any reference to Virgin in [my] files'. Staff in sensitive areas have been briefed on 'anti-trust' laws and how to respond to a sensitive situation involving Virgin. Actually, the current situation is verging on paranoia!

Peter Fleming had been a senior marketing executive based at BA's Victoria office. This was the first real intimation I had that British Airways had actually set up a special internal unit to discredit me, and had ordered the shredding of documents relating to Virgin. Why were those documents so incriminating that they needed to be shredded? I decided to put Peter Fleming's letter on file while we watched to see how the British Airways campaign, which became known as their 'dirty tricks' campaign, developed.

In the meantime, we had plenty to do. If Virgin Atlantic was going to operate from Heathrow, we had to set up check-in desks, baggage handlers, an engineering team, and of course we had to have a working timetable to offer our passengers. This meant being allocated slots. Only when we had the slots in place could Virgin Atlantic set up a timetable and then sell tickets. If we were going to benefit from the busy summer traffic we had to have these in place by April at the latest. Every single item was a battle. It was only through battling ferociously, and saying that we would take the entire issue of slot allocation to the European Commission, that we were eventually given the slots we needed.

While I was locked in my debate with the Heathrow Slot Committee, Jordan Harris and Jeff Ayeroff, who ran our American record label, called me to say that Janet Jackson had told them she would like to sign up with Virgin Music. This was as sensational a breakthrough for Virgin Music as winning access to Heathrow was for Virgin Atlantic. Janet Jackson was the world's top female singer and I recognised that she had the single-minded determination to stay at the top. She wanted to become even more successful than her brother Michael. Alongside talent, one of the deciding factors in a singer's success is their mental strength. And Janet had plenty of that. She had built up her success over a number of records. In many ways it is better for a band if they take a long time to build their success since they can then learn to live with it, and they have a broader, more loyal, fan base.

Although Janet told me that she would like to sign with Virgin, there was still to be an auction for her and Virgin would have to match the highest offer before her preference for us would swing it. It was going to cost far more money than we had at our immediate disposal, but I instinctively knew that we had to have her: signing Janet Jackson would confirm Virgin's position as the world's sexiest record company. I was damned if I was going to let the caution of our bankers stop us.

Throughout my business life I have always tried to keep on top of costs and protect the downside risk as much as possible. The Virgin Group has survived only because we have always kept tight control of our cash. But, likewise, I also know that sometimes it is essential to break these rules and spend lavishly. The chance of signing Janet Jackson was one of these moments: she could not be missed. After talking with Simon and Ken, I decided to offer Janet the largest amount of money ever to be offered to any singer. On top of this, I decided to break all the rules of the record industry: rather than tying her down for a number of future albums, Virgin would offer her a contract for just one album. This was virtually unprecedented. I wanted to blow away the competition. I felt confident that once Janet started working with Virgin she wouldn't want to go anywhere else.

As well as cementing Virgin Music's position as the best record label, signing Janet Jackson would send out the right message to all the people in the City and the CAA who might believe the British Airways rumours that the Virgin Group was suffering a cash crisis.

The only trouble was that we were indeed suffering a cash crisis. I knew that we would receive no help from Lloyds Bank if I asked for an extension of the overdraft to sign her, so Trevor and I looked for ways to juggle our assets and find more finance so that we could make the down payment. After a number of rapid meetings with banks, Trevor finally won the approval of the Bank of Nova Scotia, who told us that they would fund the Janet Jackson contract.

We offered Janet Jackson $15 million, with a payment of $5 million on signature. However, the auction soon topped that and we had to jump up to $20 million and finally $25 million, just for the one album. It was millions more dollars than any record company had ever paid for a single album. We pointed out to the bank that Janet was the world's top female singer and she had had more top-five singles from her last album than any other singer, including her brother Michael. The Bank of Nova Scotia assured us that they would stretch to the $25 million.

As good as her word, when the bidding levelled out at $25 million, Janet chose Virgin. The contract was ours for the signing and we had to find $11 million to pay her upon signature. I don't think Janet had any idea of the effort it took to scrape the money together, or of the wild plane dashes across the world with banker's drafts that were necessary to meet her deadline – but somehow we did it.

24 The kick boxer in the first room

April–July 1991

W<small>E DECIDED TO PAY</small> a huge sum – some $25 million – to sign up Janet Jackson. But such a huge debt caused alarm bells to ring at Lloyds Bank as they saw us take on board another load of debt, Trevor and Robert managed to sell the European licence to distribute Sega computer games back to the parent company, Sega in Japan. We needed the cash and we needed to show the outside world some of the hidden value within the Virgin Group. None of the bankers had put much value on the licence, but we sold it for £33 million. The sale was also perfectly timed: a year later the bottom fell out of the computer-games market, and the yen soared, which would have sliced the value of the licence to practically nothing.

Virgin had acquired the European licence to distribute Sega games in 1988, when we bought the company who owned it, Mastertronic. At the time we had little idea of the potential of the computer-games business. All I knew was that Holly, Sam and their friends were suddenly spending a lot of time playing computer games on the television. While Trevor was at MAM he spent time with Sega as he leased out their arcade machines. He felt sure that Sega would be able to draw upon their software expertise to rival Nintendo, and that their new portfolio of small machines to play with at home would sell well. It seemed like a good business to get into.

Mastertronic was only five years old. Frank Hermann had set it up in 1983 and acquired the rights to a number of computer games. At that time he distributed these games, which were on cassettes and played on consoles, through newsagents. Frank noticed that a new games series manufactured by Nintendo was selling well in America. He tried to sign up the licence to distribute Nintendo in Britain, but Nintendo had already signed it to Mattel, a large toy manufacturer. Nintendo had a 95 per cent share of the computer-games market in America, so Frank went to see its only other competitor, Sega. He signed up to become Sega's British distributor in 1986, and in the first year his company managed to sell 20,000 Sega Megadrives.

The next year, 1987, Mastertronic's sales of Sega were soaring but, given that Sega were charging £55 for a console, Frank needed a partner to finance the sales. Although he could sell the consoles for £99, he needed a large amount of working capital to finance the gap between the £55 outlay to Sega for supplying the console, which was cash in advance, and receiving the £99 from selling it.

In June 1987 I was telephoned by Roger Seelig, who asked me to come and meet a friend of his, Frank Hermann, who had stumbled into this rather amazing business. Trevor and Simon Burke negotiated to buy a 45 per cent stake in Mastertronic, and we put it in with Virgin Communications. Frank and Robert started working together and they bought the licence to distribute Sega in Spain, France and Germany for five years. Their challenge was to build the Sega name from scratch in Europe. Virgin marketed Sega as the cool game to play, and initially we sold it on the basis that, while your younger brother may be happy with Nintendo games such as Super Mario and Gameboy, the smarter games for smarter kids were ones such as Sega's Sonic the Hedgehog. Then, as the market developed rapidly, we found that younger and younger boys were buying Sonic: they all wanted to be like their older brothers. Our trick was to position Sega above Nintendo and force them further and further down-market. And it worked: in Europe Sega overtook Nintendo with a 45 per cent market share, compared with a tiny market share back home in Japan.

By 1991 the sales of Sega in Europe had soared to £150 million, up from £2 million in 1988. By then we were beginning to be rather terrified that the bubble might burst. In order to maintain our position we were having to spend £70 million marketing Sega each year, before the cost of financing the sales. There was always the danger that, because these games were primarily sold to an extremely narrow section of teenage boys, if another craze came along out of the blue, then Sega's sales would collapse. Peer pressure ensures that nobody wants to be left behind for a moment.

At home I noticed that Sam and Holly began to grow bored with their computer games. They spent less time tapping away at their consoles and Gameboys. Sam began to listen to music more, and Holly began to do other things. Just as they had turned us on to the idea of buying into this business, so Holly and Sam gave us the first warning signs that the market was topping out. If we stayed in the business we would have to commit to another huge budget for promoting Sega. It was time to sell.

The sale of the Sega licence surprised both the outside world and our bankers: £33 million in cash had been conjured up for a business on which they had placed no value. This was over ten times our original purchase price.

Before starting discussions to sell the Sega licence, Robert had hived off the small team who wrote the software programmes into a separate company called Virgin Interactive. In 1990 the next wave of technology would be games which were played on compact disc, and Robert commissioned a number of software writers to come up with programmes for CDs. Without Sega and Sonic the Hedgehog to worry about, the tiny team of software programmers that Robert had assembled in America began to devise a new game for CD-ROM technology. They named it 'The 7th Guest', and I noticed that people were growing increasingly excited about it. It was a game that involved battling your way through a haunted house while all kinds of attacks were launched at you without warning.

'I've no idea what happens in this game since I'm always killed by the kick boxer in the first room,' Robert told me. 'All I know is that these guys tell me that The 7th Guest is going to be big. They say it's way ahead of anything else on the market.'

As the world of virtual reality and CD-ROMs expanded and kids fought their way out of haunted houses on their computer screens, I found myself in an equally weird world in which I had to fight off a growing number of attacks that arrived from every side without warning.

'Perhaps it was just a bad day but one of Virgin's passengers was clearly not impressed with the service in upper class last week. An entry in the visitors' book read: "No wonder your boss travels round the world in a balloon."'

This was a small piece entitled 'VERDICT ON VIRGIN' among the sheaf of press cuttings I looked through one Monday morning in June 1991. The journalist was

Frank Kane, who wrote extensively about aviation and in particular British Airways; the newspaper was the *Sunday Telegraph*, of which Lord King was a nonexecutive director. I picked up the phone and called Syd Pennington, the managing director at Virgin Atlantic:

'Did you see that piece in the *Sunday Telegraph*? Please can you send me the pages of the visitors' book for the last fortnight?'

It sounded all wrong to me. We had so few passenger complaints that I felt sure that the crew would have alerted me to this one. I found the entry in the visitors' book. It read exactly as Frank Kane had quoted it, but he'd missed out the punch line: 'But seriously, I had a great time.'

All the other quotes in the book about that flight were highly complimentary. I don't mind bad press as long as it is accurate, but this clearly was not. I traced the passenger, Cathy Holland, and phoned her up to check that she'd had a good flight. She assured me that she'd had a wonderful flight and that – as she'd made clear – it was just a joke. Then I wrote to the *Sunday Telegraph* and pointed out that Frank Kane had failed to quote her comment in its entirety. I knew that many elderly *Sunday Telegraph* readers would be sceptical about flying Virgin anyway, but this snippet would put them off even more. What was a casual mean joke to a journalist meant many thousands of lost pounds to Virgin Atlantic – and to my bankers. Worse still, Carol Thatcher then read the piece out on television on the David Frost show. I wrote to her pointing out that the journalist had misled her, but the damage was done. Six million viewers did not know that this comment was taken out of context.

I called up Frank Kane to complain and he was apologetic.

'Oops, I'm sorry about that misquote,' he said. 'I looked over a neighbour's shoulder and that's all I could see.'

'That's all right,' I said.

'There was another comment in the book,' Kane went on. 'It said, "I couldn't get a seat on the BA flight because they were giving tickets away today. I'm glad. I shall fly Virgin from now on."'

On 7 July Virgin started flying in and out of Heathrow. As Hugh Welburn had predicted, our sales on the three routes we offered, JFK, Tokyo and Los Angeles, rapidly increased by 15 per cent. On 14 July, British Airways' internal magazine, *BA News*, published an article entitled 'VIRGIN OUT TO SNATCH MORE SLOTS', and once again said how unfair it was that a lower-priced competitor should be allowed to compete with them.

Then, on 16 July, Lord King stood up at the British Airways Annual General Meeting and announced that British Airways would stop making its annual donations to the Conservative Party. Lord King had failed to spot that this gave away the fact that they thought that donating money to the Conservatives in the past had helped them secure various privileges. Some critics pointed out that these same donations, which totalled £180,000 since BA had been privatised in 1987, had helped secure a sympathetic hearing whenever British Airways needed to speak to the Department of Transport. If an airline in Nigeria gave money and free air tickets to the ruling party in return for being granted a monopoly, it would be scorned in the West as being blatantly corrupt. 'It's impossible to do business in Africa!' people would retort. 'Look at the Nigerians: they're so damned corrupt!' The round of applause that British Airways won for this announcement at its

Annual General Meeting on 16 July struck me as amusing.

Indeed, BA's influence went further than merely giving money to the Conservative Party. During the summer I gave a presentation to a group of MPs about the lack of competition in British aviation. Afterward, I was having a drink with the MPs and found myself chatting to two of them about their holiday plans.

'Have you seen your travel agent yet?' one asked.

'No, I'm just going to give them a call to get my free ticket.'

'Who's this travel agent?' I asked.

'British Airways, of course!' they chorused.

When Lord King stopped British Airways' donations to the Conservatives, I hoped that it would put British Airways as firmly out of favour as the previous donations had clearly kept them in favour. I also hoped that the government would start encouraging more competition. The day after BA's AGM, Sir Michael Bishop, the chairman of British Midland, and I released a press statement which congratulated the British Government on freeing up Heathrow, and supported it against British Airways' criticism.

Despite the excitement of starting our Heathrow operation in July 1991, it was clear that Virgin Atlantic would be unable to expand any further for a while. In the event, we couldn't offer a new route for another three years, until we started flying to Hong Kong in 1994. This was due to one of the fiercest, most focused and vicious attacks ever launched by an airline against a smaller competitor.

25 'Sue the bastards.'

September–October 1991

W<small>E WERE UP AT MILL END</small> one weekend in September 1991 when it really looked as if my world was falling apart. After the high point of signing Janet Jackson and getting into Heathrow earlier in the year, everything was now going wrong. With the burden of funding the Janet Jackson deal, even Virgin Music was having difficulties. And the airline was stretched almost to breaking point by trying to operate out of both Gatwick and Heathrow. On top of that, the rumours about Virgin's financial troubles were mounting. It was rather like being engulfed in a bush fire: although I kept stamping out flames, I was aware that more and more people were talking about my impending bankruptcy. I had taken so many telephone calls from journalists demanding to know whether our cheques were bouncing that I could barely think straight. I needed some fresh air and privacy, so I walked round the lake several times to try to work out what to do. I felt overwhelmed by the problems I faced.

Although we had signed Janet, I was growing increasingly worried about Simon's commitment to Virgin Music. He had stopped going out to clubs to search for new talent and, as a result, Virgin had failed to break any significant new bands for a couple of years. In many ways, breaking a new band is the acid test of how dynamic a record company is. I knew that Simon was worried that the value of his shares in Virgin Music was at risk if something went wrong with Virgin Atlantic. But, equally, I was worried that his lack of commitment to Virgin Music would damage the value of my shareholding. His heart wasn't in the business any more, and he seemed more interested in his own personal projects.

Virgin Atlantic was having an extremely hard time competing with British Airways. Our engineering teams were now driving three or four times a day between Heathrow and Gatwick to service each flight, and if a flight was delayed at one airport it had a knock-on effect in the other. Will had heard that Lord King was going around announcing proudly that the 'battle of Fortress Heathrow has been won – Virgin's about to collapse'.

On top of all this, BA was now blatantly poaching our passengers. We had two reports that BA had called up a Virgin Atlantic passenger at home and tried to persuade them to change their flight from Virgin to BA. Our staff had also seen BA staff approaching Virgin Atlantic passengers at the terminals and trying to persuade them to switch to BA.

I was caught in the middle between Virgin Atlantic and Virgin Music. I was alone in being the only person with a foot in each camp. The only other thing that bound them together was Lloyds Bank, in that the loans which Lloyds had made to Virgin Atlantic were guaranteed by Virgin Music. This was the crux of Simon's worry, but the airline would not have been able to function any other way.

Our troubles at Virgin Atlantic brought the question of the future of Virgin Music to a head. Throughout the summer, Simon, Trevor, Ken, Robert and I had tried to work out what to do. I had effectively put the idea of the possible sale of the record company to the back of my mind, but with the rumours about Virgin Atlantic mounting into a great wave I realised that something had to give.

'Have you seen this?' Will brought in the new issue of *Fortune* on Monday morning. It had a photograph of me lounging on the floating deck chair in Necker Island. I was holding a book entitled *Mavericks in Paradise*, and the caption was: 'Richard Branson, founder of the Virgin Group, savours the billionaire's life ... in the British Virgin Islands naturally!'

I read with interest that I was worth $1.5 billion.

'I hope Lloyds read this.'

'They may read it,' Will said. 'But will they believe it?'

'It's in the papers,' I laughed. 'It must be true!'

'WILL RICHARD BRANSON'S BALLOON BURST?' was the headline on Wednesday 2 October. The entire page of the *Guardian*'s business section was devoted to discussing my debts. 'Behind the Man with the Midas touch there is a picture of a highly indebted and not-very-profitable conglomerate,' it read. The subheadline was: 'THE MELODY LINGERS BUT WON'T MEET INVESTMENT NEEDS'. This article had come out of the blue. Normally when journalists do a profile, even for a hatchet job, they contact me to go over some of the ground. But this *Guardian* journalist had never made contact.

I started reading: 'The latest available accounts for the Virgin companies show an alarming picture of faltering cash flows failing to meet the companies' investment requirements.' I looked through the article with a horrible feeling that this could inspire a host of other newspaper stories along similar lines. If it looked to informed financial journalists that Virgin was in such trouble, then the bankers would head straight back to their vaults, taking their money with them.

'Virgin therefore remains highly exposed,' the article concluded. 'It remains tiny by comparison with its key competitors. Its main businesses are in highly volatile industries. The legacy of the buy-back, together with the ballooning growth of the empire, keep debts at stubbornly high levels. The Branson balloon appears to be pursuing a dangerous path to the stratosphere. It is an exciting journey, undertaken with no shortage of panache, but Mr Branson's balloon journeys are unfortunate models for any business to follow.'

This article had caught us at our most vulnerable. All the accounts were shown in the worst possible light. To the world at large, or at any rate to the *Guardian*'s readers, it looked as if I was in the same boat as Alan Bond: Richard Branson was sinking fast.

The phone started ringing with other journalists asking for my reaction, and I went through the response which Will and I had drafted. We tried to emphasise how factually inaccurate the figures were, how the article ignored the intangible value of Virgin Music's contracts, and how it put no value on Virgin Atlantic's aircraft. I was due to fly to Japan that day and, with the flight leaving at 5p.m., I didn't have much time to respond to the *Guardian*. I began scribbling a letter to the newspaper's editor. I tried to shrug off the article:

There are many inaccuracies that could have been avoided in your article 'WILL RICHARD BRANSON'S BALLOON BURST?' if your journalist had had the courtesy of speaking with me before writing it. Since I'm off to Japan in a few minutes (amusingly in the context of this letter to be made a doctor of economics!) I'll spare your readers a long list of them. However, to give you but one inaccuracy, our profits didn't 'plunge' as a public company – they doubled!

I went on to argue that the net worth of all my companies after repayment of every debt was around £1 billion. Will came down to discuss the letter.

'It's got to be more than a letter on this one,' Will said. 'You've been attacked with a whole-page article. What I want to do is get them to give you a whole page to defend yourself.'

'They'll never do that.'

'They might. It'll cause a commotion and that's good for the *Guardian*. It's better than a letter tucked away on page 27 that nobody will read.'

Together, we wrote out a whole article rebutting the *Guardian*'s piece, but before I could finish it I had to leave for Tokyo. The moment I arrived there Will was back on the phone:

'OK, we've got half a page,' he said. 'It's better than nothing. I'm faxing you the draft. The *Guardian* thought we might sue them so I think they were relieved when we asked for the right to reply.'

I called up Trevor and asked what Lloyds thought of the piece.

'Funnily enough, they're quite relaxed about it,' he told me.

When I telephoned Lloyds I found out why.

'Yes, I did see the piece,' John Hobley said, 'but I don't think many other people did. In any event, nobody I know takes the *Guardian* very seriously. If that piece had been in the *Daily Telegraph* or the *FT* it would have been a different matter.'

'Now, what's your decision on the loan?' I tried to sound casual, as if I really didn't mind one way or another.

'The board have passed it,' Hobley said. 'We've got a mechanism which will give us precedence over your assets in the retail operation.'

I put the phone down, lay back on my hotel bed and

shut my eyes. If that article had appeared almost anywhere else, the City's reaction would have been very different. It is a frightening truth, but perception is everything with some of these bankers. Normally we have been able to use the perception of Virgin to our advantage. But for the first time the boot was on the other foot and we were fighting to restore confidence. If such an article had appeared in the *Financial Times*, the banks could well have pulled out their loans and brought the Virgin Group crashing down.

I was in Japan to receive an honorary doctorate. The university had asked me to fly out to meet the students and suggested I do a question and answer session rather than a formal speech. As I sat in front of a thousand students, the professor asked for questions. There was a deathly hush which lasted for nearly three minutes. To break the ice I said that the first person to ask me a question would get two upper-class tickets to London. Fifty hands shot up. For the next three hours I was kept very busy.

I was also looking at a possible site for a Virgin Megastore in Kyoto. Mike Inman and I took the train from Tokyo to Kyoto. This train was called the 'Shinkansen', popularly known as the 'Bullet Train'. It was rather like being on board a plane: there were audios to listen to, steward service and even vending machines.

'Why can't trains be like this in the UK?' I wondered. I jotted down some notes about trains in Britain and trains in Japan and then turned my attention to the Megastore site.

Back in London the next week, Will's telephone rang on Friday evening. It was Toby Helm, the transport correspondent on the *Sunday Telegraph*. He asked Will

347

whether Virgin would be interested in operating trains if the government privatised British Rail. Will came down to ask me.

'Well, are we?' I asked back.

The more we talked, the more sense it made. Railways had to be one of the answers to all the traffic problems. Every new motorway was immediately clogged up; driving from London to Manchester was a nightmare.

'Tell him that we are,' I suggested. 'It can't do any harm.'

The headline of the *Sunday Telegraph* read 'VIRGIN TO GO INTO TRAINS' and explained that Virgin wanted to operate the east-coast franchise and do a joint venture with British Rail. It became the story of the week – a useful distraction from our cash problems and an excellent counter to all the negative publicity we had suffered. It showed us thinking about expanding rather than worrying about our finances. It was a crucial release of pressure for us, and for a while journalists stopped going on about our finances and imminent collapse, and started taking an interest in our bold plans for the future.

All kinds of people called us up on Monday, including Siemens and GEC, and among them was someone who introduced himself as Jim Steer from Steer Davies Gleave, transport consultants. Will immediately recognised that Jim knew what he was talking about.

'You've got to follow this through,' Jim told Will. 'I suggest that you get together with Intercity and offer a joint service on the 125s.'

We registered three possible trading names, 'Virgin Rail', 'Virgin Express' and 'Virgin Flyer', and asked Jim to commission an artist's impression of a Virgin train. We warned him that our budget was zero, but he went ahead anyway and then put us in touch with a venture-capital firm called Electra who he said might put up some seed money to investigate the idea. Will and I went along to Electra and met someone called Rowan Gormley who agreed to put up £20,000 to commission a feasibility study.

Armed with a small business plan and a mock-up of a Virgin train, Trevor, Will and I, together with Jim and Rowan Gormley, met Chris Green, the director of British Rail's Intercity service; Roger Freeman from the Ministry of Transport; and John Welsby, the chief executive of British Rail. We talked about the possibility of Virgin running some railway services, but British Rail weren't keen. John Welsby was against any kind of privatisation and he saw our proposal as the thin end of the wedge.

As he walked out of the meeting, he turned to one of his companions and made a comment which was picked up on the intercom and broadcast all over the office. He said, 'I'll be in my grave before that fucker gets his logo on my trains.'

Throughout the week of 21 October, I stood in for Angela Rippon on her early-morning LBC radio show. This was not my ideal job since it entailed getting up at 5a.m. and heading off in the dark to the LBC building near Euston. I was in the studio from 6a.m. to 8a.m. and then went home for breakfast.

The radio-show producer called up Lord King to invite him on the show to debate with me the problems which British Airways and Virgin were having and the sorts of tactics that British Airways was employing against us.

'Tell him we're not prepared to lower our standards that much,' Lord King snapped at her. 'And you can quote me.'

It was the first time I had approached Lord King since our exchange of letters in January and February, but his reply had lost none of its sting. My invitation to Lord King to debate what was going on was only half tongue in cheek. The previous week I had been called by Joseph Campbell, who ran a limousine service for Virgin Records.

'Richard,' he said, 'I'm sorry to bother you but I thought you should know that something rather sinister has happened. One of the ladies who works for us has a daughter who works for a company of private investigators. And she told her mother that the company has just started spying on you. They followed you to Claridges last week and sat at the next-door table.'

I flicked back my diary: I had indeed had lunch at Claridges. I thanked Joseph and wondered what to do. Should I call the police? I put the telephone down and looked at it. All my life the telephone had been my lifeline. But now I wondered whether anyone was listening in to my calls. I wondered whether these private detectives were following my children to school. Or sifting through my dustbins. I wandered over to the window and looked up Holland Park. Perhaps the British Telecom van parked there was a fraud and was actually packed with listening devices. Perhaps I had been reading too many spy novels.

Then I pushed the thought out of my mind. I couldn't change the way I lived and I had nothing to hide. If I tried to second-guess these detectives and whoever was employing them, who I was sure had to be British Airways, then I would drive myself mad. I couldn't live like that. If I started thinking that I was being continually followed, I'd rapidly become paranoid. I decided I would carry on my life as normal. I wouldn't even stoop to their level by having my telephone checked for bugs.

All week I was up at 5a.m., and by Friday I was feeling rather exhausted. In the middle of the afternoon I went back to my office to find a note on my desk from Penni: 'Chris Hutchins from *Today* called about a potential gossip story. Wanted you to call him back.'

Chris Hutchins was a gossip columnist with *Today* newspaper who had a known drink problem.

I called him back.

'Richard, first of all I want you to know that I've done Alcoholics Anonymous,' Chris said. 'I'm clean, so you can take what I say seriously.'

I began to listen and picked up my notebook.

'I've spoken to Brian Basham.'

'Who's he?'

'BA's PR man. He is to Lord King what Tim Bell is to Lord Hanson. I know Basham's wife Eileen quite well because she used to work for me here. She called me to say that Brian might have a good story about Branson and drugs.'

'Great,' I said sarcastically.

'I called Basham up and he told me that he'd been doing a detailed study for BA on Virgin's operations, its strengths and weaknesses. He also mentioned an unsubstantiated story about Heaven and suggested that I check out the drug position there for myself. He said he didn't particularly want to put you out of business; in fact the last thing BA wanted was to be seen to have your blood on its hands.'

This struck a chord. I tried to remember which other journalists had been asking about Heaven and suddenly it came to me: among them was Frank Kane, the financial journalist on the City pages of the *Sunday Telegraph*.

'He then told me that I should also look at the recent piece in the *Guardian* about your cash position. Well, finance isn't my thing and I wasn't that interested.'

'Well, perhaps you should turn the tables on BA and investigate them,' I suggested.

'I could consider that,' Chris said, 'but it's not really my style. I just write a gossip column. Anyway, I'm having lunch with Brian Basham on Monday at the Savoy.'

'Will you come and see me over the weekend?' I asked. 'I'd love to chat this through with you.'

'Sure,' Chris said.

I buzzed the intercom up to Will.

'Chris Hutchins called me.'

'He was the one in 1989 who caused all that fuss by claiming you were in for a knighthood: "ARISE, SIR RICHARD". Remember?' Will said.

'He sounds like he's cleaned himself up. He called me with a story about BA and their interest in us.' I read from my notes. 'Have you heard of Brian Bingham?'

'No,' Will said, nonplussed.

'Well, he is to Lord King what Tim Bell is to Lord Hanson.'

'Never heard of him,' Will said.

'Basham,' I corrected. 'Brian Basham, and he's talking about drugs at Heaven.'

'Brian Basham! Christ! I'm coming down.'

Will always looks flustered, as if he's itching to get on and make the next telephone call, but when he stormed into my room he looked in a flat panic.

'Brian Basham is bad news,' he said. 'He's one of the most influential PR men in the business. If he's up against us we're in deep, deep shit. He's got closer ties in Fleet Street than anyone.'

26 Barbarians at the departure gate

October–November 1991

B RITISH AIRWAYS WAS OBVIOUSLY gaining access to computer information that should have been off limits. It was confirmed when, out of the blue, Peter Fleming from BA wrote a second letter in which he detailed a number of things that British Airways had done. Dated 29 October 1991, it covered a wider range than his letter from earlier in the year. He started off by repeating how a management task force had been set up to discredit the 'Branson image'. 'This, I felt,' he wrote, 'would have originated as a strategy at a very senior level within BA. I was shocked that the company could be so open about this and state it in such an uncompromising way.' He went on to say:

> However, not long after when Virgin took some
> concerns to the European Courts there was a
> noticeable backlash which swept the whole
> company. At this time I was told to destroy all
> documents that had any references to Virgin, not
> once but four or five times by different people from
> managers to managers' secretaries. Again I was
> reasonably shocked that BA's senior management
> could be so concerned about its activities that it felt
> that all references to an airline should be destroyed
> in this way. I did not destroy anything myself, as I
> did not feel that my files had anything of a damaging
> nature, but I know that other people in my

department did destroy material because of this directive.

Peter Fleming had already described these two aspects of BA's campaign, but I was still surprised to see them set out in black and white. More interesting were the further details he highlighted: 'The following points are the issues that I was aware of in respect of BA trying to squeeze Virgin out of the picture. They do not necessarily constitute anti-competitive behaviour but this is something for you to decide.'

The list included British Airways deliberately applying for slots to Japan and Australia that it didn't need for the sole purpose of stopping Virgin getting them; a special sales force getting business in the Gatwick area and offering low fares from Gatwick to squeeze yields for all airlines there (while continuing to operate a high-fare monopoly from Heathrow); refusing to process bookings for passengers who had flown from Japan to Gatwick by Virgin and then wanted to switch to BA, so that they would have to fly BA all the way; and accessing our booking information by delving into the computer reservations system.

'In my opinion,' Fleming wrote, 'BA lacks integrity and this stems right from the top of the organisation with Lord King, and unfortunately permeates the whole structure.'

With Peter Fleming's evidence, I now knew some of what British Airways was doing behind the scenes; when I also got hold of Chris Hutchins' tape of his conversation with Brian Basham I also knew what they were doing in the press. Although I was caught in this two-pronged attack, at least I knew exactly which tactics BA was using. It was sinister, but I could begin to think about how to retaliate.

'BRANSON ATTACKS BA "TRICKS"' was the headline in the *Sunday Times* on 3 November 1991. This wasn't exactly what I had in mind but it was true nonetheless. I'd been hoping that the *Sunday Times* would stick their neck out and say how scandalous they thought BA's tactics were rather than just repeating my claims, but it was a start. For the first time in the campaign, Brian Basham was publicly linked with British Airways, blowing his cover. Insight reported how Basham had given his confidential report to a number of journalists. I was quoted as saying that I had a list of one hundred complaints which I would take to the European Commission unless British Airways stopped their dirty tricks. And Nick Rufford made no mention of the cash-for-fuel story which had started his investigation.

27 'They're calling me a liar.'

November 1991–March 1992

'RICHARD YOU'RE NOT GONNA believe this about BA,' Ronnie Thomas told me.

'Try me,' I said. 'At this particular moment I'm prepared to believe almost anything.'

Ronnie Thomas runs his own limousine company in New York. Twenty years ago he started out as a regular cab driver in Manhattan and slowly saved enough money to trade in his clapped-out yellow cab for a smart limousine, which he offered as a chauffeur-driven service specialising in collecting and dropping off passengers at New York's two airports. By the time I met him in 1986 he had a successful limousine service with over 200 cars. He had called me as soon as he read that Virgin Atlantic was going to offer a limousine service to all upper-class passengers, and he pitched for the entire account. He won it, and over the years Ronnie has never let us down.

In the previous few days he and his drivers had been finding that, when they dropped passengers off at the kerb, British Airways staff were meeting them and offering them 'incentives' to fly BA instead of Virgin. Ronnie had had a flaming argument with them, and later got a call from BA banning him from BA's own terminal at JFK.

'Have you ever come across anything like this before?' I asked Ronnie.

'No, man,' he said. 'I thought that American carriers

weren't exactly gentlemen, but this is another ball game altogether.'

I had no idea whether this was illegal or not, but it was certainly the most blatant attempt yet to poach our passengers.

After the *Sunday Times* had exposed some of British Airways' tactics, the next paper to follow was the *Guardian*, with a front-page headline: 'BA UNDER FIRE FOR VIRGIN CAMPAIGN'. There was a full-page analysis of British Airways' tactics entitled 'VIRGIN'S COMPLAINT TO EC CASTS MORE DOUBT ON BA'S PRACTICES'.

In spite of the articles, the dirty tricks carried on. No matter how many accurate press stories were published, British Airways had always been immune to criticism. To the world at large, they shrugged off my allegations as the hysterical overreaction of a man who couldn't take competition. Their arrogance was overwhelming. As it became clear that British Airways was intent on seeing the back of us, I knew that I had to fight back even harder. In mounting desperation, I began to look for any legal action that we could take against British Airways.

'It would amount to an anti-trust case in America,' Gerrard concluded when we'd finished going through what BA was up to. 'But there's no equivalent legislation here.'

There is a surprising lack of legislation governing competition in the British aviation industry. The Monopolies Commission and the Office of Fair Trading had no jurisdiction over BA in this instance, since they could investigate only an airline merger, and the CAA had little jurisdiction beyond the safety angles involved in servicing aircraft and supervising the prices of air tickets. Although BA was a privatised monopoly like British Telecom, there was no government watchdog like Oftel to supervise it. We had lodged a complaint with the European Court, but although there were some grounds for this court to rule against BA under Article 85 of the Treaty of Rome, which deals with the principles of fair competition, in practice it lacked the teeth to enforce any request that might make a company change its business tactics. In effect, our list of complaints to the European Court was useful only as a publicity exercise.

I didn't want to take British Airways to court. I knew that it would be expensive and risky, and that they would employ a top-flight team of lawyers to try to overwhelm us and the jury with the great weight of statistics that a vast airline can muster. I simply wanted the dirty tricks to stop and, as I cast about for other ways in which to persuade British Airways to call off their campaign, I thought of the nonexecutive directors. Since I had already written to Lord King without success, I hoped that the nonexecutive directors of British Airways might be more impartial. If I asked them to investigate what was going on in their company, then in principle they would have to take that request seriously. A nonexecutive company director has the same legal responsibilities as an executive director, but they typically look after the shareholders' interests if there is a conflict between the directors and the shareholders. As British Airways was now being accused of behaviour that could create such a conflict, and accused by the press as well as by Virgin Atlantic, the shareholders deserved an explanation of what their company directors were doing.

The British Airways nonexecutive directors comprised Sir Michael Angus (a director of Thorn EMI at the time and formerly chairman of Unilever), Lord White (who ran Hanson Trust with Lord Hanson), the

Honourable Charles Price, Sir Francis Kennedy, and Michael Davis. Their names read like a Debrett of business. The letter took me over a week to compose, and set out everything we knew about what British Airways was up to. On 11 December 1991, I eventually signed and sent off an eleven-page document which outlined the facts and concluded:

> I have found it hard to believe that a major public company like BA could be behind the sort of conduct identified in this letter whose primary purpose can only be the discrediting of a competitor and the damaging of its business. I am writing to you because I doubt whether you would want a company of which you are a director to conduct itself in such a way and in the hope that the directors of BA would wish to be absolutely and unequivocally disassociated from any such activities because they would agree that it was not the proper way to run a business.
>
> I would like you to investigate the matters raised in this letter, provide detailed responses and give me your assurance that you will ensure that the conduct revealed to you on investigation or any similar conduct is stopped and never again repeated.
>
> I would have thought that British Airways' experience of trying to eliminate the competitive threat posed by Laker Airways was sufficient deterrent against trying to do the same to others. I am sure you remember the impact upon BA of its actions towards Laker Airways. BA's privatisation plans were disrupted; the directors in the United States were threatened with criminal prosecution; there was a huge waste of management time; BA attracted considerable adverse publicity; millions of dollars were spent in legal expenses and BA made

the biggest single contribution to the massive legal settlement fund.

I attached an eight-page appendix which covered all the details I knew, and divided the dirty tricks into six sections: the press campaign, spoiling tactics, engineering matters, sales and marketing, dirty tricks, and private investigators(?). I put a question mark on the final category since I still found it impossible to believe, and wrote, 'Bizarre incidents have been taking place recently more suitable for an episode of *Dick Tracy* than the airline industry.' I related the snippets I'd picked up and asked, 'Can you shed any light on any of these incidents? I cannot believe that a major public company like British Airways is behind this sort of conduct.'

As the letter was sent, I had no idea what reaction to expect. I did not wish to sue British Airways. There was enough to do without having to spend eighteen hours a day fighting British Airways. I was acutely aware that I was having to ignore all the other businesses within the Virgin Group as we fought this battle.

I wondered whether the nonexecutive directors would assume that I couldn't compete with Freddie Laker's court case, which had produced over a million legal documents. Sir Freddie had sued British Airways only after he had gone bust and had time to devote all his energy to the lawsuit. But, by then, of course, BA had accomplished their task. The court case may have delayed their privatisation and forced them to pay £10 million compensation, but this was nothing compared with the profits they made on the transatlantic route by hiking prices as soon as Laker's planes were grounded. I was trying to stop British Airways while simultaneously running the airline, but BA might not back off until Virgin was grounded too.

Whatever their reaction, I felt sure that the nonexecutive directors could not ignore the eight-page attachment which detailed their company's dirty tricks. Since they were also responsible to their shareholders, we released copies of this letter to the press to ensure that their shareholders would have the chance to read it too.

To my amazement, I received a reply from both Sir Colin Marshall and Sir Michael Angus the very next day. Sir Michael Angus wrote a disclaimer saying that it would be 'wholly inappropriate for the nonexecutive directors of a public company to report to a third party in the manner that you request', and concluded that 'the proper course of action is for any such allegation to be directed to the board as a whole'.

Sir Colin Marshall's answer was equally patronising. His letter flatly denied that British Airways was involved in a deliberate attempt to damage Virgin or sought 'to compete other than through normal marketing and promotional efforts'. He suggested that our 'allegations' were made to gain publicity, and that I should devote my 'undoubted energies to more constructive purposes'.

Given the time these two directors had taken to respond to my letter, they could not have begun to investigate any of its contents.

I replied to Sir Colin Marshall on 16 December 1991 and urged him to reconsider his dismissive attitude to my allegations. I did not accuse him of masterminding the dirty tricks or even condoning them, but merely asked him to look at the facts. I wanted to give him every chance to put a stop to what was going on. I wrote:

I had always hoped that you personally had no knowledge of the worst that had been going on at

361

British Airways. However, having read your response to my letter I'm no longer sure, for your letter continues the lies that we at Virgin have had to contend with. The allegations are certainly not 'unjustified'. In fact many of them are not our allegations but matters that first came to our attention from reports in the *Sunday Times* and the *Guardian*. I notice that you have written to neither paper refuting them. They also came to our attention from Virgin passengers who were shocked that BA could get their home phone numbers and offer them incentives to cancel their firm Virgin tickets and switch to BA ... How can you dismiss them out of hand without any inquiry? I ask *you* to take the matters raised seriously and respond to my letter point by point. We can then get on to competing in a fair manner.

But Sir Colin Marshall wrote straight back as if he had barely bothered to read my letter: 'I see nothing to be gained from further correspondence.'

For a time afterward it looked as if British Airways' version of events was gaining ground. Sir Colin Marshall was quoted everywhere saying that my allegations were 'utterly without foundation' and, although he never said that Marcia Borne or Ronnie Thomas were figments of my imagination, people outside Virgin could have been forgiven for assuming that there was an element of truth in BA's denial.

My allegations against British Airways had passed the point of no return. Unless British Airways apologised and put an end to their dirty tricks, I would have to follow up my open letter to the nonexecutive directors with some kind of legal action. The difficulty was finding the appropriate grounds upon which to sue.

The row between us had one immediate casualty that I should have foreseen: Virgin Atlantic was completely unable to raise any money. Salomons, our American investment bank, were trying to raise £20 million of capital by privately offering some of the equity for sale. But, in exactly the same way as it had been impossible to sell equity in British Airways while the Laker court case dragged on, so nobody would touch Virgin Atlantic while it looked as if we would go to court against BA. And we were still losing money. While we had been frantically busy trying to piece together what British Airways was up to, our consortium of lending banks had continued to watch the cash flow. And in the depths of winter the numbers looked much worse.

I realised that, to this extent, I'd played straight into British Airways' hands. One of their objectives was to stop me expanding Virgin Atlantic, and the only way I could do that was by refinancing the airline. The louder I complained about their dirty tricks, the less any other airline, venture-capital house, or other investor wanted to invest in Virgin Atlantic. Outsiders probably thought that there was no smoke without fire. We lost both ways: nobody wanted to invest in a small airline if it was being squeezed out by a vast organisation like British Airways; and nobody wanted to invest in an airline that might embark on lengthy and expensive litigation against one of the world's largest airlines.

Without funds forthcoming from the City, Virgin Atlantic continued to be starved of capital. By Christmas 1991 Virgin Atlantic was ploughing through the difficult winter months and losing money. Our six main lending banks continued to write to Trevor reminding us that our loans were due to be repaid next April, and Lloyds Bank, which was our clearing bank and so saw wide fluctuations as money came in and went out, grew increasingly anxious. Perhaps British Airways gambled that, even if we did announce a legal action, they could spin it out long enough so that we would go bust in the meantime. Even after my letter of 11 December, British Airways was brazen and laughed off my allegations.

For once I did not know what to do. I spent a lot of time thinking and became very quiet. Will went the opposite way and spent all day in a fury about British Airways, shouting and ranting in his frustration at not being able to land a proper punch on them.

On 21 December a letter arrived from Lloyds Bank which heightened the sense that we were under siege. It reminded us that we had recently exceeded our £55 million overdraft facility, and spelt out that the bank had allowed the excess only because the money had been needed to pay salaries and because IATA had confirmed that £7.5 million was due into our account the following day. We were warned that the bank might not 'respond favourably to another request to break the £55 million limit'. It finished by wishing us a happy Christmas and 'a less stressful New Year'.

If that £7.5 million had been delayed by a week Lloyds might well have bounced our salary cheques. If Virgin Atlantic went bust, I couldn't even be sure that Virgin Music would remain intact. I doubted that Janet Jackson or Phil Collins would be impressed by the airline's collapse.

As we talked about where we could find sufficient funding to replace some of the bank debt, it became increasingly clear that we had to find some radical solution rather than always arguing with banks over small amounts of increased debt. Virgin Music was our only seriously profitable business, and it was our only chance to save the airline. With the weight of bad publicity caused by BA hanging over us, we couldn't sell

Virgin Atlantic as a going concern, but we could sell Virgin Music as one. Selling Virgin Music would save the airline and leave two strong companies. Closing down Virgin Atlantic would leave one strong company and one bust company, with 2,500 redundancies and the Virgin Group's reputation as a company and a brand name in tatters.

I called up John Thornton, who was still talking to several companies that were interested in acquiring Virgin Music. I had watched his progress with a growing sense of foreboding, unable either to feel any enthusiasm for it or be able to stop it. John told me that Thorn EMI was now offering £425 million upfront with an earn-out starting from the second year. This was still below the level at which David Geffen had sold his record label to MCA. In March 1990 he had sold his record company for $520 million, which then represented 2.6 times annual sales. On a similar multiple, Virgin Music was worth 2.6 times our sales of £330 million – over £850 million.

Throughout January 1992, Lloyds increased their pressure on us to reduce our overdraft. John Hobley from Lloyds toughened his stance considerably. Since we had mentioned the possible sale of Virgin Music a year ago, that was all he wanted to hear about: Why wasn't there more progress? Could they talk to Goldman Sachs themselves? From their point of view, if the sale didn't happen then Virgin Music would remain a collection of music contracts – intangible assets. They couldn't understand why there was such a long delay. Was there something wrong with Virgin Music? Had the bidders walked away? Was the company really worth the $1 billion we had airily mentioned? Their patience was wearing thin, and they wanted to see their loans to

Virgin returned to their vaults as real cash. One of our problems was that a large amount of our debt was due to be repaid in April, and Trevor and I felt doubtful that we could persuade the bank to roll these loans over to a later date.

The bank's correspondence reminded me of some of the letters I had received from Coutts when they were losing their nerve about their client with shoulder-length hair who had padded barefoot into their offices to discuss a loan to buy a manor in Oxfordshire. My hair was now shorter and Virgin was bigger, but the bank remained uneasy. Although we had never failed to make a payment, they had other clients collapsing on them and they were concerned.

The investment atmosphere of early January is summed up by this stock-market report:

> Attention is now focusing on Lonrho's debt
> mountain and the attitude of its principal lenders,
> Lloyds, Standard Chartered, Barclays and Nat West.
> Lonrho's director, Paul Spicer, insists Lonrho's
> relationships with its bankers are 'in good order' and
> the group 'is under no pressure from them'. But,
> after the debt debacles at Polly Peck, Brent Walker
> and Maxwell, there is hardly a banker in London who
> lives comfortably these days with large lines of credit
> to entrepreneurial companies driven by a powerful
> individual. Rightly or not, Rowland is being squeezed
> by 'the tycoon factor'; and his position is made worse
> by the recession, which had slashed the value of
> Lonrho's assets at a time when the company must
> sell businesses to raise cash. The old maestro has
> escaped from tight corners before, and nobody can
> say that he will not do so again. This time however
> the pressure is really on.

The ingredients of the story looked ominously similar to ours.

As Lloyds saw their money at risk to an entrepreneurial company, John Hobley made one more effort to control our overdraft. In a letter dated 3 January, he pointed out that our overdraft had continued to rise and that Lloyds was 'not in a position to fund this outflow'. It was clear that Lloyds expected us to sell Virgin Music within the month. John reminded us that our overdraft had to be paid off in full by the end of the month and that in the meantime we could not extend our overdraft facility again. He expressed surprise that we had even considered holding on to Virgin Music in the hope of a better offer than Thorn EMI's.

This was as bad as the Coutts crisis in 1984. Even then we had time and were able to see some other banks to form a syndicate. But January 1992 was as bad a month for bankers and airlines as January 1991 had been, when Air Europe and Dan Air went under. All the bankers were in a tailspin and it was difficult to remain calm.

We owed £55 million to Lloyds. As we headed into February and March the airline would need cash funding of a further £30 million. The winter months are the most expensive since we have to pay for all the major aircraft maintenance at the same time as the number of passengers drops off. So much for the unsecured debt. Looking at the cash coming in, we knew that Virgin Music had sales of £330 million that year, making operating profits of £38 million; next year we were forecasting sales of £400 million with operating profits of £75 million. But Lloyds were not willing to wait. I could see that something had to give.

A second Thames Television programme about the battle between British Airways and Virgin Atlantic was due to be broadcast at the end of February. This time it was Thames Television's flagship national current-affairs programme, *This Week*. Will and I had first met the producer, Martyn Gregory, at the beginning of January, when he had come to see us about the documentary. We had told him as much as we could about British Airways, and then left him to carry out his own independent research. Martyn had spoken to Peter Fleming, along with various other ex-British Airways staff whom we had not come across, and had managed to verify many of my accusations of BA's dirty tricks. British Airways refused to participate in the programme and their legal director, Mervyn Walker, wrote to Martyn Gregory and accused him of falling 'into the trap of being used as a vehicle for Richard Branson's propaganda'. Nothing could have been guaranteed to infuriate an independent television producer more.

I was in two minds about the programme. I could see that by showing people all the dirty tricks we were up against they might have two responses. One possible response was that they would be able to see our vulnerability and thus might back away from Virgin Atlantic as a likely loser. Just the words 'A plane will fall out of the sky', even if they were spoken by Brian Basham, who was working for British Airways, might remain in people's minds and worry them about flying Virgin Atlantic. But, equally, the public might rally round and support us as the underdog. This was my main hope. Gerrard also pointed out that, since the television audience is so wide, it might jolt some people's memories and prompt them to telephone Virgin Atlantic and tell other stories that would help us as we compiled all our evidence against British Airways. I organised thirty salespeople to sit at the switchboard of our sales office in Crawley on Thursday 27 February in case anyone telephoned us.

The *This Week* film, 'Violating Virgin?', opened with a bird's-eye view of all the mothballed planes lined up in the Mojave Desert, which is like an aeroplane morgue where the planes are parked in the dry air so that they will not rust. They are drained of their oil, stripped of some of their parts, and then their engines and valves are sealed with silver foil. Over this haunting picture came the narrator's voice:

'Virgin Airways is crying "Rape!" and Richard Branson claims that British Airways is putting him out of business.'

'There's fair competition and unfair competition,' I said to the interviewer. 'And I can't believe that British Airways is resorting to these dirty tricks.'

The documentary interviewed Peter Fleming, with his face completely concealed and his voice distorted, as he described the special unit British Airways had set up to discredit me, and the mass document shredding which had taken place. A similarly concealed American witness described how BA had shredded documents relating to Virgin in the USA. In New York, Ronnie Thomas told the story of BA buttonholing Virgin passengers as they were dropped off by his limousines, and a Los Angeles travel agent described how passengers were switching to BA since they had heard that Virgin was about to go bust. Then, with subtitles to spell out what he was saying, we heard Brian Basham telling Chris Hutchins that Virgin was a 'dicky business – just dicky'. Sir Freddie Laker repeated his advice to sue the bastards.

Thames Television interviewed me standing next to one of the Tristars in the Mojave Desert. I was dwarfed by a line of over twenty PanAm planes spanning almost a mile. I stood underneath one of the seven marooned British Airways planes. It was odd to think that my entire fleet consisted of only eight aircraft.

'I know a lot of these stories come from Brian Basham, who's employed by British Airways, and Brian Basham reports to a man called David Burnside, who is the head PR person at British Airways, who then reports to Lord King,' I said. 'I've never sued anyone in court for anything. We've probably got a good case to say that someone's tried to damage our business, but you know it takes hours of management time. I think our best bet is to get it out into the open and hopefully there'll be people at BA who'll realise it's counterproductive, and that they should not carry on in the future behaving in this kind of way.'

British Airways staff were doorstepped by *This Week*. Dick Eberhart, one of BA's vice presidents, was confronted in New York, and David Burnside outside his London home in Chelsea. Both men refused to answer any questions. The final shots of the documentary were aerial views of the dead aeroplanes stretching across the desert, gleaming impotently in the Californian sunshine, just where BA would like to see the Virgin fleet.

'Perhaps it's time for Richard Branson to put up or shut up,' said the final voice-over, 'or Virgin Atlantic's planes could end up like Laker's: in the desert sand.'

'Violating Virgin?' was seen by over 7 million viewers and that evening the Virgin switchboard received over 400 calls. Most of the callers just wished us well and said that they would never fly BA again, but among all the well-wishers were many people who said that they too had stories to tell of being approached by British Airways at the airport as they tried to check into Virgin. And then we hit the jackpot.

On 6 February Yvonne Parsons was at home when someone purporting to be from Virgin's reservations department called her to say that her flight was overbooked. Since she hadn't been issued with a ticket, would she mind changing to a British Airways flight? This was the last straw. Yvonne Parsons had flown to and from the States four times in the last eight months, and each time there had been an alleged 'booking error' with Virgin. The previous October, Parsons had been called in her New York office by a 'Virgin representative' who gave her name as 'Mary Ann' and told her that her Virgin flight was overbooked and, to compensate for the inconvenience, she could fly – at no extra cost – the following day on Concorde. Parsons refused. She flew to and from New York and London regularly, and she preferred Virgin – once she got on to the plane. She was a valuable customer, and she was rather surprised that Virgin was being so casual about her. She asked to be wait-listed for her flight and asked Mary Ann to call her the next day to let her know whether she was on or not.

As with 'Bonnie' from Virgin in August, who had told her that the flight was delayed, and 'Larry' from Virgin in September, who said that all nonsmoking seats were full, Mary Ann failed to call Yvonne Parsons back. So Parsons called up Virgin reservations and asked to speak to Mary Ann.

'There's no Mary Ann here,' she was told.

'Then who called me yesterday and said that I was bounced off the 16th of October flight?' Parsons asked.

'The 16th of October? No, you're confirmed on that flight, nonsmoking.'

Yvonne Parsons was baffled. She was also furious with Virgin and switched to American Airlines and United for her flights for the rest of the year. When she decided to give Virgin one last try in February, she couldn't believe it when another member of the Virgin reservations staff called her to tell her that the flight was overbooked and would she mind flying British Airways.

Then she watched 'Violating Virgin?' The next day she called up Virgin and was put through to our lawyers. She told her story to Gerrard.

'As I watched the programme,' she told him, 'it suddenly dawned on me that I must have been the victim of an elaborate and disgraceful deception by British Airways. I'd always been offered flights on British Airways, never on other airlines. I wondered whether these people were British Airways staff impersonating Virgin.'

'We've got an amazing statement,' Gerrard told me after taking down this story. 'We could build a court case around her alone.'

To drive the point home, I wrote to Sir Colin Marshall the day after 'Violating Virgin?', 28 February 1992, and asked him to reconsider my letter to the nonexecutives of 11 December 1991. I pointed out:

> Given the haste of your reply, I take it that you did not have sufficient time within which to investigate the matter. There have been numerous further independent reports in the media on this subject which have all supported the complaints that Virgin have made, culminating in the broadcast on ITV last night of the *This Week* television documentary. *This Week* have independently uncovered many more facts which go to prove that our allegations are totally correct. The content of the programme speaks for itself and in fact confirmed that the problem is even more serious and deep-rooted than we originally thought. The least your shareholders can

now expect is a full and proper explanation as to what exactly has been going on within British Airways and of the activities of Mr Brian Basham and those to whom he reports at British Airways.

I asked him directly whether he would now intervene:

I should now like from you in your role as deputy chairman and chief executive of British Airways a clear assurance that you will make certain that the activities that have been highlighted will immediately cease and that you will give a clear apology.

Well, I thought, it wasn't too late – just. But he'd better make sure that his apology was a good one.

I was up in Kidlington on Friday when Will rang me. 'Richard,' Will said. 'I'm in a call box. I've just landed at Gatwick and I've picked up a copy of *BA News*. The front-page headline says, "BRANSON 'DIRTY TRICKS' CLAIM UNFOUNDED". They're calling you a liar.'

Will had been on a skiing holiday when the programme was broadcast. The dates of both the programme and his skiing holiday had been changed several times so that they didn't coincide, but as luck would have it they still did. Since so many people were calling us, I had asked Will to come back to manage the PR storm which was brewing. In response he had just landed at Gatwick.

The *BA News* article went on to say:

Thames TV's current-affairs programme *This Week* last night devoted its programme to Richard Branson's allegations of 'dirty tricks' by British Airways against Virgin. British Airways was invited

373

to take part but declined after careful consideration for reasons explained to Thames's producer Martyn Gregory in full in a letter from Mervyn Walker, legal director.

The rest of the article reproduced the letter from Mervyn Walker which accused Thames Television of falling into my publicity trap and said that BA would not be 'provoked into playing Mr Branson's futile game and must therefore decline to take part'.

'What a load of bollocks!' we said together. 'They're calling me a liar and this is libel.'

It was the last straw. Will faxed me the article from Holland Park. We tracked down Gerrard, who immediately agreed that they had libelled me. Suing BA for libel would be a far easier case to bring to court and make clear to a jury than a highly complicated case about BA abusing its monopolistic position at Heathrow. It would also push everything out into the open.

On Monday morning I discovered that Lord King had written personal letters back to any viewers who had written in to question him about British Airways' dirty tricks, and he'd assured them that there was no truth whatsoever in my allegations. In effect, it was the same libel repeated, and once again to members of the public. I decided that I should sue Lord King as well.

That morning, I also received a letter from Sir Colin Marshall. He called my accusations 'unjustified', said he had nothing to add to his previous letters to me, and asserted that the allegation of a 'dirty tricks' campaign was 'wholly without foundation'.

I stared with amazement at the letter. Perhaps Sir Colin Marshall had been unable to watch 'Violating Virgin?' Perhaps he had been stuck in a traffic jam or on board a delayed flight. Perhaps he remained blithely unaware of what was going on in his company. If so, it seemed very odd: by reputation Sir Colin Marshall was a workaholic, a man who was obsessed with detail, who knew every single thing that went on in any of the companies where he worked.

The next week the sale of Virgin Music finally overtook me.

28 Victory

March 1992–January 1993

T HERE WAS £560 MILLION – $1 billion – on the table, but I didn't want it.

'They need to know by 2p.m. this afternoon,' John Thornton told me. I rang off and looked across at Simon and Ken. We had spent the last twenty years building up the company but nothing had prepared us for selling it.

In many ways the signing of The Rolling Stones was the culmination of everything I had ever wanted to do at Virgin Music. We had been fighting to sign them for twenty years, and now at last we had the greatest rock and roll band in the world on our label. From being a start-up label back in 1973 that had relied on the genius of Mike Oldfield, we had now come of age: now we were the label of choice for many of the world's biggest bands. Artists had seen how we had launched Phil Collins' solo career, and how we promoted UB40 and Simple Minds, what we had been able to do with Culture Club and Peter Gabriel, and they wanted to sign with us. But, just as we reached this height, it was over.

'Ken?' I asked.

'It's your call,' he said.

'Simon?'

'Take the cash. You've got no option.'

Whenever anyone tells me that I've got no option, I try to prove them wrong. Over the last few days Thorn EMI's offer had changed from an all-share offer, which would have left me as the largest shareholder in Thorn EMI with 14 per cent, or a lower cash alternative, to a higher cash offer. Even though Thorn had now switched tactics and was offering more cash than shares, I was more attracted to the share exchange since it would mean that I could keep a stake in Thorn EMI which I might use in the future as the basis to bid for the company. The difficulty was that everyone told me it would be too risky to use this stake as security to borrow any more money to support Virgin Atlantic. Shares in Thorn EMI were not seen as a cast-iron security. Although I had already drafted a letter to the staff explaining that I was going to take up Thorn EMI shares and so keep an interest in the company, I reluctantly had to change my mind and go for the cash offer.

Before finally agreeing, I called up Peter Gabriel and broke the news to him. I wanted his advice, and I was also aware that the sale would affect his career.

'Don't do it, Richard,' he said. 'You'll wake up one night in a cold sweat and wish that you'd never done it. You'll never get it back again.'

I knew that he was right. It was exactly what Joan had been saying. But the pressure from BA was too great. By now I felt so sure that Lloyds was going to foreclose on us that I had no alternative. I was also aware that Simon wanted to sell, and that he wanted to take cash rather than prolong his involvement with the Group by taking shares. If taking shares in Thorn EMI would prolong the agony at Virgin Atlantic, then it would defeat the whole point of the exercise. My overriding objective was to save Virgin Atlantic from going under, and – cruelly – the only reason I was selling Virgin Music was because it was so successful. If I sold Virgin Music, the Virgin name would be saved. Rather than having one struggling airline and a record company, there would be a secure airline and a secure record company, albeit owned by Thorn EMI. And, although I knew that Simon would leave it, I could stay on as president of the company. Most importantly, Ken was going to remain in charge of Virgin within Thorn, and he would safeguard the Virgin reputation.

I called up Trevor, who confirmed the bank's line:

'Cash is the only choice,' he told me. 'It means that we can pay back all the debt and start afresh. It'll give you complete freedom. And, when thinking about Thorn shares, remember what happened in the stock-market crash.'

That made up my mind. If I took Thorn shares and they fell dramatically in value, I could be powerless to stop the bank moving in. Sir Freddie Laker had reminded me how it happens so fast that it takes your breath away. Rather like Virgin, his airline had fought a long battle against British Airways and, just when he needed their support, the banks pulled in their loans. He was invited in to see the banks, expecting them to agree to a small increase in his overdraft on the back of an expected boom the following year, but when he arrived he was shown into a side room. Nobody came to see him for thirty minutes. Finally, he managed to get hold of the bank director, who then invited him up to another room. One look at their faces as he walked in made him realise that something terrible had happened.

'We've put Laker Airways into receivership,' they told him.

It was all over. There was nothing Sir Freddie could do to prevent the receivers from sacking all the staff, changing the locks on the buildings, confiscating all company property, leaving passengers stranded and handing the planes back. The Laker check-in desks at Gatwick vanished overnight and the sales desk stopped taking bookings. The telephones were unplugged and a lifetime's work disappeared in six hours. It was Sir Freddie's experience which more than anything else made me hold back from pushing the banks too far. Once I let them take control, Virgin Atlantic would be finished. It would be scant consolation to know that $1 billion had once been on the table.

Obstinate as I am, I recognised that there is a time to back down. 'Live for the present –' I heard my parents' old maxim in the back of my head '– and the future will look after itself.' My instinct for continued involvement with Virgin Music and taking Thorn EMI shares was tempered by the need for financial security. John Thornton, who was advocating that I should take the shares, did not know the whole picture; nor did Peter Gabriel, who was arguing that I shouldn't do it at all. And so, pushing Virgin Music into the past tense, I picked up the phone and called John Thornton at Goldman Sachs.

'I'll take the cash,' I heard myself say. 'I'll leave the rest to you.'

'Fine,' he said. 'The lawyers are on their last round now. I'll call you when it's time to come over.'

Although I had saved the airline, I felt that I had killed something inside me. Looking at Simon and Ken, I was saddened that we would each go in separate directions. In some ways I was happiest for Ken: he was going to stay with Virgin within EMI, and would soon be releasing records by Janet Jackson and The Rolling Stones. I had no idea what Simon would do, but I suspected that he would enjoy a quieter life. I knew that, as soon as Virgin Music had gone, I would have to come back out of the corner and slug it out with British

Airways. I'd already lost count of the rounds we had fought and was beginning to feel punch-drunk and exhausted.

We had to wait before signing contracts, since Fujisankei, our 25 per cent shareholder, had a pre-emptive clause that allowed them to match any offer for Virgin Music. We also had to decide whether to accept Thorn EMI's offer of £510 million in cash and taking on Virgin's debts fixed at £50 million; or £500 million in cash and whatever debts were in the company at the date of completion in four weeks' time. Although we had to continue to run Virgin Music in the normal manner, Ken felt sure that by completion the debt would be smaller.

'There are some good sales going on at the moment,' he said. 'Let's take all the money now.'

And so we opted for £510 million plus £50 million of debt in Virgin Music. In the event Ken was right (as always!) and we earned an extra £10 million by choosing this option. In the meantime, we had to wait until 3a.m. before Fujisankei finally threw in their lot with us and opted for Thorn EMI's cash. We signed contracts as dawn was breaking. The next morning Thorn EMI announced the purchase of Virgin Music for exactly $1 billion – or £560 million.

Simon, Ken and I went to see the staff at our Harrow Road offices.

'It's like the death of a parent,' Simon said to me as we went inside. 'You think that you've prepared for it, but when it happens you realise that you're totally unable to cope.'

I felt that it was more like the death of a child. Simon, Ken and I had started Virgin from scratch, kept it going through all the times when it looked as if it was coming to an end, and reinvented it with every generation of music so that it continued to be the most exciting record label in the business. While other record labels such as Apple still symbolised The Beatles and Abbey Road, Virgin had leapfrogged from Mike Oldfield and Gong to The Sex Pistols, then Boy George, then Phil Collins, then Peter Gabriel, then Bryan Ferry, then Janet Jackson and The Rolling Stones. Throughout each era – hippie, punk, new wave – Simon's taste had prevailed and Ken had kept everything together.

Ken now stood up and told everyone that they would become part of Thorn EMI, and that he would be staying with EMI to ensure Virgin's independence. Simon started to speak but instead burst into tears. Everyone looked at me. I stood up, on the verge of tears myself. It was no good. I was in an impossible situation. I couldn't tell them the real reason why their company had been sold. If I told them the truth about the bank's attitude to Virgin Atlantic, then the airline and the rest of the Virgin companies would be damaged by lack of confidence. Airlines are all built on confidence, and an admission of weakness would scare away passengers. And so, hating myself for appearing to have cashed in, I stood there and offered everyone a job at Virgin Atlantic if they were unhappy with EMI, and assured everyone that Ken would look after them. When Jon Webster proposed a vote of thanks to me, Simon and Ken for 'the best years of our lives', I could bear it no longer. I left the room and set off at a sprint down Ladbroke Grove, tears streaming down my face.

Oblivious to the stares of passers-by, I must have run for almost a mile. When I passed a newspaper stand I saw an *Evening Standard* poster that should have dried the eyes of most grown men: 'BRANSON SELLS FOR £560 MILLION CASH'. I ran past it, tears still streaming down my face, and somehow made my way home. Joan was out, so I went into the kitchen and put on the kettle. It was a cold March morning, but the cherry trees at the end of the garden and in Holland Park were just beginning to blossom. As I stared outside, a fox broke cover from the hedge and trotted across to the back door, where Joan left out scraps for it. It picked up a chicken carcass and then turned on its heel and vanished into the undergrowth. The last photograph I had seen of Lord King had shown him on horseback, resplendent in full hunting gear.

'Feeling thoroughly depressed,' I wrote in my notebook about my decision to go for cash rather than shares. 'Decided to go for the conservative route for the first time in my life. All my advisers (bar John Thornton) were advocating it.'

As well as picking up an extra £10 million by choosing the fixed-debt option, Ken also gained us another £9 million profit over the currency transfer to Fujisankei. Thorn EMI paid us the £510 million in cash, of which we had to pay £127.5 million to Fujisankei. Fujisankei wanted their money in yen, so we had to change it. We had a month's grace between taking the money and passing it on at completion on 1 June. We had to choose when to switch into yen. Simon and Trevor wanted to do it immediately so that we all knew where we stood. Ken and I were a little more relaxed and inclined to gamble with it. We kept it in sterling and, as luck would have it, sterling appreciated against the yen. We let it run and changed it at the last moment, earning ourselves a further £9 million profit. Nothing like a bit of luck!

And so the crisis was resolved. From the original cash purchase price of £510 million, Fujisankei received £127.5 million, and we received more than £390 million. Simon and Ken took their share of the proceeds and went their separate ways. I used my proceeds to repay the bank and invested the remaining cash in Virgin Atlantic. Rumours about Virgin Atlantic having to pay for fuel in cash were now well and truly scotched. We had more disposable cash than British Airways.

The banks immediately started calling me with renewed impatience – no longer to demand their money back, since we had returned their debt to them, but to offer to put my funds in high-interest deposit accounts, offshore accounts; to invest it; to invite me for lunch; to do some kind of business with me; and – of course without seeing the irony – offering to lend me as much money as I wanted to finance any future deals!

It took a while for me to understand the implications of the sale. For the first time in my life, I had enough money to fulfil my wildest dreams. In the immediate future I had no time to dwell on this, because that very week the British Airways story took a turn that occupied all my attention. In some ways I was pleased that I didn't have time to think about the sale of Virgin Music. I hate living in the past. I particularly didn't want to think about all the lost friendships. But the weight had been lifted from my shoulders and at the back of my mind I was aware that the Virgin Group was now free to develop in whichever direction we chose. Virgin Music may have gone; Ken and Simon and I had split up; but the best was yet to come.

'Penni,' I asked, 'please can you give me Freddie Laker's number in Miami?'

I dialled the number.

'Freddie,' I said. 'It's Richard here. I've decided to take your advice: I'm suing the bastards!'

'Go for it!' said Freddie.

* * *

As we embarked on the court case, the single thing that I had to keep reminding myself was that this was a libel case, not an argument over business practices. I had to clear my name.

Marshalling the evidence happened in three stages: we had all our own evidence which we already knew; we received a vast collection of documents from British Airways under the rules of legal disclosure; and a great deal of evidence began to materialise from disillusioned British Airways staff. It was this evidence that was the most powerful.

Out of the blue, Gerrard received a call from an ex-BA employee called Sadig Khalifa who had worked in the airline industry since 1974, when he was employed by British Caledonian in Tripoli. When British Airways took over B-Cal in 1988, Khalifa joined a division within BA called Special Services which dealt with any special passenger problems. In 1989 he started work as a check-in agent at Gatwick Airport and then joined the Helpline section, which was ostensibly there to meet BA passengers, help them transfer between flights, and look after elderly people. Another more clandestine activity was to try to poach other airlines' passengers. There was an equivalent team at Heathrow nicknamed the 'Hunters'.

In April 1990 the Helpline team was taken over by Sales and Reservations and the new boss, Jeff Day, came into the Helpline office and announced to Khalifa and his team of fifteen staff that 'money doesn't come from helping old ladies to the gate. What you have to do is get out and get more passengers from other airlines.' Khalifa told Gerrard about a second meeting in August which Jeff Day specified had to be a 'closed meeting': no non-Helpline staff could attend or were to hear about it.

At this meeting, Jeff Day told Khalifa and his colleagues that Helpline had a new task: to accumulate as much information about Virgin Atlantic as possible. This included flight information: the number of passengers booked on flights, the actual number of passengers who went on board the aircraft, the mix between upper class and economy, and the time of departure. At the end of each shift the Helpliners had to fill out a form on each flight and personally give it to a Mrs Sutton, who gave it to Day. And how were they to get the information? Jeff Day told the Helpliners that they could get it by using the Virgin flight numbers to gain direct access to the British Airways Booking System, known in the trade as BABS. This was something they had assured Virgin that they wouldn't do. The locks on the Helpline room were changed, and they were to keep the nature of their activities secret. One woman working alongside Khalifa refused to join in these activities since she thought that they were immoral, and the rest of the team covered for her.

Gerrard took a statement from Khalifa, and we sent it across to British Airways. It was set to become one of the main planks of the court case.

Immediately after Khalifa's affidavit arrived with BA's lawyers, I received a call from Michael Davis, a BA nonexecutive director who was a long-standing friend of my parents. He asked me whether we could meet for breakfast.

At our meeting, Michael began talking about 'egg on face'. This was the first hint of apology. He had obviously been singled out as the one nonexecutive who could talk to me. Lord King and Sir Colin Marshall were still clearly unwilling to bring themselves down to my level and acknowledge that there was any truth in my accusations, but Michael Davis – as a family friend – had

385

been designated the person who could best finesse the difficult idea that BA might have made some mistakes.

'I think the three of us should have a little chat,' Michael said. 'A little chat. The three of us – you, me and Sir Colin.'

'Sir Colin?'

'Yes, he's going to be around for the next ten years, you see. You see, the King is dead; long live the Marshall. I think it would be a sensible thing to do to meet up, the three of us, and see if anything sensible can come out of it.'

I watched Michael Davis grope for the appropriate words. Reading between the lines, he was telling me that Lord King's days at British Airways were over.

'You see, certain people at British Airways recognise that there's been a certain amount of egg on face,' he confessed. 'There has been an acceptance of that egg, but if we're going to have a sensible relationship in the future I think you, me and Sir Colin should sit down together.'

As I listened to his tortured syntax and his attempt to offer me a deal, I realised that I was listening to someone talking about somebody else's money and somebody else's livelihood. Michael Davis, Sir Colin Marshall, Robert Ayling and Lord King would receive their salaries no matter what they had initiated at British Airways. The BA shareholders would stump up money to pay for Brian Basham, to pay for the detectives, and to pay for their lawyers when I sued them. Perhaps it was a good investment: if they had managed to put Virgin Atlantic out of business it would have been money very well spent. But Virgin Atlantic was primarily my own company. It was a private company and, if BA poached an upper-class passenger to New York, that was £3,000 that Virgin would lose:

£3,000 that we couldn't reinvest in the business. And, unlike BA, I had no vast corporate reserves I could draw on to fund salaries. So, for all his talk of 'egg on face', Michael Davis was missing the point: BA had tried very hard to put me out of business and my staff out of their jobs. They had also forced me to sell Virgin Music, which had affected a whole group of other people who had nothing to do with the airline. It made me furious. I was not going to sit back over a gentleman's breakfast and agree that it was all just a certain amount of 'egg on face'.

Throughout the entire dirty-tricks episode I had been accused of being 'naive': naive to believe that British Airways could behave in such a manner, naive to think that British Airways would ever stop behaving in such a manner, naive to believe that I would ever be able to bring British Airways to court, naive to think for a moment that I could win a court case. The word 'naive' echoed round and round in my head and at some points had almost undermined my resolve to go on. Sir Michael Angus told Sir Colin Southgate that I was naive to take on British Airways 'as if it was a *Boy's Own* story'; Jeannie Davis told my parents that 'Ricky should learn to take the rough with the smooth'; and even people like Sir John Egan of the BAA told me 'not to shake the money tree'. Perhaps I was naive in fighting for the justice I wanted; perhaps it was idealism; or perhaps I was just plain stubborn. But I knew that British Airways' activities were unlawful and I wanted compensation. I was determined to make all those people, who had dismissed my stance as 'naive', eat their words.

I called Gerrard Tyrrell after the breakfast and told him how sympathetic and persuasive Michael Davis had been.

'Rubbish,' he retorted. 'BA had the chance to settle at the beginning but they didn't. It's only because their lawyers are now looking into a black hole of guilt that they're being forced to consider settling.'

I had never heard Gerrard sound so angry.

'You'll never have a better opportunity than now to nail them,' he went on. 'Don't cave in now.'

'Just testing you,' I said. 'Of course I won't cave in.'

The next week we met George Carman, our formidable QC who was preparing our case. With his white hair and impeccable manners, George seemed like everyone's favourite uncle outside the courts. Inside, he had the subtlety, tenacity and killer instinct of a praying mantis. People went to extraordinary lengths to avoid him.

'What do you think of my opening line of address?' George asked us. 'The World's Favourite Airline has a favourite pastime. It's called "shredding documents which are liable to be misconstrued".'

I called Michael Davis and told him that I couldn't agree to let my accusations slip under the carpet. The court case was set to start in January and the British Airways directors would be cross-examined by George Carman. I didn't even need to hint at how much George Carman would relish this. Sobered by this prospect, Michael Davis put down the phone.

By now I felt really confident that we could beat BA. Not only had we discovered so much about their dirty tricks, we had also found out details of an extraordinary BA undercover operation.

Someone contacted my office to say that he had some information about an undercover operation set up by BA involving various private detectives. He said that he had a computer disk containing a diary of everything the private detectives had done. He insisted that I meet him personally before he handed over the disk.

I felt rather strange as I climbed into the car with one of my assistants, Julia Madonna. This was partly due to the fact that I was wearing a microphone hidden in my crotch area so that I could tape my conversation with the contact. I knew how vital the tape of Brian Basham's meeting with Chris Hutchins had been, and I wasn't going to leave anything to chance with this meeting. When I set up Virgin Atlantic I had no idea that I would have to resort to *James Bond*-style activities in order to run it!

I scribbled in my notebook as our contact talked:

> Trying to find out what we were up to [but] didn't want to give that impression. Not at Lord King's level ... Being careful not to be seen to do any investigation only putting up defences.

Most importantly, our contact gave us the computer disk. When I had it printed out it was a revelation. The private detectives had kept an extremely detailed log of what they had been up to and who they had been reporting to at British Airways. The log revealed that the operation had been codenamed 'Covent Garden'. The first entry, dated 30 November 1991, stated, 'First sight of Project Barbara report seen in S1's office in Enserch House [BA's central-London HQ].' 'S1' turned out to be the codename for David Burnside, and 'Project Barbara' was the report on Virgin that Basham had given to Chris Hutchins.

Most of BA's top management had been named, but they had been given alphanumeric references so that their real names never appeared in print. I found it relatively easy to establish who was who: Lord King was 'LK' or 'C1'; Colin Marshall was 'C2'; and Basham was 'S2'. There were others, 'R1' and 'R2', who were unknown to us. They turned out to be the private detectives, Nick Del Rosso and Tom Crowley, who were leading the team under the guise of trying to find the mole inside BA who was leaking information to us. Operation Covent Garden was supposedly run by Ian Johnson Associates, 'international security management consultants'. The log detailed how Johnson and Del Rosso briefed BA's director of security, David Hyde, and the legal director, Mervyn Walker, on the progress of operation Covent Garden. It also recorded meetings with Robert Ayling and Colin Marshall.

The log contained astonishing details of how the team of detectives had convinced some of BA's senior management that we were running an undercover operation against BA. The amount of money they estimated we were spending on our nonexistent operation was £400,000. We later found out that BA was spending £15,000 a week on Covent Garden.

The sheer absurdity of the operation was revealed by details of how the detectives had staked out the Tickled Trout Hotel in Lancashire with secret cameras and sound-recording equipment. The idea was to secretly record a meeting between Burnside and an 'agent' that the Covent Garden team had convinced themselves was working for Virgin. The log recorded how their plans came unstuck when Burnside failed to turn on his bugging device! I could have spared BA the trouble: I never have employed private detectives and never will. That is not how I or Virgin operate.

When I had finished reading the Covent Garden log I felt as if I had returned from a parallel universe – one created in the imaginations of BA's hired conspiracists and senior management at the cost of thousands of pounds. I really began to look forward to the libel case, which was being heralded as the 'mother of all libel trials'.

7 December 1992

'BA have collapsed,' George Carman told me. 'They have today paid just under half a million pounds, £485,000 to be precise, into court. They've admitted in effect that they're entirely guilty as charged.'

We later discovered that, just before the court case was due to start, BA's lawyers had told them that they had no hope of winning. If they wanted to avoid the humiliation of having to stand in the witness box and be cross-examined by George Carman, and seeing all their activities written up in the press, then their only option was to make a payment into the court and start negotiating an out-of-court settlement.

At first I was in two minds over whether to accept the money. I was innocent, and we could put all the BA directors in the witness box and destroy them. But then, as we talked about it, I realised that, although this was tempting, such a move could be seen to be vindictive and was highly risky.

'You've got to remember why you brought this case,' George Carman advised me. 'You wanted the dirty tricks to stop and you wanted to clear your name. BA have admitted that you are totally right. You've cleared your name.

'If you persist with the case, then two things may go wrong. The jury might award you damages but they might think that you were such a rich man that you didn't need £500,000 and just award you £250,000. That would be seen as a failure for you and a triumph for British Airways. If the jury award you less than British Airways have paid into court, then you will have to pay both sets of costs. So you may win the case but lose a lot of money, and people will be confused as to why Virgin Atlantic has to pay £3 million of costs.'

This last part of George's advice was very persuasive. Although in some ways my decision to settle out of court could be something of an anticlimax, in that we wouldn't have the satisfaction of watching George Carman cross-examining the directors, by deciding to accept BA's offer we won a completely clear-cut victory with no risks attached and were immediately free to get on and run the business.

'What do we have to do now, then?' I asked.

'We have 21 days in which to take the money out of court if we're going to accept it.'

'So we'll do that?'

'Good Lord, no,' George said, looking shocked. 'I'm not going to accept it. I'm going to get them to give us at least £600,000. If they've given £485,000 they can go up to £600,000. Every £100,000 makes an inch bigger headline.'

George spent a week negotiating over the payment. On 11 December 1992 we agreed the terms of the highest uncontested libel payment ever made in British legal history: £500,000 to me personally to compensate for the personal libel, and £110,000 to Virgin Atlantic to compensate for the corporate libel.

11 January 1993

'VIRGIN SCREWS BA' was the *Sun*'s headline. There wasn't much room for anything else on the front page.

'I'd have preferred it the other way round,' Kelvin MacKenzie, the *Sun*'s editor, told me. 'It would have made a better headline.'

I was in George Carman's chambers with Gerrard Tyrrell and my father, whom I was delighted to share in the triumph. We walked round to the High Court in the Strand and jostled our way through the mass of photographers outside. The corridor outside court eleven, where the hearing would take place, was teeming. Inside the court it was very quiet. British Airways were noticeable by their absence: Lord King, Sir Colin Marshall and Robert Ayling, the three main protagonists, weren't there. David Burnside was absent. Brian Basham had gone abroad, but his lawyers were there making a last-ditch attempt to have his name removed from the statement of apology. The judge listened to the plea and then asked British Airways' counsel their opinion. They agreed with Virgin that Brian Basham's name should be included in the apology. The judge ruled that the apology should stand as prepared.

George Carman stood up and read the agreed statement. When he came towards the end, there was complete silence in court:

'British Airways and Lord King now accept unreservedly that the allegations which they made against the good faith and integrity of Richard Branson and Virgin Atlantic are wholly untrue. They further accept that Richard Branson and Virgin had reasonable grounds for serious concerns about the activities of a number of British Airways employees, and of Mr Basham, and their potential effect on the business interests and reputation of Virgin Atlantic and Richard Branson. In these circumstances, British Airways and Lord King are here now by leading counsel to apologise and to make very substantial payments to the plaintiffs by way of compensation for the damages and distress caused by their false allegations. They also seek to withdraw their counterclaim against Virgin Atlantic and Richard Branson.

'In addition, British Airways and Lord King have agreed to pay Richard Branson and Virgin Atlantic's legal costs in respect of the claim and the counterclaim and have undertaken not to repeat the defamatory allegations which are the substance of this action.'

George Carman paused and took a breath. The court held its breath.

'British Airways and Lord King are to pay Richard Branson £500,000 damages and are to pay Virgin Atlantic £110,000 damages.'

George had to raise his voice to make himself heard above the sudden noise in the court:

'In the light of the unqualified nature of the apology and the payment of a very substantial sum by way of damages, Richard Branson and Virgin Atlantic consider that their reputation is publicly vindicated by agreeing to settle the action on those terms.'

I saw tears running down my father's cheeks as he listened to the settlement. He had a large silk handkerchief in his breast pocket and he took it out to wipe his eyes. I clenched my fists under the table to stop myself from jumping to my feet.

The single jarring note was in the British Airways apology when, although they apologised unreservedly, they then went on to absolve themselves of any blame:

'The investigation which British Airways carried out during the course of this litigation revealed a number of incidents involving their employees which British Airways accept were regrettable and gave Richard Branson and Virgin Atlantic reasonable grounds for concern. I should however like to emphasise,' their counsel said, 'that the directors of British Airways were not party to any concerted campaign against Richard Branson and Virgin Atlantic.'

A number of people in the court snorted with derision. It had been the one phrase that British Airways had refused to take out of the apology.

'Let them leave it in,' George Carman had finally

advised me. 'People will see exactly what it really means. We haven't heard the last of that word "concerted".'

Then, with the judge's permission, Basham's counsel stood up to point out that his client did not accept that the references to him in the foregoing statement were an accurate summary of his actions on behalf of BA.

Outside, in the mad hustle of journalists and photographers, I held up both hands and shook my fists in triumph.

'I accept this award not only for Virgin,' I said, 'but also for all the other airlines: for Laker, for Dan Air, Air Europe and B-Cal. They went under and we survived British Airways, but only just.'

Back at Holland Park the party started. I decided to share the £500,000 damages which had been given to me among all the Virgin Atlantic staff, since they had all had to suffer from the pressure which British Airways had put us under, in the form of reduced salaries and cuts in their bonuses. The television was on in the corner and every news programme covered the Virgin success as the main story of the day. ITN even interviewed Sadig Khalifa and Yvonne Parsons. The party stopped to cheer them momentarily, and then went on.

Much later, I was in the middle of talking to someone when a wave of exhaustion hit me. I realised that we had won. All the stress relaxed out of my shoulders; I smiled a wide, happy, contented smile, toppled sideways and fell deeply asleep.

29 Virgin territory

1993–1998

NINETEEN NINETY-THREE was a watershed for Virgin. From that moment onwards, and for the first time, we had the luxury of money; and in 'Virgin' we had a strong brand name, which could be lent to a wide variety of businesses. We faced uncharted territory, but at last we could afford to follow our instincts, rather than spend all our time persuading others to do so. Once we had made the lateral and surprising jump from Virgin Records to Virgin Atlantic, we could try our hand at anything. We were a long way from when we first copied out an old record contract on the houseboat and signed Mike Oldfield. Times had changed and we had £500 million in the bank. But I didn't believe in leaving it there.

At this point I could of course have retired and concentrated my energies on learning how to paint watercolours or how to beat my mum at golf. It wasn't, and still isn't, in my nature to do so. People asked me, 'Why don't you have some fun now?' but they were missing the point. As far as I was concerned, this was fun. Fun is at the core of the way I like to do business and it has been key to everything I've done from the outset. More than any other element, fun is the secret of Virgin's success. I am aware that the idea of business as being fun and creative goes right against the grain of convention, and it's certainly not how they teach it at some of those business schools, where business means hard grind and lots of 'discounted cash flows' and 'net present values'.

Even though I'm often asked to define my 'business philosophy', I generally won't do so, because I don't believe it can be taught as if it were a recipe. There aren't ingredients and techniques that will guarantee success. Parameters exist that, if followed, will ensure a business can continue, but you cannot clearly define our business success and then bottle it as you would a perfume. It's not that simple: to be successful, you have to be out there, you have to hit the ground running; and, if you have a good team around you and more than your fair share of luck, you might make something happen. But you certainly can't guarantee it just by following someone else's formula.

Business is a fluid, changing substance, and, as far as I'm concerned, the group will never stand still. It has always been a mutating, indefinable thing and the past few years have demonstrated that. But it is only when you come to write a book such as this that you discover how far you still want to go. That's how I see this book: a comprehensive account of the first fifty or so years of my life – the struggling years – but also a work and a life in progress. This book was never intended to be as dry as a balance sheet, but will, I hope, give an idea of what has been important to my life and to the people around me thus far.

Virgin has expanded over the last few years, perhaps more quickly than any other European group, and has developed radically in the process. Our way of doing business may remain the same, but the context has changed dramatically. After the sale of Virgin Music and our victory over British Airways in January 1993, I realised that, for the first time in my business career, I had climbed the wall and could at last peer into the promised land. It hadn't always been possible. For anyone who starts without financial backing there is a very thin line between success and failure. Survival is the key priority. No matter how many successes Virgin had had, there was always the danger that the cash would run out. Virgin has made money, but I have always invested it in new projects in order to keep the group growing. As a result, we had rarely had the luxury of spare cash to use as a cushion.

Over the years we have clung on through three recessions; we have suffered losses; we have closed down some businesses and, in some instances, we had to make some staff redundant. But after 1993 no bank would ever again be able to dictate to us how to run our business. We had financial freedom. I was one of a rare breed: most entrepreneurs don't manage to survive that far or for that long. In the process of gaining that freedom, we had to overcome all kinds of obstacles thrown without warning into our path.

When we were established as a mail-order record company, and thus dependent on the post, out of the blue came a six-month postal strike. If we hadn't reinvented ourselves, we would have gone bust. There was no choice. Within days of the strike we had opened our first Virgin Records shop. It may have been up a dark, narrow flight of stairs above a shoe shop and have consisted merely of some shelves, a shabby sofa and a till, but in its own small way it taught us all we now know about retailing. I can draw a straight line from that tiny shop to the Virgin Megastores in London, Paris and New York. It's just a matter of scale, but first you have to believe you can make it happen.

In the same way, as the record label gathered momentum through those early years, every deal was make-or-break. We may have failed to sign 10cc, but we were still willing to put the company on the line when we tried again with the next band. We launched the airline on a wing and a prayer, and when the engine blew up on our test flight it might have been over before it had begun. We were lucky: each time something went wrong, we were the smallest jump ahead of the banks.

However tight things are, you still need to have the big picture at the forefront of your mind. The most vivid proof of this came during the depths of the recession in 1992. At the time, I was trying to raise money to install individual seat-back videos in all our aircraft – I have always believed that Virgin should offer the best in-flight entertainment. We needed £10 million to install the equipment. Nobody at Virgin Atlantic could raise the necessary funding and we were all sitting down at Crawley one day in despair, on the point of giving up, when I thought I would try one last gamble.

Nervously, I picked up the telephone, called Boeing and asked to speak to the CEO, Phil Conduit. I asked him whether, if we bought ten new Boeing 747-400s, he would throw in the individual seat-back videos in economy class. Phil was amazed that anyone was thinking of buying planes during that recession, and he readily agreed. I then called Jean Pierson at Airbus, and asked him the same question about the new Airbus. He agreed. After a few further enquiries, we discovered that it was easier to get £4 billion credit to buy eighteen new aircraft than it was to get £10 million credit for the seat-back video sets. As a result, Virgin Atlantic suddenly had a brand-new fleet of planes, the youngest and most modern fleet in the industry, at the cheapest price we've ever been able to acquire planes before or since.

The Virgin Group has always had a life of its own and I have always tried to think ahead with it. When I tried to sell Student to IPC Magazines back in the early 70s, they shied away from me because I started talking about all the other business opportunities I wanted to explore: a Student travel company that would offer cheaper travel than the existing airlines, a Student bank because I thought that students were being ripped off when they had no income to protect them. I even wanted to hire trains from British Rail because their tickets were so expensive and their trains were always late. Even then, I was attempting, with limited resources, to explore what was possible by wanting to go into some of these businesses and turn them upside down. At the time, it was all theoretical and beyond my capacity, but some interesting ideas emerged from the process. I may be a businessman, in that I set up and run companies for profit, but, when I try to plan ahead and dream up new products and new companies, I'm an idealist.

My grandiose plans didn't work for Student. But, following the sale of Virgin Records, I was once again ready to start pushing at the barriers. This time it was rather different: I didn't have just a few pounds in the Student biscuit tin – which we ended up spending on takeaway curries – but a treasure chest of hundreds of millions of pounds. In an intoxicating moment, everything seemed possible. We had the finance, and, even more importantly, we had the name, 'Virgin', which already had a track record of reinventing itself. There was nothing to stop us becoming something else.

I give free rein to my own instincts. First and foremost, any business proposal has to sound fun. If there is a market that is just served by two giant corporations, it appears to me that there's room for some healthy competition. As well as having fun, I love stirring the pot. I love giving big companies a run for their money – especially if they're offering expensive, poor-quality products.

In the early 1990s, there were already scribblings in my notebook about the possibility of launching a range of Virgin soft drinks, led by Virgin Cola, which could take on the might of Coca-Cola, one of the world's top ten companies. The Cott Corporation specialises in bottling own-label colas and was looking for a brand that could have global appeal.

'You've got the X factor, the Y factor – you've got every factor there is,' Gerry Pencer, the chief executive of Cott Corporation, said to me. 'People like Virgin; they trust the name; they'll buy a product because it's a Virgin product. So how about it? We've got the recipe; you've got the name. What do you say to Virgin Cola?'

As usual, when people warn me against doing something once my mind is made up, I grow increasingly determined to try it. In this case we all recognised that it would be an inch-by-inch fight along the shelves of the supermarkets but, once we established that there was minimal financial risk if we failed, we decided to proceed. We knew that the product was as good as either Coke or Pepsi, and the first blind tasting we had at the local school, which was followed by many across the country, established that most people preferred Virgin Cola to the others. And so we went into Virgin Cola. Within a few months we were selling £50 million worth of Virgin Cola across the country and had grabbed 50 per cent of the market in the outlets that stocked it. We went on to launch it in France, Belgium and South Africa, and we even managed to place a Virgin Cola machine right underneath the Coke sign in Times Square, New York. This was after we'd driven a Chieftain tank through a wall of Coca-Cola and Pepsi cans, and fired at the Coke sign hanging above Times Square!

Initially Coca-Cola head office didn't take Virgin Cola seriously as a threat so we had no opposition from them. What I didn't know was that based in Atlanta, in Coke's head office, was an English lady working in a senior position for Coca-Cola. She warned the management there that Virgin had the power and the brand to rock Coke on a wordwide basis and she persuaded her directors to let her set up a SWAT team in England to try and stamp us out. Within days she and her team had moved to England. Retailers were offered unbeatable terms from Coke to take their cola over ours. Smaller retailers were threatened with removal of Coca-Cola fridges. The campaign from Coca-Cola was even more potent than the dirty tricks campaign from British Airways to stamp out Virgin Atlantic but Virgin Cola survived. Ironically this very same lady now holds a senior position at Virgin's main clearing bank.

Looking to the future, I had no idea whether Virgin Cola would become a global leader in soft drinks or not, but, as with all of our businesses, I keep an open mind. But I do know that Virgin Cola, which has now expanded to become Virgin Drinks, is indicative of the Virgin philosophy – beneath all the fun and razzmatazz of selling it there is a sound business plan. The decision to launch Virgin Cola was founded on three key things: finding the right people, the positive use of the Virgin brand name, and protection of the downside.

The business plan for Virgin Cola was clear: we would never lose much money selling it. It is so cheap to produce that, unlike most other products, the manufacturing cost is negligible. We could therefore balance the advertising and distribution costs directly against the sales. One look at Coca-Cola's balance sheets is enough to reveal what a profitable business it is, and with that kind of margin we knew there must be plenty of room for someone else to come in with a decent cola to sell alongside Coke and Pepsi.

Once I was convinced that we had protected the downside – which is always my first concern – the other significant question to resolve was whether the move into Virgin Cola really enhanced the Virgin brand name. Despite objections from colleagues, I was persuaded that cola has a number of attributes that people associate with Virgin: fizz, fun and freedom. Not only that, but ours was a better, cheaper cola than the others. We thrived on the fact that we were small and a newcomer up against the two giants. And it meant that we kept the brand alive in the youth market.

'All right,' people admitted, when they heard my defence of Virgin Cola. 'I can see that cola is fun. It's fizzy and profitable and fits the Virgin image. But surely not life insurance? What on earth are you doing selling life insurance, mortgages and investments?'

I have to admit that some healthy discussions about life insurance took place before we decided to launch Virgin Money. 'Life insurance?' everyone snorted when they heard the idea. 'People hate life insurance. All the salesmen seem so unscrupulous, barging into your home and taking secret commissions. It's a terrible industry. It's definitely not a Virgin kind of business.'

'Exactly,' I said. 'It's got potential.'

It is no secret that I love playing devil's advocate. I could see all the bad points about the financial-services industry. The idea of setting up Virgin life insurance and a Virgin bank would have horrified our original staff at Albion Street, or our customers who lounged about on the beanbags at the record shop. And yet, whenever I see people getting a bad deal, I want to step in and do something about it. Of course, this is not pure altruism – there's a profit to be made, too. But the difference is that I'm prepared to share more of the profit with the customer so that we're both better off. The maverick in me was also quietly amused that the guy who brought you The Sex Pistols could sort out your pension, too. Another part of me was equally amused by the idea that we were going to set up our own bank to give those very banks that nearly foreclosed on us a run for their money.

My attention had first been brought to the financial-services industry by Rowan Gormley, a venture capitalist I had asked to work for Virgin to identify new business opportunities. One of the first things he did was review the Virgin pension policy, which he told me made no sense. When he asked six different pension advisers to give quotes as to how best to restructure it, he was the bemused recipient of six different answers.

'I don't understand it,' he told me. 'I've three degrees in finance, but none of what they're saying makes sense.'

Instinctively, I felt that the world of financial services was shrouded in mystery and rip-offs and that there must be room for Virgin to offer a jargon-free alternative with no hidden catches.

As with our other ventures, we needed a partner who both knew the industry and could put up the money to go alongside the Virgin name. Despite some of our past difficulties, I still believe that a fifty-fifty partnership is the best solution to financing. When something goes wrong, as it invariably will at some point, both partners have an equal incentive to put it right. Such is not always the case. At worst, such as with Randolph Fields and Virgin Atlantic, Virgin will buy out the partner entirely. At best, as with Sprint, our partner with Virgin Mobile in America, it stays at fifty-fifty and both sides remain content. In between these poles there can be many variations and we have tried out most combinations. Ultimately, you never know what to expect when dealing with other people and, although you might both appear to go into a project with the same enthusiasm, situations can change. Knowing when and how to renegotiate a contract is all part of the challenge of business.

Virgin Money, our financial-services company, started off as Virgin Direct with Norwich Union as a fifty-fifty partner. After Virgin entered the financial-services industry, I can immodestly say it was never to be the same again. We cut out all commissions; we offered good-value products; and we were practically trampled by investors in their rush to buy. We set up a new office in Norwich rather than rent a gleaming tower block in the City of London. We never employed fund managers, some of the world's most highly paid people, since we discovered their best-kept secret: they could never consistently beat the stock-market index.

We launched aggressively and the initial signs were good but, in spite of our success, we realised that we were going faster and further than was comfortable for Norwich Union. It looked like we would be three times the size we had originally predicted. After a short time we arranged for Norwich Union to sell their shareholding to a partner who shared our ambitions, Australian Mutual Provident (AMP). Together with AMP and our great team at Virgin Money, we had cut a broad swathe through the financial-services jungle. From a standing start in 1995, it is staggering to think that Virgin Money had become the country's most popular investment house, and 250,000 people had trusted us with over £1.5 billion, and all this had been achieved within three years.

The success of Rowan Gormley and his vision for Virgin Money illustrates one of the great strengths of the Virgin Group: we thrive on mavericks. The quality that I recognised in Rowan when I first asked him to work for Virgin was that he would make things happen. When he started work perched at a desk on a half-landing at 11 Holland Park, neither of us had any idea that a few months later he would start up a financial-services company. When – unsurprisingly, with hindsight – he alighted upon financial services, we arranged a company structure that gave him and his team a shareholding in the business and let him get on with it. Like all the managers of Virgin companies, Rowan was given a high incentive to succeed because he could clearly see the wealth that success would bring him and his team.

Virgin Money may appear to have been an incongruous departure for Virgin, the rock'n'roll company: it was a lateral leap in the same way as it had been from records to airline. But it was still all about service, value for money and offering a simple product. The vision I have for Virgin does not run along the orthodox lines of building up a company with a vast head office and a pyramid of command from a central board of directors. I am not saying that such a structure is wrong – far from it. It makes for formidable companies from Coca-Cola to Pearson to Microsoft. It is just that my mind doesn't work like that. I am too informal, too restless, and I like to move on.

People have always asked me what the limits to Virgin are, and whether we haven't stretched the brand name beyond its natural tolerance. With monotonous regularity, they point out that there is no other company in the world that puts its name to such a wide variety of companies and products. They are absolutely right, and it remains something of which I am proud.

It doesn't stop me thinking about the question

nonetheless, and the answer isn't easily explicable. I have always lived my life by thriving on opportunity and adventure. Some of the best ideas come out of the blue, and you have to keep an open mind to see their virtue. Just as an American lawyer called me to suggest setting up an airline in 1984, a Swedish ballooning fanatic asked me to fly across the Atlantic with him in 1987. The proposals come in thick and fast and I have no idea what the next one will be. I do, however, know that, if I listen carefully enough, the good ideas somehow all fit into the framework that Virgin has become. By nature I am curious about life, and this extends to my business. That curiosity has led me down many unexpected paths and introduced me to many extraordinary people. Virgin is a collection of such people and its success rests on them.

The more diffuse the company becomes, however, the more frequently I am asked about my vision for Virgin's future. I tend either to avoid this question or to answer it at great length, safe in the knowledge that I will give a different version the next time I am asked. My vision for Virgin has never been rigid and changes constantly, like the company itself. I have always lived my life by making lists: lists of people to call, lists of ideas, lists of companies to set up, lists of people who can make things happen. Each day I work through these lists, and it is that sequence of calls that propels me forward. Back in the early 1970s I spent my time juggling different banks and suppliers and creditors in order to play one off against the other and stay solvent. I'm still living the same way, but I'm now juggling bigger deals instead of banks. Once again, it is only a matter of scale.

As anyone in my office knows when I've misplaced it, my most essential possession is a standard-sized school notebook, which can be bought at any stationery shop on any high street across the country. I carry this everywhere and write down all the comments that are made to me by Virgin staff and anyone else I meet. I make notes of all telephone conversations and all meetings, and I draft out letters and lists of telephone calls to make.

Over the years I have worked my way through a bookcase of them, and the discipline of writing everything down ensures that I have to listen to people carefully. Flicking back through these notebooks now, I see some ideas that escaped me: I was asked to invest in a board game called Trivial Pursuit and a wind-up radio. But, when I turned down the offer to become an underwriting name at Lloyds Insurance, my guardian angel must have been looking after me.

Whenever I'm on a flight or a train or in a record store, I walk around and ask the people I meet for their ideas on how to improve the service. I write them down and, when I get home, I look through what I've written. If there's a good idea, I pick up the phone and implement it. My staff were maddened to hear that I had met a man on the airport bus who suggested that we offer onboard massages – and please could they organise it? They tease me and call it 'Richard's Straw Poll of One', but, time and again, the extra services that Virgin offers have been suggested to us by customers. I don't mind where the ideas come from as long as they make a difference.

I also insist that we continually ask our staff for any suggestions they might have, and I try my hand at their jobs. When I tried pushing a trolley down the aisle of a jumbo, I found I crashed into everyone. When I talked to the crew about this, they suggested that we introduce a more waitress-style service and keep the trolleys to a minimum. As it turned out, by getting rid of trolleys altogether in Upper Class, we were able to use up some of the aisle space to provide the longest and largest seats in the air.

My vision for Virgin was ultimately summed up by Peter Gabriel, who once said to me, 'It's outrageous! Virgin is becoming everything. You wake up in the morning to Virgin Radio; you put on your Virgin jeans; you go to the Virgin Megastore; you drink Virgin Cola; you fly to America on Virgin Atlantic. Soon you'll be offering Virgin births, Virgin marriages, Virgin funerals. I think you should rename Virgin the "In and Out Company". Virgin will be there at the beginning and there at the end.'

As ever, Peter, who is an astute businessman as well as a gifted musician, was very close to the truth. He had no idea at the time that we had two hundred people down in Eastbourne working on a range of Virgin cosmetics, another team designing a range of Virgin clothes, or that we were just about to bid for two British Rail franchises that would make us the largest train operator in Britain. I doubt that we'll ever go into Virgin funerals, but Virgin Births has a certain ring to it. If there's a good business plan, limited downside, good people and a good product, we'll go for it.

In some ways it all boils down to convention. As you might have noticed, I do not set much store by such so-called wisdom. Conventionally, you concentrate on what you are doing and never stray beyond fairly narrow boundaries when running a company. Not only do I find that restrictive, I also think that it's dangerous. If you only run record shops and refuse to embrace change, when something new like the Internet or MP3 is launched you will lose your sales to the person who makes use of the new medium. Even in the heady days of 1999 I felt it was far better to set up your own Internet operation to which your record shops lost business than lose it to somebody else's Internet operation. Various outside advisers did try to get us to launch an Internet site, bizarrely suggesting that we do this without using our name. 'This is the age of Currant Bun, Handbag and Jamjar,' they said. They just didn't understand brands.

This partly explains the jigsaw of companies we have. As well as protecting each other, they have symbiotic relationships. When Virgin Atlantic starts a flight to South Africa, I find that we can launch Virgin Radio and Virgin Cola there. In the same way, we can use our experience in the airline industry to make buying train tickets easier and cheaper. We can draw on our experience of entertaining people on planes to entertain people on trains.

Despite employing around 40,000 people, Virgin is not a big group – it's a big brand made up of lots of small companies. Our priorities are the opposite of our large competitors'. Convention dictates that a company should look after its shareholders first, its customers next, and last of all worry about its employees. Virgin does the opposite. For us, our employees matter most. It just seems common sense to me that, if you start off with a happy, well-motivated workforce, you're much more likely to have happy customers. And in due course the resulting profits will make your shareholders happy.

Convention also dictates that 'big is beautiful', but every time one of our ventures gets too big we divide it up into smaller units. I go to the deputy managing director, the deputy sales director and the deputy marketing director and say, 'Congratulations. You're now the MD, the sales director and the marketing director of a new company.' Each time we've done this, the people involved haven't had much more work to do, but necessarily they have a greater incentive to perform and a greater zest for their work. The results for us have been terrific. By the time we sold Virgin Music in 1992, we had as many as fifty subsidiary record companies, and not one of them had more than sixty employees.

But there is little point in looking back, except to note that, since then, Ken Berry consolidated and made Virgin Music the most profitable jewel in EMI's crown, before moving on early in 2002. For us, we were now free to start again with V2 Records, using the same techniques and skills. Our first signing may not have made quite the same impact as Mike Oldfield, but The Stereophonics were still named Best Newcomers in the Brit Awards for 1998, and have gone on to great things since.

The Virgin way has been to develop many different ventures and grow organically. For most of our companies, we have started from scratch rather than merely buying them ready-made. We want each of the Virgin subsidiaries to be an efficient, manageable size. When it comes to setting up new companies, one of my advantages is that I don't have a highly complicated view of business. When I think about which services I want to offer on Virgin Atlantic, I try to imagine whether my family and I would like to buy them for ourselves. Quite often it's as simple as that.

Of course life becomes more complicated when you move away from organic growth. In recent years Virgin has bought companies to add to the ones that we have set up. The purchase of MGM Cinemas was the first big acquisition we made, and we also bought two substantial British Rail train franchises. While we were able to fix the cinema chain relatively quickly, before selling it to the French company UCI, the trains are a much longer-term prospect. In some ways we became a victim of our own success in that the train passengers expected that, as soon as Virgin had taken over the running of the trains, miraculous change would take place. Unfortunately, the logistics of the task were against us: our two train companies had 3,500 employees and we needed to build a completely new fleet of trains and at the same time negotiate with Railtrack over how they could upgrade the tracks and signalling.

Despite a difficult time in the railway industry as a whole, we're confident that Virgin Rail will come to be seen as one of the best things Virgin ever did with its brand.

30 Diversity and adversity

1998–2005

AN ENORMOUS AMOUNT has happened in the last decade. This book opens with my first attempt to fly around the world in a balloon, a trip that ended up in the deserts of Algeria. It was my last ballooning trip, at the end of 1998, however, which finally knocked some sense into me. I realised that it was perhaps time to put to better use everything I'd learned during my personal adventures. However, it had been a magnificent trip.

When we were about to set off, someone suggested to me that I keep a diary, and I've dusted that down to use here. Rather than cut it, I'm going to let you see it as I wrote it, so that you can get a sense of what it's like to be adrift, thousands of feet above the surface of the Earth, with just the wind to power you.

Day 1, 18 December 1998

This is a daily diary for Theo, my godson, who saw us lift off today from Marrakech, for Lochie, India, Woody, for all my special nephews and nieces, and for my children Holly and Sam.

The delightful Moroccans welcomed us like brothers. Holly and Joan arrived at the airport. The balloon looked like a magnificent mosque and the sun was rising up over the Atlas Mountains. Strangely, I wasn't enormously nervous on this occasion: we'd had such a good team planning this. We'd been through so much heartache in the past that I really felt that this time we had a good chance. The only serious problem was that last night the Americans and British had started bombing Iraq. And we are due to fly along the Iraqi border in thirty hours' time – some fifty miles from it.

We have Bob Rice, the best weatherman (meteorologist) in the world. He believes he can help us find the winds to carry us right along the border without crossing into it. I've promised him that we will stuff him instead of the turkey this Xmas if he gets it wrong. That is if we are not already stuffed ourselves.

Almost all of my closest friends and family, except Sam, who had to be at school, had flown in to see us off, after having just travelled all the way with us to the Caribbean the day before to go on holiday. The moment we arrived there, I was told to go all the way back because we had found the perfect weather. Weather so perfect that, if nothing goes too wrong, we could be back on my grandfather's birthday – Boxing Day.

We arrived to a wonderful welcome of musicians, camels, jugglers and even flying carpets. Alex Ritchie's children, Alistair and Duncan, my daughter Holly and Per's daughter Jenny were together to press the button to launch us into the air. We put on our parachutes. We said our goodbyes – to my mum and dad, my brother-in-law, my daughter and my friends. Tears were in their eyes.

Countdown – 10-9-8-7-6-5-4-3-2-1 – then lift-off!

We gently climbed 2,000 feet. The door was still open. Everyone was clapping and cheering. Then suddenly we started to sink: we had hit a weather inversion. We burned hard to warm the helium. We burst through the inversion. I realised we had overburned.

We were shooting up and the bottom of the balloon

was smouldering – 1,700 feet a minute, 1,800 feet, 1,900 feet – until at last we were slowing, but the liquid burners had burned holes in the bottom of the hot-air balloon. Fortunately for us they were right at the bottom. It was the helium balloon that was the critical one. We could fly on: ugly holes, but nothing to stop us.

It's wonderful. We are flying up with the birds and we are on our way. Everything seems to be working: we are up to flight altitude and the capsule has pressurised and the balloon has not burst. We are on our way at the beginning of a magnificent adventure, and there below us are the beautiful Atlas Mountains covered in snow.

Day 2, 19 December 1998

For hours we had a magnificent flight watching the massive range of the Atlas Mountains that stretches across the whole of the north of Africa, from Morocco across Algeria, Libya and almost, I believe, to Egypt. We bade farewell to the Moroccans after about seven hours of flying and then headed out over Algeria.

Algeria has become a very sad country due to a terrible civil war that is going on. We were plunged into that two years ago when our balloon failed at night and we had to land. But tonight we're flying along the Atlas Mountains, over the rugged desert where Alex and I had once had to throw everything we had out of our balloon to stop a rapid descent – we even threw out an envelope full of dollars! Alex saved our lives on that occasion by climbing out on the roof and releasing fuel tanks just before we hit the deck.

This time everything seemed to be going well.

Almost too well! When it began to get dark and the helium above us cooled, we turned on the burners. Instead of plunging, as we had on our last attempt around the world, the heat stopped any descent and the flames lit up the Arabian skies around us. We had to be careful not to fly higher than we had during the day or the heat would vent the helium and shorten the time we had in the sky. So we took it in turns to fly during the night.

Then, very tired, we suddenly had a major spanner thrown in the works. A message from Libya came through saying they had withdrawn our right to fly over their country. It was night-time, pitch black, and we could never land before crossing their border. Steve, Per and I debated what we could do about it. If we had gone very low we might have been able to crawl around the south of Libya, but that would mean abandoning our dreams. In the end we decided to slow up the balloon by dropping lower to give us time to try to persuade Colonel Qaddafi, who rules Libya, that ours is a sporting mission undertaken in the interests of peace. The King of Jordan had been a great help to us previously, and I had also been honoured in the past to know Nelson Mandela – and I knew he knew Colonel Qaddafi quite well. So my wonderful secretary Sue opened up my office in the early hours of the morning and got hold of their telephone numbers.

Our next concern was the realisation that they would all be asleep. The King of Jordan is unwell with cancer, and Nelson Mandela is not a young man, so I decided to write one of the most important letters in my life to Colonel Qaddafi.

Excellency
I am making this personal and direct appeal to you from the ICO Global Challenger Balloon in which the general post and telecommunications company of Libya has a significant investment.

A mutual friend of ours, his Royal Highness King Hussein of Jordan, spoke to you about my plans to try to circumnavigate the globe in a balloon. You graciously granted us permission to cross your country.

Early today we took off from Morocco in the certain knowledge that we had permission to overfly your country. We would not have done so had we not had the permission and goodwill of both Algeria and Libya. We are currently over Algeria and we will cross your border in the early hours of this morning.

Libyan overflight clearance permit OVG11@01001 was graciously extended on 20 July 1998 to us for this flight. Your Air Traffic Control personnel have just informed us that this permission has been rescinded. We obviously understand that they have every right to do this, but I'm afraid that it is impossible to land a balloon at night due to the icing that forms on the helium valve. We are unable to vent the helium to descend.

Because of this emergency condition, we simply do not know how to avoid crossing your airspace. We hope that you will grant us emergency permission under these circumstances via your air-traffic control services.

Thank you for your understanding of this problem.
I am, sir, your most obedient servant,
Richard Branson

By that point we were all extremely tired and purposefully flying much slower than the balloon was capable of, to give us time. Then the onboard phone rang and we were told that, even though it was one o'clock in the morning, Colonel Qaddafi had granted us permission to go on. Although our route to go around the world had been made more difficult by the slower path, the bigger, immediate problem was that by slowing down we had changed direction and were headed towards a storm over Istanbul in Turkey. Hopefully we could ride above it.

Whether through the pressure of all of this, or some bug, I was beginning to lose my voice. We decided I should go on a course of penicillin just in case.

Per remains as calm as I have ever seen him. His dream, that started so many years ago, is finally coming true. And Steve is a pleasure to have on board. He is the only one of us who ventures into the kitchen, producing an excellent 'Steve Soup'.

Morning has now broken and we have crossed the Libyan border. Miles and miles of desert and a warm welcome from air-traffic control in Tripoli. No military planes. Thank you, thank you, Colonel Qaddafi, from all of us in the ICO Global Balloon team.

Day 3, 20 December 1998

I haven't slept since I last wrote my diary 24 hours ago. With good reason. Let me share these 24 hours with you. I only wish right now that you could be up here with us. However, there were some moments in the day I would not wish on you.

Let me first explain the challenge that faces all us balloonists who want to go around the world. It is not just the elements, or the technological challenge. Sadly, it also involves people and politics. As always in life, it is not the ordinary people who get in the way. It's a handful of politicians at the top who selfishly make their country and this world a sadder place to live. After all, this is a sporting challenge and a mission flown in peace.

Let me begin by suggesting that you pull out a map; imagine you are a balloonist in Switzerland, in America or in Morocco as we were. Then cross out some of the countries whose politicians say you cannot cross: Russia, Iran, and Iraq (remember, two balloonists who did cross the Russian border three years ago were cruelly shot down and killed).

Imagine you're in a race to be the first around the world, and there are seven other balloonists waiting to take off. All of them will likely go well south of Russia and Iraq. You know that they will not experience the same hold-ups that you have, so every second counts and taking a risk becomes a necessity. So, when your weatherman says he believes he can squeeze you between Iran and Russia, instead of saying no, you take that risk. Even though it means flying down a 24-mile-wide piece of land that is 2,600 miles from where you are taking off, and which is owned by Turkey and flanked by two countries in which you are not welcome.

Remember, a balloon has no propulsion except the wind. The only way of steering is to change height as you go along to try to find winds going in a different direction. It helps you to have the best weatherman in the world.

That weatherman tells you he thinks it can be done. You and your team decide to go for it. Then the night before you launch you are told that the British and the Americans are bombing Iraq and you are British and Steve Fossett is American. And this particular path is within fifty miles of Iraq.

You would probably be certifiably mad to continue and until an hour ago I thought we were mad. But we knew our weatherman – we had worked with Bob Rice before over the Atlantic and Pacific – and we knew that, if anyone could help get us through this narrow crack between two countries in which we have no permission to fly, it would be him. And the very minute I am writing this diary, we are coming out of the other end of the crack, with Iraq and Iran on one side of us and Russia on the other. We, with the help of our magnificent team back at base, have miraculously crept through.

Twenty-four hours ago we said goodbye to Libya as it was getting dark and headed out over the Mediterranean towards Cyprus. An RAF Hercules flew overhead. They said they were on their way to bomb Iraq. They wished us good luck, and we wished them the same.

I had just tried to lie down to get some sleep when Steve shouted, 'Get your parachute on – we've been told there's a very high thunderstorm ahead.' Steve had lost his balloon in a similar thunderstorm over the Pacific only two months before, so he knew only too well what havoc they could wreak. By climbing, the wind would blow us over Iraq. What was worse – a possible storm ahead or the 'storms' of Iraq? In the distance, we could see the traces of anti-aircraft fire. We decided to risk the thunder and pressed on. Somebody was looking over us. We not only missed the storm but also missed Iraq by thirty miles, Iran by seven miles and Russia by ten miles. Right now our weatherman can do no wrong. If he gets us home for Boxing Day, the champagne is on me.

The views from where we are flying are breathtaking. We are crossing the snow-clad Armenian mountains; below us is a little village called Ararat, where Noah landed in his Ark. Over our headsets came the crackly sound of the air-traffic controller from Armenia: 'On behalf of all the Armenian people we would like to say welcome.' It was said with such genuine friendliness. If only all countries could be so welcoming.

About 2,600 miles gone – the width of the Atlantic Ocean – 20,000 left to go. Everybody feeling incredibly exhilarated. I for one need to borrow somebody else's nails for the rest of the trip – because I no longer have any of my own left!

Day 4, 21 December 1998

We are still flying, and our voyage becomes more awesome by the minute. We have moved from Turkey through our secret passage out into Armenia and over Mount Ararat. From there we went through Azerbaijan, a new independent state in the former USSR, out across the Caspian Sea, through Turkmenistan and Uzbekistan (what wonderful names these states have). We then passed over Afghanistan, where a bloody civil war has raged for years. Afghanistan was one of the countries that Alexander the Great once conquered.

Then, early this morning, a wonderful but rather frightening prospect dawned on us: the winds had unexpectedly changed, and we would not now be able to fly to the north of the largest mountain range in the world, but would have to go straight across them.

These were the awesome Himalayas, never crossed before by a balloon. We would cross Nepal, a remote kingdom between India and Tibet. Nepal is where the Buddha was born, but is also known for the largest mountain on earth – Mount Everest – which soars up to nearly 30,000 feet.

This sounds wonderful, but, as with everything about trying to fly a balloon around the world, there was a catch. It is what's known as 'deadly curl-over'. A balloon can be grabbed by the wind and literally smashed into the other side of the mountain, as one crosses it. To avoid this we will need to fly 1,000 feet above the mountain for every 10mph we are travelling.

We did our calculations based on our present speed of 80mph, and this meant we had to fly 8,000 feet above the mountain. At present we couldn't fly more than 30,000 feet, so we would have to fly 40,000 feet over Everest to avoid being smashed on to the other side of it.

We couldn't do that. Could we and our team back home steer us between Everest and the next highest mountain, K2?

Well, we won't know for a few more hours, so tomorrow if we succeed I'll let you know.

Day 5, 22 December 1998

Well, I'm still here writing my diary, so we must have missed Everest and K2. In fact we steered right between them – more by luck than skill this time, since the mountains had taken control of our direction and they were not going to let us go.

We spent the last twenty-four hours following the beautiful mountain range. In the day they were exquisite. At night having them a few thousand feet below was an eerie feeling. Adding to our problems were masses of ice forming on top of the balloon, blocking the helium valve.

As daytime approached, enormous clumps of it would fall down on to our capsule. It was actually very beautiful and I've made a wonderful film of our crossing of the Himalayas. Hannibal would have been proud of us.

Because the winds died on us we didn't suffer the deadly 'curl-over effect' that I wrote about in yesterday's diary.

Day 6, 23 December 1998

We were three hours from crossing the Chinese border when they dropped a bombshell on us. 'We're revoking your permission to cross China. You will not enter.' We had no choice. We couldn't land in the Himalayas. That would mean almost certain death. But to fly into China when specifically told not to can also mean very serious trouble.

The Chinese had originally given us permission to cross the south of China. Because we had been sucked into the Himalayas we were going to enter China 150 miles north of where they had asked us to.

So we had three hours to try to persuade them to let us in. I knew Sir Edward Heath, who was once Prime Minister of Britain and who had excellent relations with the Chinese. So our people first contacted him and he was good enough to speak to his contacts. I got through to Saskia in my office and asked her to contact Tony Blair. 'But I don't have the number for Downing Street,' she said. Tired out, and, to be frank, pretty worried by now, I raised my voice. 'Dial 192. Get it from Directory Enquiries!'

Tony Blair was good enough to write a personal letter to His Excellency Premier Zhu Rongji. I also contacted Peter Such – the head of one of our rival airlines, Cathay Pacific – who was based in Hong Kong, and who was also very helpful. And our British Ambassador in Beijing and his team were enormously helpful. Finally – a half-hour before we crossed the border – we got the word that we could enter as long as we stayed in the very bottom section of China. We soon realised this would be impossible. The winds would take us towards Shanghai – coincidentally a city I visited only two weeks ago, and a city that Virgin Atlantic has recently applied for permission to fly to.

We then had word that the Chinese had held a press conference in Beijing and had stated that we had violated their airspace without permission – if we did not rectify this promptly the consequences could be severe. At the same time we received a message from our base in London, going through the probable sequence of actions that an escort fighter plane would adopt. We went through the sequence of events that we would try to adopt ourselves in order to comply.

We were high over snow, cloud, mountains – to land would be suicidal. We then received a message from the Chinese Civil Aviation Authorities:

> PLEASE BE INFORMED THAT YOU MUST LAND AT LHASA
> AIRPORT AND CANNOT CONTINUE FLYING OVER OUR
> AIRSPACE BECAUSE YOU CANNOT OBEY OUR REQUIREMENTS.
> PLEASE CONTACT LATER. YOU MUST OPERATE THE BALLOON
> AS REQUESTED BY LHASA ACC. THANKS FOR YOUR
> CO-OPERATION.
> BEST REGARDS@OPS OF CAAC

Well, the words 'thanks for your co-operation' were the only friendly words we had heard in a while. A balloon cannot land at an airport. The weather conditions were atrocious, it would be dark in two hours, we were over mountains, and we were carrying five tons of propane. We were being asked, in effect, to commit suicide. I wrote back to Virgin ICO Global Balloon Base asking them to contact the Chinese, explaining all our problems. We received a response one hour later:

> PLEASE BE INFORMED YOU MUST LAND. YOU CANNOT
> CONTINUE OVER OUR AIRSPACE.

We were in a Catch-22 situation: to attempt to land

would mean certain death, but to continue, without permission, would mean that we'd almost certainly be shot down.

I contacted the British Ambassador in Beijing and explained our predicament. He promised that he and his team would stay up all night to try to resolve it. I sent the Ambassador a note to pass on to the Chinese:

WE KINDLY ADVISE THAT IT IS NOT POSSIBLE TO LAND NOW WITHOUT SEVERELY ENDANGERING THE LIVES OF THE CREW AND ANY PERSONS ON THE GROUND. WE CANNOT STEER THE BALLOON AS IT GOES WHERE THE WIND TAKES IT. WE HAVE FULL CLOUD COVER AND CANNOT SEE THE GROUND. WE CANNOT DESCEND THROUGH CLOUD AS IT WILL CREATE ICE ON THE BALLOON RESULTING IN US CRASHING. WE KINDLY BRING TO YOUR ATTENTION THAT WE ARE DOING EVERYTHING IN OUR POWER TO RESOLVE THE SITUATION AND APOLOGISE PROFUSELY FOR NOT BEING ABLE TO COMPLY WITH YOUR INSTRUCTIONS. WE ARE NOT BEING DISRESPECTFUL TO THE CHINESE AUTHORITIES. WE ARE JUST IN AN IMPOSSIBLE SITUATION THAT WE CANNOT RESOLVE AT PRESENT WITHOUT ENDANGERING LIVES. WE KINDLY REQUEST THAT YOU GIVE OUR TEAM MORE TIME TO WORK ON THIS PROBLEM.

OUR PILOTS HAVE TRIED EVERY FREQUENCY THAT YOU HAVE GIVEN TO US BUT ARE UNABLE TO CONTACT YOU. THEY WILL CONTINUE TO TRY. PLEASE CAN YOU ADVISE SOME MORE HF OR VHF FREQUENCIES.

WE KINDLY REQUEST A RESPONSE TO THIS MESSAGE.

We flew on nervously. After all the personal pleas from so many world figures, we hoped the Chinese wouldn't do anything too dramatic.

In the early hours of the morning, to our great relief, the following fax came through:

SINCE THE VIRGIN GLOBAL CHALLENGER HOT-AIR BALLOON
HAS INFRINGED THE PRINCIPLES AGREED BY THE TWO SIDES
AND THE PROMISES MADE BY THE UK SIDE AND DID NOT
ENTER THE AIRSPACE WITHIN THE DESIGNATED AREA THE
CHINESE SIDE HAD NO OPTION BUT TO DEMAND THAT IT
SHOULD LAND. IN RESPECT OF THE APPEAL MADE BY
AMBASSADOR GALSWORTHY THE CHINESE SIDE HAVE MADE
EVERY EFFORT TO OVERCOME ALL DIFFICULTIES AND HAVE
NOW DECIDED TO ALLOW THE BALLOON TO CONTINUE ITS
FLIGHT. BUT THEY REQUEST THAT IT SHOULD LEAVE CHINESE
AIRSPACE AS RAPIDLY AS POSSIBLE. IF THE CHINESE SIDE
HAVE NEW REQUESTS THEY WILL BE IN TOUCH WITH THE
BRITISH SIDE.

We cannot thank the Chinese enough. Thank you.

Day 7, 24 December 1998

A bizarre thing happened to me as we left the Chinese coast. I received word from England:

MANY CONGRATULATIONS! VIRGIN ATLANTIC HAS BEEN
GIVEN PERMISSION TO BE THE ONLY AIRLINE TO FLY TO
SHANGHAI DIRECT FROM ENGLAND. BRITISH AIRWAYS HAS
BEEN TURNED DOWN. HURRY HOME.

It's a strange world. One minute terrified of being shot down over Shanghai in a balloon, the next being given permission to start flying a 747 there!

It would have been delightful news if we hadn't found ourselves heading for North Korea. It seems that every country that did not welcome balloonists had a magnetic attraction to them. And North Korea is one of the most closed, heavily militarist countries in the world. We had been told not even to bother to apply for overflying rights.

Bob went into overdrive to find winds to take us south through South Korea. In the meantime, Kevin Stass – who with Erin Porter had been battling back at base to get our overflight rights – thought, give it a go, and contacted the North Koreans.

To the surprise and delight of all of us, a quick response came, welcoming us to overfly. Maybe as a nation they are now ready to become part of the wider world. For whatever reason, we were extremely grateful. They were the last political headache we had to face before heading home. We now had 'only' the biggest ocean in the world to cross – 5,200 miles of the Pacific, America, and then the Atlantic Ocean.

After everything that had happened, in the first five days we had only travelled a third of the way around the world. The Pacific has claimed many other hot-air balloonists who have attempted a crossing. The day before Per and I successfully crossed the Pacific in a hot-air balloon, ten years ago, a delightful Japanese balloonist attempted it and perished. Only three months ago Steve Fossett hit a thunderstorm over the Pacific and was brought down near Fiji.

We therefore all have enormous respect for the Pacific Ocean, and yet strangely we were so relieved to have got through the political problems of the last few days that we felt somehow we would have a drama-free trip. It started well: we ended up crossing South Korea as it turned out, since Bob had already been working on changing our track successfully before North Korean permission came through. We then travelled on to a beautiful dawn over Mt Fuji, and Kansai in Japan. We could see literally thousands of people thronging the streets looking up at the balloon as we passed overhead. Will Whitehorn, my right-hand man, who was in Kansai, contacted the balloon and said that 'it was one of the most remarkable sights of my life – standing and watching the whole place come to a halt'.

The winds began to pick up, to our great relief. We found speeds of between 150 and 180mph. We were being sucked into the jetstream and we needed it. We had used up a lot of fuel flying over the Himalayas and had to race home. We had no more than five or six days' duration left, and two-thirds of the way to go. But, with these speeds, we calculated we could cross the Pacific in less than forty hours; a day to cross America, another to cross the Atlantic and then home. Our spirits were high; we really thought we were in with a chance.

Then we received an urgent message from Bob Rice. It began: 'We have a potential problem that is giving me great concern.' If Bob had great concern about something then so should we. 'Specifically,' he went on, 'there's a trough out there that will have an elongated shear line from around Hawaii, northeastward. The result of a pattern shift like that will take the balloon southeast towards Hawaii and back into the Pacific Ocean. We need to get to the trough before it starts to shear. Maximum speed is critical: more so than on any other occasion.'

We knew what he meant – if we did not get through on time, we would be turned southward and end up in the water. Or, as Mike Kendrick, our base commander, said five minutes later, 'This is a matter of saving you going into the drink, so, for God's sake, fly.' So we went as high as we could to get extra speed, but we could only find ten knots more at altitude. We have had a long night's flying towards this trough. Bob reran the figures to see if ten knots was sufficient to push us through and on into America. If not, it is fortunate that the capsule was built to float. But I have no plan or wish to test it!

The diary ends here, just as things started to turn for

the worse. I didn't complete it as we were too busy just trying to stay alive. I remember just before going to sleep on that last day when we had all but crossed the Pacific and had the States ahead, with the weather forecasters saying that we would be home in two days. The winds were so strong, about 200mph, and it looked as if we were going to cross America on Christmas Day, with Father Christmas dangling far below us, and be home for Boxing Day.

As I was going to sleep, I thought that this was almost too much for one person in their lifetime, to have such fantastic experiences, and to be so fortunate. It was only when I woke up that I realised that fortune was not going to shine on us this time and that we were going to end up landing in the Pacific rather than being the first to travel around the world in a hot-air balloon.

The wall of bad weather that we tried to beat had got there before us. We went as high as we could to get through it; we went as low as we could to get through it. But to no avail. It was as if a solid brick wall had been built right down the coast of America to stop us.

We were very fortunate to find winds that took us back out into the Pacific, towards the only islands for thousands of miles – Hawaii. Once we were sixty miles from them, we crashed into the sea. The balloon dragged over the waves, bouncing 300 feet each time, like the bombs in the *Dambusters* film. Pushing the dome on the roof open, we climbed out, hanging on for dear life. Then, finally, as the balloon hit the sea for the tenth time, we threw ourselves off, once again to be plucked out of the sea by helicopters, which just managed to reach us. No wonder Virgin sponsored London's helicopter ambulance service!

On Christmas Day I landed in Hawaii and decided to get to Necker Island, where all the family were. On

Boxing Day I landed to find a slightly surreal thing happening when I arrived. Nobody was in the big house. All my best friends and relatives were gathered at the very far end of the island, having a children's party. The reason it was surreal was that I'd written my will the day before I'd taken off in the balloon and in it I'd instructed that, if the balloon had gone down and my body had been recovered, I was to be buried at that end of the island. I wanted my best friends and family to be at my funeral, and I wanted to be laid for ever in this very special place. And so it was strange to be there in person, looking around and thinking, My God, what a different kind of party this could have been.

And it was at that time that I thought, OK, I've had these incredible experiences; somebody has been kind to me and I've survived them. These exploits had helped me put Virgin on the map, put me on the map, and given me some fantastic memories to tell the grandchildren one day. But I'd pushed my luck as far as I should. Now I could see that if I could use the position in which I'd found myself – where I could pick up the phone to President Mandela or Bill Clinton or Tony Blair and get straight through – I might be able to do something worthwhile. To use that power and position to try to fulfil my original dream – from when I was fifteen, starting the magazine and writing in my first editorial – about trying to change the world. I have always tried to use my position to help charities. When Diana died I was flying back from America and, like everyone else, I was deeply affected by her death. But, as a great friend of the princess, I felt it was important that I try to find a way to make something positive come out of her death. So I decided to put together the best album ever in her memory and pledged 100 per cent of the profits to a Diana memorial fund. Eric

Clapton, Sting, George Michael, Chris de Burgh and Paul McCartney all contributed willingly. But I also wanted a fantastic song that would reflect Diana's life and which could be sung at her funeral and then go on the album.

I knew Elton John was a friend of Diana so I asked him if he would be prepared to perform 'Candle in the Wind' at the funeral and if Bernie Taupin would adapt the words to make them more appropriate for the occasion. I also made it clear that I wanted the song to go on the tribute album. All of this had to be cleared not just by Diana's family and the Queen, but also by the church. Three frantic days of negotiation followed but the Queen was minded not to allow it so I called Tony Blair and asked him if he would intervene. Fortunately he did, because Elton's performance of 'Candle in the Wind' captured the imagination of the entire world and made what was already a terribly difficult occasion almost unbearably poignant.

At the time Elton John's career was in a lull, but imagine my surprise when, a few days later, Elton withdrew permission for the single to go on the charity album. I wrote him a long letter expressing my anger which I decided not to make public. But, as is the way of these things, someone unscrupulous found it when rummaging through Elton's dustbins and inevitably it found its way on to the front page of the *Sun*. Fortunately our tribute album went on to make millions of pounds and was the biggest single contributor to the Diana, Princess of Wales Memorial Fund. And 'Candle in the Wind' ended up by being the largest-selling single in the history of music, selling some 33 million copies.

What I'd always thought was that Virgin should be more than just a money-making machine, and that, as Virgin has the wealth of a small nation, we should use that wealth to tackle social issues more than we had in the past. Companies do have a responsibility to tackle them. Bill Gates, over the last few years, has invested enormous amounts of money trying to develop vaccines to stamp out deadly diseases. Despite the difficult time he's had, and the bad press Microsoft has received, he's given an awful lot back to the community. He's a tremendous example to all other entrepreneurs.

When I was last in South Africa, I visited some hospitals, particularly ones in Soweto. It was devastating to see the number of people whose lives have been destroyed by HIV/AIDS, including the millions of orphans who have become heads of households at the ripe old age of nine. After the launch of Mates in the UK, Virgin continued to support a number of organisations in the fight against HIV/AIDS around the world – but after this trip I vowed that we would in some way do even more to help stop this disease from wiping out entire generations.

In Africa, I'm also a supporter of an organisation that's trying to make sure that the 2 per cent of Africa currently set aside for wildlife is increased to 4 or 5 per cent, giving the wildlife of Africa more wild areas in which to roam – areas that are not just given over for cattle and farmers. Among my favourite animals in the world are the African wild dogs, a dying breed of animal, which I find fascinating. It would be a fantastic legacy for the next generation if twice as much land as is currently used can be fenced in for wild animals, giving them a greater chance of long-term survival.

Another area of the world that has seen more than its fair share of trouble is Northern Ireland. Although there will always be extremists from both factions – Catholic Republicans and Protestant Unionists – by the 1990s the public were increasingly getting tired of years of sectarian bombings and killings. In May 1998 Mo

Mowlam was appointed Northern Ireland Secretary – an inspired choice. Mo is a completely down-to-earth woman who could relate to the ordinary man and woman in the street (literally – as it turned out). She decided to go above the heads of the politicians and directly to The People to hold a referendum on the future of Ireland. If she won, permanent peace was a strong possibility. If she lost, the alternative was to go back to the last 30 years in which 3,500 people had been murdered. The referendum proposed that Northern Ireland would remain part of Great Britain but that, if one day the majority of citizens of Northern Ireland ever wanted a unified Ireland and they voted for it, they could have it.

Two days before the vote the outcome looked uncertain. Mo is an old friend of mine and she rang me to ask if I would walk the streets with her. I think Mo felt that I was popular in Ireland because of my ballooning and boating adventures and that I had no political or religious associations; she may also have wanted to send the message that with peace would come prosperity in the form of investment in business.

Either way, the next day I set out for Heathrow with one of our PR staff, Wendy, who happened to be from Northern Ireland herself. In the lounge she turned to me and said, 'Richard, I'm sorry. I just can't come with you. My dad will kill me if he sees me with you campaigning for this peace treaty.' I'd never thought of her as Protestant or Catholic, just a delightful Irish girl. It brought home to me just what a difficult job Mo had ahead of her.

In the end I persuaded Wendy to come. She bravely stayed with Mo and me for the rest of the day. By the end of the day Wendy was so convinced by the arguments that she decided to vote 'yes' and also persuaded her mother and sisters to vote 'yes' as well. Unfortunately, she realised her dad was a lost cause.

That night, having walked the streets of Northern Ireland and shaken hundreds of hands, we all went back to Hillsborough Castle, the Northern Ireland Secretary's beautiful residence, for dinner and bed to await the outcome. At least I knew my trip had secured four extra votes!

The next day the good news came through – the 'yes' vote had been won. Peace finally had come to Ireland. Since it was a peace voted by the people this time it felt like it just might hold.

In my life, I've come to expect the unexpected. It sounds easy enough to say, but all the things that have happened to me, to the family and to Virgin have taught me that you have to be prepared at all times to deal with surprises. You just develop a way of picking up your feet and getting on with it. But nothing I've ever faced made me ready for what happened on 11 September 2001.

It was a quarter past three in the afternoon in Brussels, and I was about to stand up to address yet another European Union inquiry into competition. I've sat through dozens of meetings like this, and there was nothing out of the ordinary about that September day. The same grey suits, it seemed, sat there, ranged against us. I knew the strength of our position, so I was already thinking ahead of that meeting, about getting home, settling back into the routine at work after a summer break with the family on Necker. This time it was not about an airline, nor was it about the music business, retailing or the railways: it was about the incredibly 'interesting' subject of 'block exemption' for

European car manufacturers. In other words, about the fact that the people who make cars rip us all off by controlling who sells them, and at what price they're sold on to us. I was there because, as the years rolled on and the world of the Internet and call centres lowered the cost of distribution, it had become possible for Virgin to sell and deliver cars direct to the public at prices up to 25 per cent cheaper than the corner garage. In the previous year, we had sold more than six thousand.

As I was about to launch into a withering attack on the vested interests of those who were sitting all around me in the room, someone quietly handed a note to the chairman, who looked up with an ashen face and announced to the shocked room that there had been a terrorist attack in New York, which involved a number of aircraft. He then asked me if I wished to continue. None of us there knew quite how serious things were but they did not sound good; there was also some concern that the European Union building could be a target. Nonetheless, I decided to carry on, deliver the speech, and answer questions from the members of the European Parliament, knowing full well that everyone's mind would be on New York.

An hour later I was about to board a Eurostar train back to HQ, when I finally managed to get through to London. 'It looks like Middle Eastern terrorists took over four aircraft,' Will said. 'The Twin Towers have just come down and there could be over ten thousand dead. Reports are also coming in of other aircraft being hijacked. They've closed US airspace. In your absence, we turned the planes back; only three had passed the point of no return. Since then they've shut US airspace. I suggest we talk in more detail once you're back and all gather tomorrow morning first thing at Holland Park.'

As I sat on the train with the chief executive of Virgin Cars, the full horror began to sink in. There was a woman sitting opposite us who was a banker, and was frantically phoning friends in London and New York to find out what she could. She began to give us a blow-by-blow account of what she knew: that the brokers Cantor Fitzgerald had been completely wiped out; that several French and American banks may have had severe casualties. Her distress was evident and I did what I could to help her. I still had not seen any pictures, but I could tell from her tears just how awful things were.

Only that morning, I'd run my mind over how the businesses were going. In the run-up to 11 September, Virgin Atlantic had continued its remarkable success story. Singapore Airlines had become our partners, paying a record £600 million for a 49 per cent stake in March 2000, and we had remained the only profitable airline flying across the North Atlantic in 2001. The business felt so good that year, as others struggled with out-of-control costs, unfriendly service and ageing fleets. Indeed, I felt so confident about the business that I had continued expanding by starting a new airline in Australia almost exactly a year to the day before the Twin Towers tragedy. It is called Virgin Blue and was based on the low-cost model of Southwest Airlines. Despite the weak Australian dollar and high fuel costs, it had thrived, driving airfares down and doubling the number of people flying on its routes.

This was not the only new investment of the previous few years. We had done a lot to rationalise Virgin and its brand in the late 1990s and, by 11 September, we had a clear strategy in place, based on the concept of 'branded venture capital'. Instead of being a conglomerate with lots of subsidiaries, Virgin had become a diverse investor. So we'd choose business sectors carefully, trying to bring more competition to sectors that would benefit the consumer. Then we'd find good partners and managers to take the businesses forward, with the eventual aim of letting them stand on their own two feet, just as companies like Virgin Records and Virgin Radio had already done.

But we were also turning our attention to whether we could make a difference in other areas. For nearly 250 days of the year I travel around the world, trying to make Virgin the most respected brand in the world; not necessarily the biggest, but the best.

We had also built a great management team, both at UK and international levels, that could act as our eyes and ears across all the businesses, so the new investments had come at breakneck speed over the previous couple of years. Virgin Active had become the world's third largest health-club chain; thetrain-line.com, selling rail tickets via the Internet across all the networks, had 5 million customers by 11 September. Virgin Mobile was Europe's fastest-growing mobile-phone company and, on the fateful day, was on the verge of doing a deal with Sprint to take our no-nonsense mobile offer to the American public.

As part of the expansion of Mobile, we had also finally consigned the Our Price brand to the dustbin of history. Since we had bought the business from WHSmith in 1998, we had taken the decision to rebrand it as Virgin to sit alongside the successful Megastore chain. It, and Virgin's other presence on the high street, helped Virgin Mobile to achieve nearly 2 million customers by the beginning of 2002, and now over 5 million customers.

One of the first things I'd checked, on hearing about the terrorist attacks, was whether or not anyone we knew had been involved. Frances Farrow, who had worked for us on the airline business over here and then moved to New York to marry her fiancé only that spring, lived near the Twin Towers. She was helping out on the deal with Sprint for Virgin Mobile. We lost contact with her for three days; later, we found out that she'd been driving near the World Trade Center just as the first tower started to fall. Luckily for us, all the other relatives and friends called to let us know they were OK.

But it wasn't the same for so many others, and I had a taste of this when I was called by Howard Lutnick, the chairman of 'Cantor's', as they were known in the city. On the Friday night, James Kyle of Cantor Fitzgerald, the firm that had lost literally hundreds of employees in the tragedy, had called Will Whitehorn. They urgently needed to fly dozens of grieving relatives to New York but, since their entire operation had been wiped out, they did not know whether they would have a business, when the markets reopened, to pay the bill. On the Saturday morning we agreed to carry as many people as they needed across the Atlantic. Whatever problems we had, it was so very much worse for them.

Howard rang that afternoon to thank me personally. I couldn't begin to imagine what a hellish time he was having, facing the loss of most of his close colleagues. 'Thanks for everything you're doing for us,' he said. 'It means a lot to everyone at Cantor's.' I felt embarrassed that we could do only this much, especially when I learned, after his emotional and gracious phone call, that his own brother, Gary, had died in the devastating attack.

I see from my diary entry on the computer for 12 September that all it says is 'RB – meeting all day at Holland Park'. And it was a gloomy group of us who met in my house that morning. Present in the sitting room were Richard Bowker, Patrick McCall, Will Whitehorn, Mark Poole and Simon Wright. Ironically, nobody was there from Virgin Atlantic. Steve Ridgway – the managing director – and his senior team had already enacted their emergency procedures and begun an urgent 72-hour review of the entire business, with a view to making recommendations by the Friday of that week as to what we should do. But all of us sitting around the table in Holland Park knew we were going to have to do something fast. With transatlantic routes closed to us, and the sudden drop-off in passenger numbers, Virgin Atlantic was set to lose £1.5 million a day. That morning I had spoken to BA's new boss – a delightful Australian called Rod Eddington – who had told me that BA could lose up to £8 million a day. I suggested that we work together in our approach to government to see what assistance we might get, once American airspace opened again. I was heartened by his straightforward reply: 'Good on ya, mate! I'll call you at the start of next week.'

The fact that BA may have been in even worse trouble than we were wasn't much consolation to the six of us sitting around my drawing-room table in the bright September sunshine. As we drew up lists of what we were up against, it was clear that we had enough cash in the various companies to see ourselves through the worst, but that the potential black hole at Virgin Atlantic needed to be plugged as quickly as possible. The other uncertainty was what was going to happen to our competitors. We knew that Sabena in Brussels and Ansett in Australia were going into administration, but would they survive?

That weekend, the plans we'd had ready for such an emergency were used for the first time. The team at Virgin Atlantic did a fantastic job in their assessment of

439

the 'market failure' between the UK and the USA, and, as a result, drew up an emergency restructuring plan. There were some painful bits to this: more than 1,200 jobs would go at the airline in the UK, but they did what they could to make the thousands of others secure. Most importantly, they switched larger aircraft, such as the 747-400s, on to booming routes in Africa, and put the smaller Airbuses into service across the North Atlantic.

On the Sunday morning we pressed the button to go ahead with the restructuring and told the staff on the Monday. I will never forget the good grace and professionalism with which they took the news and then got on with the job. The months that followed were sticky but we had called it right in the first week: by Christmas it was clear that Virgin Atlantic was through the worst and would survive. This was no mean feat given that our American competitors went cap in hand to their government, and received massive cash handouts from them. This may be what got them through, but all we saw was that it gave them leeway to behave more anti-competitively than they usually do.

The irony of the situation was this: not only had we built up such a fantastic team of people but, until 11 September, we'd been profitable. My biggest worry at that point was how morale in the business would react to these enforced redundancies. It was a testament to everybody involved that, not only did a lot of the older and part-time staff come forward and volunteer, but those who stayed really buckled down in the spirit that undoubtedly made Virgin Atlantic what it is today. The innovative nature of the airline – using bed-seats and in-flight masseurs, to make passengers more comfort-able – now meant, ironically, that we were the first to install bulletproof Kevlar cockpit doors, to further ensure passengers' safety.

It would have been harder for Virgin Atlantic's management to be as single-minded as they were if they had to worry about short-haul operations as well, but under Virgin's investment model they didn't have to. We have two other airlines, Virgin Express in Brussels and Virgin Blue in Brisbane, Australia, both of which are separately run and publicly quoted. The effects of 11 September on these businesses were entirely different but equally challenging. In the case of one, it faced the collapse of the main state-owned carrier (Sabena), and the other the collapse of its main competitor (Ansett). Both have had to move quickly to reshape and grow their businesses. In each case they were able to focus completely on their own issues.

Similarly, Virgin Mobile faced challenges early in the twenty-first century: growth in the UK market, a recession in Singapore and the decision as to whether or not to press the button to expand in the US. If Virgin Mobile were one conglomerate there could have been paralysis in these decisions but, as each is under a separate joint-venture structure, once again the management teams could concentrate on the job in hand. By October, we took the momentous decision to go ahead with launching Virgin Mobile in the US in partnership with Sprint, and began a fundraising exercise to help finance the $500 million venture.

This was not as daft as it may seem. It was clear that the US economy was going into recession but what was also clear was that mobile-phone sales were finally starting to boom in America after the uncertainties that followed the tragedy of 11 September. Virgin's low-cost model of prepaid phones seemed an ideal solution to help attract a youth market, one that had not warmed to mobiles and text messaging in the way that the European, African and Asian youth markets had.

Within another two weeks, on 7 October, the war against the terrorists started in earnest as the bombs and cruise missiles started to rain down on their enclaves in Afghanistan. It's always hard to stay focused at times like these, as I knew from the first Gulf War, but people still had jobs to go to. So it was another shock when Virgin Rail Group's biggest supplier, Railtrack, went bust. It was a blow to the railway-using public and to Virgin, which was at the time trying to negotiate a deal to save the upgrade of the West Coast mainline. Yet again, the consequences were quickly understood by a dedicated management team, who did not have to worry about the rest of some amorphous plc's other activities.

However, another shock was to follow when the government pinched Richard Bowker to become head of the Strategic Rail Authority. As co-chairman of Virgin Rail, he had done a fantastic job in co-ordinating our new train orders, as was proved when the first of our tilting trains were delivered from the factory, on time and to budget, in November 2001. By way of contrast, Railtrack's cost for the upgrade had gone up fourfold, and was going to end up being years late.

It was a proud and tearful moment, standing in the Alstom factory in Birmingham on a cold and sunny November day, watching Joan name one of our new trains *Virgin Lady*. It was an even better moment sitting by the fire that evening watching the *Six O'Clock News* and hearing the words I had waited five years for: 'Virgin has delivered on its promises.' This was no mean feat, as the orders had been placed in 1998 and, despite all the technological difficulties, Virgin had produced the world's most advanced train, which tilted round corners at speeds of up to 140mph (225 kph). Of course the sting in the tail was that the track would not be ready for 125-mph operation until 2004!

The winter of 2001 saw yet more midnight oil being burned by Virgin Rail's finance team as they negotiated with Railtrack, its administrators, the Strategic Rail Authority, the Department of Transport and the train suppliers to ensure that our trains got the track they deserve – and the public the service it deserves. I thought how ironic it was that every critic of our deal to upgrade the railway in 1997 had predicted that we would never get the new trains to work and that we would go bust in the process of trying. As it was, about the only tangible successes of privatisation were Virgin's electric Pendolinos and diesel Voyagers. The railway experts who had also predicted in 1997 that upgrading the track would be easier than the trains were dumbfounded.

Meanwhile, in Australia, the effects of 11 September continued to be felt in the airline business. Following the collapse of Ansett, Virgin Blue suddenly found itself Australia's second-largest airline. Its chief executive, Brett Godfrey, had been steadily building the business for a year but almost overnight was running an airline that promised to be more profitable than easyJet and had enormous opportunities, if only he could raise the finance. Our corporate finance director, Patrick McCall, was on a plane to Australia within three days of the Twin Towers attack. One month later Virgin Blue had announced the appointment of Goldman Sachs to prepare for a flotation in 2003 with a potential valuation being talked about of over AUS$1 billion.

It nearly did not turn out this way as Ansett's parent company, Air New Zealand, had made an offer to buy Virgin Blue for US$250 million shortly before 11 September. Our friends at Singapore Airlines had a 20 per cent stake in ANZ, so it was the CEO, Dr Cheong (CK), who telephoned me to make the offer. 'Richard, I really think you should accept this offer,' he said. 'It is a very generous valuation and if you don't take it we'll put the money into Ansett instead, and they will wipe out Virgin Blue within six months.' Was he bluffing?

It was a difficult decision. My instinct told me that the company was worth more than that, but it wasn't an ungenerous offer. However, there was something in the desperate insistence in CK's voice on the long-distance phone line that made me hesitate. I decided to be a little mischievous, and to call a press conference. I wanted the competition authorities to understand how strongly the public felt about the need for healthy competition. I announced, with a sombre and straight face: 'This is a sad day, but I've decided to sell up. This means that cheap air tickets in Australia will be a thing of the past – others won't want to follow what we tried to do. It will, of course, mean that our staff will be part of Ansett, and that there will be redundancies. But, anyway, I've done well out of it, so I'm off back to the UK right away with my $250 million profit.' There was a deadly hush, and the packed room seemed in deep shock. A journalist from the Press Association rushed off to file her copy. And then I caught sight of some of our staff across the room, who were not meant to be at the press conference. I realised they were in tears. 'Only joking,' I added quickly, and publicly tore up the US$250 million cheque.

Five days later, Ansett went bust and Brett could barely contain himself on the phone as he enthusiastically outlined his plans for rapid expansion of what had become, overnight, Australia's second-largest airline. It was that call that made me realise that Brett's team had built a truly Virgin business: it had revolutionised the market for Australian air travel; it had built a fantastic reputation for quality; and all this had been done as a small-scale, venture-capital start-up, with only AUS$10 million.

By December 2003 this AUS$10m start-up had captured over 30 per cent of the market and was the first of our new generation of companies to float. This was a remarkable achievement given the chaos in the aviation market and the tragic terrorist attack in Bali the previous year, which had dented Australians' confidence in their immunity from the problems of the rest of the world. By the time we took the company public on the Australian stock market we had a new partner in Virgin Blue called Chris Corrigan, and, with his investment and the float, we had made over $780m in just over three years of trading. After the float Virgin retained a 25 per cent stake and the company continued to prosper for over eighteen months until Qantas finally woke up to the destruction of their domestic market and, like all good monopolists, they launched a low-quality clone of Virgin Blue in the spring of 2004 called JetStar. By January 2005 Virgin Blue was locked in a price war. Despite this, Virgin Blue is still one of the world's most profitable airlines. Indeed, one of the remarkable achievements of 2004–5 was that Virgin Blue and Virgin Atlantic both remained profitable at a time when most of the US airlines finally went into Chapter 11 bankruptcy.

Even our newer dotcom businesses – those launched since 1998 – seemed to go from strength to strength after 11 September, largely because they were modelled on a real brand, selling real things. Virgin Cars sold its six thousandth vehicle that winter and, despite a blip after the New York attacks, car sales actually improved in the run-up to Christmas. The same was true of thetrainline.com. Again, sales rocketed as nervous executives decided that a train from Manchester or

Newcastle was a better bet than a plane. By the beginning of 2002 these and several other of our e-commerce businesses had turned cash-flow-positive. There was only one exception, Virgin Wines, which, despite winning 100,000 customers, still could not get the margins it needed in a cut-throat market; but we're confident that it will turn the corner soon enough.

Virgin Wines was a good example of our management philosophy of giving our people the chance to become entrepreneurs in their own right. Rowan Gormley, of Virgin Money, had begun to feel by the end of 1999 that our financial-services business was maturing and needed a different sort of manager. The former venture capitalist had been bitten by the entrepreneurial bug and simply wanted to start something new – an online wine retailer. I sympathised with him and, in spite of our misgivings about entering such a different sector, we decided to back him almost as a matter of principle. Virgin Wines was established as a joint venture by Virgin and Rowan.

I could go on, but hopefully the point is well made. By investing in separate businesses with partners – 'ring-fenced', as the bankers keep telling me – we had been able to withstand the management pressures of 11 September, spread risk and take what we hope have been a lot of good decisions. Couple these with a venture-capital private-equity model of creating individual companies with their own business case, shareholders and financial resources, and you have the Virgin that existed in 2001, and continues to exist now.

It's been interesting, with the collapse of Enron, to see how people still want to build enormous companies; but if something major goes wrong the whole lot falls. What we are trying to do at Virgin is not to have one enormous company in one sector under one banner, but to have two hundred or even three hundred separate companies. Each company can stand on its own feet and, in that way, although we've got a brand that links them, if we were to have another tragedy such as that of 11 September – which hurt the airline industry – it would not bring the whole group crashing down. So we've managed to avoid the danger that we might wake up one day with one awful thing going wrong that threatens to bring all the companies down.

As it turns out, we've never let a company go: we've always paid off its debts; we've always managed to keep our reputation as an organisation that honours its obligations. But in the event of an absolute catastrophe we could let a company go; we could cut it out and, because of that, the rest of the group would not be affected. Obviously, our reputation would suffer, and we wouldn't want it to happen, but at least it would avoid a disaster and the loss of 40,000 jobs.

The sheer diversity of Virgin's businesses has proved the test of time and circumstance. With each management team focused on its own business and entrepreneurial goals, we can achieve just about anything, as long as it is right for the brand. I had learned a lot in the late 1990s and I had come to realise that sticking our name on products was not the best way to create value. Virgin Vodka might sell well on the planes and at the airports, but we did not have the worldwide distribution of firms such as UDV or Scottish Courage to back it up. However, find entrepreneurial managers like Frank Reed and Matthew Bucknall at Virgin Active, and give them the resources, and the sky will be the limit.

The omens were not good when Virgin Active opened its first club in Preston, Lancashire, in August 1999. A fire swept through the club, doing tens of thousands of pounds' worth of damage, and a distraught Frank phoned me to give me the bad news. However, one can often turn bad news into good news. When he said it would give them a chance to do one or two things differently and have longer to train the staff, I was relieved. I was also beginning to get the measure of why Frank had such a strong reputation in the leisure industry.

At the same time, Frank helped me fulfil a pledge of many years' standing to invest in South Africa. One of the first casualties of the stock-market decline that preceded the Twin Towers attack was a quoted South African company that happened to own the country's largest chain of health clubs. I was in the bath when Nelson Mandela called, and explained that it would be a particular blow to have eighty health clubs owned through a black-empowerment scheme closed down with the loss of several thousand jobs. He asked whether we could rescue it, and save those people's livelihoods. We could, and we did, so that, by the end of 2001, Virgin Active had mushroomed through growth and acquisitions into one of the top five health-club operators in the world.

In the years that followed, Virgin Active became one of the silent success stories of the Virgin empire. Even internally very few people knew how well it was doing. We brought venture-capital partners into the business and, by the beginning of 2005, it was making a profit of £34m a year.

Our method of expansion through branded venture capital may not suit everyone, but it is heartening to see that one entrepreneur is now following a not-too-dissimilar model. EasyJet has been so successful that it now has a stock-market quote and its entrepreneurial founder, Stelios Haji-Ioannou, is developing new businesses using the same brand, such as easyCar, through his separate private venture-capital vehicle easyGroup.

In the aftermath of the attacks of 11 September, Virgin Atlantic has completely restructured its operations, whilst BA's main response was to wrap itself in the Union Jack and pursue the government to back yet another attempt for it to create a transatlantic monopoly with American Airlines. Instead of trying to prevent more than 60 per cent of UK–US airline traffic and slots at Heathrow from falling into the hands of one monolithic structure, it was clear that the British Department of Transport was going to help!

On a warm and sunny November day in Washington, while I was presenting our case against the deal in front of the Senate, the transport department's hypocrisy was brought home to me. The British Embassy put out a press release supporting the merger, and an attendant 'Open Skies' deal – amazing considering the only beneficiaries were likely to be the two airlines creating the monopoly. With considerable pomposity, our diplomats tried to capture the pro-British mood on Capitol Hill with the words, 'Two allies, united in so much else, should be able to reach agreement on something that would be to their mutual benefit.' If anyone could have told me what 'mutual benefit' the attempt to create a North Atlantic airline monopoly had for two allies locked in conflict with the Taliban and Osama Bin Laden, I would happily have given them a free Upper Class ticket for life.

That was not the end of it, though. In trying to defend the deal, BA made the ludicrous claim in the *Sunday Telegraph* that there was no shortage of slots at Heathrow; this was, in the immortal words of Sid Vicious, 'bollocks'! Virgin responded by offering to give £2 million to charity for every slot that Lord Marshall managed to procure for us. Naturally, he was unable to rise to the challenge, and he must have groaned when the United States Department of Justice slammed the deal as anti-competitive and confirmed that its investigations concluded that the shortage of slots was a major reason why the deal should not go ahead as proposed.

It was not until late January 2002 that BA's game with American Airlines finally played itself out. The US Department of Transport announced that it would let the two monopolists merge their operations if BA gave up slots to the other American carriers. The problem was the price: the US regulators realised that Heathrow was overcrowded and that they would have to give their airlines a lot of access as the price of the deal. For BA, though, the price was too high; in the last week of January they abandoned their merger plans and went back to the drawing board on the whole 'Open Skies' issue.

Since the start of their attempted merger in 1996, BA had wasted thousands of man-hours, not to mention tens of millions of pounds, on a hopeless scheme, more in tune with the 1970s view of the airline business than the modern world of deregulation, competition and low-cost airlines. Rod Eddington wisely bit the bullet and, instead of trying to create a monopoly to get out of difficulties, announced the 'Future Size and Shape' project to restructure BA.

One of the things I've learned over my years in business is that, once you have a great product, it is essential to protect its reputation with vigilance. It's not just a question of getting it into the marketplace. As a result, every day I receive a bundle of press cuttings – everything that mentions Virgin. These – and staff letters – are the first things I read in the morning. When I launched the airline, I realised that I would have to use myself to raise the profile of Virgin Atlantic and build the value of the brand. Most companies don't acknowledge the press and have a tiny press office tucked away out of sight. If an inaccurate story appears in the press and is allowed to run for more than one issue of the paper, it becomes fact. Then, every time your product is mentioned, this same story will be repeated.

My reputation has been threatened on two major occasions – first by British Airways, which I've covered in detail, and second by Guy Snowden and his company GTECH, the driving force behind the creation of Camelot, which won the franchise to run the British National Lottery. For both companies I was a spanner in the works, costing them millions of pounds in lost earnings.

The GTECH incident was a particularly crucial one in terms of reputation. I met Guy Snowden in 1993 when the British Government had finally agreed to go ahead with the National Lottery. Various commercial consortia were beginning to form, but I felt strongly that the Lottery should be run by a company that would donate all the profits to charity. This would be possible because it would be a monopoly with no risk involved at all. I had asked John Jackson, with whom I had worked on the Healthcare Foundation when he was chief executive of Body Shop, and with whom I had launched Mates condoms, to pull together our charitable bid. GTECH was the leading supplier of lottery equipment, so we thought that we should meet them to see whether they would be interested in supplying us in the event that their consortium failed to win the contract.

John Jackson and I met with Guy Snowden for lunch on 24 September. The conversation we had has since become the stuff of legal legend. After we reached a stalemate, in that Guy Snowden didn't want to quote for supplying equipment to us and I didn't want to join his consortium, there was a pause. Then Snowden pointed out to us that if we went ahead with our bid it would cost the GTECH consortium millions of pounds, since they would have to reduce the percentage they were going to charge as the operators from the 15 per cent of turnover mentioned in the government guidelines to 13 per cent and possibly lower. Assuming that the annual sales of Lottery tickets reached £4 billion (which they did), each percentage reduction of the operators' slice was worth £40 million a year. There was a great deal of money at stake.

We were sitting in the conservatory in the garden at 11 Holland Park, and I noticed that Snowden began to sweat. He shifted in his seat and looked at me.

'I do not quite know how to phrase this, Richard.'

I looked across at him, wondering what he was going to say.

'There's always a bottom line. I will get to the point. In what way can we help you, Richard?'

I didn't know what to say. Snowden clarified his intentions.

'I mean, how can we help you personally?'

My mind reeled at the question. I was being offered a bribe.

'What on earth do you mean?' I said, astonished and angry and trying to give him the chance to stop. But he didn't.

'Everybody needs something in life,' Snowden said.

'Thank you,' I answered. 'I'm quite successful. I only need one breakfast, one lunch and one dinner a day. The only way you could have helped was by providing technical services for our bid.'

And with that I stood up and left the conservatory. I

wanted no further part in this man's world. While John and I were trying to pull together a bid for the National Lottery that was intended to give many millions of pounds to charity, this man was trying to bribe me to stand aside and enable his bid to go through, which, as well as giving less money to charity, would simultaneously enrich him and his company.

I bounded down the stairs and into the loo. There I scribbled the words he had used on to a piece of paper. I had never been offered a bribe before. Then I went back upstairs, and John and I ushered Snowden out of the house.

'I wasn't mistaken, was I?' I asked John. 'That was a bribe, wasn't it?'

'It most certainly was,' John told me.

Later, John told me how he nearly fell off his chair when Guy Snowden said those words. To cut a long story short, in the court case that ensued, the jury found in my favour against Guy Snowden and GTECH. In his summing-up, the late George Carman QC pointed out to the court that, above any commercial success one might enjoy, one's reputation for honesty is the most important thing. Guy Snowden had 'picked the wrong man, said the wrong thing, in the wrong place at the wrong time'.

I decided in 1999 when the licence for the National Lottery again came up for tender that I would bid once more with a not-for-profit consortium to take over the Lottery. I was convinced that New Labour's commitment to the not-for-profit approach we had taken in 1993 would ultimately be honoured. As before, most of my close Virgin advisers tried to persuade me not to bid because of the risk to the brand that a fight with Camelot – which few of them believed we could win – could do. Nonetheless, I felt so passionately about this that I decided to go ahead, and kicked things off by picking up the phone to my old friend Simon Burridge. He had spent the intervening years at the J Walter Thompson advertising agency as managing director, but had lost none of his enthusiasm for either the principle of a People's Lottery or the inevitable fight with Camelot that would follow the decision. Simon was not a man to mince words: 'I've been following things at Camelot very closely, Richard, and all our predictions in the 1993 bid are coming true. Sales are falling like a stone, the GTECH technology is crap, their games are unexciting and with the right suppliers I think we can do it!'

He set to work immediately and brought together everybody from Anne Leach and John Jackson right the way through to Colin Howes at Harbottle & Lewis. The only exception to the previous team was Will Whitehorn, who again felt strongly that there should be a clear demarcation between Virgin and what was to become known this time round as the People's Lottery. We were in the middle of investing in a whole new range of businesses, which, with the exception of the airline, might not see profits for the first couple of years. Will told me that he thought they would really go for the jugular and try to destroy my business reputation. He wanted to concentrate on fighting that bigger picture – the PR for the group and the brand – and suggested instead using an outside PR agency for the People's Lottery.

And so we assembled a new team of suppliers, agencies and people, built around the core team from the 1993 bid. In all, we ended up with more than twenty suppliers, from Energis and Microsoft to J Walter Thompson, JP Morgan and our previous rivals, AWI. Camelot, for its part, had brought in the Post Office as a shareholder to replace the now disgraced GTECH, although it still intended to bid with its equipment. Camelot had managed to improve one thing during their otherwise lacklustre six years: they had brought in the formidable Diane Thompson as chief executive. Diane was a good example of the new generation of senior female executives who began to make an impact on Britain's staid boardrooms in the 1990s. I relished the idea of a fight with her but, having heard her on BBC Radio 4's highly respected *Today* programme several times, giving John Humphrys and Jim Naughtie a run for their money, I knew she would not be a pushover.

At the time, I was freshly back from our final, failed, round-the-world balloon attempt of Christmas 1998, and I didn't appreciate one crucial difference between the Camelot of 1993 and that of 1999. Having won the bid to run the Lottery and run it for six years, they were prepared to do anything to keep it. More importantly, because most people thought they would win it again, we ended up being the only rival bidder, which meant they (and their friends) could concentrate all their firepower against us – and me personally.

The end game played itself out in the summer of 2000, while we were on our family holiday on Necker. A fax arrived from the boss of the Lottery Commission, Dame Helena Shovelton, telling us that we had not won, but we had sort of won. We were given a period of exclusivity to negotiate a deal. If we could guarantee enough money to cover any potential downside and clear up a few points, then the Lottery would be ours.

If only it had been that simple. Simon and John saw the danger signs fairly early on in the process and were right in predicting that Camelot could take a judicial review against her decision. They did. And, what's more, they won it, which then threw the entire process into chaos that autumn, with the danger of there being no time to hand over the Lottery to us. A very bitter Dame Helena resigned and was replaced by Terry Burns, a former Whitehall mandarin. In a few short weeks Burns reversed Dame Helena's entire approach to the Lottery, and came to the (I felt) ludicrous conclusion that the licence should go to Camelot.

None of us could believe it and, as the weeks went on into 2001, it became clear that the British public could not believe it either: they began to desert Camelot in their thousands. By the time 11 September shook the world, sales were falling at a rate of 20 per cent per year. I took no satisfaction from this, because, of course, it was not Camelot that suffered, but rather the many good causes – sport, the arts, charities and other organisations – that simply got less money.

Camelot's new licence to run Britain's National Lottery came into effect in January 2002, amid falling numbers of people playing. Diane Thompson, the chief executive, said that this was because people found it boring – how sad, that someone who has the job of making many millionaires a week can't make it exciting.

It also emerged that Camelot had managed to win the renewal of their licence by pledging to raise £15 billion for good causes, but the government hadn't asked them to guarantee this. Within a week of winning, Camelot were publicly looking for excuses as to why they wouldn't raise anything like £15 billion. 'We were distracted by the bidding process' etc. etc. But it was too late. They had their licence. It was a staggering outcome and one for which I think the government should hang their heads in shame: they had pledged at the election that the Lottery would be run with all the profits going to good causes – and they'd reneged on that pledge.

* * *

The restructuring of Virgin Atlantic after the tragedy of 11 September really began to pay off in the years that followed and the confidence of the management was if anything enhanced by the ability of the airline to withstand the shocks that followed – the after-effects of the war in Afghanistan and the double whammy the following year of SARS in Asia and a second war in the Gulf. Virgin Atlantic truly came of age during these events and managed to return to profitability after April 2002, despite having lost nearly £100 million in the months that followed the Twin Towers tragedy.

We also launched our secret weapon in the so-called 'battle of the beds' with British Airways. In the summer of 2003, Virgin Atlantic unveiled its Upper Class Suite, which is the world's only first class-style truly flat bed in a business class. It took off in every sense of the word and the summer of 2004 we were making significant in-roads into our rivals' market share.

The project to create the beds had the usual Virgin characteristics. We took the brave move to design the unique product ourselves and the task fell to Joe Ferry, Virgin Atlantic's head of design. He achieved the holy grail of airline seat manufacturers, which is to make a comfortable seat into a genuine bed through its unique flipping mechanism. The risk paid off, and Joe's design won six of the world's biggest industrial design awards during 2004 and had the effect of moving thousands of British Airways regular travellers to Virgin Atlantic.

As Virgin Atlantic continued to recover, I felt a great deal of unease about the 'war on terror'. It had long been the desire of the so-called neo-conservatives in America to conduct a more interventionist role in the Middle East to 'stabilise' that region. By the autumn of 2002, it was clear that the Bush administration had taken a decision to intervene in Iraq regardless of what world opinion thought of the matter and, by early 2003, it was clear they would do it even if the UN did not back their decision.

I found the whole episode deeply depressing and had a real foreboding about what I believe was an unjustified invasion. Apart from the obvious human cost of a conflict, I was sceptical about the weapons of mass destruction and could not fathom why the US government would possibly find Iraq so easy to democratise when so many others had failed before. George Bush continued to state on television, and at press conferences, that 'War was a necessary evil' – it is my belief that most 'necessary evils' are far more evil than necessary. Though, after 11 September, Will Whitehorn had counselled us against public opposition to the Bush administration over the issue of Iraq on the basis that it was inevitable. By February 2003 I'd hatched a personal plan to try and persuade Saddam Hussein to stand down before the dogs of war were unleashed. With a heavy heart I called Nelson Mandela and followed this with this simple letter.

Dear Madiba

As always it was very good to talk to you. I thought I'd send you a very brief note setting out our discussion.

America and Britain have definitely decided to go to war. Inevitably there will be many civilian casualties.

I believe there may be only one way to stop a war in Iraq and I believe you may be the only person in the world to achieve it.

If Saddam Hussein could be persuaded to retire to Libya (or somewhere else), with full immunity, I do not believe it would be possible for America to press ahead with war. If he were to make this sacrifice to avoid his people going through yet more suffering he would enhance his reputation considerably. The personal alternative will be the fate of Noriega, Milosevic or worse.

Knowing your close relationship with President Qaddafi and the respect you are held in in Iraq you are perhaps the only person who could organise this.

I believe that you would have the credibility to persuade Saddam Hussein to step down. By flying out with you – to, say, Libya – he could leave with his head held high. It would be the best thing he could ever do for his people.

If it helps you I would be happy to send you a plane to take you there and back (hopefully via Libya!).

I'll talk to you once you've spoken with Thabo.
Kind regards as always
Richard

It was a bold plan that might just have worked. But time was running out.

Nelson Mandela wanted me to get the approval of Kofi Annan, the United Nations Secretary General, and the blessing of his own President Thabo Mbeki. I wrote to Kofi Annan and followed up with a phone call. He gave the idea his full support. On 17 March we positioned two pilots and a Lear Jet in Johannesburg to take Mandela to Baghdad. We had managed to get the hostages out of Iraq some years before by sending Edward Heath. This time Nelson Mandela – the world's most respected person – had spoken out strongly against the upcoming US invasion. If anybody could persuade Saddam it would be him. Enormous numbers of lives could be saved and injuries avoided.

Sadly time ran out and two days later events overtook

us. On 19 March 2003 the US bombed Baghdad and the rest is history. There is nothing in my life that I regret more.

But what I realised from this experience – and from friends with vision, like Peter Gabriel – is that the world needed a group of elders – such as Nelson Mandela – who could step in on behalf of the world community in situations like this. I decided that, over the next couple of years, I wanted to help bring together a group of individuals who could serve as global 'Elders' to deliver a voice to the people of the world.

In late 2003 Joan, Holly, I and some of the team from Virgin also had the wonderful opportunity to attend and help organise Madiba's '46664' concert in South Africa. Madiba was generous enough to use his prison number, 46664, as a symbol for hope in the fight against HIV/AIDS. Sitting next to him and his wonderful wife while listening to Peter Gabriel sing 'Biko' for the first time in South Africa was one of the most moving experiences of my life.

Before this concert, but not long after the war was over, I saw a microcosm of Iraq first hand when we took the first relief flight into Basra. Appropriately, it was piloted by Mike Abunalla, an Iraqi exile whose family had fled Iraq twenty-two years earlier. Our mission was to deliver over 60 tons of generously donated medical supplies to the hospitals of Basra which Saddam's army had stripped bare in their rush northwards. During the flight we were all struck by the devastation of any infrastructure on the ground and the sheer emptiness and enormity of the country.

The whole project had been a remarkable co-operation between an Iraqi exile, Luay Shakarchy, who was based in the Midlands, in Birmingham, our own Jackie McQuillan and Air Marshal Brian Burridge. The spirit of co-operation between the British forces on the ground in Basra and a small team of operational staff from Virgin Atlantic was remarkable; in a matter of weeks they managed to open Basra Airport for a 747, getting this much needed aid into the country. I spent a lot of time talking to the servicemen and women in Basra and I could tell that many of the British forces had a strong sense of foreboding regarding the situation unfolding with their American counterparts in the north of the country. How true that sense of foreboding turned out to be.

Many of us were moved by what we saw and experienced during this first civilian flight into Iraq since 1990. Not least Jackie who, joined by three Iraqi exiles who are now doctors in Britain, went downtown to visit some of the patients in Basra General Hospital. It was there she saw first hand not only the pain and suffering inflicted on civilians during war, but also the fact that there is always hope and beauty no matter how horrific the situation. In the hospital she met a young woman of twenty who had been severely wounded in the legs and stomach by shrapnel. Despite her agony, she could not drag her eyes away from her beautiful little baby girl, who had been born by emergency caesarean section two days before. Seeing Jackie's tears of sympathy the woman said: 'Please don't cry for me, God has given me the greatest gift of all and in her eyes is only innocence and love.' They were some of the most poignant words relayed to me that day.

The Pentagon suggested that the cost of the conflict in Iraq would be approximately $75 billion per year over ten years. In accepting the Niwano Peace Prize on 8 May 2003, Dr Priscilla Elworthy, of the Oxford Research Group, said, 'We must compare this $75 billion to the costs of building international security in other ways.

'(a) In the year 2000 world leaders estimated that it would require $25 billion to $35 billion annually to raise levels of health and welfare in Africa to Western standards.

'(b) Unesco estimate that all the world's children could be educated if we were to spend $7 billion dollars per year for ten years.

'(c) Clear water and sanitation could be provided for everyone in the world for $9 billion annually.

'(d) HIV and Aids now claim 5,500 lives a day around the world – more than the Black Death – and twelve million children in Africa have been orphaned by the disease. Kofi Annan has called for $10 billion annually to address the Aids epidemic.

'So all these goals could be reached, all this suffering prevented worldwide for less than the United States spends on military action in Iraq.'

However, she ended on a positive note by quoting Dr Müller, the Chancellor of the University of Peace in Costa Rica, and the Dalai Lama.

'Dr Müller, in a speech earlier this year, said, "I'm so honoured to be alive at such a miraculous time in history. I'm so moved by what's going on in our world today. Never before in the history of the world has there been a global, visible, public, viable, open dialogue and conversation about the very legitimacy of war. What will be the consequences? The costs? What might be the peaceful alternatives? What kind of negotiations are we not thinking of? What are the real intentions of declaring war?"

'Many millions of people in the world seem to have found a new voice. Maybe some good may emerge from the decision to invade Iraq after all.

'And finally the beautiful quotation purportedly from the Dalai Lama: "If you wish to experience peace, provide peace for another. If you wish to know that you are safe, cause others to know that they are safe. If you wish to better understand seemingly incomprehensible things, help another to better understand. If you wish to heal your own sadness or anger, seek to heal the sadness or anger of another.

'"Those others are watching for you now. They are looking to you for guidance, for help, for courage, for strength, for understanding and for assurance at this hour. Most of all – they are looking to you for love."'

Back in London in the spring of 2004, it was business as usual in the Virgin empire. Gordon McCallum, previously Group Strategy Director for the Virgin Group, was busy preparing Virgin Mobile for its flotation on the London Stock Market with an expected valuation of £1 billion. It really had been a remarkable story. In only four years we had created the world's first virtual mobile-phone network and established a base of 4 million customers who were the most satisfied in the industry. Even more exciting, in some ways, was the huge success of the US mobile venture, which we had started in the dark days of post-11 September America. Even by 2004, it was clear that Virgin Mobile USA could eventually be more valuable than the UK operation. It had become the fastest-growing company in the history of corporate America to reach a billion dollars and had done so in under three years. Hot on the heels of the US, other colleagues, Robert Samuelson and Max Kelly, were beavering away in Canada recruiting the team for yet another mobile venture to launch there in 2005 in partnership with Bell Canada. By mid-2004, it was becoming obvious that the model really worked and we could provide a better deal for consumers, through leveraging our brand off other networks' excess capacity. As the year drew on, more and more opportunities began to pop up in places as diverse as Africa and China.

In July of that year Virgin Mobile UK floated on the stockmarket. In the five years since the company had started, it had become a major force in the UK mobile industry, gathering over 4 million customers and becoming one of the most profitable companies in the industry based on its simple and cheap 'virtual network' model. As usual our timing was impeccable! The stockmarket was the worst it had been since 11 September and flotations were getting pulled on a daily basis on both sides of the Atlantic. To add insult to injury, the only other company floating on the stockmarket in Britain at the time was the manufacturer of Branston's pickle – so it won't take much for you to imagine the headlines that accompanied our dilemma on whether or not to float Virgin Mobile. I was on holiday on Necker when we took the final decision to go ahead at a reduced price of £2 per share. The psychology was very important to us in that the Virgin Group had once been quoted on the stockmarket in Britain and we had always said that, if we came back, it would be with a single company focused on a particular business. I'm glad to say that, in the winter of 2004, the Virgin Mobile shares went from strength to strength. This has resulted in a huge amount of interest in our US mobile business and proposals to float it, which we did in late 2007, with a share price of $15. Two thousand and five was also the year that we began to take the mobile concept around the world on the back of the success of the UK, Australia and the USA. The first big new mobile launch was in Canada in the spring with South Africa to follow in the winter and deals being done for launches in China, India and other parts of Africa.

Not only had the successful flotation of Virgin Mobile allowed us to consider indulging in riskier projects such as space travel, but it also gave us the chance to try out one or two fun sponsorships of the type that Virgin had not been able to do since 11 September. Steve Fossett's Virgin Atlantic Global Flyer was only one of these. In early 2005 we agreed to back a unique archaeological project to survey ancient Alexandria using the latest geophysical equipment – a georadar. Many important historical buildings, such as the tomb of Alexander the Great, the Great Library and Ptolemaic Royal Palace, have lain hidden and undiscovered somewhere under the city of Alexandria since late Roman times when an earthquake destroyed the whole area. It felt like old times for me as Martyn Gregory, with whom I had become a friend since he had written his book about BA's dirty tricks and another, *Diana, The Last Days*, on the death of my friend Princess Diana, presented the idea. He had credible research behind his belief that a group of young archaeologists could unmask the secrets that lie below the modern city using ground-penetrating radar. It would take until 2006 to find out whether he was right and if we would be part of the greatest archaeological discovery of all time or yet another forgotten sponsor of an ill-fated expedition to find one of the wonders of the ancient world.

Despite 11 September, we did not ignore the airline industry where it was clear there were still opportunities to create really exciting businesses. By the summer of 2004, Fred Reid, who used to run Delta Airlines, was recruited to lead one of Virgin's boldest moves in its 35-year history – an all-out assault on the bankrupt US domestic air-travel market. Because of the historic protectionism of the US domestic market I would have to play a relatively minor role in the creation of Virgin America as an airline, with the majority of the funding and the management coming from US institutions and companies. It was, therefore, bizarre – but deeply satisfying – to wake up one morning in May 2004 to read that my new airline was going to be called Virgin America. For me, Virgin had come of age. We had the confidence to invest in the world's toughest aviation market and be prepared to not have full control of the company's destiny. The very rules that had made the US such a barrier to entry to us in the past and which BA had tried to use to seal a monopoly, no longer held any fear for us. Over the years we had witnessed some of the most anti-consumer and monopolistic practices by the big US carriers. It finally appeared that the tables were turning. But for some the desire to keep the barriers up to new players within this underserved market is still great. In July 2004 I received a letter from a friend who had attended the ACTC Aviation Conference in Washington. In attendance at this event were the chief executive officers of the leading five American carriers. During the meeting one of these gentlemen was heard to remark: 'All we need now is Branson and the cookies will get very burnt.' This sounds vaguely familiar. If not flattering!

However, it was not the new airline but another unique aviation event that took me back to America during mid summer that year. On a cold morning on 22 June 2004, I was fortunate enough to witness one of the most amazing sights I have ever seen as the world's first privately funded spaceship streaked into the skies above the little town of Mojave in the Californian desert. SpaceShipOne was the truly remarkable brain-child of Burt Rutan, a friend I had known for many years. Burt is one of the world's true geniuses and his designs for numerous aircraft had been groundbreaking for decades. He was already working with Steve Fossett and me on the Virgin Atlantic Global Flyer, a unique and beautiful aircraft that we were planning for Steve (or myself, if he got ill) to attempt the world's first non-stop solo flight. The aircraft looked amazing, but not as amazing as the little spaceship I had seen hidden in the hangar earlier that year and was now streaking into space at 3,000 miles an hour above our heads in the desert.

Another friend, Paul Allen, who is one of the founders of Microsoft, had funded Burt's vision of a cheap reusable spaceship for some years. Like Burt, Paul is a visionary. He was visibly excited as he watched his sci-fi dream unfold and become tomorrow's reality. Mike Melville, an incredibly brave pilot, took the little spacecraft to 328,000 feet (100km) above the Earth. I watched with awe and realised that our own vision of cheap space tourism might finally be becoming a real possibility. At dinner with Burt and Paul the night before, we had discussed the future of private space flight through a partnership with each other and I left the evening feeling uplifted. I had always felt that the government monopoly on space was a danger to mankind rather than the benefit often touted by cynical politicians and self-serving missile manufacturers. Monopolies don't work in any industry whether public or private. Here was a chance for Virgin to take on the final frontier. I'm sure you won't be surprised that we had registered both the trademark rights and a company for space travel ten years earlier – to be called Virgin Galactic Airways. The Virgin Group – 'To Infinity and Beyond'! 'You must be joking,' people said to me. 'OK,' I responded, 'Virgin Intergalactic Airways!'

All in all, 2004 turned out to be a hugely important year for Virgin on every front. The Virgin Galactic joke became a very serious reality in September of that year. After months of intense negotiations Paul Allen agreed to sell the rights to the technology, which had made SpaceShipOne, to Virgin Galactic, which was officially born as a company on 15 September 2004. Within two weeks SpaceShipOne, carrying the Virgin banner, had completed two flights into space – the first-ever repeated private space flights – winning Burt and Paul the X-Prize, a US$10 million aviation incentive prize designed to jumpstart the space tourism industry. The media went wild and Burt rightfully took his place as an all-American hero. It was one of the proudest moments of my life to stand with Paul and Burt on a cool, still desert morning in Mojave to watch the second flight successfully completed. There was something about that day that just made you realise that we were watching history unfold and it reminded me of one of my favourite films of all time: *The Right Stuff.*

It wasn't easy to persuade my level-headed colleagues at the Virgin Group of the sense in investing over $100m in building a spaceship. In fact, amusingly, I intercepted an email between some of these 'level-headed' colleagues by mistake, which said that I should be called 'Dr Yes' because I said 'yes' to everything. By now, Stephen Murphy, who had worked for Virgin in the early 1990s and had since returned to work with us again, had become the nearest thing that we had to a real chief executive and, for the past three years, he had led a committee who scrutinised all of our investment decisions. When Will Whitehorn had to present them with the notion that I wanted to launch commercial space flights by 2008, they were just a little bit sceptical! Unless you have met Burt Rutan and understand his achievements, it would be hard for anyone to believe that a small group of buildings in the Mojave desert could possibly manufacture and safely fly a cheap private spacecraft. But, as the deal to launch Virgin Galactic unfolded, so did the credibility of the project, and, by the beginning of 2005, even my hardheaded bean counters began to accept that the project was viable. As readers of this book will know, I've often been accused of talking ahead of myself, but I do believe that in the near future we will be taking the world's first private astronauts regularly into space both safely and for $200,000 or less each.

The unique features of Burt's spaceships that give me so much confidence are the safety of both his rocket motor and his feathering device for re-entry into the Earth's atmosphere. In both cases his genius has been to take very old ideas and apply modern technology to them. Let's start with his rocket motor. It is unique in that it burns laughing gas and rubber; by themselves both inert, put them together and you've got a perfectly credible rocket motor, which is also much safer than the highly combustible liquid-fuelled rockets of NASA. One cynic did point out that, if anything ever happened up in space, at least we'd die laughing.

The other feature turns the spaceship from a streamlined supersonic craft into the equivalent of a sycamore leaf or shuttlecock whilst in space. This allows the craft to re-enter the Earth's atmosphere much more slowly than a space shuttle would, which removes the risk of overheating.

The final feature of Burt's design is his use of plastic and what are called composite materials; neither the mother ship that launches his spaceship nor the spaceship itself are built of metal, but instead use new heat-resistant materials that are lighter and safer than aluminium or steel. The net result is a spaceship launch mechanism that is safe, cheap and environmentally friendly. To have the same impact on the environment as one space-shuttle launch would require many tens of thousands of launches by our spaceship. This means that the vision of millions of people – that they may one day be able to visit the stars – can finally be realised. However, this won't be true of Joan Branson, who has not volunteered for the first flight, despite the fact that both my mum and dad and Holly and Sam all want to go. I suppose I should hardly be surprised as Joan still crushes my hand every time we fly anywhere together. My dad will be in his nineties when he flies. When asked whether he was worried about going into space, he responded by saying that, given his age, that was the least of his worries.

If my confidence in Burt Rutan's unique status as the Einstein of aerodynamics needed any reinforcing as we geared up to build the world's first truly commercial spaceship, it happened at the end of February 2005. When Steve Fossett had approached me in 2002 to be his back-up pilot in case of illness I readily agreed, and was equally pleased to fund and manage the building and flying of the world's first high-altitude global circumnavigation aircraft. We could not have dreamed that three years later the project would also have produced one of the most extraordinarily beautiful aircraft ever built, the Virgin Atlantic Global Flyer. It was Steve's ambition to fly it solo around the world in less than eighty hours, using a combination of one of the most efficient aircraft designs ever built and Burt Rutan's legendary ability to build large composite aircraft not containing any metal.

It was a freezing evening on Monday 28 February when Steve Fossett took off from Salina, Kansas, to attempt his heroic flight. The aircraft looked magnificent as it trundled down the runway with 18,000lbs of fuel on board out of a total weight of little over 21,000lbs. Thousands watched the take-off and all of our hearts were in our mouths for ten seconds when, having lifted off, Steve drifted back down towards the runway, but, before the fatal moment that we all saw in our mind's eye, he swooped away like a beautiful swallow into the night skies of the Midwest.

I followed him up for the first few hours in the chase plane, and was due to be dropped in Toronto by Will and the team in order that I could launch Virgin Mobile the next day in Canada. As we headed into a freezing blizzard, it was clear that all was not well with the plane: in the climb out from Kansas, Steve had definitely lost some fuel and there seemed to be a problem with his GPS system as he crossed the Canadian border. I was unceremoniously dumped on the tarmac by the chase plane team and left to head into Toronto not knowing if Steve was going to make it. But, like most things at Scaled Composites (Burt's company in the Mojave desert), every contingency had been thought of, and over the next twenty-four hours John Karkow, Burt's brilliant aircraft designer, crunched the numbers and came to the conclusion that if the jetstream winds remained strong around the Earth then Steve could still make it. For sixty-seven hours Steve battled with the elements and, at one point, flew as high as 49,000 feet above the Earth in order to try and catch the best fuel efficiency and winds.

Having left Kansas in freezing, wintery conditions on the Monday night, he arrived back at the same airport, having not slept or landed anywhere on the planet's surface, to the beautiful sunshine of a spring day. It was one of the happiest moments I've ever had and, even though I hadn't participated in the attempt directly, I felt not only proud of Steve, but also a strange comradeship with his achievement – the type you can only feel if you've been there once before with him.

There was no doubt about the importance of his achievement. For Steve it was a world record but, as importantly for a major international airline, we had proved the point that you could build a light, highly efficient aircraft with no metal in its fuselage or wings and achieve sustained high-altitude flight. The Global Flyer used less fuel per hour than an American four-wheel-drive truck. If the lessons of this flight could be transferred to civil aviation and become integral to the cultures of Boeing and Airbus, commercial flying could finally become the most environmentally friendly way to carry large numbers of people around the planet.

The future of the airline industry around the world also took a leap into the dark in January of 2005 on a cold clear winter's morning in Toulouse. It takes something really special to bring a British prime minister and a French president together in the same place since relations between the two countries haven't exactly been their best once the war on terrorism began. But, that morning, I was privileged to stand and watch Tony Blair and Jacques Chirac open the doors on the most amazing aircraft I'd ever seen in my life. It was the huge Airbus A380, and it is a monster. My mind slipped to the movie I had watched only two days earlier called *The Aviator*, which was about the life story of American businessman Howard Hughes. This Airbus was the first plane built that made his giant 'Spruce Goose' flying boat of 1946 look small. In the A380, Airbus had built the world's largest-ever aircraft capable of carrying over 800 people, although Virgin loyalists will be pleased to hear that our version will only carry 550 – so there will finally be room for the double beds, gymnasium and casino that I have long wanted to put on long-haul flights. Unlike Howard Hughes, who never really had a market for his white elephant, I looked at the Airbus A380 with confidence. Knowing the history of the dirty tricks affair, readers will not be surprised to learn that most of these giant A380s are going to end up at Heathrow where, in 2005, BA still controlled nearly 50 per cent of the landing slots, and where anyone who has had to sit stacked up waiting to land will know just how precious they are.

In the summer of 2004, I also brought myself one step closer to my dream of using the strength of the brand and our people to change the world for the better by launching a new part of the group called Virgin Unite. This new organisation was built by Virgin staff around the world and will be a vehicle to pull us all together, hopefully to make a difference with some of the tougher social challenges facing us. Holly volunteered to spend whatever time she had during her final year at medical school to help out with sexual health issues facing young people in the UK – right back to where I started some forty years ago when I opened the Student Help Centre, which I'm happy to say is still providing free counselling on Portobello Road in West London.

The run-up to the war and its aftermath did not hold back the Branson household. Holly had sailed through her A-levels and fulfilled her (almost) life-long ambition to go to university to study medicine. She celebrated her twenty-first birthday and our son Sam his eighteenth. Though Sam perhaps hasn't got the same sense of purpose at school as Holly had, he certainly knows how to party, and (perhaps taking after his father here) knows how to enjoy life to its full.

Joan and I were incredibly proud of how well Holly

was getting on in her medical degree so we decided to throw a big party for her twenty-first. The weather was beautiful in Kidlington in Oxfordshire that cold November night and Holly looked lovely in her white evening gown. Joan and I had to pinch ourselves thinking back to the little baby girl who we had brought back to our London houseboat in the Regent's Canal back in 1984. It was not many months later when Sam had his 18th, which was a considerably more 'laddish' affair in the Roof Gardens in Kensington. To say that his friends' speeches were risqué would be the understatement of the year. On this occasion Joan and I had to put our fingers in our ears, rather than pinch ourselves.

Our day in Toulouse with the Airbus A380 has since brought my mind back time and time again to Howard Hughes and that film and has made me realise just how slim the line is between genius and insanity and between determination and stubbornness. Yet again, I thank my lucky stars to have had the stability of a family around me during all the years of turmoil that Virgin has had to navigate without the balance sheet of a multinational corporation or the luxury of a cosy state monopoly. Poor old Howard Hughes didn't really have anyone he could turn to for honest advice or the friends and family whose wit, charm and wisdom can so often help all of us in life to keep our feet on the ground while we look at the stars.

I have also taken a conscious decision to spend more time with my parents, in particular my father, Ted, who is the eldest. Though they are both well into their eighties, they are still on and off aeroplanes, travelling around the world. They have enormous affection for Africa, as do I, and in 1999 we bought a beautiful game reserve called Ulusaba in South Africa, where we've built a lovely house up on the hill looking over the jungle. We run this as a business, but make sure that we all find the time to go and visit it ourselves. These are the times that you remember and cherish. Over the previous decades, I had more and more come to appreciate Ted's wisdom. One example had been his very wise counsel about the war in Iraq, which he had also been vehemently against, but on which he had also reinforced my own views – that, once the shooting started, we had to stand by and support the many brave young men and women from all the allied countries who were 'following orders' in Iraq.

By the spring of 2004, Ted had fully recovered from a complex hip replacement operation a few years earlier and I took a short sabbatical from the world of Virgin to go camping with him in the Serengeti. It is an awesome place where you can really feel that nature is still in charge of her destiny. Having been there, I can fully understand why so many anthropologists believe the region is where man originated as a species. We spent ten days following the wildebeest migration and the predation of the lions upon their herds. For those of you who have not spent ten days in a tent with your father – if you are fortunate enough to be in a position to do so – I can thoroughly recommend it in every way. I think we developed an even better understanding of each other as we talked long into the evening.

More than anything, I marvelled at the sense of humour of a man who had seen it all! One fantastic example of this was early one morning on his birthday; we'd all just woken up and were quite grumpy after a night in the tent but Dad was beaming. We were all intrigued until he said: 'If I was Catholic I'd be doing penance today. I had the most wonderful dream. It involved a girl.'

'Did you misbehave with her?' I asked.

Quick as a flash Dad replied: 'I don't know *what* you mean. Well *I* behaved. *She* was outrageously naughty!' And this from a man in his eighties!

There are many influences on my life that affect the way I feel about things. Ulusaba is one of them. Ulusaba means 'Place of little fear' because it's a kind of rock citadel or watchtower rising out of the jungle where the original warriors who lived there could make a stand when attacked by their enemies. To me, it is a place of great peace where I can sit around a campfire at night with my friends and family and listen to stories and make plans – just like the people of this ancient landscape have always done.

I spend a lot of time in Africa and have been fortunate enough to get out into the jungle. I think there is nothing more beautiful in the world than being out there and seeing the early morning sunrise. The air feels cleaner than anywhere else in the world and you're completely in touch with nature. I remember one dawn when I was down in the river bed at Ulusaba and for a long time watched two three-month-old lion cubs playing with their enormous mother. When she got tired of them she picked them up in her teeth and went back into the thicket again. I marvelled at how gentle she could be. We continued on foot and soon saw the dominant leopard which has been in our game reserve for such a long time we've given her a name – Makwele. She was also playing with her young cubs as they ran up trees together, fell out of them and chased each other in circles. Their agility, grace and playfulness were astonishing.

The first time I went to Ulusaba was when I was in South Africa to open a Virgin Atlantic route to Cape

Town in 1999. At the time, I was looking for somewhere very special in the bush and I was directed to the Sabi-Sand region. As we drove, massive rocks emerged dramatically from the bush, pushed out by some ancient convulsion of the earth. Having chosen the area, we asked Mark Netherwood, a friend who used to run Necker Island, to work with us to create something dramatic and beautiful yet unspoilt out of the jungle. There's nothing quite like Ulusaba in Africa. Rock Lodge is high on a rocky ridge with spectacular views of the jungle and game, while down in the river bed is Safari Lodge, which has a wonderful Robinson Crusoe walkway through the trees to a dam where hippos and crocodiles wallow. There is so much game in this region of Africa; you're almost guaranteed to see most species without going very far. You can get up early in the morning or in the evening and go for a drive or even walk (with a guide!), and you'll always find things to see and marvel at.

As I write this, I can see giraffes walking by and elephants in the distance. I have a particular affection for the elephants because they are so intelligent and playful. The young ones are just like children or teenagers. They love a tree called the marula, which bears a small red fruit that elephants find irresistible. Just this morning, I spent hours watching a young bull elephant shaking the tree to get at the fruit. They were falling like sweeties, just ready to be hoovered up. But at the point at which he got a carpet of them ready to eat, his brother came along and tried to sneak in. They ended up having the most almighty fight. The first young bull seemed to roar, 'How dare you take my sweeties!' – just like any human being. Elephants will never damage their sweet shop – the marula tree – but their numbers are growing and they do great damage to other trees. People want to have the elephants culled. We have tried to come up with an idea to help the elephants in order to avoid culling and I noticed that nobody has actually replanted trees in the jungle. So, partly with our global warming hats on, partly to avoid the need to cull elephants and partly to create jobs for Africans, we're setting up tree nurseries and will work hard at getting trees replanted in the jungle. Many will be trampled or eaten by the elephants or giraffes, but some will survive.

For the past forty years I have worked hard at developing Virgin as a major global business. On the way, along with some great successes, there have been many challenges, tempered by fun, and for a long time it seemed enough. But, while I had always been aware of the need to be socially responsible, perhaps I am growing older and wiser because, gradually, I feel I should do much more, on a far wider scale, to help people. Setting up Virgin Unite was part of the process of my development as a social entrepreneur. One of my first trips with Virgin Unite was to South Africa with Brad Pitt. With HIV/AIDS at the top of our agenda, we took Brad to visit some of the 'hospitals' in different townships and in very rural areas. When we arrived at one hospital we saw that the walls were plastered with posters of competing undertakers. Inside, I was shocked when I saw hundreds of people who seemed to be almost resigning themselves to dying from HIV/AIDS. People were waiting in the corridors for the beds of the dozens who had died the night before – it was like a conveyer belt of death. There seemed no end to the suffering because even the hospital workers appeared to accept the outcome as an inevitable part of 'Africa'.

The figures, which have been published for some years, but often ignored, have always seemed too big to be comprehensible, which I think makes a lot of people switch off. It is too much to accept when you read that 15,000 people are dying every single day from HIV/AIDS, TB and malaria, most of them in sub-Saharan Africa. If this were happening in the UK or the US, we wouldn't allow it.

I was outraged by this ridiculous situation. These diseases are treatable, yet they aren't being treated. Africa seemed to have so many insurmountable issues – how could they be turned around at a greater speed? We were rather subdued when I took Brad to meet with Nelson Mandela at his home to discuss the 46664 AIDS campaign, in which Mandela used his prison number to call on South Africans not to allow AIDS patients to be reduced to statistics. It is easy to ignore statistics because you can get information fatigue when too many figures are thrown at you. A lighter moment was when I introduced Brad to Mandela by saying, 'Brad Pitt's in film,' and Mandela turned to Brad and said, with a twinkle, 'Oh, what kind of film do you do?'

Then, while Brad was posing next to Nelson Mandela for a picture, dressed in a 46664 T-shirt, someone said, *sotto voce*, how lucky the former president was because so many young ladies would give their eye teeth to be sitting where he was. Deliberately misunderstanding, Brad grinned and replied, 'So many young men as well!'

Later that day, we took Brad to meet Taddy Bletcher, a man who single-handedly started up CIDA, Africa's first free university, in downtown Johannesburg. Taddy had started with nothing, but got the idea that, if he could be given an empty building and if he could keep the costs down by asking the students to run the school and do all the cooking, the cleaning and the administration, and if he could get businesses to lend their top staff to come and do the lecturing, then he could offer students a fully accredited business degree at almost no cost. Most Africans had never had the chance to have this kind of education because they are all from very poor rural areas or townships. Poor children from the townships or rural communities have never stood a chance to get their feet on the first rung of the ladder, but 1,600 students a year are now being educated through CIDA to degree standard for under $300 for the full course, including books and accommodation. I appreciated what Taddy was doing and we soon started working in partnership with CIDA, Love Life and Life College, three small social entrepreneur organisations, to build a graduate programme called Women on the Move. This helps young women with peer education and mentoring. Once they are educated, they go back into their communities and find thirty other young people who they then have to mentor and educate. In this way, we have started to build an army of people across South Africa who are being educated. Part of the rationale behind it is that they will spread a serious message of health education, much needed in Africa.

Many things had collided and come together during that trip to make me want to put more effort into working towards change, but it was the visits to the hospitals and overcrowded orphanages that had the most impact on me. I decided then to devote a more significant part of my time – about 50 per cent – to social and environmental issues. I felt I had come a long way in my personal journey to Africa in the five years since I had found Ulusaba.

My African journey had been one of many miles and many experiences. Death has always been a part of the landscape, and, while animals might stalk and kill each other in the jungle, there is no reason why so many Africans should die of preventable diseases.

Some opportunities to help come out of nowhere. I was returning from Africa on Virgin Atlantic one day and, as always, I strolled around, chatting to passengers. A lovely lady sitting in economy class met my eye, and smiled. She invited me to sit next to her for a moment. Her name, she told me, was Marianne Haslegrave, and she was the Director of the Commonwealth Medical Trust. Little fazes me, but even I didn't expect to be discussing fistulas with her.

She spoke to me about fistula, which was the first time I'd even heard of it. Fistula happens, she told me, when very young girls – often as young as twelve and thirteen, as is the custom in some areas of countries such as Nigeria and Somalia – struggle to give birth without any assistance. A tear in the vagina wall – called a fistula – leads to permanent incontinence; consequently, these young women are divorced by their husbands and shunned by their families. Thanks to good maternity care, the last case of fistula in the US was in 1890, but it is still a common problem in Africa.

Marianne has devoted her life to trying to help these girls. I knew I had to do something and asked Jean Oelwang, who runs Virgin Unite, to look into it. Jean went to the United Nations Population Fund (UNFPA) to see how we could help. This coincided neatly with Natalie Imbruglia, who is a good friend, coming to me and saying she wanted to do something to help young women. I invited her and Jean to lunch and Natalie agreed to champion a campaign to promote the repairing of fistulas because no one else of her stature was behind the issue.

We took her out almost immediately to Ethiopia and Nigeria so she could see the problems for herself. At the same time, I put some money in and through the wonderful work and dedication of the team at the

UNFPA, we did a fistula fortnight in Nigeria, where, over a two-week period, 500 young women were repaired and we upgraded the hospitals. Since then, Natalie has worked tirelessly for her adopted project and I am proud of the way in which she rallied round when she was needed. The fact that she is a young, beautiful woman with an enormous talent who is willing to help such an unfashionable issue makes her a great role model. She also uses her music to promote fistula awareness and fundraising – and this gave us an idea to launch the Music Movement, which is a community of musicians willing and able to get involved with tough social issues. Natalie told me that seeing the young women first hand was one of the saddest journeys she's been on. It is the worst thing that can happen to them – many of them are just little girls, living as outcasts, shunned by the community. Some of them have lived in a hut at the back of their family house for twenty years or more. It is outrageous that this still happens when the problem can be repaired so easily. It could be avoided with more birth control and fewer girls marrying so young, but it is difficult for us to impose our views on other cultures – but at least we are allowed in to help make things better and to provide education and help improve the health infrastructure.

I do try to be tactful, but sometimes you just have to speak your mind to make a point, as was the case when I went to speak to the US Senate towards the end of 2005, as part of a project to develop a coalition on HIV/AIDS. On the way there in the taxi, Jean briefed me: 'There are some issues with the Bush government regarding condoms. They have committed a huge amount to HIV/AIDS, but they're unwilling to use it to buy condoms.'

I nodded. 'Yes, I see.'

'So you might need to be a bit careful about how you speak about this at the Senate today,' Jean continued.

As soon as she said that, I smiled.

It was slightly surreal to be in the amazing Senate House, with all its history, and to be discussing sex. Someone used the word 'grazing' to describe how HIV could be spread by having sex with multiple partners – like a bee going from flower to flower. One of the Republican senators reared to his feet and declared that people should abstain from sex.

I stood up and said, 'That's lovely, but it's not realistic. People are going to graze – but they should wear a condom when they graze. No glove, no love.' I could feel Jean bring her hand up to her face to hide a wide grin.

I was hopping into a van outside the CIDA campus one afternoon, having just met the wonderful Dalai Lama for the first time, when, out of the blue, Taddy grabbed me on the pavement and said, 'Hey, Richard, I've got a great idea. Why don't you start the Branson School for Entrepreneurship?'

Taddy is an inspirational man and, when he speaks, you find yourself nodding in agreement. Inspired by his almost throwaway words in the street, I decided I would set up my first 'school'. CIDA City Campus already provides specialised accredited business administration degrees to disadvantaged students, and I resolved that Virgin Unite would work with Taddy to launch a separate school at CIDA to help young people start their own businesses. One of the first things we wanted to do was to raise a seed fund, to be used as a kind of revolving loan for the students' enterprises. As soon as they started to make money, they would repay the loan and, in that way, the fund would continue to work for those who followed behind.

My model for this was Muhammad Yunus, who for some thirty years had successfully been operating a micro-credit system for some of the poorest people in the world, through the Grameen Bank – known as the Poor Bank. He was first approached by a group of craftsmen in 1976 when he was a professor of economics in Bangladesh to lend them $27 to start a business. He did so, fully confident that they would pay him back – as he said, 'The poorest of the poor have a great sense of responsibility.' He even lends to 55,000 beggars under a Struggling Members Programme. Professor Yunus's long-term vision is to eliminate poverty. So far, he has lent $1.5 billion to three-and-a-half million people, principally women, and has had very few defaulters.

Virgin Atlantic sponsors the *Sunday Times* Fast Track initiative, which brings top entrepreneurs together for dinner each year at my house in Oxford, to act as mentors to fledgling businesses. I auctioned off two spaces on our Wake Up Trips to Africa. Two British entrepreneurs, Tom Bloxam and Leo Caplan, bid £120,000 each to go with us. This launched the seed fund for our students' businesses, to help start them off in the world. Most people cut ribbons or break bottles of champagne when launching something new. Instead, along with Tom and Leo, in October, I found myself taking my shoes and socks off and leaving my footprints in concrete at the entrance to the newly opened Branson School of Entrepreneurship. I felt quite emotional as I glanced at our footprints – which were supposed to inspire the students to 'walk in the footprints of global entrepreneurs'. The first footprints of people were found in the clay of African shale beds. But, to me, the more important thing was that this very building at 27 Harrison Street was where Nelson

Mandela had worked as a young man before his long years of imprisonment. His autobiography, written after he was freed, was titled *Long Walk to Freedom*; the students would also have a long walk on their road to economic freedom against so many odds.

Capitalism – which in its purest form is entrepreneurism even among the poorest of the poor – does work; but those who make money from it should put back into society, not just sit on it as if they are hatching eggs. Every single person at the Branson School soon had an idea to fill in a gap here, to fill in a gap there. Any opportunity, they soon realised, is worth pursuing. Students will sell lollies, set up dealerships, be tour guides, open street cafés and restaurants – anything that will give them a leg up out of the townships and slums. I often pop in when I'm in South Africa and I was both taken aback and moved once to find some of the kids had taken it upon themselves to fill in the holes in the road and then stand by the side of the road and see if anyone would be good enough to pay them for filling in holes. It was a good example of capitalism at work.

When Sam reached the age of eighteen and left school, he thought he might take a gap year off and do some travelling. I thought it was a great idea and asked if I could tag along for a while. I'd been working pretty diligently since I was fifteen years old, not wanting to let people down, and missed out on a gap year of my own. Fortunately, we're the kind of family who choose to go on holiday together, rather than separately, and Sam and I are very close, so it wasn't a matter of 'getting to know him' but of having some fun together. I had to be in Australia for some meetings, and afterwards we headed off down the coast to Byron Bay, the most easterly point of the Australian mainland. We stayed in a flat above Rae's, an exotic little hotel, more Mediterranean Moroccan than Alice Springs, right on Watego's Beach and went for a walk along the Cape Byron Lighthouse track, which meanders through some fabulous rainforest. As the forest opened out on to the headland, we saw a manta ray idly cruising along and a small school of sharks.

In the small town of Byron itself large groups of hippies roamed the wooden Western-style sidewalks. There were more head shops and bongo drum shops than in San Francisco and the haze of marijuana hung heavy in the air, like a time warp back into the Summer of Love.

The first morning, we were up early and ran down to the beach with a couple of surfboards to 'catch a few waves'. Sam and his friends were old hands, but I had never surfed before. I could kite surf and thought that surfing would not be hard. You just waited for a wave, climbed up on a board and it would carry you along to shore. The first day, I couldn't get up. The second day, I couldn't get up. My mind idly remembered the sharks out there beyond the headland.

'It's easy – look, you do this, Richard,' Sam's suntanned friends chortled as they cruised by on a long, curling wave.

I was determined to crack it, but was still struggling on the third day when someone on the board next to me said, 'Hey, Richard, two guys are hiding in the bushes over there with telephoto lenses.'

Instantly, ego got the better of me and, on the next wave, I got up, balanced like an old pro and sailed smoothly in. It was like riding a bicycle. You struggle and struggle, then suddenly you're off and never look back.

It was a perfect day, one of the very few times in my

life when nothing seemed that important. I didn't make phone calls, didn't think about a thing. I was out on the waves, with not a care in the world. Such days are rare and all the more precious for that. I remember when Holly was about five, the two of us went off for a week down to the fishing village of Bantham, in Devon, without Joan. It was a special week for both of us.

Several years after successfully surfing that day, Sam and I drove sixty miles up into the mountains together, goofing around, saying silly things, cracking bad jokes and laughing, more like two best friends than father and son. We were so exuberantly happy, we didn't want the day to end.

31 Changes

2006

M ANY THINGS CAME together in the summer of
2006 to make me focus on the two linked
issues of global warming and rising fuel prices.
I had first seen warning lights when the figures showed
me that Virgin's fuel bill was rising by half a billion
dollars a year.

As early as my teens, perhaps because of the influence
of one of my relatives, Peter Scott, who founded the
World Wildlife Fund, I was interested in the environment. I was drawn to the Gaia Theory, a hypothesis
formulated by James Lovelock almost forty years ago,
which states that the Earth is a living entity, like a single
cell, and, like a single cell, everything it needs for its
existence is contained within it. Professor Lovelock
believes that the planet can heal itself if damaged, but,
even with Gaia, there is a point of no return, beyond
which the damage could be irreversible. We at Virgin
knew what dangers came from wasting resources and
carelessly burning fossil fuels but, for many reasons,
even among the greenest of the greens, there was no real
sense of urgency. I'm afraid that it wasn't until it began to
affect me personally that I sat up and took more notice.

I first got interested in looking for alternative fuels in
the 1990s when I became more aware that oil was a
finite resource. Britain's own North Sea oil was running
out and most of the rest of the world's supplies were in
the hands of OPEC in a very unstable Middle East,

which could make oil both vulnerable and expensive. The war between Iraq and Iran in the 1980s raised the price of oil from an average of $16 a barrel to a spike of almost $70. When Saddam went after the Kuwaiti oilfields in 1990, it confirmed oil's vulnerability to war. As someone who is heavily involved in the transport business, I needed to be aware of the cost and availability of oil and I looked into the alternatives. Virgin used over 700 million gallons of jet fuel between the four airlines, and large amounts of diesel in Virgin Trains. In 1997, when we were investing in a new fleet of trains, I asked the manufacturer, Alstom, to ensure they were fuel efficient. As a result, our Pendolino trains are the only ones in Europe that put 20 per cent of electricity back into the grid every time the train brakes. And our Voyager diesel/electric trains are being converted to a biofuel blend of rape and soya.

Then, after Hurricane Katrina in 2005, when the US drilling platforms in the Gulf of Mexico and the huge refineries along the Gulf coast were damaged or destroyed, the price of refined fuels in the US went through the roof. With a major capacity shortage, I started to look into the potential of investing in our own oil refineries and, in fact, issued a press release to announce that we were building one hopefully to bring the price down.

Ted Turner is an interesting blend of capitalist, environmentalist and philanthropist, who is as well known for founding the CNN news channel as he is for owning the Atlanta Braves and for being an Olympic yachtsman and winning the America's Cup. I had last met him at the Time Global Health summit a few months earlier, alongside Bill Gates, Madeleine Albright, Paul Wolfowitz, Bono and others – and after I announced my intention to build an oil refinery, Ted rang me and said, 'Richard, have you thought of the alternatives?'

'What do you suggest?' I asked.

'Why not build a refinery for clean rather than dirty fuel? Come and meet my people. They will convince you that there is another way.'

Ted invited me to Washington to lunch with some members of the United Nations Foundation, a think-tank he had started up with a hefty donation of $1 billion to look into environmental issues and push biofuels in the US. Around the lunch table with Ted were Senator Tim Wirth, the UNF's president; John Podesta, Bill Clinton's former chief-of-staff; Boyden Grey, George Bush's legal counsel (shortly to be appointed US ambassador to the EU); and Reid Detchon, head of the Energy Future Coalition.

The subject almost immediately turned to biofuels. I already knew a fair bit about fuels in general, but wasn't yet as knowledgeable about biofuels as this group was. While they talked, I made my usual cryptic notes in the notebook I always carry, and, by the end of the meal, I decided that they were right. Instead of investing in conventional forms of refining, the more sensible thing for Virgin to do would be to invest considerable sums in alternative fuels. I am lucky – once I make up my mind, I can generally do something about it: I joined the steering board of Ted's Energy Future Coalition; and went back to my team at Virgin and asked them to look into plant-based ethanol. The result was that I became hooked on the potential of biofuels as an environmental necessity and as one way forward to loosen the world's dependency on oilfields. Both environmentally and economically, it made perfect sense that individual countries should grow their own fuel and use it at point of origin, without transporting it halfway around the world – thus saving even more on financial costs and CO_2 emissions.

I formed Virgin Fuels in early 2006 and began an

investment programme in research and development of biofuel. Our first investment was to back a California firm, Cilion, which makes bioethanol from corn. We started to build biofuel refineries in both the American West and Tennessee, at both the point of origin and of use, and then moved into Brazil. The next stage will be to expand into the US East Coast and elsewhere in Europe.

I wasn't being entirely altruistic. Alternative fuels should be a good business move – investing in them puts pressure on fossil fuel prices and acts as a hedge for our airline and train companies. If the price of oil remains high, we can make very decent returns on both our research and development and our investment in the cost of building refineries. It also makes perfect sense over the next five or six years to replace some or all of our conventional fuel with our own fuels.

In the early summer of 2006, Virgin Fuels had already made its first investments but I still wasn't fully aware of the urgency of global warming. But nothing wakes one up more to the issues at hand than the former vice president of the United States coming all the way to your home in Holland Park, London, to give a personal lecture on global warming. When the film *An Inconvenient Truth* came out some months later, I realised that he'd test run it on me at my home that day.

We sat down at the low table in the sitting room and Joan brought in tea and sandwiches. Al perched on a corner of the table and pulled out his PC and switched it on. I sat in a big armchair, with Will Whitehorn leaning over behind me and Steve Howard of the Climate Group seated on the other side, and we all looked at the screen. It was quite an experience having a brilliant communicator like Al Gore give me a personal PowerPoint presentation. Not only was it one of the best presentations I have ever seen in my life, but it was profoundly disturbing to become aware that we are potentially facing the end of the world as we know it. The impact on humanity and the natural world could be so great that we have no choice but to do something drastic, first to stop it and then turn it around.

During our intense discussion, Steve Howard said that we need to make people confident that this is a problem that can be solved. Some people think dealing with climate change could destroy the economy and is therefore an insoluble problem; but there is a lot we can do. We really have no choice in the matter: we have to do it.

Al agreed. Looking directly at me, he said, 'Richard, you're known the world over. You could help to lead the way with me in dealing with climate change. Without the politicians we need business leaders to take the lead.'

Al Gore's lecture was a polemic, but it had enough good science around it to work really well. It was the first time I'd been presented with the full enormity of the effects of climate change. I saw at once that if we don't do something fast to fix carbon emissions, in a very short space of time most of the Earth will be uninhabitable and the planet's population will plummet. Most animals and plants will become extinct and life will be wretched. 'I'm just about to launch a new air route to Dubai,' I said. Usually I like doing that kind of thing – but now I could see the paradox of it. We want a connected world, we want to be able to fly, but we must also beat climate change.

'How much time do we have?' I asked.

Al replied, 'Scientists say that we may have as little as ten years before we cross a tipping point, beyond which it will be too late. We have to make a massive and determined start. If we do, it is possible to start levelling out CO_2 within the next five years. Part of it is evolution. Our brains are good at perceiving danger in the form of fangs and claws and spiders and fire but we find it hard to deal with dangers that can't be seen until it's too late – like the world heating up. Most of it is happening right now at the poles, where very few people see it and so couldn't care less.'

Al was very persuasive and remained good-humoured, despite his argument with Will as to when Lovelock had first written Gaia Theory. Sometimes it's interesting to be in a room with two people who both think they're right!

After Al Gore left, Will and I had a long discussion about the way in which Virgin could take a lead in dealing with global warming. Obviously, with over 50,000 people working for us and their livelihoods at stake, I didn't want to make any drastic changes that would mean we would run unprofitably; but I saw a way forwards in which we could act responsibly by making small changes – such as using long-lasting light bulbs and becoming paper free – as well as major changes, like switching to biofuels as and when possible. We coined the phrase 'Gaia Capitalism' to describe this. The concept of Gaia Capitalism is all about solutions: we wanted to take an apparent contradiction and show that it worked and made real sense. We were able to do this efficiently because Virgin is like a massive ecosystem. The parts are separately run and managed, and even have their own share-holders, but there's always the linkages between them.

Three months later, Bill Clinton rang me to see if I would make a pledge to his Global Initiative. That night in the bath I had an idea. Al Gore had said he needed leadership from me. What if I pledged 100 per cent of all profits the Virgin Group made from our airline and train companies and invested them in developing alternative fuels? That could make a big difference and perhaps get other business leaders on board too.

As a result of my conversation with Bill Clinton, two months later I flew to New York to attend the Clinton Global Initiative. On 21 September, the second day of the conference, I joined Bill Clinton and Al Gore to personally pledge $3 billion to develop clean fuels. As I was about to sign the commitment document, I looked up at President Bill Clinton and, with just the right degree of dramatic pause, pen poised, said, 'That's an awful lot of noughts.'

It was a firm commitment, intended not just to move the Virgin Group forwards, but to inspire others. The idea is to pinpoint our transport companies to fund this investment, but, if it's not met from that direction, the money will come out of our other existing businesses as well. We will do it, whatever it takes. One of the things I stressed was that this wasn't philanthropy or charity. Our entire Gaia project is based on sound commercial sense. I didn't want the media to give the impression that this was some kind of donation to environmental causes – but they did, painting me as some kind of universal benefactor. Charitable donations do have their place, but to me it seems far more sustainable to invest seed money in order to generate money for the future so that the ball continues to roll and we can have a better chance of competing with the oil and coal companies.

After my public announcement, which, within moments, was beamed around the world, Steve Howard said, 'Richard, we work with lots of different organisations, but the pace of change at Virgin is without parallel. It is really impressive to see the Virgin machine unleash itself.'

Someone asked me what I felt about soaring oil prices. To the disappointment of my airline's executives, I said, 'I think that soaring oil prices are the best thing that has happened to this world. It forces governments and big business to find new ways of reducing their dependency on oil. We needed something like this to happen to bring a halt to an almost suicidal dependency on fossil fuel. If we could get it right, it might stop Middle East wars in the future.'

I love the challenge of learning about industries I know nothing about. At school, I had no interest in chemistry. Now I wanted to learn everything there was to know about ethanol, cellulosic ethanol, ISO butanol, methane and carbon; the best products to make fuels from – sugar, corn, switch grass, willow trees and waste product; about wind power and solar power; and about hydrogen and geothermals. By the end of a three-month crash course of asking questions, I felt I was equipped to start fulfilling my $3 billon pledge by ramping up Virgin Fuels as a global force. But the best way of learning was to get on and do it: to try to turn Necker and Moskito into the first 100 per cent carbon neutral islands; to build our first corn and sugar ethanol plants; to try to develop clean ISO butanol for planes, and so on. I wanted to do for renewable energy what private capital did for mobile phones two decades ago, by turning a small idea into a universal phenomenon.

Towards the end of 2006 I invited Tim Flannery to Necker to speak to all managing directors of Virgin worldwide on the environment. Tim is a brilliant Australian scientist and explorer, whose groundbreaking book, *The Weather Makers*, had started me thinking about the climate in the first place. I think what Tim will do for us is to help give us the scientific background to the path we've now embarked on, and give our people a much better understanding of why we are on it. It is not just about having green credentials; I have made a firm commitment that this is going to be an industrial strategy for Virgin in the twenty-first century. I'm sure that I'm going to get a lot of criticism. I can hear people saying, 'If CO_2 emissions are the problem, why doesn't Richard Branson just stop his planes from flying?' But people want to fly and, if we stopped, we'd leave a gap that somebody who might have no sense of responsibility at all would fill. We want to be the people who fly, but in a responsible way. Towards this, by the end of the year, we were aiming to save fuel when planes took off. If they were towed to and from the end of the runway while waiting to take off, they wouldn't need to stand around so long with their engines spewing out CO_2. We started the ball rolling by experimenting at Gatwick and Heathrow. If every airline did the same, we estimated that it would save up to three tonnes of aviation fuel per flight, and, together with other efforts, airlines could cut aviation carbon emissions by about 25 per cent worldwide.

A case in point was the Virgin Atlantic Global Flyer. It wasn't made of metal; instead it was built of a carbon composite, which is very light but capable of operating safely at very high altitudes to improve fuel efficiency dramatically. I had been there just a year earlier in Salina, Kansas and saw it off on its dazzling flight. I chased it to the freezing wastes of Canada and I was back in Kansas when it landed, sixty-seven hours later. I was excited when I saw for myself how it could circle like some glorious eagle, far above the world at 49,000 feet, and use less fuel per hour than a four-wheel-drive vehicle. This stunning achievement led us to starting up Virgin Galactic and investing in space, the final frontier. Without space, and the work of organisations such as

NASA, we would not even know or understand the realities of climate change or feed the current population of the world. Satellites beam back information from space that allows farmers to look at long-range weather forecasts and plan their planting and harvesting to the best advantage. Space also provides the answer to necessary future travel without atmospheric impact. However, sadly, the technology is still in the dirty, polluting and carbon-intensive Cold War era and there has been no private investment in viable space-launch systems using renewable fuels. We aim to change that as well.

Using the Virgin Atlantic Global Flyer as a model, Virgin Galactic's fleet was green from the word go. In addition to the spaceship's construction from carbon composite materials, the launch system prototype relies on a fuel derived from laughing gas and rubber, and, because of the unique piggyback launch system, we can do thousands of flights for every one of NASA's.

One of the big corporate events of recent years has been Virgin Galactic getting going. We had the concept of course, developed by Burt Rutan as a very benign space-launch system – but the first exciting thing was the realisation that this could be a new space-launch system to take payload and scientists into space. The second was that I could also clearly see a vision of the future and answer many people's questions: why does space really matter; and why have you got involved in it? Many people seemed to think that Virgin Galactic was some kind of challenge, a personal plaything, albeit an enormously expensive one. The truth is that space is the future of mankind. Everybody, from Dr Tim Hansen at NASA's Goddard Institute, who is one of the fathers of space science, right the way through to

Professor Stephen Hawking, the father of modern physics, agrees that better access to space and the utilisation of space is going to be crucial to the reorientation of the world's industries in coping with climate change.

For a start, we wouldn't even know about climate change if it hadn't been for the work that was done from space on proving that the climate is changing. Ground-based science is unable to prove climate change in the way that satellites have done. Secondly, very few people realise that we couldn't feed the current population of the world without observations about the climate and weather forecasts, which can only be done from space. The weather and agricultural satellites and the global positioning system in space give farmers a heads up on the weather patterns and allow an extra 15 per cent productivity to actually reach people's mouths. Crate-loads of food don't spoil at the docks any more; farmers can choose to mill their corn a day earlier, farm it a day earlier, plant it a day later. The first thing many farmers in the American corn belt or the plains of India or the middle of China do every morning is to go on the Internet and check out what the long-range agricultural satellites are saying they should be doing that day or that week. Access to space has allowed us to increase food production over the past fifteen years by about 10 per cent – which has just about coped with the population growth.

One of the most crucial things we are going to have to face as a civilisation is population growth. It is the key to our survival on the planet. We can't find the solution scientifically and technologically unless there's a willpower to find it. The real problem is that the environmental lobby hasn't really grasped the fact there are 6.5 billion people on the planet.

Tim Flannery sees the Earth as a spaceship circling through space. This is what he has to say on the subject of Spaceship Earth's population in *The Weather Makers*:

In 1961 there was still room to manoeuvre. In that seemingly distant age there were just 3 billion people, and they were using only half of the total resources our global ecosystem could sustainably provide. A short twenty-five years later, in 1986, we had reached a watershed, for that year our population topped 5 billion, and such was our collective thirst for resources that we were using *all* of Earth's sustainable production.

In effect, 1986 marks the year that humans reached Earth's carrying capacity, and ever since we have been running the environmental equivalent of a deficit budget, which is only sustained by plundering our capital base. The plundering takes the form of overexploiting fisheries, overgrazing pasture until it becomes desert, destroying forests, and polluting our oceans and atmosphere, which in turn leads to the large number of environmental issues we face. In the end, though, the environment budget is the only one that really counts.

By 2001 humanity's deficit has ballooned to 20 per cent, and our population to over 6 billion. By 2050, when the population is expected to level out at around 9 billion, the burden of human existence will be such that we will be using – if they can still be found – nearly two planets' worth of resources. But for all the difficulty we'll experience in finding those resources, it's our waste – particularly the greenhouse gases – that is the limiting factor.

Over the next century as we go into a population of

nine billion we've got to be mindful of space. During 2006, as I travelled to the crowded big cities of the world – to China, India, Africa, the US – I looked and saw and pondered. I am someone who believes in humanity and in the value of each single human life. I can't bear human misery and will do all I can to eradicate poverty, disease, suffering – yet a population of nine billion is simply unsustainable. The sheer weight of numbers and overuse of resources will end up killing us. I didn't know where the answer lay, or what the way forwards was. I knew that there was an urgency to stop climate change as fast as possible for us to just win some breathing space before we could even start to think of population numbers.

Our plans for Virgin Galactic were soaring ahead at a great speed. We had broken ground on a space station of the future in New Mexico. It was like science fiction. Futuristic designer Phillipe Starck came up with a dramatic eye logo – a bright blue iris with black pupil – and this has been inlaid on top of a flat disc that covers an enormous underground silo. The disc slides back silently in a very *Star Trek* way, to reveal the launching pad below. But some things that should have flown smoothly ground to a depressing halt – thanks to archaic laws and human resentment.

Back in 2004, when we first discussed launching Virgin USA in the US as a low-cost alternative airline to the existing domestic carriers flying long-haul between the East and West coasts, and ordered Airbus planes to show our intent, we expected some opposition in the way of healthy competition. What we didn't expect was to be sandbagged by an old xenophobic law. In the early days of flying, America was worried about 'foreign planes' flying in American skies and, in order to prevent that, in 1926, they passed the Air Commerce Act, which requires that all domestic airlines remained under the control of US citizens. This was boosted by the Civil Aeronautics Act of 1938 that says that no more than 25 per cent of the voting shares of any airline company based in the US shall be in foreign hands. This meant that 75 per cent had to be under the 'actual control' of US citizens, and we were told by the US Department of Transportation (DOT) that we had to restructure.

We tried to comply, but I had no idea that endless problems would be put in our way. Two years dragged by with legal argument and eventually, in 2006, I asked Fred Reid, former president of Delta, to run the new carrier, which would be under the control of a US company, VAI Partners, which would own 75 per cent of the capital stock and would appoint two-thirds of the voting members of the board of directors. We separated Virgin America from Virgin Atlantic and all our other airline companies, including Virgin Galactic, or any company that shared the Virgin brand name. In addition to ordering new planes, we budgeted about $200 million for start-up marketing in the US, we moved our base of operations from New York to San Francisco, and I thought we were finally on track to fly.

However, I had agreed to be the very visible face of the airline. I was ready to get out there and promote it, as I have always done with all Virgin companies. Perhaps I was too visible. We received massive opposition from labour unions and all major airlines in America: Continental Airlines, American, United, the lot! Our DOT certificate was withheld for months thanks to this protectionist opposition, while we did everything feasible to comply with every new hurdle every step of the way. Even though Virgin America would be run by a board that was largely made up of US citizens, the opposition claimed that it was a ploy and I would still be in charge. As 2005 dragged on into 2006, we were told that, 'Virgin America's responses to inquiry were not sufficient to prove that the airline is a "US citizen".' Our opponents urged the DOT to require us to produce additional documentation. Whatever we did, however, it seemed it wasn't enough.

Again, we proposed that the airline be restructured, with the voting shares held by a trust approved by the DOT and with only two Virgin Group directors on the eight-person board. In addition to removing the Virgin Group's veto and consent rights, Virgin America said that it would remove me from the board, and possibly even drop the Virgin brand entirely. Then the new board said they would be prepared to remove CEO Fred Reid, 'should the DOT find that necessary'.

By that point, I had stepped back, although I was kept informed as a shareholder. I was very gratified that there was also a groundswell of populist support for Virgin America. California governor Arnold Schwarzenegger, Gavin Newsom, the mayor of San Francisco, and Hillary Clinton all said the new airline would create a thousand new jobs in its first year of service (estimates say this would rise to 50,000 new jobs across the US by the fifth year). Even the San Francisco Giants came out in support. The biggest surprise, though, was the 50,000 letters sent in our support to Congress and DOT. As many as 25,000 Americans signed a petition in our favour and there was a website, www.letVAfly.com, where people could check on news. There were T-shirts and mugs on sale with the slogan, LET VA FLY.

I think people realised that Virgin America would keep prices down and improve the quality of flying. In fact, a study by the Campbell-Hill group showed that if Virgin America had been allowed to fly in 2006, it would have saved US consumers more than $786 million, or an average of $88 per round trip for that year alone. It would also have led to discounting in most, if not all, new markets. This was the opposition's problem. As Fred said, 'In the old school of airlines, we're everybody's nightmare. They want to kill a powerful new airline in its infancy. Maybe they need to pay attention to what their customers are saying about their level of service.'

All our efforts seemed in vain; by the end of 2006, Virgin America was still grounded. Rumours were circulating that we would only be allowed in the air if the US got 'open skies' access to Heathrow and other European airports, even though the two issues were totally unrelated.

At the end of September 2006, I was in South Africa again, when Brad Pitt and I met with Nelson Mandela to help lend our support to a new landmines initiative with the appropriate name of the Sole of Africa – motto: 'It's time to put your foot down'. The other patrons included Mandela's wife Graça Machel, Queen Noor of Jordan and John Paul DeJoria of John Paul Mitchell Systems. The Sole of Africa was working with the Mineseeker Foundation to get rid of the 100 million landmines that are buried in the earth and kill or maim someone every twenty minutes. A quarter of a million square miles of land in the world is useless – much of it in Africa, particularly in Mozambique. Graça was born into a farming family in that lush and beautiful country, so she was eager to be involved with the project. We would be starting in Mozambique to clear the land and return it to agriculture. As soon as the land was cleared, 'Sole' co-operatives would train local villagers to plant and harvest crops, which in turn would feed them and allow them to make a living by selling their surplus.

The British Ministry of Defence had created wonderful new radar technology that used airships, built by a Virgin company, the Lightship Group, to locate landmines. Before, only 40 square metres of land a day could be cleared, but the brilliant airship technology allowed 100 metres of land to be scanned per second. What would have taken 500 years would now take a decade or less. When Mozambique was returned to its farmers, then we would move on, country by country.

Graça is also an advocate for children, and she and Mandela discussed with us the issue of the huge numbers of AIDS orphans in Africa. Again, the figures were hard to comprehend. Brad was shocked when Mandela turned to him and said, 'There are a million children whose parents have died from AIDS. More than 1,000 a day are orphaned in South Africa alone. Six, seven and eight year olds are now the sole breadwinners for their family.'

The sheer quantity could seem overwhelming, but there is a story, which I find appealing. It goes like this: a young girl is walking along a beach where the sea has washed up hundreds of starfish which are dying on the shore. As she walks, she stoops and picks up the starfish and throws them back into the sea. An old man is passing and says to her, 'Why are you doing this? It's not going to make a difference because there are hundreds there.' She looks back at him and says, 'If I can make a difference in one of their lives then it's worth it.'

This story is the parable that founded Starfish, a small organisation that opens and runs AIDS Community Day Care Centres in South Africa. Virgin Unite has been working at a grassroots level and finding ways within the community to take care of these orphans. Africa is full of incredible, strong women, who seem to hold things together in a very Earth Mother kind of way. Nora is one. I can remember the first time I met her in a small village some forty-five minutes outside Johannesburg. There, in a dirt clearing, was a small tin shack and, in it, Nora, an elderly woman, was cooking food for the 200 orphans who lived with her during the day. Somehow, she achieved enough to feed them all by going out and finding the food, then cooking it on a tiny little stove. We were just standing there looking and all I could see was this sea of two hundred heads, tiny people and their eyes – so huge in hungry faces. They have no one, and are petrified to be picked up and hugged.

Just one woman. There's no way she can take care of 200 children, yet she does. It was scary. One way we can help is to invest in these women, who have seen the need and set up as surrogate mums and housemothers. It's a huge issue and no one has really contemplated the results of what's going to happen to children who grow up without the individual love and attention needed by a child who is developing emotionally. I looked around at so many children, playing or tucking into a simple meal, and I could see at once that there simply wasn't enough room for them to sleep in the tiny shack.

I asked, 'Where do all these children sleep, Nora?'

She laughed. 'Oh, they're like roosting birds. They scatter in every direction at night and find somewhere safe to sleep. In the morning, they come back like starlings to eat breakfast – and somehow I always manage to find something for them.'

I felt humbled and emotional, but I also felt angry. If their mothers had been given antiretroviral drugs, they would have been there to bring up their children, instead of being used to line the pockets of the undertakers. Starfish was already helping Nora, but we gave them some money to help with expenses. Working with volunteers from Virgin Unite, we expanded Nora's shack and built an extension on the side to let children sleep there, and then we provided her with a very big stove and promised her a constant supply of cooking fuel. We can't give all of Nora's children a family of their own, but we can help Nora and women like her.

Sadly, the African continent is one of the few places in the world where the HIV prevalence rate continues to rise. By 2010, it is estimated that approximately three million children will be orphaned in South Africa alone. We support two Community Day Care Centres now. In October, we supported five more with the Loomba Trust. Cherie Blair came on that trip with us and launched them. If you think of the UK and US, we have so many resources. It's very frustrating and we all need to do everything we can to stop this ridiculous situation from continuing. I certainly have let this passion boil over a few times, including at the formal dinner given by the Loomba Trust. People should not be dying from preventable and treatable diseases – no matter where they live in the world.

The death from AIDS of one of our waiters at Ulusaba some years ago brought this home to me. HIV/AIDS was treatable in the West and the death rate had dropped dramatically. This, as I had already seen, was far from the case in Africa. To have someone in our midst die in this way was a shock. Despite his sickness Donald Makhubele had remained positive, composing poetry, music and songs. He'd written some beautiful words, which I read after his death, feeling choked that such a talented young man had been lost to us.

The following writings were composed by our friend – Poet and Musician, Donald Makhubele. He passed on as a result of an AIDS-related illness. His music and his thoughts, along with these beautiful words, shall live on and enlighten others. He had hoped to reach people while he was alive and well, living with HIV, but the Universe deemed he would speak from beyond ...

KNOW THE TRUTH AND THE TRUTH WILL
SET YOU FREE

A SHORT HISTORY ABOUT DONALD'S SICKNESS!

The day 14 September 2003 was my second day of my employment at Ulusaba Private Game Reserve. It was summer, but in the middle of the night I started to feel cold. It felt like it was winter. I was bound to go knock on David's room. David stayed next door, so I asked him for a heater because I could no longer stand the cold.

The following morning David gave me some money to go to the doctor for a consultation. The doctor did not tell me what was killing me. He suspected Malaria; it was not Malaria. I came back to Ulusaba with a Doctor's Note. I was not able to work until the days that were given to me to be off sick, came to an end.

I returned back to work but since then my life was shacking. Every time I had to be absent from work because I was not feeling well. I've tried Songomas, Private Doctors, but all that was unviewed or fruitless.

Then it happened one day after I went on annual leave I started to realise that my stomach was so big and very painful. Then I went to the Private Doctor, Dr V Hlatswayo at Hazyview. He helped me a lot, because he encouraged me to go to the Matikwane Hospital.

'ADMIT & HUMBLE YOURSELVES IN ORDER
TO GET HELP'

The doctor and I agreed that I would go to the hospital. When I arrived there I was bound to be admitted because I was in a bad condition. They took me to have an X-ray, but the end result of that was that they did not find anything. They also did a blood test and still nothing, until they drained some of the water from my stomach; my stomach was full of water. They sent some to the laboratory so I was just waiting for the results. The result was that I have TB PLEURA.

After the results I started to take TB Tablets they gave me (Rifampin) and, I must be honest with you, these tablets helped me a lot. I did manage to gain my body weight again. I gained my appetite, but my condition started to get worse, after I stopped the Rifampin. I took five tablets daily and changed to two tablets but it started again. I felt dizzy, losing my energy and I was sweating a lot. When I went back for a check-up I told them how I was feeling but they just didn't take me into consideration. They were just doing their own things. I took the TB treatments for almost nine months, until I went back for another check-up for the last time, and then I asked them to do an HIV Test.

'MY PEOPLE ARE DYING BECAUSE OF THE LACK OF KNOWLEDGE'

They conducted the test and, after the results, they told me that I am HIV Positive, but they cannot give me any treatment because they are still waiting for my CD4 Count Results; only then they can see what to do. They also said that they couldn't treat me if my CD4 cells are above 200; they will only give me treatment if it's below 200.

MY POINT OF VIEW

As far as I am concerned about this the Government are supporting HIV/AIDS to do their job of destroying the

Nation. They told me that my CD4 count is above 200, which means that my system is still strong and that's why they cannot help me. So I thought, that is totally wrong. Why wait until my CD4 cells go down, before they'll help me? Why can't they make sure that the virus does not cross the boundary to go from HIV to AIDS?

'BLESSED ARE THE PEOPLE WHO ARE EAGER TO HELP BECAUSE GOD WILL GIVE THEM WISDOM'

Because of everything that I have experienced during my sickness and until now, I know what is killing me, I feel like I can Rise and Shine. So that people can know the truth and the truth can set everyone free. It took me time to decide whether I should do the test or not. Because I was scared that if they told me that I'm positive I'd start to worry and people will laugh at me. But I must tell you that now I know my status I've accepted it. I forgave myself and asked God for forgiveness and I have put everything behind me as I'm coming from X to next. I'm very bold and strong to live with it and I'll never die as a Coward, but as a Hero.

By the way, I'm a songwriter who writes about HIV and AIDS so I had to know my status so that I can practise what I preach. I just want to be an example, especially in our area as it is a rural area and the people are still scared to expose themselves. The virus will spread all over if we hide it from others.

Let us work together as one, to be proud of ourselves and have the same purpose in order to defeat our enemy. This is not a disease but it is a war that is in Africa, aiming to destroy our continent. I'm pleading to everyone who can read this message to consider it and come out with something to help the nation.

*   *   *

I'M DONALD THE AFFECTED ONE

As a man who is living with HIV, I'm always thinking about positive things in such a way that there is nothing painful happening to me anymore and I don't have a room of disappointment in my heart as I've had worse disappointments in my life before. No more for the second time.

I'm proud of myself, I love myself, and I'll always look after myself for better health and I live for the lives and future of others. I'm now fully aware that I'm responsible for my family and myself and hope to be well again. I really didn't believe that you can live with HIV and AIDS for a long time, but I believe that I have lived life with it for a period that I did not know about my condition. Now that I know, I promise you that it will be cured and it will leave me like a free man. Like a man who has been freed from jail or from Chains. I'm telling you that I'll rise again. God said that he would give power to the weak so that they can fly like an Eagle.

If this can work for me again I know that it can work for you, my friend; don't even be scared to go and do the test because it is helpful, especially if you are unsure of your life status. This is a good time to go ahead and be brave enough to fight the sickness, and, listen, united we will stand, but divided we fall so let us work together in order to become victorious at the end of the day.

The actual cause of Donald's death was AIDS-induced TB; but malaria is also a major killer. After Donald died, I swore that no other Virgin employee would die unnecessarily. As a result of Donald's moving words, and finding out more myself, I decided that it was wrong that any company anywhere in the world should lose any of its staff from AIDS, and that every company in the world should pledge that they would encourage their staff to be voluntarily tested and make sure they get antiretrovirals in time to avoid HIV ever becoming AIDS. The first thing was to try to get our own house in order. So my wife Joan and I started the process by pulling in all the people who worked for us together in the bush. We then took an HIV test in front of everybody and we tried to get as many people as possible to take it. Most of them did; and we also asked young people who had HIV to come and explain how antiretroviral drugs had saved their lives, as an example to everyone of how the programme worked. We made two films, particularly for Africans, explaining, in simple and straightforward terms: how the body works; how antiretroviral drugs work; how the immune system works; what happens when the CD4 level drops below 200; why people are dying; how they can avoid dying; and that condoms save lives. In a test in one of our businesses in South Africa, nearly 24 per cent were HIV positive. I'm afraid that it's about average, which basically means that 24 per cent of our staff would die within six to seven years if they did not have access to antiretrovirals. We made it clear that we would supply anybody who had a CD4 count that dropped below 300 with antiretroviral drugs free of charge. We also rolled out the 0% Challenge across all our businesses worldwide, focusing on ensuring that no Virgin staff members would ever die from AIDS, that 0% would become HIV positive, and that 0% of HIV positive pregnant mothers would pass on HIV to their baby. This also includes 0% tolerance of any discrimination against HIV positive people within our businesses.

Donald said, 'This is not a disease but it is a war that is in Africa, aiming to destroy our continent. Let us work together as one, to be proud of ourselves and have some purpose in order to defeat our enemy.' In memory of Donald, I've decided to set up a 'War Room' to help co-ordinate and unite all the organisations in Africa who are trying to defeat African diseases. The 'War Room' will map out the problems, seek out best practices, and move and maximise resources. It will get on with the job rather than arguing and debating. It will alert the world to new diseases like AIDS before they get out of control. It will fight HIV, malaria, TB and fistula. It will mobilise experts, movers and shakers to get out to particular areas fast by pulling in contacts, governments and founders. Its ultimate aim is to make sure there are no more Donalds and that, through his death, thousands of others live.

After Donald died I happened to visit the local hospital with my mum and, by chance, came across a delightful man called Dyke, who used to be a game driver for Ulusaba. He was lying in a bed without hope, basically just a skeleton with no body fat left on him whatsoever. When he saw my mum, there was a glimpse of recognition and happiness in his eyes. We instantly put him on antiretroviral drugs. His improvement was immediate. He completely recovered. Thanks to getting proper medicine and treatments, he went from literally death's door to leading a normal life again. Everyone who has AIDS should have this opportunity of being reborn. Very sadly, Dyke has recently died from a bout of malaria that he contracted on a trip to Mozambique – which has made me even more determined not to let a small insect continue to wipe out thousands of people in Africa every single day.

I did some research with Virgin Unite and a wonderful man from Anglo American called Dr Brian Brink into finding a blueprint of hope and, amongst treeless, rocky hills and the dismal poverty of the dusty rural townships of Elandsdoorn in Limpopo Province, we came across the Ndlovu Medical Centre. It is run by Dr Hugo Templeman, an earnest Dutch physician, who has dedicated the past fifteen years to treating HIV/AIDS, as well as the other big diseases that kill Africans: TB and malaria.

One of the first things I noticed when I was shown around was the cluster of small development projects outside Ndlovu hospital, including a bakery, a repair shop, nappy manufacturing, pre-schools, computer school, car washes, a gym, all offering employment to locals. Hugo saw I was impressed.

'Yes, we're all about hope – and we want people to know that they will get well. They also need to make a living to keep themselves and their families while they are being treated.'

Dr Brink had fought a stubborn battle over many years to get antiretroviral drugs prescribed free of charge to any of Anglo's tens of thousands of workers who needed them. He finally won by pointing out that the loss in trained staff cost more economically than the costs of the drugs themselves. Once he won that battle he then said, 'Now, what about the miners' families, who have HIV and AIDS?'

I admired his forthright attitude and, with Hugo and Virgin Unite, we discussed what it would take to build a hospital to serve the Sabi-Sands district around Ulusaba. My first venture in helping to control the spread of HIV was in the early 1990s when I launched a charity, Mates condoms. It was a big step from free Mates condoms to joining with Anglo American to create a one-stop healthcare centre. We decided that the new hospital would be named the Bhubezi Community Health Centre after the Zulu word for lion. It would serve 100,000 people. Treatment for HIV, TB and malaria would be free, but other medical services would have a modest charge that will help ensure that the clinic becomes sustainable over time. The 100,000 people around Ulusaba would be protected. However, for those who live far from the hospital, the treatment needs to get to them.

It is difficult to reach that 'last mile' in remote areas with health services. So we kicked off a campaign called Heaven's Angels across the whole Virgin Group to raise money to buy and maintain motorbikes. The businesses, especially Virgin Trains and Virgin Atlantic, have done a wonderful job raising over $1m (US) to put over 100 bikes on the road. The working model we are building is that someone from a village buys the bike through a loan; in return, they are trained and paid to deliver healthcare on the motorbike three days a week, and the rest of the week they can use the bike for their own entrepreneurial activity. In this way, it becomes sustainable and creates jobs for people within the communities. In 2007 we began to test this model with a great partner called SHEF, who have already built over sixty-four sustainable clinics and pharmacies across Kenya – all owned by local people. We'd like to scale that up to help with healthcare delivery across Africa, with not hundreds, but thousands of biking medical outreach workers, and by showing the people themselves how they can earn a living, help each other and go that last mile.

On the one hand, I was working hard through Virgin Unite to try to help the developing world with some of the problems they face; and on the other hand, I was working hard at taking our space-launch programme forward. It was a strange but fascinating dichotomy. Virgin Galactic had caused a great stir and people had already signed up for our first flights. Then something remarkable happened in my personal journey to space.

I was on Necker in November with Burt Rutan, the designer of the spaceship, and a group of our founding customers, who had come out to find details of the project directly from Burt's own mouth. Will called from London to say he had just listened to Professor Stephen Hawking on the *Today* programme on Radio Four.

Will said, 'Stephen Hawking has just done an amazing interview, about why man needs to be in space – and why he still wants to go and why if possible he'd like Richard Branson to take him there!'

I gathered all of our founding customers and Burt around a set of speakers and we linked up to the Internet and played Stephen Hawking's podcast from the BBC site to them: 'The human race must move to a planet beyond our solar system to protect the future of the species. Life could be wiped out by a nuclear disaster or an asteroid hitting the planet. Once we spread out into space and establish colonies, our future should be safe. There are no similar planets to Earth in our solar system so humans will have to go to another star. Current chemical and nuclear rockets are not adequate for taking colonists into space, as they would mean a journey of 50,000 years. I discount using warp drive to travel at the speed of light for taking people to a new outpost.

'Instead, I favour matter/anti-matter annihilation as a means of propulsion. When matter and anti-matter meet up, they disappear in a burst of radiation. If this was beamed out of the back of a spaceship, it could drive it forward. Travelling at just below the speed of light, it would mean a journey of about six years to reach a new star. It would take a lot of energy to accelerate to near the speed of light.

'My next goal is to go into space; maybe Richard Branson will help me.'

There was a ripple of excitement amongst our budding astronauts. We all felt privileged to be part of a project he felt so enthusiastic about. I never cease to be amazed by Professor Hawking – a man I admire greatly. I have met him a couple of times over the years, so I picked up the phone and called him. I explained that we had not given away any free tickets on Virgin Galactic to anyone, despite the large number of celebrities approaching us, but if Stephen really felt up to it and was medically shown to be fit to fly, it would be a privilege to carry him into space.

Using his computerised voice he explained that mankind simply had to get into space if we were going to maintain life on Earth. 'There is a threat to life on Earth posed by humans. The two main causes of concern are global warming and the genetic alteration of vaccines and other microorganisms. Because we now have enough knowledge of the things that could happen to this planet to know that we need to use the resources of the rest of the solar system if we're going to survive as a civilisation. And we need also to have the incentive to go out and explore; and it can't only be about robots going into space although that is part of the answer. People have to be able to go there.' He added, 'Virgin Galactic is a step towards taking access to space out of the hands of the chosen few.'

At my request, Stephen Attenborough, head of astronaut relations, went to see Dr Hawking with our Chief Medical Officer to discuss the logistics of arranging a simulation gravity flight for him as soon as possible.

Continuing on from Dr Hawking's interest in our project, we looked into many other aspects of why space matters. There is the short-term reason of understanding climate change and providing us with the communications and information to keep the planet producing food it needs for its burgeoning population. But, as he said, in the long term we also need to be in space to provide the future sources of energy for the planet and possibly even some of the solutions to climate change. For example, many exciting ideas are being developed, such as solar umbrellas. They are not as big as people might think, but small crystalline structures made of transparent film that are scattered in space like bubbles at the Lagrange Point, which is halfway between the sun and the Earth. Here, the umbrellas would reflect back about 5 per cent of the sun's rays, which in real terms is a lot. People also think that the Internet is somehow energy free; but it emits masses of greenhouse gas. Scientists have been looking into Serva farms, for example, which are fuelled by solar panels and beam back radio signals from space direct to computers, saving a massive 80 per cent in electricity. One of the things I am also very interested in is the possibility of taking a Virgin Fuels research team to the moon – then building a fleet of spaceships so we can work there. This might sound like science fiction, but at the start of the decade I had no idea that I would be running a spaceship fleet and would be taking a suborbital flight into space with the most brilliant physicist alive today. In keeping with Stephen Hawking's opinion that our future could lie in space, I have been looking at a space-age fuel: Helium-3. It is an incredibly rare form of helium on the surface of the Earth, and freely available at the Earth's core, far beyond our present capabilities to tap. But there is a rich abundance of it in moon dust. When I considered that just a single spaceship load from the moon would power the US for a year, it did make me pause and do more research into the possibilities. Helium-3 is made under extreme pressure and extreme heat. It was made when the moon ripped out of the Earth and flew into orbit around it, and continues to be made by solar winds down countless millions of years. Scientists can make only minuscule amounts, at a cost of billions of dollars, in the accelerator at Cern. Getting it from the moon – where it would be 'mined' from the dust and then heated to release the gas itself – would not be wildly expensive, nor beyond our ability. Helium-3 could supply all of the Earth's energy needs way into the future by using fusion, which is both clean and safe. It would allow the land being earmarked to grow biofuels to be given over to growing food. As far-fetched as it might sound, Helium-3 could one day save humanity.

In February 2003, when it had looked inevitable that the US and UK were going to invade Iraq, I decided that I could not just stand by and watch. I had to do something to try to stop it. Sadly, before I could, America began bombing Iraq. But it got me thinking: maybe we should gather together a group of global Elders, in the hope that their voices and wisdom and negotiating power could avoid such conflicts in the future.

At the same time, at his home near Bath, my good friend Peter Gabriel had a wonderful vision that technology was propelling people into one large global village – yet there was no one there to lead this village and use technology as a powerful force for good. Many of today's leaders are not there to do the right thing for humanity, but instead most of them have some other type of agenda linked to political, military, economic or religious power. Our ideas converged on a poignant trip to South Africa in November 2003 when we were helping Mandela launch his 46664 campaign. Since then we have been on a deeply satisfying journey with the help of some amazing individuals to build a dream of pulling together a group of Global Elders. We believe that men and women who have shown moral integrity and leadership have a great deal of wisdom to offer. It is the kind of wisdom that has always been historically passed down by tribal or village elders. Ancient, intuitive wisdom is what our frantic, high-tech, global village needs. When Mandela and his wife Graça Machel agreed to be the Founding Elders and Archbishop Tutu agreed to chair the group, we knew that we had the core of something very special.

In July 2006 on Necker, we held a gathering of some of the top leaders in the fields of technology, philanthropy, business, science, the arts and many other areas, all of whom had come together to debate the Elders concept and to take it forward to the next stage.

Peter and I opened the first day by explaining where the idea for the Elders had originated. Peter said, 'I see it based on African tribes, who look up to the elders in their village. But now we're way beyond the little village. Now there's Google and Wikipedia and all the other links to connect people.'

I nodded. 'There have been individual Elders operating alone for a long time. Good men and women who speak out. The idea is if the most respected people in the world work together as a group, they will be more effective. Instead of the power of one, we'll have the power of twelve.'

It was two weeks filled with incredible ideas and debates, but most of all the overwhelming confirmation that the world needs a group like this. It was the most fantastic experience to be in the presence of some wonderful individuals like Archbishop Tutu and President Carter. Both of them added such deep insights into the Elders concept, and Tutu of course added a playful sense of humour. I will never forget some of the magical moments, like Peter playing 'Biko' on the grand piano in the living room of the Great House with Tutu and his beautiful wife Leah dancing. Or when Peter, in a long, white flowing shirt, was teaching Tutu how to swim in the ocean. He seemed to enjoy it because he spent some time with Peter and me practising in the pool.

'I've got a pool at home I don't use. My wife and children do, so perhaps now I can join them,' he said, smiling broadly.

We also had the pleasure of having some amazing grassroots Elders join us to give their views on how the Global Elders could make a difference. Zachie Achmat from the Treatment Action Group inspired us all with his passion to ensure that everyone who is HIV positive has access to antiretroviral drugs. He has truly given up his whole life to fight for the lives of others, refusing to take treatment himself until everyone can get the drugs. Hopefully the Global Elders can play a role in amplifying the voices of people like Zachie and Taddy Bletcher – individuals doing impactful work who need their stories heard around the world to help them scale up their efforts. Everyone spoke freely and frankly, putting forward strong and sensible opinions and points of view.

Jean Oelwang led off one session by commenting about Mandela. 'This is an amazing time in history. Mandela has true moral courage. He'll say the same thing behind closed doors and out in public. He's focused on what's best for humanity, and he's demonstrated leadership, not just through a course of action but through compassion.'

She handed over to Archbishop Tutu. He got up with difficulty from a low seat and joked, 'That happens when you are at this age. You have to have a discussion with your body and say, Body, we're about to get up now, how about it?'

I gave him a shoulder rub – but joking aside, all of the things Tutu said were moving. 'I'm glad I'm not God. God must be weeping; God is omnipotent but seems weak. We wonder why he doesn't zap people who do wrong. But there are people who rise up and do good things – they overthrow apartheid. Sometimes, like sun shining through the rain, God looks and smiles. He's smiling today on this island. I firmly believe this is a moral universe. Despite all appearances to the contrary where it often seems so clear that evil is on the rampage. But in the ultimate end, good prevails. Compassion, caring, are what will ultimately have the last word.'

One important issue we discussed was what difference the Elders could make, without replicating the role of the United Nations, or the important work of the World Health Organisation (WHO). I started the ball rolling by saying, 'We have all discussed the idea that the Elders would cover areas that the UN and nation states are not covering.'

Obviously, Jimmy Carter had personal experience not only of working through the UN, but also working through his own foundation, the Carter Center. He said that one of the problems that beset the UN was the veto, and that there was a lot of horse trading behind the scenes to get some resolutions through. 'You can't get past the veto in the UN. It would be feasible for the Elders to bypass this. There isn't anywhere now people can go for conflict resolution. To further the peace process. To provide experts on how do you negotiate peace. There are organisations – Harvard, the Carter Center – but you can't go to the UN because you know the US will veto one side, Russia, China, the other. So the Elders as a peace foundation or whatever, so that people will say as a first response, Why don't I go to the Elders to help prevent this war? If we had a perfect UN we wouldn't need it. But the UN isn't dealing with peace or the alleviation of suffering, or human rights violations, the oppression of women. You can't get them to debate the oppression of women because many Muslim countries are against that. Christians too. This is the kind of thing Elders could address without constraint and the hell with the fact that it isn't being done. I bet that Kofi Annan would be saying Amen on all this. The Carter Center worked to set up a High Commission on Human Rights which the UN didn't want. We are talking about an organisation that could supercede the UN and avoid the inherent constraints of a two-hundred-member organisation.'

It was heavy stuff. We had a consensus during that session that the Elders should seek to reinforce women's rights, and to do it from a position of being above politics.

'But with no authority,' Jimmy said. 'That's important. Only moral authority.'

Where the work of the World Health Organisation was concerned, it was thought that the Elders would need a broad agenda to look at controversial issues, such as HIV/AIDS, helping to ensure clean drinking water for all – 80 per cent of the developing world does not have access to clean drinking water – and disease. While the Elders would support eradicating malaria, for example, only WHO would have the authority to use the term 'eradicate'.

Jimmy said, 'The Elders could try to promote the quality of life in the poverty-stricken world. If they don't want to create something, they can help with the structure of something. Alleviating suffering through disease eradication is part of that.'

Every day was like that – filled with solid debate and discussion, each time moving the concept and our dreams forward a little. We all understood exactly where he was coming from when Peter said, 'The world is a living mirror. Astronauts say from space you see the Earth as something you can hold in your hand, a little blue ball. Light bounces off it; everything is reflected. My four-year-old son was telling me a story. He said, when people get touched, they light up. When they don't, they go into the shadows; so we should try to get everyone touched. They're not numbers and statistics, but real people.'

Ideas seem to stimulate ideas. It was as if we'd had these hopes buried inside, just waiting to burst out. Even just before Jimmy Carter left, he turned back with some last-minute thoughts. 'Elders can be the conscience of the world. They can be a guide to the world, an entity that is recognised for putting forth ideals of peace and justice. Being here has been delightful. It has been an inspirational, exciting, unpredictable and gratifying experience.' Then with a wave and his characteristic broad smile, he went up the steps and the helicopter lifted him and his wife Rose up and away.

Back at the house I asked Tutu if he would like some tea. 'No, I'm not English,' he replied with a twinkle.

'Oh, you'd like Peter's tea. He has more time to make tea than I do,' I joked.

A month later we met with Graça and Mandela at their home for them to make the selection for the initial group of Elders. Grandchildren scurried around us, and Jean and I walked out of this wonderful meeting, feeling that the Elders was finally a reality. We went on to Ulusaba and had a wonderful celebration signing the invitation letters. It was even more emotional as my father and mother were there to share this special moment with us. The dream that Peter and I had so many years ago was gathering momentum.

32 Flying high

2007

I N MOST OF THE Western Hemisphere that February morning of 2007, it was bitterly cold, with reports of snow, high winds and ice storms. Meanwhile, my mum was enjoying her morning swim in the crystal-clear waters inside the reef at Necker – being in her eighties has never stopped her from doing anything – and I was gazing northwest towards an island that I couldn't see, but had just bought for £10 million, which was a far cry from the modest £180,000 Necker had cost in 1976. Having a fresh challenge gave me a buzz and my head was filled with plans.

Now, you might think that one paradise island would be enough for anyone, and you'd be right. However, I had bought this second pristine jewel of an island to prevent it from being ruined by overdevelopment. Moskito is named after the original Moskito Indians who had lived there back when Sir Walter Raleigh arrived and named the Virgin Islands after Queen Elizabeth I. It has one slightly scruffy dock and a few small buildings that looked as if they might blow over in a light breeze – but, other than that, the island hasn't been touched almost since time began. It is a beautiful place and I wanted to do the minimum possible to make it comfortably habitable. An island is a perfect microcosm of the world – and this could be a Utopian model for dealing with global warming. Towards this end, I asked Dan Kammen, a professor at Berkeley, and

Ken Kao from Harvard University to do a study to come up with suggestions that would turn Moskito into the greenest island in the Caribbean.

I bought Necker more than thirty years ago, when I was just twenty-eight years old. I wanted a desert island hideaway where my friends could roam around with bare feet. Consequently, Necker has remained an unspoiled Eden, a family home where our friends could come and share with us in peace and privacy. I had already asked the people on Necker to use environmentally friendly materials, such as long-lasting light bulbs and organic cleaning products. We have planted an organic vegetable garden, are using biofuels in the generator and have wind and solar power. One bonus is that we've proven these natural methods are cheaper than conventional fuel. But Moskito was a clean slate, where I could do a lot more.

When I walked over Moskito for the first time as its new owner, I was filled with excitement. I don't think you ever get over that desert-island feeling. There are many beautiful birds and masses of flowering trees, a small Caribbean rainforest, hills that are higher than on Necker with magnificent views, and some dramatic cliffs. I found a large salt-water lake that had silted up and one of the first things we did was to fill it with water to encourage birds and fish. I decided there and then that all the materials we used would be green and renewable. Vents open to the windy side of the island would provide free air conditioning.

Living inside an ecological experiment will be a challenge. If you go around the world saying that, in order for the world to survive you have to make huge changes in your way of life, it does help if you yourself walk the walk and talk the talk. Moskito will be a role model for the chief minister of the British Virgin Islands; and, after, it could be a model for the Caribbean as a whole – perhaps even for the world. Someone suggested that I should change its name though!

Sometimes, I feel bad about the number of times Joan packs and unpacks suitcases as we travel around the world, and I wondered once, 'Don't you get tired of always having to pack?'

'Oh, it's all right,' she said matter-of-factly, folding another sweater, 'I know how to do it properly. When I was younger I used to work in a pawnbroker's shop in Glasgow. I'd unpack everything when people brought it in to pawn it on a Monday, and repack it when they came in on Friday to redeem it.'

I laughed. What a different life she'd had since being brought up in a caretaker's flat and working for a pawnbroker in Glasgow. But the matter-of-fact way she'd compare our travels to working in a pawnbroker's and her straightforward approach to life is one of the things I love about her. Shortly after I had signed the Climate Initiative with Bill Clinton, I was sitting on the end of the bed watching a discussion on the TV news about the urgency of global warming. Joan was behind me, packing yet another suitcase that lay open on the bed.

'James Lovelock believes we may have already gone past the tipping point and that the amount of CO_2 in the air means mankind is doomed,' I said to her.

'Man created the problem. Man should solve the problem. There must be somebody out there who can sort it out. There are a lot of good brains out there,' Joan said, as if it were blindingly obvious. I turned around and stared at her. She was right. If you look at the history of scientific and industrial development going right back to the seventeenth century, most of the big innovations of the past 400 years have come about as a result of offering big prizes. I had enjoyed reading Dava Sobel's book *Longitude*, which is about the first-ever industrial prize of the modern era. The British government offered £20,000 at the start of the eighteenth century to whomever could develop a portable clock so accurate that sailors at sea could tell where they were on a line of longitude anywhere in the world. Navigators had always relied on the position of the sun and stars for plotting their course on charts, but, when it was overcast and cloudy, they often went miles off course, got lost or were shipwrecked. Maps were inaccurate, and arriving at one's destination was more miss than hit. A foolproof method of accurate navigation would be of great value to the English whose colonies stretched over half the world. The man who eventually won was a clockmaker, John Harrison – but without such a huge prize he probably would not have bothered to spend half his life solving the puzzle. Prizes became the main way in which almost all modern industrial development has taken place. The first cars – and, ironically, also aeroplanes – were spurred in their development by prizes.

Sometimes prizes were offered by governments – as was the case with the longitude prize – or by individuals, as in the Blue Riband that I had helped win some years previously. But prizes were the spur to science of the eighteenth and nineteenth centuries. And, of course, it was even a prize that inspired the design of the Spitfire in the early 1930s. After World War II governments took over and they paid scientists to come up with solutions; big prizes offered by individuals slowed to a trickle.

Virgin itself has been a beneficiary of the X prize, that was set up to stimulate affordable private space travel. Burt Rutan and Paul Allen had successfully won the $10 million prize by developing a prototype spaceship called SpaceShipOne. It was that very prize that led directly to us investing in developing SpaceShipTwo with Burt – and, ultimately, to Virgin Galactic.

If we had gone beyond the tipping point because of the amount of carbon and methane already in the Earth's atmosphere, perhaps we could challenge scientists and brilliant minds to come up with a way to extract it.

I picked up the phone and called a group of people to sound them out and to make sure I wasn't mad. I spoke to Will, who has a good grasp of science and is running Virgin Galactic for us; to Josh Bayliss, our in-house lawyer; and, finally, I spoke to Shai Weiss, CEO of Virgin Fuels, to ask their opinions. All of them sounded cautious notes of optimism. They agreed that it certainly sounded possible, but that I should probably ask a scientist. So I asked James Lovelock, Steve Howard of the Climate Group and Tim Flannery. They told me that some work was already being done with capturing CO_2 gas in various parts of the world and the stimulus of a major prize would be very good. So Joan's almost casual comment quickly took the shape of a $25 million prize to find a way to actually remove carbon dioxide from the atmosphere. This is not to be confused with stopping CO_2 getting into the atmosphere in the first place. Our prize is for taking CO_2 that is already there out of the atmosphere, and this will include methane and greenhouse gases generally.

We are not looking for an agricultural solution to the problem because those methods are already known among scientists and have their constraints. By agricultural solution, I also mean using the sea, such as algae seeding in the ocean, although it's a very interesting area. There have been some experiments in the South Pacific–South Atlantic areas, off New Zealand and Brazil: algae captures CO_2 and, when depleted, the algae sinks to the bottom, theoretically out of harm's way. The problem is that there is always the law of unintended consequences and it's not known what possible effect large areas of algae could have on the fish population.

People are already planting more trees, and we're going to continue that process. We have also suggested using 'set-aside land' in Europe to grow trees. We are talking about maintaining the biodiversity of the Amazon rainforest, the African rainforests and the Asian ones – although, even as I write, in the next twenty-four hours, deforestation will cause as much CO_2 as eight million people flying from London to New York. One of the old ideas on climate change was to seed silver iodide to make clouds rain, and that's not what we are looking for either because it's not new. What we are looking at is a way to find a process using the forces of nature or something else to literally take CO_2 out of the atmosphere – something absolutely innovative that has not been thought of. And let me assure you now that no reader will win this prize by sending me an acorn in the post tomorrow morning!

Our proposed Climate Prize seemed to tie up extraordinarily well with a range of projects we were working on linking back to Gaia Capitalism, the Clinton Initiative and Virgin Fuels, then linking forwards from the Climate Prize towards Virgin Galactic. Once I had all the information and was assured that it made sense and had arranged a trust fund to be put in place for the prize itself, I telephoned Al Gore and asked him if he would launch the prize with me.

'I'd be glad to, Richard,' he said without hesitation.

A mere six weeks after my conversation with Joan, on 9 February 2007, Al Gore and I held a press conference in my London garden to announce the $25 million prize, the 'Virgin Earth Challenge', to inspire innovations in the field of combating climate change. Al said to the media gathered there, 'What we are facing is a planetary emergency. So some things you would never consider otherwise, it makes sense to consider.'

As we were filmed tossing into the air a beach ball that was painted to look like the Earth, as seen from space, I said, 'The prize will go to whoever comes up with the most innovative way of sucking harmful greenhouse gases out of the atmosphere within three years. The Earth cannot wait sixty years. We need everybody capable of discovering an answer to put their minds to it today.' It also occurred to me that, while finding a solution to carbon dioxide in the atmosphere might be as hard as finding a cure for cancer, if something does come of it, we could all enjoy life and not feel guilty about leaving the light on or putting coal on our fires.

I was gratified that many scientists agreed with us. As Tim Hansen, a climatologist and director of NASA's Goddard Institute for Space Studies in New York City, said, 'It makes much more economic sense to find ways to address the climate problem directly by reducing the pollution that causes it.'

The judges of the Virgin Earth Challenge include a NASA scientist and several top environmental researchers from around the world, including James Lovelock, Sir Crispin Tickell and Tim Flannery, who told me he was very excited by the potential. Almost as soon as the prize was announced, the entries started coming in – 5,000 in the first month alone! We had so many entries that we asked a team at the University of

Cambridge in England to appoint some of their people to work full-time at going through them to assimilate and analyse and see if there were any real break-throughs. It was agreed that it would be remarkable if any of the first applicants struck lucky. We are sure that we will get some crackpot ideas – but, promising or potty, it will only take one to win.

In the meantime, the US government, by doing nothing to tackle the problem, is helping to kill our beautiful world. 'They go on in strange paradox, decided only to be undecided, resolved to be irresolute, adamant for drift, solid for fluidity, all powerful to be impotent,' said Winston Churchill about the Chamberlain govern-ment, who didn't believe another threat in the 1930s was real. 'The era of procrastination is coming to a close. In its place we are entering a period of consequences,' he concluded.

Three weeks later, I was enjoying a peaceful holiday with my family in Switzerland. We had spent the day – Friday 23 February 2007 – skiing and, late that night at 11 p.m., we were relaxing in the lovely little cinema in Zermatt, watching a French film with subtitles. The cinema had sofas and you could eat your supper from low tables. It was a very comfortable place to be after a hard day on the piste and I felt a little sleepy. My phone was off, but I felt it bleeping and vibrating in my pocket. It stopped after eight or nine bleeps and I carried on watching the film.

During my very first year of being in the travel business and owning an airline, if I ever had a call late at night I'd always be particularly worried. But now, I realise how wonderfully safe planes and trains are – and that night I felt I had no real reason to be worried when I got a late call. But there was something about this call that niggled in my mind so I finally decided to leave the cinema and stand outside to check my voicemail.

I was alarmed when I was told that there had been an accident involving a Virgin train in the wilds of Cumbria – a remote, mountainous region in the northwest of England. I went back into the cinema to tell Joan and the kids and we hurried back to the hotel, where I was able to phone around to arrange things.

One of the first people I tried to reach was Will Whitehorn, who is also a director of Virgin Trains, but his phone just kept going to voicemail. Eventually, I found my list of emergency numbers and reached Will's wife, Lou, in East Sussex. I could hear chatter and laughter in the background.

'It's Will's birthday, we're having dinner at a friend's house,' Lou said, handing the phone over to Will.

For the first time in twenty years Will had left his phone behind. He remembered it as they drove out of the gate, but his wife, in hindsight memorably, said, 'Don't worry – nothing's going to happen tonight.' But he knew that something must be up if I had gone to the trouble of tracking down Lou's number and he was instantly alert.

Briefly, I explained that there had been an accident to the 5.15 p.m. London Euston to Glasgow service. At that stage nobody knew how bad any injuries were or how many people had been hurt. I was told the train had gone down a ravine and the rescuers were having difficulty in reaching it. I said I was getting back to the UK as quickly as possible, but all the airports were closed. The first plane left Zurich for Heathrow at about 5 a.m. UK time.

'I'll see if I can find out more this end,' Will said. He advised me that if it were a major accident – as it appeared to be – we wouldn't be able to get a train north from Heathrow to near the crash site. In the end, it proved easier to fly to Manchester and for him to meet me there.

From Zermatt, I got a taxi for the five-hour drive down the mountain to Zurich and managed to get a direct flight to Manchester. I had plenty of time to think during that long night. I knew how disastrous train accidents could be. Even on a flat stretch of track, people were often killed and scores could be horribly maimed and injured.

By 2005 Virgin Trains had come out of the crisis period of the collapse of Railtrack and the formation of Network Rail. It had been tough, but things were running smoothly and our trains had fulfilled their promise. One of the things I was very proud of was the fact that the design of our Pendolino trains was unique. We had discussed our expectations with Alstom, the manufacturer, and outlined what we wanted. One thing we insisted was that we were designing a train that should be the most environmentally friendly train ever built – and, in service, it had proved that. Despite the fact that their electricity comes from the British national grid, Pendolino trains boast the same carbon efficiency as the nuclear-powered French TGVs (the supremely fast 'train à grande vitesse'). In Britain we instead use a much bigger mix of oil, gas, wind and some nuclear power, but, because our Pendolino train is more efficient than the TGV and has regenerative braking – the same as a Toyota Prius car – as well as an aircraft-type aluminium body shell, it emits 78 per cent less CO_2 than the equivalent airline seat to Manchester or Glasgow.

The other feature we designed into the train was safety. When we asked Alstom to build it and gave them the specifications, we said we wanted them to look into every successful innovation in safety around the entire world and incorporate it into the new train. They were to do nothing that hadn't been tried and tested and shown to work somewhere in the world. I said to Tony Collins – at the time he was Alstom's managing director – 'I want you to bring together the best of all innovation in the rail industry in the design of the train. We want a train that should be able to survive an accident at full speed, regardless of the cause, and the passengers should be able to walk away from it.'

It was a very tall order, but I didn't see why it couldn't be achievable. Passengers are entitled to know that all that could be done has been done to ensure their safety. Consequently, there was innovation at every level. The design of the linkages between each carriage; the design of the carriages themselves; the design of all the interior fittings; the design of the windows – if there was an accident, the windows wouldn't smash open and kill the passengers, or the passengers wouldn't be hurled out of the train, as had happened in the Clapham disaster in 1988. The list of specifications was long.

The other thing that happens in a lot of train disasters involving old rolling stock is that, because of the design of the bogies – the links that hold the wheels on underneath – and the linkages (the connectivity) between each carriage, one carriage rides over the other one in accidents, crushing the carriage in front. Also, because of the old design of chassis with a body shell on top, one train can ride over another and push the body shell across the top of the chassis and kill the people trapped inside – again, as happened in the Clapham disaster. So we decided to build exceptionally strong carriages, even though it made for a heavier and more expensive train. In turn, to keep down the weight, we ordered what is termed monococh construction. That is, each carriage was a total aluminium cell, integral with the people in it. In effect, the passengers were in their own life-support system, even down to things like the lighting, which was designed to stay on after an accident, and run off automatic batteries for three hours. I knew we had tried to do all we could to make the train as safe as possible; nevertheless, having received little information from the front line of the accident at Cumbria, I was worried.

While I was making my way to Manchester, Will drove to Heathrow. The place was deserted, so he had a quick sleep under the British Midland check-in desk until he was woken up by the check-in staff, who put him on the first plane to Manchester. Will and Tony Collins – the man who had made the Pendolino at Alstom and who now ran Virgin Trains – met me when I arrived. We didn't say very much. We got in a hire car and the first thing we did was switch on the radio to listen to the early morning news. The BBC had a running commentary and we would learn anything new as it happened. They didn't know how many people had been killed but, to our great relief, there were already police reports from the scene that stated that the train was remarkably intact, which had contributed to the large number of survivors.

I turned to Tony and said, 'Well, Tony, you built a bloody good train.'

We sat and listened to the radio for about another five minutes, but there was still little information. I said to Will, 'Are we going to the train or to the hospital first?'

'The first thing we're doing is going to go to the hospital,' Will replied. 'I don't know what we'll find there. We've phoned ahead and they're expecting you. They've taken the people to two separate hospitals.'

It was a long drive that cold and dank February dawn.

England looked grey and grim compared to the dazzling Swiss Alps I had left. My mood was very introspective. As the chairman of the company I felt it was important to take a lead, to get out there, talk to the emergency services, talk to people and treat them as you might members of your own family who had been caught up in a disaster. I knew I had to go to the hospitals, and was dreading finding how badly injured people might be. The fact that they had used two hospitals sounded ominous.

The thing that had shocked the staff in each hospital – and both the registrars mentioned it – was that when they heard about the accident and the conditions under which it had happened and as the pictures began filtering back that night from the scene from the helicopters flying to pick up the injured, they geared themselves up for over one hundred dead. The first reports from the scene were that there were over seventy to eighty casualties. As it turned out, of that number, only twenty-five went to hospital. By the time we arrived in the early morning, there were only eleven people still in hospital with serious, though not life-threatening injuries, many of which were caused by a whiplash effect when the carriages rolled down the embankment. The driver, Iain Black – a former Glasgow policeman – was the most seriously injured, with a broken neck. It had taken two hours to release him from the cab, although the cab itself remained intact. The other two seriously injured people were the children of a lady in her eighties, who had sadly died after she was brought to the hospital of heart failure.

I remember the registrar at the first hospital we visited, the Royal Preston in Lancashire, saying, 'It's incredible. Our experience of train crashes and the reality of what has occurred here is nothing short of a miracle.'

Miracle was a word we were to hear often as the morning unfolded. We visited the intensive care unit, but were unable to speak to the driver because he was unconscious and being prepared for an operation. But we met the surgeon and he said he thought the driver was going to be all right. We were leaving that hospital when we got accosted by a reporter from the *News of the World*. I said a few words to them and went on to the Royal Lancashire Infirmary, where we found that most people had been discharged. Again, I offered my help; and then we went quickly on to the scene of the accident. The surrounding lanes and fields were very waterlogged and the site was inaccessible by car. The police had cordoned off the approach and, displaying a little bit of bureaucracy, they asked who I was. I told them, but they still refused us access until they had radioed ahead to make sure that it was OK for me to go and look at my own train. Escorted by police, we walked about a mile towards the railway line, which lay across fields. As we got closer, we could see smoke rising and I instantly remembered the dreadful flash fire of the Clapham disaster.

When you don't know what to expect – when you don't know how many people are going to end up as casualties, whether your driver will live or die, or whether there is something that has been done or not done by your crew – and when you arrive at the scene and you see the train looking like a Dinky Toy set thrown everywhere, there is a sense of unreality. It was ghastly; but wonderful that it had stood up to the accident so well. It was impossible to prepare yourself for this. You think about the world of public relations and suchlike and how people have written statements and seem so controlled. But my experience is that you can never be prepared for situations like the one we were walking towards. It was important to avoid the 'don't apologise' industry approach by appearing on the scene of the accident to apologise, to reassure and to make it quite clear that we would take responsibility if responsibility had to be taken and that we would discover what had caused the accident. It seemed to be the logical and the human way to handle the situation. But, of course, lawyers and insurance people always advise people not to do that.

We knew a lot about the history of rail accidents because we had studied them. One of the big issues was the appalling communications, which made things worse, especially for families and friends. So one of the models we tried to create when we planned for a potential accident scenario was fast, efficient and honest communications from the word go. When we arrived at the scene there had been very little in the way of communication from anybody who was there, apart from the police, who had already held a press conference that morning at the site. They'd said that they suspected it was track failure at the points and the train was not at the centre of their inquiries. This was a great relief for us; though obviously not for the chief executive of Network Rail who was already there – a very nice man called John Armitt (who has gone on to run the infrastructure of the British Olympics). Robin Gisby, director of operations and customer services for Network Rail, who was with John, explained to us again that the cause was most likely points failure. The nine carriages had rolled off the bank but most of them had managed to stay upright – clearly they had been thrown into the air while travelling at 95 miles an hour – and most of them seemed intact. John and Robin showed us where it had happened and how the train must have come off the tracks before travelling for some distance along the stone chippings.

John just looked at me and simply said, 'Sorry.' I knew exactly how he felt and how overcome he must have been.

It was time to make a statement to the gathered press, who had been herded at a safe distance below the embankment by the police. I had always laughed at funny films and cried at sad ones and my children always took a box of tissues for me. Mum always said, when public speaking, don't think of yourself but of who you are talking to. Thankfully, as I faced the press, my emotions didn't get the better of me. Obviously, it would have been far more difficult if the cause had seemed to be something we were responsible for. It was still an emotional moment, though, when one reporter said there was a hundred-foot viaduct seconds away and it was pure luck, a matter of seconds, that the train had stopped in time.

I didn't know a great deal at that stage of what had actually occurred, but I praised the bravery of the driver who stayed at his post and managed to slow and control the train as much as possible: 'It is a very sad day because of the loss of one life and the injuries caused to other people. The actions of the emergency services, the RAF and the police in dealing with the crash were wonderful. The driver of the train, Iain Black, deserves recognition. He came around a corner to find the line defective before the train started to leave the line. He carried on sitting in his carriage for nearly half a mile, running the train on the stone. He could have tried to get back and protect himself but he didn't, and he's ended up quite badly injured. He is definitely a hero. In the sober light of day we will have to see if he can be recognised as such.'

I continued, 'The train itself was magnificent – it's built like a tank. I think, if it had been any of the old trains, the injuries and the mortalities would have been horrendous. Each carriage is built like a motor racing car with rolling bars. Not one of the carriages has crumpled; hardly any of the windows have been broken. Everyone is going to have to learn from this incident and Network Rail are going to have to look at this track problem and make sure nothing like this ever happens again.'

When asked why I had come to the scene of the accident in person, I replied, 'You know, the thing is I'm here not as the boss of this company. I am here because I am a human being and, if my children had been in that train, I would have expected the owner of the train company to come and learn from it and to go to the hospital and show sympathy to the relatives. And I think people would expect the same of me. You keep asking me whose fault it is. We don't know the answer to that yet; but, clearly, it is some form of track failure and the train is not at the centre of the investigation. That will come out in the fullness of time. The only thing that we have to take away from today is to learn lessons for the future, to make sure that something like this never happens again.'

After talking to the press I went to visit all the emergency services that remained. The helicopters and ambulances had gone and the remaining services were winding down from the night's activities and were getting ready to do the more forensic work on the train. Chief Superintendent Martyn Ripley of the British Transport Police said forensic experts, engineers, scenes of crime officers and accident investigators were working on the scene. 'All of us who were involved were amazed that we didn't get more fatalities at the time. We were very, very fortunate.' This opinion was backed up by Superintendent Jon Rush, of Cumbria

Police, who said, 'It is a scene of devastation. We were very surprised that there have been so few fatalities.'

After the uncertainty of the morning, I felt a great relief that things were far better than we had originally imagined – even though I continued to feel very aware of the poor woman who had died, and the others who were injured. As we walked away from the scene of the accident, Tony said, 'Richard, you probably won't remember this, but you were the one who sat at the first meeting we had as the train manufacturer and said, "I want to build the safest train in the world."'

Next, we went to the farmhouse next to the track to thank Geoff Burrows, the farmer who owned the field where the train crashed, for his help. He had supplied the passengers with sandwiches and tea and had helped the rescue effort by pulling cars and ambulances out of the muddy ground with his tractor. Finally, we went back to the Royal Lancashire Infirmary to meet the family of Mrs Margaret Masson, the lady who had died. They wanted to meet me in the morgue. However difficult it might have been for me, it was obviously far worse for them and I knew it was the right thing to do to be there and talk to them – as much as one can in those circumstances. I sat with them feeling deeply moved. They never looked to me for an explanation. We shared their grief together.

Obviously, as a company, we later analysed how everything was handled and how we could learn from the accident. I was genuinely very proud of the way the Virgin team had handled things. Long ago, we had put emergency plans in place and they had swung smoothly into action. Because the entire London to Glasgow line had to be closed, some twenty to thirty thousand passengers were stuck up and down the railway line. We hired virtually every spare taxi in Britain and every single passenger was home in a taxi by one o'clock that morning. We had carers on the scene at the hospital and the site of the crash. The counselling of the injured people and the families was carried out on a one-to-one basis by the staff – that is continuing as I write. How people deal with adversity is important and they did so well. The driver was released from hospital after a month and I was told he would fully recover. Hopefully, he'll be back driving.

During our analysis a great irony surfaced: we'd had to fight the government to allow us to build our Pendolino train to high specifications. When the media repeatedly reported that the survival rate in the accident was 'a miracle' I wanted to say it wasn't a miracle. If it was a miracle, it was a miracle by design, in the sense that if you plan properly for some eventuality and make no compromises to the solutions to that possible eventuality, then you can build unprecedented levels of safety into any transport system. Virgin has a proud record of safety – we've never lost a passenger in an air accident in twenty-five years of flying. And we'd had ten years of operating trains by the time Cumbria happened and never lost a single passenger – until now. Mrs Masson's death was a real tragedy and I was angry that every argument we'd had over those trains, ludicrously, was with the government, with many civil servants advising minis-ters that we had 'overspecified' the train. And as a result, they'd said it was 'too heavy' and 'too expensive'!

That train went into that accident with no faults whatsoever – yet they insisted that we'd had 'needless' systems built into it, such as an automatic computer system that monitored the entire train and sent back a satellite signal to our headquarters in Birmingham which would inform headquarters if any fault ever developed on any Pendolino. Unlike in previous accidents in the rail industry – where people were kept waiting for years to find out the answer, which causes enormous distress to families – we could walk into that situation in Cumbria and honestly report that that train had arrived there with no faults on it. To compare, the technology that Network Rail has to monitor its tracks and points is still decades behind the train that's travelling on them.

If you look at the health and safety regulations in Britain, the Virgin Pendolino surpasses the regulatory minimums for safety in its systems by a factor of three. That was what the civil servants meant by over-specified. It was built well above and beyond even current safety standards in the UK. It's now causing a lot of hand wringing in government, with people wondering what to do about the fact that new trains are being built right now that are not to the same standard of safety specifications as the Pendolino.

Whilst the tracks our trains are running on aren't as modern, there is no excuse for bad maintenance. But at least it was good to see the head of Network Rail taking it on the chin and accepting responsibility within twenty-four hours.

The handling of the accident has become a BBC case study for new journalists on standards that BBC reporters should expect from corporate organisations. They said Virgin had set a new standard for the management and the handling of emergencies of this nature. A director at the BBC was on the train and, while still stuck in her carriage, she witnessed the way the accident was handled – and how the events unfolded afterwards and how they were in turn dealt with. As an eyewitness she was highly impressed by the conduct of our people, by the procedures that were followed.

Very few people knew that we'd taken some big decisions in the previous twelve months about whether or not we wanted to stay in the rail industry. Now that the Pendolino was up and running and we were growing passenger numbers fast and taking real market share from the airlines on routes like London to Manchester, Liverpool or Glasgow, the business was finally becoming profitable – and there were lots of people out there who wanted to buy it from us. We had had to decide whether or not to stay in rail. In the early years, until huge sums were poured into upgrading the railways, we had caught a lot of flak from critics. This had caused problems for the Virgin brand and we had had many discussions over whether or not to expand in the business. The delivery of the Pendolinos and then getting them into service convinced us to stay in. Interestingly, by the time the Cumbria accident had happened, we had decided to expand in the business and start bidding for other franchises. In 2007 we made a bid to run the East Coast line and take it over from GNER, whose parent company went bust, but the route was awarded to National Express.

I'm a great believer in rail – and I do think a new age of the train is coming in Europe. I would go further and say that I think that we are going to get to the stage from an environmental perspective whereby decent fast and efficient train services should operate between cities in the future, instead of domestic airlines. It will require continued investment for both Britain's network and the rest of Europe's. Ironically, despite the public perception, Britain is investing more into railways than any other country in Europe now and our railways are becoming the best in Europe. As the *Financial Times* pointed out in a major editorial piece in the spring of 2007, the general public only sees the French TGVs.

What they don't realise is that most French commuter trains are now over fifty years old and are providing a terrible service to commuters into Paris and the other major cities of France. Britain may not have the fastest railways, but they are at last on their way to becoming amongst the best. It's a trend that will only become a reality if that investment continues, however.

For the travel industry managers who are reading this, the whole value of the Pendolino contract was £1.2 billion. We set up the contract in a unique way in that the manufacturer had to take responsibility for maintaining the train and looking after it throughout its life: it was called a 'design, build and maintain' contract. They only got half their money for building the train; the other half they would get over the life of the train for safely maintaining it. Now the motive of that, which had never previously dawned on the rail industry, but which we had begun to learn in the airline industry, was that, if you're a manufacturer and you've built trains which you then hand over to somebody, the incentive to build to the very best standards can never be as high as if you're going to have to maintain and be paid to maintain. Obviously, in the latter case, a manufacturer will want to make that maintenance as easy and as efficient as possible. This will also generally mean that you will also build much more safety into the regime.

Of the total of £1.2 billion, £600 million was to build the trains and the remaining £600 million was paid out for maintenance over the life of the trains. Each Pendolino cost an average of £11.5 million per train – which we were told was about £1.5 million too expensive. Part of that cost was for regenerative braking. However, we insisted on fitting regenerative braking, which puts back 17 per cent of all the electricity these trains use into the overhead wires every time they brake. At the time we decided to go ahead with that, oil was only $10 a barrel and there were certainly plenty of people in the Department of Transport who couldn't understand why we would 'waste money', given how cheap energy was. They were missing the point. If you're going to have to operate trains for twenty years you never know what the price of energy is going to be in the future, and you have to plan for more expensive energy – which was something that we at Virgin believed by 1999 was going to happen, against the trend of the time. But, even back in 1999, the more I looked to the future of energy and oil, the more I looked at environmental issues, and the more I was convinced we had to do something. That's when the regenerative braking decision was taken. The other thing that we spent more on was the safety aspect of the trains. But, if you look at the reality today, we have already paid back the cost of the regenerative braking in the lower energy use and the lower environmental impact of the trains – and, as for the safety features, this one accident alone has caused less misery and less social cost than any 100mph accident with a train anywhere in the world in history. The train that was in the Cumbria accident will go back into service – which some people find hard to believe. But only two coaches were damaged enough to be taken out of service. The rest of the train is in very good shape and has passed all safety tests.

On a further environmental note, red diesel was the low tax fuel during World War II for industry and agriculture, and has remained so for agriculture ever since. I don't see why biofuel should not benefit from this same tax break, since we are helping reduce CO_2 emissions. I went to see Gordon Brown, the then Chancellor of the Exchequer, and discussed these issues with him. I'm pleased to say that he agreed with me, and in the subsequent budget he gave us the tax break we needed, so that on 7 June 2007 the first passenger-carrying biofuel train, the Virgin Voyager – the diesel version of the Pendolino – went into service on the London to Holyhead route. It was not only a first for the UK but for the whole of Europe.

As a postscript, the final irony of the events of 23–24 February in Cumbria is that, the Monday after the accident, a letter of complaint was received at our head office from a member of the public. He wrote that he was unable to use his mobile phone from the Pendolino he was travelling in, because of the small windows and special metallic fillers. This safety feature protects the passengers from shattering glass, but does make for smaller than usual windows and damages mobile phone reception. We've not, however, had another complaint since! Having said that, in the near future new technology will allow people to use their phones uninterrupted.

Meanwhile, I had been keeping a watching brief on our work in South Africa, and towards the end of April, I flew to there to open our new hospital. It had all come about because of Donald and Dyke, and to make sure we didn't lose any of our staff or community again. It set alarm bells ringing and I was determined to make sure it didn't happen again. The doctors, Hugo Templeman and Brian Brink, who I had met the previous year, were there as well, to help with the grand opening, when Africans, in their tribal costumes, danced outside and many people from the local area came to check us out. Hugo had worked on the building plans and Brian helped us do fundraising. The entire building had gone up in less than eight months, including fitting it out, at a remarkably low cost. With the doors open, ready to treat thousands of people, it cost just a million dollars. The equivalent hospital built from scratch in England would cost $100 million and take years. We put in $600,000, Anglo American $400,000 and the US government will also be putting in $5 million over some years to pay for antiretroviral drugs and other medicines. It is a complete clinic, with four maternity wards and twenty-four-hour care for full HIV, AIDS, TB and malaria treatment, as well as all the basic healthcare services.

The vision behind the quick, efficient build was to get the hospital up and running to start treating people at once without hanging around discussing plans and issues. We just raised the money and did it. Our idea was to try to build in a much more efficient and portable way than has been done in the past, using as a model a method that converts the ubiquitous 'charity' into a sustainable business model – that is, it will ultimately become self-running and pay for itself. I feel that helping people towards self-sufficiency where possible gives them more hope and confidence and can take them out of a cycle of poverty and despair. We used as a blueprint Hugo Templeman's Centre, where he has helped HIV/AIDS patients who are being treated to set up small businesses around the clinic, so they can make a living and have some dignity. Using Hugo's model, we agreed that HIV/AIDS, malaria and TB would all be treated free; but there would be a charge for basic healthcare and less urgent treatment where people could afford it. It was important, though, for the people to know that we would never turn anyone away. Our aim ideally is to take that as a model and scale it up across South Africa, then as many other places as possible where there is real need through Virgin Unite.

Creating sustainable businesses frees 'charity' money to be used elsewhere and effectively stretches it further.

It was a few days later that I got the welcome news that scientist Stephen Hawking had come one step closer to his dream of going into space with us. On 27 April, shortly after his sixty-fifth birthday, with the help of Peter Diamandis and a team of doctors and nurses, he finally experienced zero gravity on board a commercial 727 jet that had been converted for weightless training flights – or what NASA astronauts-in-training call the 'Vomit Comet'. Just to make sure he would be all right, he took a motion sickness pill just before his flight. He was the first person with a disability to enjoy the experience – and enjoy it he did. The video beamed back to us on Earth showed a wide smile on his face as he left the confines of his wheelchair and floated free for the first time. 'It was amazing ... I could have gone on and on,' he said after landing. 'Space, here I come.'

I can't know exactly how he felt at having achieved the first part of his dream – only he could possibly know that – but I know what it feels like to float at zero-g. On first leaving the gravity of Earth, the feeling of weightlessness travels slowly through the body until, suddenly, instant bliss fills you. Everyone who has ever known it agrees that it is 'pure, sheer ecstasy' – but words alone cannot describe the pleasure. Having passed the test with flying colours, Professor Hawking was now ready to be a passenger aboard a Virgin Galactic space flight.

Not everything would go as smoothly, or even as joyfully, as flying at zero-g. Eighteen months earlier, on 11 September 2005, an interesting opportunity came my way. I was in New York for the US Open tennis finals, when I attended a lunch meeting at the Four Seasons

Hotel with Gordon McCallum, head of Virgin's
management company, Simon Duffy, CEO of the UK
cable television company NTL, and Shai Weiss, NTL's
director of operations – who now runs Virgin Fuels.
Simon and Shai had flown in that morning for the
meeting. It was the culmination of months of secret
negotiations between us to create a new powerhouse
media company in the UK to rival Sky. Our codename
for the proposed union was Project Baseball; like a
baseball pitch it had four bases (a 'quadplay') with a
diamond in the middle. The diamond was the value to
be unlocked by our merger.

Originally, NTL/Telewest had asked if we would
license the brand to them, but I thought we could do a
lot better. In discussions with Stephen Murphy, our
chief executive, I said, 'Virgin Mobile is sitting here with
4.5 million customers and a lot of rights in terms of
content. The only way I can see this working is to
integrate Virgin Mobile into the new business.' I didn't
just want to do a rebranding deal, I wanted to have
equity. As I saw it, they were going to have to rename
and rebrand anyway – and Virgin had by far the better
image.

Simon and Gordon agreed. This was that NTL and
Telewest – the UK's biggest cable providers – should
combine together with Virgin Mobile, to rebrand the
new group with Virgin's name and very successful
image. Together we would have some ten million
customers, which would enable us to do wonderful
things. The first selling point would be to launch
'quadplay' – that is, we would offer a 'four for £40
service' in one package of digital TV, broadband,
telephone and mobile telephone. I liked the fun and
business coup in this unusual reverse take-over.
NTL/Telewest was effectively buying Virgin Mobile for

a very large sum – but I would become the largest shareholder and stamp our name and logo on the entire company. I immediately saw it as a way of unlocking the huge potential in Virgin Mobile and, at the same time, having the fun of becoming a major competitor in the market place. I had tried before, when I had bid for Channel 5 (now Five) and knew how difficult it could be. It took eighteen months to fine-tune the proposal before a fifteen-page summary was sent to me early in 2007. Obviously, the structure of the deal took many more sheets of paper, but I have always preferred summaries: I am able to see at a glance whether a deal is for me or not, by cutting to the chase and skimming the main points.

During the long months of negotiation, we had managed to keep the deal secret by working through only one bank and not even telling Charles Gurassa, the independent chairman at Virgin Mobile – but ultimately it leaked. The *Sunday Telegraph* wrote: 'James Murdoch is going to choke on his muesli when he hears about this. It's going to be the battle of the brands – Virgin vs. Sky.'

T-Mobile, who were involved with Virgin Mobile, had a change of control provision in their deal with us. Obviously, with the leak about to go public, they had to be told. They weren't told everything – such as the NTL/Telewest proposal – but someone there guessed. It ended up with Gordon urgently calling Charles Gurassa and saying, 'There's something you need to know ...'

We formally became Virgin Media on 6 February 2007. Part of our strategy in order to give us content was to identify and then make a bid for ITV. It was well known that ITV was struggling in the market place, but it had a good base for us to make and buy in content. We thought we had a good chance, until we came up against quite a big player in the form of Rupert Murdoch – who owns more than 50 per cent of all UK media, from TV to newspapers. I knew we would end up locking horns with Sky, but I underestimated the speed with which Murdoch moved. His son, James, runs Sky, but there is little doubt that his strings are pulled by Murdoch senior. I get on well with both Murdochs, though I am aware of how ruthless they can be in business. Our bid for ITV suddenly fell apart on 26 April when Rupert Murdoch stepped in and bought a large slice of ITV shares at well over their value. As a result, Sky shares immediately lost £150 million in value but they didn't mind that to stop us becoming too powerful a competitor. I believe that what they did under competition law was unfair and illegal and we asked the competition authorities to adjudicate on whether Murdoch could buy those ITV shares or not. Some of the competitive reaction undertaken by Sky was also somewhat unexpected. We had three million homes against Sky's nine million homes, but, cleverly, Murdoch senior had tried to paint a picture that I was portraying myself as a David vs Goliath, whereas – according to him – it was Goliath vs Goliath. I believed that the two Murdochs and I have quite a lot of respect for each other, but the game, as Sherlock Holmes said, was afoot.

Until then, Sky and the new entity, Virgin Media, had a symbiotic relationship, in that we had channels on each other's networks. We paid quite a lot of money to Sky for their basic channels; but, with no warning, suddenly they asked us for a lot more money than the market value, or than we were willing to pay, because those channels were declining in numbers of viewers. At the same time, they decided to reduce what they paid us to use our network by tens of millions of pounds, despite an increase in viewers of our programming. As a result our customers lost some of Sky's programming, but we were eventually able to settle the issue at the end of 2008.

I hadn't been at Ulusaba very long when I became more fully aware that animals know no boundaries or frontiers. Some people talk of 'Kenyan elephants' and 'South African lions', but the reality is that most animals have always followed their old hunting and feeding paths, regardless of man-made borders. Like migrating birds, they are gypsies, going where they will. It is only when they come up against the needs of people to grow crops or to build towns that the problems develop.

Africa was divided up like a pack of cards in the Victorian era, when European colonialism was at its height. Artificial political borders cut across tribal lands and split clans; as well as across animals' migration routes, fragmenting and destroying ecosystems and biodiversity. It was to try to right this damage that national parks were established. However, most national parks are exactly that – national and within borders. Peace Parks, under the guidance of Dr Anton Rupert, went to the next stage. Together with Prince Bernhard of the Netherlands and Mandela, Dr Rupert set up the Peace Parks Foundation. Their dream was to once again create an Africa where wildlife can roam freely across international borders. Co-operation between countries would allow eco-tourists to come, bringing in money, work and prosperity to some abjectly poor people and regions. The people, animals and the land of Africa would all benefit.

According to Dr Rupert, 'We believe in the philosophy that there needs to be harmony between humans and nature. Africa without fences. We dream of ancient migration trails trodden deep by an instinct that time has never contained. We dream of a wilderness where the elephant roams and the roar of the lion shatters the night.'

Ulusaba is within the great Limpopo Transfrontier Conservation Area (TFCA) that stretches across the entire area of southern Africa, from coast to coast. But I was very attracted to the idea of the Peace Parks when I learned that they will eventually straddle the globe, taking in some of the most beautiful and remote places, from the Arctic to the Antarctic, and east to west around the globe – some 112 countries in all are involved. But although the Parks are without borders, every country retains absolute sovereignty of the part of the Park that falls within its territory. It's an amazing achievement and I loved the concept when Mandela first mentioned it to me.

In due course, in January 2006 Professor Willem Van Riet approached me to join Club 21. '21' stands for those interested in peace and development through conserva-tion in the twenty-first century. Each member of the club makes a minimum contribution of one million dollars. It's a lot of money – but I agreed with Dr Rupert's witty quip that, 'Conservation without money is just Conversation.'

But all was not wonderful in paradise. The reality, as I found, was the amount of land set aside for wildlife in Africa is tiny. Farms encroach, poachers poach and in some areas – such as a beautiful area of Mozambique – there's no game left because of civil war. But in South Africa's Kruger Park, there's too much game. The more I got involved, the more I realised how crucial the work of the Peace Parks is. One of the most exciting breakthroughs was the removal of the border fence between South Africa and Mozambique. Now the over-populated elephants of the Kruger can move freely into Mozambique and breathe life into its deserted game parks.

Things moved at great speed. By April 2007, I was flying to Kenya to finalise an initiative to lease land from the traditional home of the Masai. The plan was to pay them more money than they currently got from farming, to protect the land as well as the beautiful migrations of the wildebeest – one of the five wonders of the world – and to then train the Masai to work in game lodges, as rangers, so they continue to work on their own land. It helps to improve the environment, gives them jobs, and protects wild animals. I think that some countries realise that what they have is absolutely priceless; and this is especially true of Africa, where they have to battle with the climate as well as with famine, war and disease. Fortunately, African governments and the African people themselves are coming to see that the game and scenery is beyond value. Once you lose it, you're never going to get it back. At least 10 per cent of our profits have been put aside to invest in Africa and to create African jobs. We've set up a national airline for the Nigerians, which West Africa desperately needed, as well as health clubs, mobile phone companies and finance companies, together employing some 5,000 Africans.

As I stood in the steamy heat of Kenya, though, breathing in the rich smells of the Tropics, I mentally braced myself for the sub-zero temperatures I was about to experience on my next challenge – which was to take some time off to trek across a part of the Arctic Circle with my son, Sam, and husky dog teams. Sam had already been training for a week when I arrived from Kenya – which wasn't the best place to adapt myself to

Arctic conditions! – to join Will Steger's 1,200-mile Global Warming 101 expedition to help alert the world to what global warming was doing to the Arctic and the Inuit and the world as a whole. By the time I arrived – hotfoot (almost literally!) from Africa, to travel with the team from the Clyde River to journey's end at the Iglulik – global warming rapidly became one of the last things on my mind. The Inuits, who were our guides, keenly observed and pointed out to us some depressing changes in the permanent ice cover.

But first I had to brave the welcoming feast. A tarpaulin was laid out in the middle of the village hall. Three frozen stag heads, cut off from their frozen bodies that lay next to them, stared out at us. Chunks of raw frozen meat cut from one of the stags awaited us. Large frozen fish lay in a row. This was the feast the Inuit had laid on for us at Clyde River to help us on our way.

The next day, we headed down from Clyde Fjord – a glaciated valley that was flooded by sea water. It was awesome; certainly one of the wonders of the world. I felt completely dwarfed with our tiny sledges in the middle of this great fjord. It was a beautiful wilderness, one I had never experienced from the ground before – although I had sailed serenely overhead similar terrain in a balloon. I was also conscious of the fact that my ancestor, the man known as Scott of the Antarctic, had walked through far worse conditions to the South Pole.

Every mile we covered was through the most beautiful scenery I had ever seen, with blue ice and soaring sea cliffs; but Theo, our guide, also pointed out other disturbing signs. As the sea is getting warmer the killer whales are moving north in ever increasing numbers. The eider ducks and phalaropes are now staying north all year round instead of just the summer.

Even in the dark of winter, when there's just two hours of sunlight, they stay. The ground squirrel that used to be found 250 miles south of Theo's village Iglulik is now flourishing around Iglulik. They are getting new species of birds. Even the robin has arrived for the first time.

Theo said, 'When we first heard about global warming we Inuits thought it was good news. Our kids would have warmer winters. Now we know it's not good news. It is changing the ecosystem altogether. This beautiful world we live in is going to disappear.'

I wrote some interesting things in my journal. Here's one especially notable entry: 'My last night was particularly cold. We all have a piss bottle in our beds due to it being too cold to get out in the night. I didn't do the top of the bottle up tightly enough. Woke up to find my sleeping bag consisted of frozen piss. I told the story the next day and everyone generally agreed – since the Inuits don't allow alcohol – that I was the only person to get pissed on this trip!'

I managed to do a satellite telephone link-up and talked to my dad. Dad had spent a lot of the War in the Sahara desert, fighting Rommel. It can be very cold in the desert at night. After I had described my adventures with the frozen bottle, Dad said dryly, 'In the War we'd fill our hot water bottles with tea so we could keep warm at night and have a cuppa in the morning.' It was a good thing that I didn't confuse his story with mine.

Seeing Sam in his element, easily able to keep up with the fittest in the party – equally at home amongst the Inuit as he is amongst Africans or on the islands of the Caribbean where he has been largely brought up – made me see how very grown up and capable he had become. It's always an evocative and poignant moment when the older generation looks at the younger one and sees them catching up, or overtaking. Sam and I have avoided the subject of if he would or would not run Virgin one day. It gets very involved because I am still having a great deal of fun and, even though I have been working hard since I was fifteen, I don't see retirement looming, not even on the far horizon. I also have to consider that Sam wants to prove himself and that there are plenty of his own things he wants to do; and Holly, of course, has never veered from her dreams of becoming a doctor. Recently, she qualified and is now working as a houseman in a big London hospital. As well as attending music college – he plays good guitar – Sam spent some four months helping with the relaunch of Virgin Media, which he enjoyed. Some of our businesses, like Virgin Media, have a youthful image and, as I head towards sixty, I have to consider that as well. I am aware that a recent survey we did on the Virgin brand gratifyingly showed that it was the Number One most popular brand in the UK; but also shows that amongst young people it was losing its popularity slightly. If I am honest, I think that's a reflection of my age. Time moves on and, therefore, having a younger person in the public eye at some stage would help, though it's not as important at the moment with things like Virgin Money and Virgin Trains.

I do realise as I get older that I'm going to be able to do less to promote Virgin; and philosophically I hope I will need to do less to promote it, since the ideas inculcated in the company are enshrined enough in the way it works to make the businesses take on lives of their own – hopefully in keeping with the ideas of the founder. If an organisation is structured in the right way there is no reason why its ethos shouldn't survive the death of the founder or even a change of ownership. Look at John Lewis: it remains absolutely in line with the principles of its first founder. Marks & Spencer may have lost its way for a while but the public never lost track of its vision of what M&S should be and the company has had to return to that vision. Another example is Rolls-Royce. Long after the deaths of its two founders, its principle of engineering excellence still reassures people as diverse as airline passengers and tank drivers the world over. So, when I'm too old or incapacitated to abseil down a building, I still think the spirit of fun and adventure will be there – although I'm still constantly assured that they will be hoisting me up and down that building in a wheelchair. Still, that moment might be a very long way off. Sam certainly thinks so. When he was at Virgin Media he was asked to do an interview. Virgin PR, Jackie McQuillan, said to him, 'Well, if you want to do the interview, babe, you can, but let's just talk about you working for Virgin – not some psycho-babble about your relationship with your dad.'

To which Sam replied, 'Aw, Jackie, do we really have to push the fact that I'm working for Virgin this soon – I'm going to have to put up with another sixty years of this shit!'

After the Arctic expedition, it seemed appropriate that, while in the great North, I stopped off in Toronto to launch another campaign to combat global warming. We had designated it 'FLICK OFF', as a reminder to turn off electricity at every opportunity, including all standby buttons. A slight touch of irreverence always amuses me – and I think people do remember the tongue-in-cheek approach. However, I was bemused to find that some worthy Canadian councillors decided that the phrase was rather indecent and someone should tell me that I should 'flick off'!

After three years of dithering on the part of the US Department of Transportation, Virgin America finally got the go-ahead to fly on 19 May. It was a great relief, not just to me, but to many people whose future jobs at VA were at stake, and, particularly, to Fred and the team at VA, who had worked non-stop to do all that was required of them to appease the DOT, and the other US airlines who had blocked us for so long.

I have always believed in healthy competition as a way of driving up standards and letting customers have the best possible deal. However, we weren't fully out of the woods. Despite all the changes we had scrupulously made as and when requested, the DOT insisted that we had to replace Fred Reid as CEO within six months and to limit the influence of the Virgin Group over VA's operations even further. Since we had already distanced ourselves from VA, there didn't seem much more we could do – but we were willing to comply. However, VA asked for the decision over Fred to be reversed. He was, after all, an American and he had previously been the president of Delta (one of the airlines that had been opposing Virgin America). It didn't make sense. Nevertheless, being passed to fly was very welcome, and we started working hard on a mid-summer launch. VA currently offers flights be-tween San Francisco International Airport and John F Kennedy International Airport in New York as well as services to San Diego, Las Vegas, Los Angeles, Boston, Seattle and Washington's Dulles International Airport. Within five years, VA hopes to add other cities so it's an ambitious roll-out.

Simultaneously, Virgin Atlantic shifted strategy to defer our order for the Airbus A380 – which was very behind schedule – for four years, from 2009 to 2013. We still have confidence in the jumbo, but, in keeping with our safety and performance strategy, we want it to be in service elsewhere before finally committing ourselves. Instead, following our environmental lead, on 26 May, I signed a contract with Boeing chairman Jim McNerney to buy forty-three shining new Boeing 787 Dreamliners, worth $8 billion. It was the biggest order Virgin Atlantic has ever made, and they are the first carbon-composite aircraft in commercial service. Looking back, to the Virgin Atlantic Global Flyer, the world's first all-composite aircraft, in which Steve Fossett flew around the world, I felt more than happy that we had paid for the Flyer to be built – to prove the point that all carbon-composite aircraft could fly long distances at high altitudes on a teacup of fuel (just joking ...). But the press suddenly picked up a joke that was slipped into the hefty contract that Jim McNerney and I signed; in this case, the deal between Virgin Atlantic and Boeing included a clause pledging that Jim and I would each lose a stone in weight to help reduce our carbon footprints when flying.

The clause reads: 'The parties hereby agree that each of the signatories will lose at least one stone in weight within the next four years in order to reduce carbon dioxide emissions by over 36lb on the delivery flight.' Apparently, our legal team had put it in as a joke to see if we would read the small print, and when we missed it on early readings, nobody had thought to take it out.

Tongue in cheek, Virgin's communications director, Paul Charles, said: 'Clearly, neither of them reads contracts properly before they sign them. We are doing our bit to tackle carbon emissions, but losing weight was an additional element thrown in for added effect. If you are carrying lighter people in the plane, you need even less fuel. Perhaps the Government should consider adopting it as a way to combat obesity and climate change in one go.'

When asked by the press how much I weighed, I was

honest and gave my correct weight at the time. But, as I pointed out, I was about to head to the Arctic and had deliberately added thirty pounds as a fat reserve. I don't know what Jim's excuse was, though!

At the same time as I signed the Dreamliners contract, I also signed an agreement with Boeing and General Electric, who are the engine manufacturers, to work on a joint development of a biofuel for aviation, which to me represents a sensational prospect. People always said that biofuels could never be developed for aeroplane engines. We've been working on a new biofuel for general use called ISO biobutanol, which may have some of the right characteristics to make a biofuel for aviation, and will continue with it. But – and this is top secret – we're also working on developing another fuel that could be a stunning breakthrough. There is no doubt about it – I am hooked on science in a way I never thought possible. I also smile at the irony of being in partnership with Boeing. When I think of how I had telephoned them once out of the blue and naively asked if I could rent one of their jumbos, it makes me realise that the future is a highly intriguing place to look back from.

With the possibility of clean aviation fuel at the end of May, I offered £1 million to a group founded by former Concorde pilots and executives to help Concorde to fly again. I have always thought that Concorde was one of the most beautiful of all aeroplanes and it was a sad day when the last one flew on 24 October 2003. I was disappointed when my offer to buy each plane for £1 million was turned down by British Airways. It seemed ludicrous that a supersonic plane that had flown for thirty years should be consigned to mothballs.

When Concorde was grounded I vowed that I would

keep up the campaign to keep Concorde flying, and told the press, 'At the very least a heritage trust should be set up to keep Concorde in the UK so future generations can see it. It would be terrible if future generations could never see it fly.'

It seemed to me that in turning me down BA was keeping our long rivalry going – a rivalry that continued to April 2007, when, bizarrely, they censored me from the latest James Bond film. The *Daily Telegraph* wrote: 'In Soviet Russia anyone who fell out of favour with the ruling elite was airbrushed out of history. Now it appears that British Airways has adopted the same approach towards its corporate nemesis, Sir Richard Branson. The Virgin Atlantic chairman, who makes a brief cameo appearance in *Casino Royale*, the latest James Bond film, is somehow missing from the version shown on British Airways flights.'

We would never in a million years dream of censoring any of our in-flight films. Our philosophy is that we expect parents to guide their children. Obviously, we don't show porn, but we do show adult or serious films. For instance, we are the only airline in the world to show Al Gore's *An Inconvenient Truth*. Will telephoned Paul Charles, the head of communications at Virgin Atlantic, and said, 'Look, if anybody phones you about this, remind them that in the Bond film, *Die Another Day*, there's a big scene showing a BA plane in Miami with the BA logo all over it. Tell them we never censored that out.' I was amused that BA overreacted like that.

Early in June, I returned to Kenya to welcome Virgin Atlantic's first daily flights to Nairobi, which will carry thousands of passengers and export Kenyan agricultural produce, worth $100 million a year to Kenyan farmers. I also launched another step in the Peace Parks initiative, by contributing an 'elephant highway' to allow some 2,000 elephants to freely move on their traditional migratory routes to and from Mount Kenya. Their search for the mineral salts they need in their diet takes them through the hundreds of small farms that have mushroomed all over the skirts of this beautiful, snow-capped volcanic peak and farmers have been shooting elephants to prevent them from trampling their crops. The Virgin Mount Kenya Elephant Corridor will stop conflict between farmers and these magnificent creatures, and allow them to survive.

At the launch, I said, 'The African elephant has roamed across the continent from South Africa to the Mediterranean coast but its population is under serious threat. We can create a vital lifeline for the entire animal and human population in the region.'

It was a very happy day. Not only did I get to dance on the wing of the first Virgin Atlantic plane into Nairobi with some African dancers and a Kenyan air hostess in their colourful robes – well, Virgin's distinctive red cabin staff outfit – but I was also made an elder by the Masai people in a very moving ceremony. Afterwards, with my 89-year-old dad and Sam, I took to the skies in a hot-air balloon. It was the first time I had been in a balloon since my round-the-world attempt in 1998, when I splashed into the sea off Hawaii. It was amazing, to sail high above the vast African landscape, following the route of the elephants towards Mount Kenya. At over 17,000 feet it is the second highest mountain in Africa and until recently – despite being almost on the Equator – it has always been covered in snow. The scenery and the experience could not have been more beautiful. Three generations of Branson men in a balloon – it was a moment to relish.

It seems a huge step from Stone Age elephants and hot-air balloons to spaceships, but today the world is a dazzling place where you can go back in time and forward into the future. As I write this, Virgin Galactic is preparing to start its test flight programme, with Brian Binnie as the test pilot for the first 100 flights. We know the system is intrinsically safer than launching a rocket from the ground, but will be only able to prove that by actually flying it. The two most exciting aspects of the spaceship system are safety and its low environmental footprint. But ultimately I agree with Professor Hawking – that we really need to be in space long term because ultimately humanity will have to find a second home somewhere in space. Simple physics tells us that one day we will be struck by an asteroid or that we could suffer from a catastrophic volcanic event, either of which would create a nuclear winter which our dense population may not survive.

So as Professor Hawking said, 'Let's use the next 1,000 years to boldly go where no one has gone before.'

It is with family and my social challenges in mind that I spend less and less time promoting the Virgin brand through dangerous world-record attempts; sitting at home, writing this, I think it's unlikely I will do another project on the scale of the round-the-world balloon flight.

I spend much time travelling and so treasure the moments the family are together. In many ways we are closest when we are all on Necker. It has developed from being the jewel that symbolised the feelings Joan and I have for each other into being a place where the whole family feel at home and at peace. We try to go for Easter, summer and Christmas holidays. With my parents, my sisters and their families, our closest friends, and quite a few people from all the different Virgin companies, it is like a melting pot where we all take stock of what is happening and get away from everything apart from the fax machine.

I've taught the children to play tennis there, and to swim, snorkel and sail. When we're there we're there for each other. It's a time to relax and reflect on what we're all doing, because we know that when we're back in London it's back to work.

My favourite time of day there is the early evening. By then it's midnight in London and it's virtually impossible to speak to anyone in Europe. The fax and telephone are silent, and the sun sets quickly. In an hour or so the daylight changes from brilliant, almost white sunshine to dusk, with a deep orange blaze across the horizon. Sitting on the veranda, I can watch the last small flock of pelicans dive for fish and flap creakily away to roost. Within minutes the sky turns a velvet midnight blue, and the first handful of stars are out. The sea in front of me becomes inky black and everything falls quiet.

We generally have supper on the terrace. Everyone is suntanned and happy. It's great to be together, and I wonder what the future holds for all the kids here. I look over at Holly and Sam and realise that I don't want to plan their lives for them. I just want them to be happy. I know that other businessmen such as Rupert Murdoch and Robert Maxwell had their children reading annual reports and financial accounts before breakfast, but I want none of that. Holly has been single-minded about her dream of being a doctor and she has taken her first big steps by qualifying and has a job in a big London hospital; while Sam has happily dipped his toe into the Virgin pool, by working for some months at Virgin Media in London, and is about to start working in Africa at our game parks – but the choice is entirely his whether or not he sees Virgin as a career for the future. His love for music might compete with the family business! I wonder, too, what it will be like to not spend so much time on Necker. I am building a new, greener family home on Moskito and can visualise being as happy there as we have all been on Necker. But, whatever the future holds, I am as excited and curious about it as I have always been. It is that curiosity and sense of adventure about the unknown with all its challenges that drives me. And with huge issues like AIDS and global warming and the conflict issues, the challenges grow more urgent. But at moments like these, surrounded by my family in another Necker sunset, I am happy to forget about my notebook, with its constant burning list of things to do and people to call, and relax into being among people I love and care about.

Even as we sit here, I know that one of our jumbos is heading from Heathrow to JFK, a route that was, until 2002, operated by *Maiden Voyager*, our original jumbo. She had been flying from London to New York since 1984 and had become the backbone of our airline and the linchpin of our success. Her retirement marked the end of an era, but also the beginning of a new one, with the arrival of our new A340-600 in the summer of 2002. *African Queen*, one of our first A-340 Airbuses, is humming through the night to Nairobi, our latest destination; and *Lady in Red*, our first Airbus, which was christened by Princess Diana, is heading overnight towards Hong Kong. Virgin Atlantic's offices at Crawley will be deserted save for the cleaners, and the night shift will be drinking their second or third cup of coffee at Heathrow and Gatwick. There will be queues outside Heaven nightclub, and I wonder who is performing tonight and what the future holds for them. The Japanese and Paris Megastores will be shut, but late-afternoon crowds will be leafing through the racks of CDs at the New York Megastore, before buying a can of Virgin Cola from a nearby vending machine. Meanwhile, in London our team at Virgin Books will be wondering why a certain 'author' is late with his manuscript! And of course, in the Mojave desert, my dream for affordable space travel and a new era in human history will gradually be becoming a reality. Space really is virgin territory.

At the outset, each of those individual ventures was a step into the unknown for the company – a bit like the loss of one's virginity. But, unlike really losing your virginity, in whatever world you make for yourself, you can keep embracing the new and the different over and over again. That's what I have always wanted for Virgin and, whether it's achieved by judgement or luck, I wouldn't have it any other way.

On 26 May 2007, Nelson Mandela arrived at Ulusaba for the first meeting of the Elders. He walked in amongst all these people waiting to greet him. How incredibly humbling it was to be in the presence of people who truly live with moral courage and who consistently put the betterment of humanity above anything else in their lives. When Madiba arrived, all the 150 members of staff at Ulusaba and guests from the meeting formed lines up and down the path to welcome him – singing and dancing and showing their love for him. His goodness and moral leadership shone from the moment he stepped out of the car.

He was fragile and tried to dance along with them, though his legs are worn out from having to kneel down, breaking stones during almost twenty-eight years of imprisonment on Robben Island – but the rest of his body still danced.

Peter and I had been working towards getting the Elders launched for a long time, so the realisation that it was finally happening – all these extraordinary people gathered to greet Mandela and to be at the birth of the Elders – was truly one of the most emotional moments of my life. I was hopeful that history was being made at that very moment. It was all our wishes that the Elders become a powerful force for good in a very uncertain world and that they will go from strength to strength, sometimes to bring peace out of chaos; to calm dangerous flashpoints; and to help when plague, famine and disasters strike.

As a collective humanity, it is unbelievable that we are allowing thousands of people to die every day from preventable and treatable diseases, and allowing people to kill their brothers and sisters due to lack of natural resources and blindly waiting and doing almost nothing as the perils of climate change are rapidly approaching.

Yet we do have the power to change all of these things. Hopefully, this group of Elders, with Mandela and Graça at the helm, can bring some hope and wisdom back into the world to play a role in bringing us together to stop unnecessary human suffering and to celebrate the wonderful world that we are so privileged to be a part of.

After a short introduction by Archbishop Tutu, Nelson Mandela opened the historic meeting by saying:

> In today's world many of the problems we face are global in nature; these include climate change; pandemics such as AIDS, malaria and TB; and of course that entirely human-created affliction, violent conflict. Destructions we have to deal with. These

actions need to be taken. And remember, who needs your help the most? It is those that have the least, that suffer the most. It is they that are rarely heard. This group of Elders can help them and make sure they are not ignored.

I know that you will support courage where there is fear, foster agreement where there is conflict and inspire hope where there is despair. This initiative cannot have come at a more appropriate time, it will bring together an extraordinary collection of people with the skills and resources to undertake what is now required. I am proud to be here, at this groundbreaking first meeting of the Global Elders. As I have said, I am trying to take my retirement seriously, and though I will not be able to participate in the really exciting part of the work, analysing problems, seeking solutions, searching out partners, I will be with you in spirit. I thank you.

Index